Lecture Notes in Computer Science   11222

Commenced Publication in 1973
Founding and Former Series Editors:
Gerhard Goos, Juris Hartmanis, and Jan van Leeuwen

Editorial Board

More information about this series at http://www.springer.com/series/7408

Kyungmin Bae · Peter Csaba Ölveczky (Eds.)

Formal Aspects of Component Software

15th International Conference, FACS 2018
Pohang, South Korea, October 10–12, 2018
Proceedings

Springer

Editors
Kyungmin Bae (iD)
Pohang University of Science
  and Technology
Pohang
South Korea

Peter Csaba Ölveczky (iD)
University of Oslo
Oslo, Norway

ISSN 0302-9743   ISSN 1611-3349   (electronic)
Lecture Notes in Computer Science
ISBN 978-3-030-02145-0   ISBN 978-3-030-02146-7   (eBook)
https://doi.org/10.1007/978-3-030-02146-7

Library of Congress Control Number: 2018957278

LNCS Sublibrary: SL2 – Programming and Software Engineering

This Springer imprint is published by the registered company Springer Nature Switzerland AG
The registered company address is: Gewerbestrasse 11, 6330 Cham, Switzerland

Preface

This volume contains the proceedings of the 15th International Conference on Formal Aspects of Component Software (FACS 2018), held at Pohang University of Science and Technology (POSTECH), Korea, during October 10–12, 2018.

Component-based software development proposes sound engineering principles and techniques to cope with the complexity of present-day software systems. However, many challenging conceptual and technological issues remain in component-based software development theory and practice. Furthermore, the advent of service-oriented and cloud computing, cyber-physical systems, and the Internet of Things has brought to the fore new dimensions, such as quality of service and robustness to withstand faults, which require revisiting established concepts and developing new ones.

The FACS series of events addresses the application of formal methods in all aspects of software components and services. Formal methods have provided foundations for component-based software through research on mathematical models for components, composition and adaptation, and rigorous approaches to verification, deployment, testing, and certification.

FACS 2018 received 32 regular and tool paper submissions. All but four submissions were reviewed by at least three reviewers. Based on the reviews and extensive discussions, the program committee decided to accept 12 regular papers and two tool papers. This volume contains those 14 papers, an invited paper by Edward A. Lee, and an abstract of an invited talk by Grigore Rosu.

Many colleagues and friends contributed to FACS 2018. We thank Edward A. Lee and Grigore Rosu for accepting our invitations to give invited talks, and the authors who submitted their work to FACS 2018. We are grateful to the members of the program committee for providing timely and insightful reviews as well as for their involvement in the post-reviewing discussions. We also thank the members of the FACS steering committee for their useful suggestions. Finally, we thank Saron Kim and Moonhyeon Jung for their assistance in organizing FACS 2018, and acknowledge financial support from the Brain Korea 21 Plus program and the POSTECH Basic Science Research Institute.

August 2018

Kyungmin Bae
Peter Csaba Ölveczky

Organization

Program Chairs

Kyungmin Bae   Pohang University of Science and Technology, Korea
Peter Csaba Ölveczky   University of Oslo, Norway

Steering Committee

Farhad Arbab   CWI and Leiden University, The Netherlands
Luís Barbosa   INESC TEC and University of Minho, Portugal
José Luiz Fiadeiro   Royal Holloway, University of London, UK
Ramtin Khosravi   University of Tehran, Iran
Olga Kouchnarenko   FEMTO-ST and University of Franche-Comté, France
Zhiming Liu   Southwest University, China
Markus Lumpe   Swinburne University of Technology, Australia
Eric Madelaine (Chair)   Inria and University of Côte d'Azur, Sophia Antipolis, France
Peter Csaba Ölveczky   University of Oslo, Norway
José Proença   University of Minho, Portugal

Program Committee

Farhad Arbab   CWI and Leiden University, The Netherlands
Cyrille Artho   KTH Royal Institute of Technology, Sweden
Kyungmin Bae   Pohang University of Science and Technology, Korea
Luís Barbosa   INESC TEC and University of Minho, Portugal
Simon Bliudze   Inria Lille, France
Roberto Bruni   University of Pisa, Italy
Zhenbang Chen   National University of Defense Technology, China
Yunja Choi   Kyungpook National University, Korea
José Luiz Fiadeiro   Royal Holloway, University of London, UK
Xudong He   Florida International University, USA
Sung-Shik Jongmans   The Open University, The Netherlands
Yunho Kim   KAIST, Korea
Olga Kouchnarenko   FEMTO-ST and University of Franche-Comté, France
Ivan Lanese   University of Bologna/Inria, Italy
Axel Legay   Inria Rennes, France
Shaoying Liu   Hosei University, Japan
Zhiming Liu   Southwest University, China
Markus Lumpe   Swinburne University of Technology, Australia
Eric Madelaine   Inria and University of Côte d'Azur, Sophia Antipolis, France

Hernán Melgratti	University of Buenos Aires, Argentina
José Meseguer	University of Illinois at Urbana-Champaign, USA
Kazuhiro Ogata	JAIST, Japan
Peter Csaba Ölveczky	University of Oslo, Norway
Catuscia Palamidessi	Inria, France
José Proença	University of Minho, Portugal
Gwen Salaün	University of Grenoble Alpes, France
Francesco Santini	University of Perugia, Italy
Meng Sun	Peking University, China
Antonio Vallecillo	University of Málaga, Spain
Dániel Varró	McGill University, Canada, and Budapest University of Technology and Economics, Hungary
Shoji Yuen	Nagoya University, Japan
Min Zhang	East China Normal University, China

Additional Reviewers

Chen, Xin	Krishna, Ajay
Chirita, Claudia	Li, Yi
Chouali, Samir	Liu, Bo
Cristescu, Ioana	Masson, Pierre-Alain
Dadeau, Frederic	Quilbeuf, Jean
Koutsoukos, Giorgios	Zhang, Xiyue

Formal Design, Implementation and Verification of Blockchain Languages (Abstract of Invited Paper)

Grigore Rosu[1,2]

[1] University of Illinois at Urbana-Champaign, USA
grosu@illinois.edu
http://fsl.cs.illinois.edu/grosu
[2] Runtime Verification, Inc., USA
grigore.rosu@runtimeverification.com

Abstract. Many of the recent cryptocurrency bugs and exploits are due to flaws or weaknesses of the underlying blockchain programming languages or virtual machines. The usual post-mortem approach to formal language semantics and verification, where the language is firstly implemented and used in production for many years before a need for formal semantics and verification tools naturally arises, simply does not work anymore. New blockchain languages or virtual machines are proposed at an alarming rate, followed by new versions of them every few weeks, together with programs (or smart contracts) in these languages that are responsible for financial transactions of potentially significant value. Formal analysis and verification tools are therefore needed immediately for such languages and virtual machines. We present recent academic and commercial results in developing blockchain languages and virtual machines that come directly equipped with formal analysis and verification tools. The main idea is to generate all these automatically, correct-by-construction from a formal specification. We demonstrate the feasibility of the proposed approach by applying it to two blockchains, Ethereum and Cardano.

Keywords: Formal verification · Formal semantics · Blockchain

Links

Runtime Verification, Inc:

- http://runtimeverification.com

Smart contract verification approach and verified contracts:

- https://runtimeverification.com/smartcontract/
- https://github.com/runtimeverification/verified-smart-contracts

---

Supported in part by NSF grant CCF-1421575, NSF grant CNS-1619275, and an IOHK (http://iohk.io) gift.

Formally specified, automatically generated virtual machines for the blockchain:

- EVM: https://github.com/runtimeverification/evm-semantics
- IELE: https://github.com/runtimeverification/iele-semantics

Contents

Tool Papers

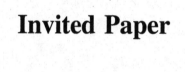

Invited Paper

What Good are Models?

Edward A. Lee[1]([⊠]) and Marjan Sirjani[2,3]

[1] EECS Department, University of California, Berkeley, USA
`eal@eecs.berkeley.edu`
[2] School of Innovation, Design and Engineering, Mälardalen University,
Västerås, Sweden
`marjan.sirjani@mdh.se`
[3] School of Computer Science, Reykjavik University, Reykjavik, Iceland

Abstract. Models are central to engineering. They are used for analysis, synthesis, and communication between humans. A given artifact or process may have multiple models with different purposes, modeling different aspects, or modeling at varying levels of abstraction. In this paper, we give a general overview of how models are used, with the goal of making the concepts clearer for different communities. We focus on the domain of track-based flow management of automated systems, and identify two different modeling styles, Eulerian and Lagrangian. Eulerian models focus on regions of space, whereas Lagrangian models focus on entities moving through space. We discuss how the features of the system, like having centralized or decentralized control or the ability to install fixed infrastructure, influence the choice between these styles. Although the choice between modeling styles is rarely made consciously, it affects modeling efficiency, and one style may be far better suited for certain modeling problems than another. For problems with a more global nature concerning the physical space, an Eulerian model is likely to be a better match. For problems that concern the moving objects specifically, where the identity of the individual objects is important, a Lagrangian view is the one to choose. In many cases, combining the two styles is the most effective approach. We illustrate the two styles using an example of an automated quarry.

1 Introduction

We are now in the era of cyber-physical systems, the Internet of Things, and smart applications. For building such systems we need a team of experts with various domains of expertise, including computer science, software engineering, computer networking, control and communication engineering, robotics, and artificial intelligence. Although all these experts have the experience of working with models, they use different terminologies and very different modeling languages. Models are used differently in different contexts, and for people with varying backgrounds, this may create confusion. With the increasing need for people with different backgrounds to work together, communication is becoming a crucial obstacle. To tackle this obstacle, in this paper we provide an overall view of modeling in the contexts of science and engineering, with different

K. Bae and P. C. Ölveczky (Eds.): FACS 2018, LNCS 11222, pp. 3–31, 2018.
https://doi.org/10.1007/978-3-030-02146-7_1

goals of synthesis and analysis, and in different directions of abstraction and refinement. We show how validation and verification provide quality assurance on multiple levels in the process of modeling.

We focus on flow management of autonomous systems, covering a wide range of application domains including air traffic control, railway systems, road traffic, automated warehouses, smart transport hubs in cities, and computer networks. The increasing traffic volume that inevitably comes with increasingly efficient use of resources makes collision avoidance and safety assurance more critical and complicated. It also increases the possibility of unpredicted changes and demands automated runtime planning. Any improvement in planning can save a huge amount of cost, which may be in the form of time, fuel consumption, or risk, and can make a system more environmentally friendly and sustainable and improve user satisfaction.

Experimenting with the design of transportation systems in the field can be prohibitively expensive and unsafe. As a consequence, it is essential to use models both for understanding how existing systems work and for determining how to improve them. There is a surprising richness of possibilities for constructing models, and the choice of modeling strategy can strongly affect the outcome. What model to use depends not only on the problem domain, but also on the goal.

In the following sections, we give an overall view on modeling, abstraction and refinement, scientific and engineering models, verification and validation, and synthesis and analysis. We then continue by focusing on actor-based models of track-based flow management systems. We show how there are similar and common concepts, features, and problems in all flow management systems. We then present two views of flow management, Eulerian and Lagrangian, and offer a discussion on how to choose one of these models over the other and how and when to combine them.

We use an automated quarry as a running example of a track-based flow management system. The case study is inspired by the quarry site used in the electrified site project at Volvo Construction Equipment, where autonomous haulers (HX) are used for transporting material in the site, see Fig. 1. HX machines are intended to perform tasks such as material transport, loading, unloading, and charging in a cyclic manner with predefined timing constraints and task priorities [1,2].

Note that there is a huge amount of work done on traffic flow management in various domains. The aim of this paper is not to serve as a literature review nor a comparative study of traffic management methods. The aim is to give an overall view of modeling of flow management systems from different perspectives.

This paper reflects the authors' collective experience in modeling different applications using actor-based modeling and simulation frameworks. Over decades of building models, we have found common patterns. Flow management problems consist of sources of moving objects, destinations, and paths. Models address safety and optimization goals, like collision avoidance, higher throughput, and minimum delay. Models also address policies for adapting to change.

For example, in a network on chip (NoC), we have to deal with a faulty router, and in air traffic control systems (ATC), we have to avoid storms. But perhaps the most interesting insight derived from our experience is that two very different and complementary modeling styles can be used for flow management problems. These two styles are called Eulerian and Lagrangian, after a similar dichotomy of modeling styles in fluid mechanics. Eulerian models focus on regions of space, whereas Lagrangian models focus on entities moving through space. When building actor-based models, an actor represents a region of space in an Eulerian model and a moving object in a Lagrangian model. Although the choice between modeling styles is rarely made consciously, it affects modeling efficiency, and one style may be far better suited for certain modeling problems than another.

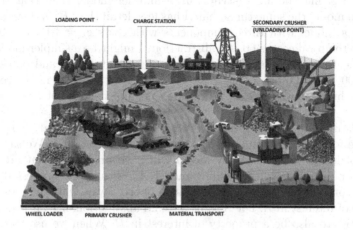

Fig. 1. The Volvo Quarry Site (from [1])

2 Modeling

A model is any description of a system that is not the thing-in-itself (*das ding an sich* in Kantian philosophy). By this definition, every human conception of a system external to herself is a model. In this paper, we focus on modeling a system that includes human-made artifacts and processes, not just naturally occurring systems. In other words, we are focused on engineering, not natural science.

In the automated quarry, the haulers and their controllers, for example, are human-made artifacts. But these artifacts are subject to natural laws, and therefore have properties and behaviors that are not human-made. Hence, our models will need to reflect both physical realities and design intent.

A naive approach to modeling such a system is to build a single ever-more-detailed model of its physicality. Such models quickly become unwieldy and incomprehensible. A more productive approach is to build a multiplicity of models, each with a purpose. But how should these models be built and how should they relate to one another? On what principles and languages should we base the models? We examine these questions in this section.

2.1   Abstraction and Refinement

Every model is designed to study some property or properties of a system. For example, we might be interested in the cost of a system, and we might construct a model where the cost is defined to be the sum of the costs of a collection of components. Here, the property of interest is cost, and this property lives within formal system of arithmetic where costs can be summed and compared.

A model A may be an **abstraction** of another model B in that they are intended to model the same thing, but A has less detail than B [3]. For example, B may be a model with three components with costs $c_1 = 10$, $c_2 = 20$, and $c_3 = 30$, so the total cost is 60. An abstraction A might be a simpler model with no components, but only a variable c, representing total cost, and an assertion that $c < 100$. A is an abstraction of B because it is intended to model cost, but it does not break down the cost by component, and it does not give a specific cost.

The abstraction A is **sound** if every property of interest that is true for A is also true for B (this is often called "property preservation"). We say "every property of interest" because any model will have properties that are not of interest. For example, when building model A, we are not interested in the number of components, so we abstract that property away. Only the total cost is a property of interest in A. For A to be a sound abstraction of B, it is necessary for total cost to also be a property of interest in B. When we use models, we focus only on some of the properties, and hence soundness is always with respect to these properties of interest.

When a model A is a sound abstraction of another model B, we can equivalently say that B is a **refinement** of A. A refinement B of A adds detail to A without exhibiting properties that are prohibited by A.

A concept that usually comes with **soundness** is **completeness**. A is a **complete** abstraction of B if every property of interest that is true for B is also true for A. While doing abstraction and refinement, we are rarely looking for completeness. Useful abstractions are usually sound but not complete. In our cost example, A is a sound abstraction of B, but if costs of individual components are also properties of interest for us, then A is not a complete abstraction, because in B we have the costs of individual components but in A we have lost that information.

There are cases where two different models exhibit the same behavior and satisfy the same properties. When building models of behavior using automata or transition systems, for example, the formal methods community uses the notions of simulation and bisimulation [4], and there are precise definitions for each concept and the spectrum of different equivalency relations [5]. Abstraction and refinement are reduced to simulation relations, while bisimulation implies both soundness and completeness.

Note that both soundness and completeness are with respect to properties of interest. Suppose, for example, that we have a model C with three components with costs $c_1 = 10$, $c_2 = 20$, and $c_3 = 30$ and weights $w_1 = 1$, $w_2 = 2$, and $w_3 = 3$. If the "properties of interest" include only *costs*, then B is a sound and complete abstraction of C.

2.2 Scientific and Engineering Models

Following [6], we distinguish models that we call **scientific models**, which are intended to reflect the behavior of a *pre-existing system*, from models that we call **engineering models**, which are intended to specify the behavior of a *system to be built*. It is important to recognize whether a model is to be used in a scientific way or an engineering way. For example, adding detail may enhance a scientific model and degrade an engineering model. An architect probably should not specify the placement of every brick, but a structural engineer studying the earthquake safety of a building may need this detail.

An engineering model may serve as a **specification** for a system to be built. It may be informal or formal and more abstract or less abstract. The purpose of the model is to give properties that the built system is required to have. Engineering models are often layered, where a less detailed model A serves as a specification for another more detailed model B. For engineering models, **verification** is the process of checking that B is a refinement of its specification A, or, equivalently, that A is a sound abstraction of B.

Scientific models may also be more or less detailed and formal or informal. The most useful scientific models are the simplest (least detailed, more abstract) that still exhibit the properties of interest. A scientific model is **faithful** if every property it exhibits is also a property of the system being modeled. Faithfulness is similar to soundness, but while soundness is a relation between two models, faithfulness is a relation between a model and a thing-in-itself.

Faithfulness is easier to achieve if properties of the modeling language itself reflect properties of the problem domain being modeled [7]. For example, a modeling language with continuous time will make it easier to faithfully model a system with continuous dynamics. Similarly, a modeling language with discrete events, concurrency, and asynchronous interactions will make it easier to model distributed software systems.

Scientific models may also be layered, although this is far less common than for engineering models [6]. If model A is a sound abstraction of model B, and model B is faithful to some physical system C, then A is also faithful to C.

Faithfulness is much harder to pin down formally than soundness because it is not a relationship between models. It is a relationship between a model and physical, real-world system, the thing-in-itself. Any property held by a real-world system is ultimately subject to measurement error, and hence faithfulness can never be more than approximately assured. Reflecting this fact, Box and Draper famously said, "all models are wrong, but some are useful" [8]. They were referring to scientific models, not engineering models. A specification, an engineering model, is by definition right, not wrong.

For most properties of interest, in science, models are always wrong, in the sense of Box and Draper, but in engineering, a physical, real-world implementation is always wrong. The specification is an idealization, and an implementation can only approximate it. For instance, every physical realization is vulnerable to failures that are not accounted for in the specification. How will a computer program behave, for example, if the computer it is running on is immersed in salt water? Whatever behavior emerges is likely not a behavior of the specification.

Consider for example the dynamic behavior of an electric hauler reacting to network command to accelerate. A scientific model may use Newton's laws to describe how the vehicle reacts to torque induced by the motor. This model is wrong, in the sense of Box and Draper, because it depends on parameters, such as the weight of the vehicle, that cannot be perfectly measured. It is also wrong because Newton's laws are wrong in that they fail to account for relativistic effects. But with appropriate assumptions, the model remains useful.

On the other hand, an engineering model for the same problem is a specification. It defines the correct behavior of a hauler being designed. But no physical vehicle will perfectly match that behavior, and therefore the real-world physical implementation is wrong. But mirroring the usefulness of a scientific model, with appropriate assumptions, the physical implementation will be useful.

2.3   Verification and Validation

According to Boehm [9], **verification** is to establish the truth of the correspondence between a software product and its specification, and **validation** is to establish the fitness or worth of a software product for its operational mission. Boehm refers to the roots of the words as well. "Verification" is derived from the Latin word for "truth", *veritasis*, and "validation" is derived from the Latin word for "to be worthy", *valere*. Informally, we might define these terms by asking "am I building the product right?" (verification) and "am I building the right product?" (validation).

Validation is comparing a model with the system, or to be more precise, comparing a model with the system projected over behaviors of interest. The model defines the "right product." Verification is comparing the model with another model reflecting more abstract properties. To avoid sinking into a philosophical quagmire, we can only formally establish "truth" by comparing models.

For engineering models, verification means making sure that a model B exhibits only acceptable behaviors, or, equivalently, that it does not exhibit prohibited behaviors. A specification A is a reference point that defines acceptable behaviors and their complement, prohibited behaviors. To formally verify B is to prove that it is a refinement of A.

Validation in an engineering process means to check whether the *specification* is written correctly, i.e. whether the model you built as the specification is really representing the system you want to be built eventually. Validation is checking whether the product meets the customer expectations and requirements.

For scientific models, validation is checking how much the model reflects the existing system being modeled, or, equivalently, how **faithful** the model is. Here, scientists rely on the scientific method to approximately validate models. Specifically, they design experiments that have the potential to expose mismatches between the behavior of the model and that of the thing-in-itself. That is, the experiment has the potential to **falsify** the model. Failure to falsify a model is the best available validation of a scientific model. On the other hand, for verification, you need two models to compare. For verification of both scientific and engineering models, you assume that the specification (which is as a reference model) is correct (valid) and verify that the other models that you build based on that are refinements.

Note that no scientific model is perfectly faithful to any physical system unless it is the physical system itself. Hence, it is not necessarily a mistake to fail to reflect behaviors of the system being modeled. All scientific models do that, in that some behaviors are ignored or abstracted away. It is a mistake to fail to reflect *behaviors of interest*, behaviors that the model was intended to explore. A scientific model can therefore be viewed as projection of a system onto a subspace of behaviors of interest.

For example in our automated Quarry, the customer has a safety and progress *requirement* that if the hauler faces an unpredicted obstacle, it has to avoid the obstacle (safety), but the system should not completely shut down (liveness). This requirement is then formulated mathematically, for example as a set of temporal logic formulas. The formulas must be written in a concrete way, for example in terms of the data received by the hauler from its sensors and cameras and commands issued to its actuators. For example, a temporal logic formula may specify that the machine halts if an obstacle is sensed, and that this halting state is temporary. Checking whether this formula is correctly capturing the customer requirements is a validation process. The formula is now a *specification* of the system. When the controller program of the hauler is being developed, the behavior of the hauler executing this program is verified against this specification.

2.4 Synthesis and Analysis

Models can be used for both synthesis and analysis. In a model-driven development approach we do **synthesis**; that is, we build abstract models that serve as a specification of a system to be built, and then we refine the models, adding details until we build the system itself. Typically, the process is iterative, with the specifications evolving along with their refinements. Models can be used along the way for different **analysis** purposes, verification, validation, and performance evaluation. If we have formal and automatic refinement techniques, we may be able to avoid introducing errors in the refined models while details are added. In this case, synthesis is said to be "correct by construction."

A classic example of correct-by-construction synthesis is what a compiler is intended to do. It translates a specification (a program) into a refinement (machine code for a particular machine), adding detail about how to accomplish the intent of the program while preserving behaviors specified by the program. If this is done correctly, the machine code will not exhibit any behaviors that are prohibited by the program. Note that the machine code is still not an implementation. It is another model, specifying behaviors that a silicon implementation of a processor is expected to exhibit. Since it is a model, not a thing-in-itself, the machine code can be formally verified, proven to not exhibit behaviors prohibited by the program. The thing-in-itself, of course, will always be able to exhibit behaviors prohibited by the program, if it is immersed in salt water for example.

Compilers that can be trusted to produce correct machine code have proven to be a spectacularly powerful engineering tool. Spurred in part by this success, software engineers continue to try to push up the level of abstraction at which systems are specified and develop correct-by-construction synthesis techniques that work from those more abstract models. These efforts have met with limited success. A commonly used alternative to correct-by-construction synthesis is to treat a model, such as a program, as a pre-existing artifact, and to construct an abstraction, a scientific model of the program. This model can be used for analysis. In some cases, the abstract model can be constructed automatically, using for example abstract interpretation [10]. We could call such a process "correct-by-construction abstraction."

For example, instead of synthesizing a computer program from a more abstract specification, say in UML, we may write a program by hand and build an abstract model of that program to analyze its behaviors. The more abstract model is, effectively, a scientific model of an engineering model. For example, a nondeterministic automaton could model a computer program. We can then perform model checking [11], which formally checks that the automaton is a refinement of a still more abstract specification model, given for example as a set of temporal logic formulas. If the automaton is a sound abstraction of the program (ideally, it is because it was built using correct-by-construction abstraction), and the automaton is a refinement of the specification (checked using model checking), then the program is a refinement of the specification.

Model checking, simulation, and building physical prototypes can all be used as methods for analysis. Simulation, which is the execution of an executable model, reveals one possible behavior of a model with one set of inputs. Model checking reveals all possible behaviors of a model over a family of inputs.

Different communities may prefer one technique over others. Some practitioners, for example, prefer physical prototypes over simulation, saying that "simulation is doomed to succeed." Rodney Brooks, for example, writing about robotics, says "there is a vast difference (which is not appreciated by people who have not used real robots) between simulated robots and physical robots and their dynamics of interaction with the environment" [12].

Indeed, simulation can be misused. A simulation of a robot may be the execution of an engineering model, a specification. If the specification is valid, then the simulation is indeed doomed to succeed. The model should not be misinterpreted as a scientific model that reveals unknown or unexpected behaviors of the thing-in-itself.

When using simulation, it is important to understand whether one is doing engineering or science. An engineering model should not be used to discover how a real physical system will behave because it will only reveal behaviors that were designed in. Faithful scientific models of robots are indeed difficult to construct because robots exhibit complex physical behaviors that are affected by phenomena such friction, plastic deformation, and acoustic propagation of vibration that are notoriously difficult to model [13]. A good engineering model of a robot, however, can be useful for validation of a specification. Does the specification, an idealized robot, exhibit desired behaviors? It becomes a separate question whether a real robot, a thing-in-itself, can be built so that the specification model is faithful.

When faithful scientific models are not available, physical prototypes are used. Physical prototypes will reveal problems that simulation based on an engineering model cannot reveal. A robot arm, for example, may be modeled as rigid and frictionless for the purposes of developing path planning algorithms. A hauler in an automated quarry may be modeled as moving at a constant speed or stopped (two states) if the purpose of the model is to analyze congestion and optimize throughput. These models should not be used to analyze precision of motion.

3 Actors

A component is a chunk of functionality that can be composed with other chunks of functionality to yield a new chunk of functionality. In software engineering, different classes of component models have evolved. In imperative languages, for example, a component is a procedure, and a program is a sequential execution of a top-level procedure that can call other procedures. Components are composed by procedure calls, a temporary transfer of the flow of control from one procedure to another. Object-oriented languages are organizations of imperative programs with information hiding. In functional languages, a component is a stateless function (free of side effects), and components are composed by function composition. In actor languages, components are concurrently executing programs called "**actors**" that send messages to one another over streaming channels. Actor languages have proved very effective for modeling concurrent and distributed systems, so we focus on those here.

The term "actor" was introduced in the 1970s by Hewitt to describe the concept of autonomous reasoning agents [14]. The term evolved through the work of Agha and others to describe a formalized model of concurrency [15]. Agha's actors each have an independent thread of control and communicate via asynchronous message passing. Each actor has a single input queue on which it receives messages, and it handles messages in order of their arrival. Rebeca [16, 17], for example, is a software framework that realizes Agha's actors, matching asynchronous and event-driven domains. It has proven particularly suitable for modeling and analyzing network protocols and applications [18–20].

The term "actor" has also been used for **dataflow** models of computation. Three major variants of dataflow models have emerged in the literature: Kahn process networks [21], Dennis dataflow [22], and dataflow synchronous languages [23]. In all three, as with Hewitt actors, a program is a network of interconnected actors. Unlike Hewitt actors, dataflow actors have explicit input and output ports, and rather than referencing a remote actor to send a message to it, dataflow actors send messages to output ports and the network handles routing that message to one or more destinations. Since actors do not have references to one another, dataflow actors tend to be more modular and reusable than Hewitt actors. The same actor can be instantiated in multiple contexts.

In Dennis dataflow, program execution is a sequence of atomic actor **firings**, where each firing consumes input **tokens** (chunks of data) and produces output tokens. In Kahn networks, each actor is a sequential program that reads from input ports and writes to output ports. In the original Kahn-MacQueen variant [24], a read from an input port will block until an input token is available and writes to output ports are nonblocking, sending data with no constraints. Various generalizations allow richer input-output semantics, for example to allow for nondeterministic merging of streams, and various specializations constrain the execution, for example to prevent unbounded buildup of unconsumed tokens in queues. Dennis dataflow can be viewed as a special case of Kahn process networks [25]. Dataflow synchronous languages differ from both of these in that, semantically, all actors in a program fire simultaneously and instantaneously. The inputs and outputs of the actors are defined by a fixed point of the function defined by the composition of actors.

The Ptolemy II framework [26,27] generalizes actors to embrace any model of computation (**MoC**) where a program is either a static or dynamic graph of components with ports, where the components are concurrent, and where the ports are connected through communication channels. In a Ptolemy II model, the execution of such a graph is governed by a **director**, a coordinator that realizes the specific MoC. Directors have been realized for Kahn process networks, several flavors of dataflow, and dataflow synchronous models. In addition, directors are available for MoCs that do not traditionally fall within the purview of actor models, but which share essential features with actor models. These include a discrete-event (DE) model, where communication is via time-stamped events, a rendezvous MoC, where concurrent components communicate by rendezvous, and a continuous-time MoC, where the communications between components are semantically continuous-time signals. Ptolemy II DE models are similar to many simulation frameworks such as DEVS [28] and hardware description languages such as Verilog and VHDL. Ptolemy II rendezvous models are similar to Reo [29] and realize a semantics similar to communicating sequential processes (CSP) [30]. The continuous-time models of Ptolemy II are similar to those in modeling languages such as Simulink (from The MathWorks) and Modelica [31]. A key innovation in Ptolemy II is that many of these MoCs can be hierarchically combined in the same model by leveraging an actor abstract semantics [32].

In any framework that supports composition of communicating actors, the specific semantics of the interaction between actors, the MoC, is a meta-model, a model of a family of models [33]. The MoC is an essential part of any modeling language. It provides designers with constructs and features to build programs and models, and the semantics of the meta-model shape the models that are built, sometimes without the designer realizing that this is happening.

Design patterns and templates also function as meta-models, using constructs and features that are provided by the modeling language and adding guidelines for how to model. They tell designers how to match entities in the problem domain to entities in the solution domain (the model we are building). Design patterns can shape the thoughts of the designer.

Broadly, these varied actor languages, semantics, and modeling frameworks provide us with constructs and features that fit concurrent and distributed systems. The varying semantics are tuned for different problem domains. In this paper, we examine how some of the relevant MoCs fit track-based flow management of automated systems.

4 Eulerian and Lagrangian Models of Track-based Systems

We now focus on the track-based flow management systems, specifically traffic management systems and transportation. By "track-based" we mean that movement through the space is restricted to pre-defined paths, as opposed to unrestricted movement in two or three-dimensional Euclidean space. Air traffic control, railroad scheduling, unmanned aerial vehicles (UAV) traffic management, smart transport hubs in cities, automated warehouses, and autonomous transport vehicles (ATVs) are examples where we have track-based traffic and transportation. Wired computer networks, like networks on chip (NoCs), demonstrate similar patterns of features, behavior and goals.

Different models and techniques are used in different application domains for flow management of such systems. The main concerns are guaranteeing safety (like avoiding collisions or running out of fuel) and improving efficiency (including multi-objective optimizations like reducing delays, maximizing throughput, decreasing fuel consumption, and minimizing environmental impact).

Design patterns help when dealing with similar problems by providing a template as the basis for designing your solution. You can reuse, customize and optimize similar techniques. We distinguish two general patterns in building models for flow management. The first pattern, called "Lagrangian," focuses on the moving objects, such as airplanes, trains, automated vehicles, commuters in cities, robots and products in warehouses, and packets in NoCs. In the Lagrangian view, the moving objects have independent identities. The properties of interest concern the behaviors of individual moving objects, including for example how quickly and safely they reach their destinations.

The second view, called "Eulerian," focuses on a region of space, and models the aggregate traffic passing through the space. In the Eulerian view, each region of space, such as a track or a section of a track, has an independent identity, and the objects moving through space are anonymous, possibly even indistinguishable from one another. The properties of interest concern the utilization of space, including for example congestion and throughput.

The Eulerian-Lagrangian terminology comes from fluid Mechanics and classical field theory, where Lagrangian and Eulerian models are well understood as alternative ways to model fluid flow [34]. In a Lagrangian model of a fluid, the observer follows an individual fluid parcel as it moves through space and time. In the Eulerian view, the observer fixes on a region of space and observes fluid mass passing through that space. For example, in studying the flow of a river, the Lagrangian view can be visualized as sitting in a boat and floating down the river, whereas the Eulerian view can be visualized as sitting on the bank and watching the boats float by.

4.1 Flow Management: A Generic View

In a track-based flow management system, moving objects are constrained to follow one-dimensional tracks within a two or three-dimensional space. Tracks can be joined and split at intersections. At any given time, a track-based system will define a network of interconnected tracks and each track will be occupied by some number of moving tokens. Sources and sinks for tokens represent the edges of the network being modeled.

The nodes in the network represent sources, destinations, and intermediate destinations. Sources and destinations can be airports (in ATC), train stations (in a railway system), hubs (in smart transport hubs in cities), shelves or racks (in a warehouse), loading or unloading positions (in a quarry), or routers in NoCs. Intermediate destinations can be places that the moving objects may or must stop, like connecting airports for airplanes or charging stations for automated vehicles. The edges in the network represent tracks and sub-tracks. There can be a capacity assigned for each (sub-)track, and minimum and maximum allowed speed. In addition to Figs. 1 and 2 shows applications where we can see the track-based flow management pattern. Figure 2a shows the North Atlantic Organized Tracks (NAT-OTS) that is used for track-based air traffic control. Figure 2b shows the subway map of Tokyo. Figure 2c shows a small example of smart transport hubs in a city and how the commuters have choices for moving between these hubs [35]. Figure 2d shows an array of routers on an NoC architecture similar to what the authors used in [18].

Moving objects form the flow on the network. Objects may have some attributes assigned to them. Apart from an identifier, they may have a maximum and an optimum speed, capacity for fuel, fuel consumption rate as a function of speed, node of origin, target node, and a pre-specified route. The model may go further than that and see each moving object as a smart agent with beliefs, goals, and learning capabilities.

Many of the problems can be formulated as an **optimization** problem, where the **goals** generally are increasing efficiency of the traffic system, enhancing mobility (which means increasing throughput), reducing delay, or minimizing cost (like fuel consumption or environmental costs). The **constraints** mostly concern safety, like keeping the necessary separation between vehicles or limiting the number of moving objects in a track.

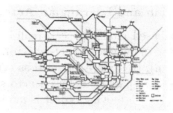

(a) By Coisabh [CC BY-SA 4.0] from Wikimedia Commons, https://commons.wikimedia.org/wiki/File:NAT-Tracks-24FEB17.png

(b) From Wikimedia Commons, https://commons.wikimedia.org/wiki/File:Tokyo_subway_map.PNG

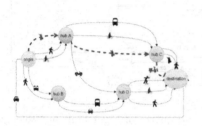

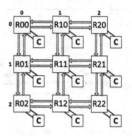

(c) An abstract schema of smart transport hubs (courtesy of Jacopo de Berardinis, Carlo Castagnari, Giorgio Forcina from a presentation prepared on the work in [35]).

(d) An abstract schema of Network on Chip (courtesy of Mahdi Mossafa, after [18]).

Fig. 2. Some applications with the common attribute of flow management.

Another common problem in flow management is **adapting to change**. Airplanes get delayed and schedules have to be updated, weather conditions change, requiring rerouting, and new flights are added, requiring re-planning. Similar changes occur in railroads, transport hubs, warehouses, and other flow management applications, and consequently, such systems have to be adaptive and resilient to change.

An Eulerian model focuses on each track, the configuration and the connecting network of tracks in a more macroscopic way, while a Lagrangian model focuses on moving objects and their behavior in a more microscopic way. The decision to use an Eulerian or Lagrangian pattern, or even a combination, can have a profound effect on the effectiveness of a model. In our experience, practitioners rarely make this decision consciously. They just build the first model that pops into their heads.

4.2   Eulerian and Lagrangian Actor Templates

In an actor-based model we can realize Eulerian and Lagrangian views using
track-as-actor or moving-object-as-actor, respectively. In a track-as-actor pattern (Eulerian), tracks are modeled as actors, and the moving objects are modeled as messages passing between actors. In a moving-object-as-actor pattern
(Lagrangian), each moving object is modeled as an actor, and actors have some
local information from their surroundings and the configuration of the system
and may be able to autonomously decide their next move.

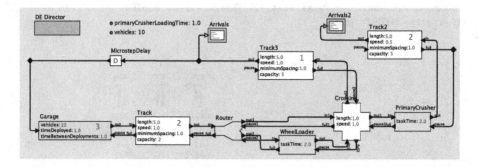

Fig. 3. Eulerian model of a piece of the automated quarry of Fig. 1 built in Ptolemy
II.

Figure 3 shows an Eulerian model of a section of the automated quarry
rendered in Fig. 1. This model is built using Ptolemy II [27] with a discrete-
event director. The actors are shown as boxes with input and output ports
through which time-stamped messages are sent. Each actor reacts to messages
in time-stamp order.

It is a matter of choice to build an Eulerian model and to use a discrete-
event model of computation. What are the consequences of these choices? Most
obviously, the active agents in the model are tracks, garages, and workstations
such as a wheel loader and crusher. The vehicles, which are electric haulers in
this model, are represented by messages exchanged between actors. This model
does not track individual vehicles, but rather models queuing and congestion
at locations in the quarry. As a consequence, this model could be suitable for
planning routing strategies, but is probably not suitable for developing or evaluating collision avoidance or battery management strategies. Note that one way
to handle collision avoidance in this model is to have tracks with a capacity of
one where the physical space is (virtually) divided in to tracks with a length
that represents the minimum safe separation between the moving objects. This
may not be a practical design, especially where we have a large space and small
safe separation, because it will create a very fine-grain model with huge number
of tracks. Also, it does not really model separation between individual vehicles,
since a vehicle at the end of one track can be arbitrarily close to a vehicle at the
beginning of the next track.

One consequence of choosing a discrete-event (DE) MoC is that the model is, by default, deterministic [36]. Building a nondeterministic model requires inserting actors with explicitly nondeterministic behavior. To model probabilistic events, the modeler has to explicitly insert sources of stochastic events, typically driven by pseudo-random number generators. In contrast, if we had chosen a Hewitt actor model, then the modeling framework itself would be nondeterministic in that messages arriving at an actor from distinct source actors are handled in nondeterministic order. In DE, the time stamps determine the order in which events are handled, and the time stamps are computed deterministically in the model.

To understand the consequences of the determinism of the modeling framework, consider the Crossing actor at the lower right in Fig. 3. This represents an intersection where haulers going left to right cross haulers going bottom to top. How should we model the situation where two haulers arrive simultaneously at the intersection? In a DE model, simultaneous arrivals is a well-defined concept (the messages have the same time stamp), and how the model handles the situation has to be explicitly specified. In the particular model shown in the figure, we chose to handle it by giving priority to the haulers traveling from left to right, but we could equally well have handled it with a Bernoulli random variable (a pseudo-random coin flip). We could also have modeled it nondeterministically by inserting into the model an actor with an explicitly nondeterministic state machine, like that shown in Fig. 4. The red transitions are both enabled when messages with the same stamp arrive on inputs in1 and in2, and which transition is taken will determine which message is handled first.

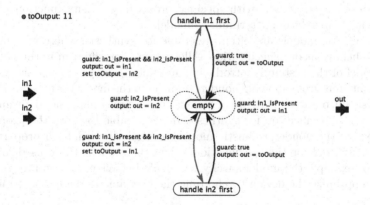

Fig. 4. Nondeterministic state machine actor built in Ptolemy II that merges streams with simultaneous messages nondeterministically into one stream.

If we wish to model the crossing nondeterministically, then a Hewitt actor model could be suitable. However, the original Hewitt actor model is untimed. To explicitly include timed behavior and nondeterministic ordering of simultaneous messages, we can use Timed Rebeca [37,38], which extends Hewitt actors with time stamps. Similar to the DE model, simultaneous arrivals is a well-defined concept (the messages have the same time stamp), but unlike the DE model the order of handling of messages with the same time stamp is always nondeterministic. Timed Rebeca has a built-in model checker that can be used to explore all the behaviors allowed by this nondeterministic semantics.

For some modeling problems, a nondeterministic MoC may be preferred because it can concisely express a family of possible behaviors that can be analyzed by exhaustive techniques such as model checking. Representing nondeterministic behavior is especially desirable in situations where we have for example simultaneous arrival of messages (vehicles, packets, ...) and no explicit priority-based policy to choose one over the other, so, the behavior of the thing-in-itself is really unknown to us. Then we build a nondeterministic model as a scientific model that shows different possible behaviors; this model will be used for analysis purposes, more specifically for model checking.

Such nondeterministic models, however, should not be used for simulation, because simulation reveals only one of many possible behaviors at a time. Unless the simulation resolves the nondeterminism in the same way that the system itself does, its choice of behaviors will tell us nothing about the likelihood of any particular behavior manifesting in the deployed system. Most implementations of Hewitt actors, for example, handle messages in order of arrival, but unless the system being modeled is actually a set of concurrent processes running on the same multitasking scheduler as the model, the fact that a particular outcome occurs in simulation would say nothing about whether that outcome will occur in the field. A nondeterministic model is about what may possibly occur in the field, not about what is likely to occur. To assess the *likelihood* of particular outcomes, an explicit stochastic model with specified probability density functions should be built, not a merely nondeterministic model.

Deterministic models are often preferable for synthesis, where we want the system to behave as our specification. Allowing nondeterminism in the behavior of the model of the system is introducing an unnecessary risk in the design process (it's different from allowing nondeterminism in the model of the environment for analysis purposes). There are occasions that we may allow nondeterministic models as our specification for synthesis. If we are able to prove the properties of interest for the nondeterministic model (basically by definition properties of interest must hold for the specification), then the model can be used for synthesis. For example the model specify what safe behaviors are, and a synthesis algorithm optimize the design by choosing the best among the nondeterministic behaviors.

A more subtle consequence of the choice of the DE modeling framework shows up as bidirectional links between components. Notice that any actor that represents a place with finite capacity, which in the model is all actors except the Garage, has to apply back pressure to any actor that sends vehicles to it. When it is full, it notifies the upstream source by sending a "full" event, which has the effect of causing vehicles to wait in a queue upstream.

An alternative MoC that would not require backwards-flowing "full" messages would be based on a rendezvous-style of concurrency, using for example the Rendezvous director in Ptolemy II or a framework like Reo [29], which realizes a communicating-sequential processes (CSP) MoC [30]. In such an MoC, a sender of a message cannot complete a send until the receiver of the message is ready to receive it. Hence, back pressure is built in to the MoC and does not have to be explicitly built in to the model. However, no mature implementation that we know of a rendezvous-based modeling framework also models timed events, despite the fact that timed process algebras have been a subject of study for a long time [39]. Without a model of time, it would be difficult to use the model to optimize throughput, for example.

For some track-based applications, such as air-traffic control, back pressure that causes upstream queuing can be problematic. Haulers on the ground can stop and wait, but airplanes cannot. A track-based DE model of an ATC scenario is given in [40], but in that implementation, the DE director was subclassed to create a global coordinator that manages the back pressure. In effect, the MoC was modified to support the application domain.

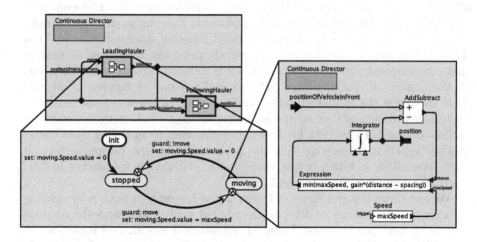

Fig. 5. Lagrangian model of a piece of the automated quarry of Fig. 1 built in Ptolemy II.

A simple Lagrangian model for the automated quarry of Fig. 1 is shown in Fig. 5. This hierarchical model is very different from the Eulerian model of Fig. 3 and could be used to answer a different set of questions. The scenario it models is two automated vehicles in a track, one leading and one following, with sensor data in the following vehicle giving it an estimate of its distance to the leading vehicle. The two actors at the top level of the model each represent a vehicle. Each actor is an instance of a class that, in this simplified model, is a hybrid system with two modes of operation, stopped and moving. In the moving mode, a first-order ordinary differential equation (ODE) models a proportional controller that strives to maintain a fixed distance to the leading vehicle but with a speed limit. This model could easily be elaborated with vehicle dynamics representing its loaded and unloaded inertia, for example, or its battery state as a function of time.

The model in Fig. 5 is a continuous-time model, using the Continuous director in Ptolemy II [41]. It could equally well have been constructed in Simulink/Stateflow, a widely used modeling environment from The MathWorks. In the continuous MoC, the messages exchanged between actors represent continuous-time signals as approximated by an ODE solver.

Comparing the Eulerian and Lagrangian models is instructive. They are very different from one another. The Eulerian model could be used to evaluate overall throughput and to develop routing and path planning strategies for haulers. The Lagrangian model could be used to design the control system for the haulers that maintains a safe distance between them and to evaluate its performance.

4.3 Eulerian and Lagrangian Actor Models in Practice

It is relatively rare, when building models, to explicitly and consciously evaluate alternative modeling styles and choose one. A notable exception is documented by Menon, Sweriduk, and Bilimoria, who advocate Eulerian models for air traffic control [42]. Although it is common to build Eulerian models in this problem domain, it is rare to see this choice explicitly defended. Menon et al. observe that the complexity of the resulting model is reduced because it depends only on the number of spatial control volumes and not on the number of aircraft. They show that the simplified model admits the use of linear control theory for analysis and design of flow control strategies. Menon et al. credit a number of authors dating back to 1955 for Eulerian approaches to modeling road traffic, which is apparently where they got the inspiration to apply the approach to air traffic control (it is worth noting that the use of Eulerian approaches in fluid mechanics goes back much further).

We encounter the two views of Eulerian and Lagrangian models by working on actor-based modeling of different distributed applications with the common pattern of flow management. Using an actor-based model, and seeing actors from an object-oriented point of view, we generally map each active entity in the system to an actor in our model. In packet routing applications on network-on-chips (NoCs), a router is an active entity, a piece of hardware and software that routes the packets through wires; and packets are passive entities that enter the network, and are routed along until they get to their destination. A natural mapping is modeling routers as actors, and packets as messages, which matches an Eulerian model. This Eulerian model represents a natural and faithful model of the system, and captures all properties of interest in order to answer the safety, optimization, and adaptation questions.

An actor-based Eulerian model of a network-on-chip is given by Sharifi et al. [18], who check efficiency and possibility of deadlock for different routing algorithms. A schematic of the NoC architecture they have analyzed is given in Fig. 2d. Ptolemy II, which we used to build the models in Figs. 3 and 5, has also been used for Eulerian network simulation [43]. The widely used network simulator ns-3 (https://www.nsnam.org/) models networks in an Eulerian way using discrete-event semantics similar to that in Fig. 3.

A seemingly different application is air traffic control (ATC). In air traffic control problems, tracks and sectors are an artifice. The space through which aircraft fly is continuous, not discretely divided into chunks. Moreover, aircraft themselves can be considered autonomous entities because pilots can override the commands received from ATC. Hence it may seem more natural to model ATC in a Lagrangian way, so that the individual entities in the model match the individual entities in the thing-in-itself. But with a more careful look, we see that a Lagrangian model may be overkill. In ATC systems we have centralized supervisory control, with a global and macroscopic view of the flow. Moreover, this macroscopic view is sufficient for analyzing optimization questions like minimizing delay and maximizing throughput. The macroscopic view is also sufficient to cover properties of interest such as collision avoidance. In an Eulerian model, collisions can be avoided in model with (sub-)tracks with capacity one; each (sub-)track becomes like a critical section where we enforce mutual exclusion. An alternative strategy is to consider a maximum load (of greater than one) for each track but leave the assurance of the collision avoidance to another Lagrangian model (as done in our Ptolemy example in Fig. 3).

Some properties which may seem to need a Lagrangian view, like preventing an aircraft from running out of fuel, can be handled using an Eulerian model by adding a few attributes to the messages (representing the aircraft). An Eulerian view works more efficiently, where we map tracks to actors, and airplanes to messages.

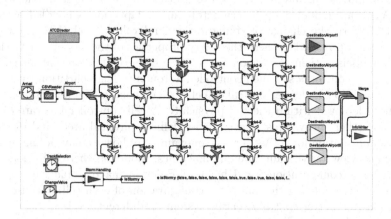

Fig. 6. Ptolemy model of the air traffic control example (courtesy of Maryam Bagheri)

Bagheri et al. show that an Eulerian actor model is effective for designing self-adaptive track-based traffic control systems for air and railway traffic [40]. Their models are used for re-planning in the event of disruptions due to weather

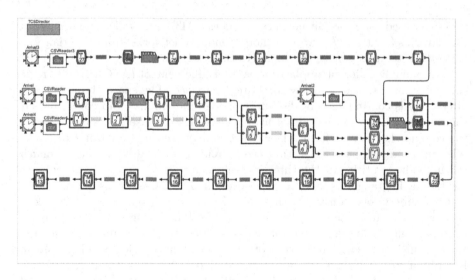

Fig. 7. Ptolemy model of the subway example (courtesy of Maryam Bagheri)

or other causes. Figures 2a and b show the two application domains tackled in [40]. An abstract view of the Ptolemy models of a simplified version of the above applications are shown in Figs. 6 and 7.

A formal actor-based Lagrangian model of a smart airport with autonomous transport vehicles (ATVs) is proposed by Khakpour et al. in [44]. Each transportation service in the airport is realized by ATVs that transport passengers between stopovers, including passenger entrances, check-in desks, and departure gates. ATVs are modeled as Rebeca actors, and adaptation is handled by policies that govern the change of configuration and role of each ATV. Analysis techniques are provided to check the safety properties of the model. They added Eulerian models to their case study to provide a balance between centralized and decentralized control, a so-called controlled autonomy. They partition the smart airport area into smaller regions called cells. A cell contains an autonomous cell controller, deployed within the cell physically. A cell controller is aware of the ATVs and other subsystems located in its defined physical area, and provides nonlocal information for ATVs. This is an example of how we have a Lagrangian microscopic view on the autonomous machines, modeling their behaviors and their different configurations; and have an Eulerian macroscopic view on the physical space, modeling the state and configuration of each cell, and use both views to have a better control over the system on different levels.

Jafari et al. give an Eulerian model for flow management of the automated Volvo Quarry with electric self-driving machines, shown in Fig. 1 [2]. The model is built in Timed Rebeca, as a scientific model for analysis purposes. The model checking tool in Rebeca is used for safety checking, it is also used for better flow planning using a reachability-based approach. Complementing the Eulerian model, Jayanthi Surendran Nair build a more detailed Lagrangian model for the Volvo Quarry site, with a focus on the behavior of each machine and the machine's architecture [45]. This model is used as an engineering model to be the basis for building the controller of each automated machine.

Castagnari et al. give an Eulerian macroscopic view of mobility services in a city with a network of transport hubs [35]. Figure 2c shows a simple schema of multiple smart hubs, the commuters, and different mobility services that they can use, like a bus, bike, or taxi. The model is used as a scientific model for efficiency and mobility analysis and can work as lightweight preprocessing to prepare for microscopic simulations where commuters are modeled as agents in a Lagrangian style [46].

4.4   Eulerian Versus Lagrangian Models

In the following, we discuss some criteria for choosing to use an Eulerian or a Lagrangian model.

Modeling efficiency. When the individual identity of the moving objects are not important, then an Eulerian model is often the better choice because it avoids unnecessary detail. For example, in [47], Bayen et al. apply the idea from Menon et al. to show that an Eulerian model is effective at predicting aircraft counts in congested airspace. Elaborating this work, Sun et al. evaluate three Eulerian models for air traffic control [48]. In ATC, a "sector" is a portion of the airspace controlled by a single human air traffic controller. According to Sun et al., traffic flow management includes maintaining the aircraft count in each sector below a legal threshold in order to ease the controller's workload as well as to ensure the safety of the flights. They say that this task is quite cumbersome and that extensive traffic forecast simulations that include all airborne aircraft are computationally too expensive. They advocate the use of Eulerian models instead.

For some problems, on the other hand, Lagrangian models are more efficient. A problem that has relatively few vehicles executing complicated maneuvers, if modeled in an Eulerian fashion, may require fine discretization of the space, resulting in many Eulerian cells that need to be modeled. In such circumstances, a model that focuses on the individual vehicles may be more efficient.

Optimization. Many models get built with the objective of optimizing a system. Some optimization problems are more naturally Eulerian, whereas others are more naturally Lagrangian. According to Bayen et al., when the objective is to come up with a more efficient use of airspace, rather than optimizing local trajectories of individual aircraft, we prefer an Eulerian model [47]. For our quarry example, we may be interested in minimizing the number of deployed haulers at a particular quarry site, and an Eulerian model such as that in Fig. 3 can be used to evaluate scenarios. On the other hand, if the objective is to derive vehicle controllers that minimize the time that electric haulers spend at a recharging station, a Lagrangian model may be more appropriate. Jafari et al. present an Eulerian model in [2] to examine different configurations for the purpose of optimization in fleet management. In the context of the same project, the authors are working on a Lagrangian model of the quarry for optimization of the properties related to each machine.

Safety. Mobility is a safety-critical problem. Models can help ensure safety at multiple levels. A safety requirement for any such system is collision avoidance, and typically this requirement is addressed at multiple levels with redundant systems. At the lowest level, on-board sensors can be used with feedback control to ensure safe distances between vehicles. Figure 5 illustrates such low-level in a Lagrangian model. At a higher level, a track (or a sector) in an Eulerian model can be modeled as a critical section. The number of moving objects in each track can be controlled by the track itself or by a (semi-)centralized controller or coordinator. In Fig. 3, for example, each track has a maximum capacity for vehicles determined by parameters shown in the figure. The safety of each track, in the sense of not being overloaded, can be evaluated using such a model. Tracks can be further subdivided in an Eulerian model so that each Eulerian node has a capacity of exactly one vehicle, and control strategies that ensure that this capacity is never violated are demonstrably safe. This method is similar to guaranteeing mutual exclusion of critical sections in distributed software systems using semaphores.

In air traffic control, the limits on the number of aircraft in a sector help reduce the risk of collisions. How to maintain these limits can be evaluated using an Eulerian model [47]. At a much lower level, ACAS systems (Airborne Collision Avoidance Systems) such as TCAS demand Lagrangian models.

Another safety problem is ensuring that vehicles reach their destinations without running out of fuel or other critical resources. Eulerian models may be adequate if there is centralized control, as there might be in a quarry or a warehouse, for example. In the domains where free movement is possible in many directions in a large space, an Eulerian approach may not not be practical.

In Lagrangian models, for guaranteeing collision avoidance, the focus is on each moving object. Using multiple sensing and actuating devices, the moving object is aware of its surroundings and keeps a safe distance from the objects around. A mixed approach can be used where each track has a maximum capacity; using an Eulerian model we avoid overloading it, and each moving object is responsible for collision avoidance inside the track.

A good example is the use of unmanned aerial vehicles for civilian operations, which is rapidly increasing. We do not yet have solid approaches to guarantee safety of such large multi-agent systems if we allow unrestricted movements, as we might with a Lagrangian model. In [49], Chen et al. describe platoons of unmanned aerial vehicles flying on air highways. They argue for track-based structuring of the airspace and Eulerian models that allow for tractable analysis.

In general, there may be many different levels of abstractions in the airspace. For larger regions such as cities, air highways may prove beneficial (Eulerian model), and for a small region such as a neighborhood, perhaps unstructured flight is sufficiently safe (Lagrangian model). Further research is needed to better understand the parameters, such as the density of vehicles above which unstructured flight is no longer manageable, or other details like platoon size.

Control and infrastructure. For many mobility applications, modeling can help explore the trade offs between centralized and distributed control. One challenge is that the structure of models may be significantly different for the two cases, thereby making comparison more difficult. An Eulerian model often matches better with a centralized control strategy, particularly when the central controller maintains an overall view of the flow that individual vehicles are unable to form on their own. On the other hand, Lagrangian models may match better when control is decentralized.

Often, a combination of models is used. For example, the air traffic control (ATC) system works as a supervisory centralized controller with an Eulerian view of the airspace. On the other hand, a pilot's view is Lagrangian. In a city, the traffic light system is distinctly Eulerian, while self-driving vehicles are distinctly Lagrangian.

The moving objects in a mobility application have varying degrees of autonomy. Goods on a shelf in a warehouse and packets in a network have no autonomy, while self-driving cars have a great deal of autonomy. When dealing with more autonomy, a Lagrangian model is often better, but again it may complement an Eulerian model.

Effective Eulerian control often requires infrastructure investment. Traffic lights in cities are a good example. Sometime in the future, when all vehicles are autonomous, traffic lights may become unnecessary. In closed (and not very big) environments, like warehouses, it is easier to build such an infrastructure. In such environments, sensors continually update the state of each track, and a centralized controller can dispatch waypoint commands to mobile agents. Once centralized knowledge of a configuration is formed, it can be made accessible to all the moving objects (or subsets of those), which can then use this additional information to supplement their own on-board sensor data to perform more effective Lagrangian control.

In an interesting blend of Lagrangian and Eulerian, Bayen et al. estimate the state of an Eulerian model of automotive traffic flow (a velocity field) from Lagrangian sensors (on-board GPS) on a subset of the vehicles [50]. They argue that this is more effective and less expensive than Eulerian sensing, where for example loop detectors or traffic cameras are placed at fixed locations.

The complexity and analyzability of control strategies may also be affected by the Lagrangian-Eulerian choice. According to Sun et al. [48], in the ATC domain, Eulerian models result in simpler, linear control-theoretic structure enables the use of standard methodologies to analyze them.

Adaptation. Mobility applications are required to be adaptive because conditions in the field and in the moving objects are constantly changing. An Eulerian model is often more appropriate when adapting to disruptions in the physical space, such as storms in air traffic control or blockages in a quarry. In such situations, the adaptation usually needs rerouting and rescheduling that may affect the whole system. On the other hand, when adapting to changes in battery status or fuel supply, a Lagrangian approach is likely more useful because the adaptation mostly affects the object itself. If the battery is low, the object may want to change its status to use less energy. It may also cause a more nonlocal adaptation, like rerouting and going towards a charging station. This example illustrates that in many cases Lagrangian models are better accompanied by some kind of Eulerian models to provide a view of the surroundings and hence provide a more solid basis for choosing adaptation policies.

Andersson et al. suggest several modeling dimensions for self-adaptive software systems in [51]. Their organization addresses "whether the adaptation is performed [or enforced] by a single component or distributed amongst several components," and ranges from centralized to decentralized; their scope is about "whether adaptation is localized or involves the entire system," and ranges from local to global. The above examples show how an Eulerian model better supports a decentralized and nonlocal adaptation, while a Lagrangian model can deal with more local adaptations.

In [40], Bagheri et al. use their coordinated adaptive actor model (CoodAA) [52], for performance evaluation and prediction of behavior of self-adaptive track-based traffic control systems. CoodAA is an Eulerian model and provides a framework for runtime analysis. If a change happens, the future behaviors of the model are explored and possible property violations are predicted. Appropriate policies can then be selected for adapting to the change. The cause of change may be anything in the physical space (like a storm for the ATC example) and the adaptation policies are rerouting and rescheduling. The adaptation decision is made in a centralized form, and causes nonlocal changes. The framework is implemented in Ptolemy II using the discrete event director, similarly to the example in Fig. 3.

The Eulerian model in CoodAA is faithful to the system, and the mapping of entities in the system to the model is simple and does not need any complex function or process. So, the changes that may happen in the system at runtime can easily be reflected in the model. This feature is important in building a runtime analysis framework because efficiency is crucial in runtime analysis. Also, the coordinated actor model reflects the central control in systems like ATC and railroad management systems.

Bagheri et al. propose a compositional runtime analysis technique, called Magnifier [53], that is based on the Eulerian view of the system. The technique is to focus on the point of change, and try to stop the propagation of effects of the change. If the propagation is inevitable, then zoom out and try the same technique. Magnifier technique can be used for adaptation of track-based flow management systems that use an Eulerian model.

An adaptive framework is proposed by Khakpour et al. in [54]. The framework is called PobSAM (Policy-based Self-Adaptive Model) and is an integration of algebraic formalisms and actor-based Rebeca models. A hierarchical extension of PobSAM is proposed by Khakpour et al. in [44]. In [44], the case study is on transportation service in the airport. Autonomous transport vehicles (ATVs) are signed in a transport scheduler service that collects passenger orders and gives tickets (pickup/drop positions, times) to the ATVs. ATVs are modeled in a Lagrangian way, where the ATVs have to collaborate and negotiate in competition on tickets, roads and charging stations. Eulerian models are added to bring in nonlocal control and an awareness of the surroundings; they for example can help the ATVs to avoid a congested area while transferring passengers. The hierarchical structure offers a form of controlled autonomy and balances agent autonomy and system controllability, for example to prevent unsafe situations caused by a selfish acting ATV.

4.5   Eulerian and Lagrangian Join Forces

Eulerian and Lagrangian patterns are complementary and can be combined effectively. A nice illustration of this is given by Claudel and Bayen [55], who introduce what they call "mixed Lagrangian-Eulerian sensing" for automotive traffic flow estimation. As we mentioned above, Eulerian sensing of traffic flow is based on installed physical infrastructure such as loop detectors, cameras, and speed radar. These are anchored to a physical location, and therefore provide information about a segment of roadway. Claudel and Bayen point out that these can be complemented with Lagrangian sensors, which travel with vehicles. In particular, they use GPS-enabled smartphones and show that even with a small percentage of vehicles so equipped, significant improvements in estimation are possible. In a personal communication, Bayen has also suggested Lagrangian *control*, not just sensing, of traffic flow. The idea is that even a small percentage of self-driving vehicles on the road can be controlled so that they affect traffic flow, complementing Eulerian control techniques such as traffic lights on freeway entrance ramps.

Consider how we might combine the Eulerian model of the automated quarry in Fig. 3 with the Lagrangian model in Fig. 5. The Eulerian model provides a macroscopic view of the overall operation that can be used to define high-level strategies. A centralized controller could distribute instructions to haulers which will then carry out the instructions using low-level Lagrangian control. The Eulerian model mitigates congestion and minimizes queuing, while the Lagrangian model avoids collisions and monitors battery usage.

Anytime a (semi)autonomous agent needs to operate in a larger context, there is potential benefit from combining Eulerian and Lagrangian perspectives. The work of Khakpour et al. in [44] is a nice demonstration of this combination. Sensors fixed to infrastructure necessarily provide different information than sensors fixed to mobile agents, and controllers fixed to infrastructure necessarily provide a different kind of control than those fixed to mobile agents. Models need to reflect these complementary properties, and engineers need to consciously choose their modeling strategies cognizant of their strengths and weaknesses.

In a different context, for setting different parameters in a planning problem, an Eulerian model is used as a lightweight model prior to using a more detailed Lagrangian model. Castagnari et al. built an agent-based simulation framework for assessing the evolution of urban traffic after the introduction of new mobility services [46]. Each commuter is an agent in the model. The agent-based simulations are computationally expensive. So, they proposed their Eulerian model [35] which they used to estimate the simulation parameters for the Lagrangian model, and save expensive iterations of executing the Lagrangian model. They implemented a tool to map the inputs to the Lagrangian model to the inputs of the much lighter Eulerian model, and compared the outcomes to show the correlation.

Acknowledgements. We would like to thank Walid Taha for listening carefully to our discussion on track-as-actor and moving-object-as-actor design patterns and pointing out the relationship to modeling patterns that have been called Eulerian and Lagrangian, terms derived from fluid mechanics. We also would like to thank Claire Tomlin and Alex Bayen for the fruitful discussions and for pointing out relevant literature.

The work of the first author was supported in part by the US National Science Foundation (NSF), award #1446619 (Mathematical Theory of CPS), and the iCyPhy Research Center (Industrial Cyber-Physical Systems, supported by Avast, Denso, Ford, Siemens, and Toyota. The work of the second author was supported in part by DPAC Project (Dependable Platforms for Autonomous Systems and Control) at Malardalen University, Sweden, MACMa Project (Modeling and Analyzing Event-based Autonomous Systems) at Software Center, Sweden, and the project Self-Adaptive Actors: SEADA (nr 163205-051) of the Icelandic Research Fund.

References

1. Volvo, C.E.: Innovation at Volvo construction equipment. https://www.volvoce.com/global/en/this-is-volvo-ce/what-we-believe-in/innovation/, 24 Aug 2018
2. Jafari, A., Nair, J.J.S., Baumgart, S., Sirjani, M.: Safe and efficient fleet operation for autonomous machines: an actor-based approach. In: Proceedings of the 33rd Annual ACM Symposium on Applied Computing, SAC 2018, pp. 423–426 (2018)
3. Manna, Z., Colón, M.A., Finkbeiner, B., Sipma, H.B., Uribe, T.E.: Abstraction and modular verification of infinite-state reactive systems. Requirements Targeting Software and Systems Engineering, pp. 273–292. Springer, Berlin (1998)
4. Milner, R.: Communication and Concurrency. Prentice Hall, New Jercy (1989)
5. van Glabbeek, R.J.: The linear time - branching time spectrum II. In: CONCUR '93, Proceedings of the 4th International Conference on Concurrency Theory, pp. 66–81 (1993)
6. Lee, E.A.: Plato and the Nerd – The Creative Partnership of Humans and Technology. MIT Press, Cambridge (2017)
7. Sirjani, M.: Power is overrated, go for friendliness! expressiveness, faithfulness, and usability in modeling: the actor experience. In: Lohstroh, M., Derler, P., Sirjani, M. (eds.) Principles of Modeling. LNCS, vol. 10760, pp. 423–448. Springer, Cham (2018). https://doi.org/10.1007/978-3-319-95246-8_25
8. Box, G.E.P., Draper, N.R.: Empirical Model-Building and Response Surfaces. Wiley Series in Probability and Statistics. Wiley, New Jercy (1987)
9. Boehm, B.W.: Verifying and validating software requirements and design specifications. IEEE Softw. 75–88 (1984)
10. Cousot, P., Cousot, R.: Abstract interpretation: a unified lattice model for static analysis of programs by construction or approximation of fixpoints. In: Symposium on Principles of Programming Languages (POPL), pp. 238–252. ACM Press (1977)
11. Clarke, E.M., Grumberg, O., Peled, D.: Model Checking. MIT Press, Cambridge (1999)

12. Brooks, R.A.: Artificial life and real robots. In: Varela, F.J., Bourgine, P. (eds.) Toward a Practice of Autonomous Systems: Proceedings of the First European Conference on Artificial Life, pp. 3–10. MIT Press, Cambridge (1992)
13. Lee, E.A.: Fundamental limits of cyber-physical systems modeling. ACM Trans. Cyber-Phys. Syst. **1**(1), 26 (2016)
14. Hewitt, C.: Viewing control structures as patterns of passing messages. J. Artif. Intell. **8**(3), 323–363 (1977)
15. Agha, G.A., Mason, I.A., Smith, S.F., Talcott, C.L.: A foundation for actor computation. J. Funct. Program. **7**(1), 1–72 (1997)
16. Sirjani, M., Movaghar, A., Shali, A., de Boer, F.S.: Modeling and verification of reactive systems using Rebeca. Fundam. Inform. **63**(4), 385–410 (2004)
17. Sirjani, M.: Rebeca: theory, applications, and tools. In: de Boer, F.S., Bonsangue, M.M., Graf, S., de Roever, W.-P. (eds.) FMCO 2006. LNCS, vol. 4709, pp. 102–126. Springer, Heidelberg (2007). https://doi.org/10.1007/978-3-540-74792-5_5
18. Sharifi, Z., Mosaffa, M., Mohammadi, S., Sirjani, M.: Functional and performance analysis of network-on-chips using actor-based modeling and formal verification. In: ECEASST 66 (2013)
19. Khamespanah, E., Mechitov, K., Sirjani, M., Agha, G.: Schedulability analysis of distributed real-time sensor network applications using actor-based model checking. In: Bošnački, D., Wijs, A. (eds.) SPIN 2016. LNCS, vol. 9641, pp. 165–181. Springer, Cham (2016). https://doi.org/10.1007/978-3-319-32582-8_11
20. Jahandoust, G., Ghassemi, F.: An adaptive sinkhole aware algorithm in wireless sensor networks. Ad Hoc Netw. **59**, 24–34 (2017)
21. Kahn, G.: The semantics of a simple language for parallel programming. In: Proceedings of the IFIP Congress , vol. 74, pp. 471–475. North-Holland Publishing Co. (1974)
22. Dennis, J.B.: First version data flow procedure language. Report MAC TM61, MIT Laboratory for Computer Science (1974)
23. Benveniste, A., Caspi, P., Le Guernic, P., Halbwachs, N.: Data-flow synchronous languages. In: de Bakker, J.W., de Roever, W.-P., Rozenberg, G. (eds.) REX 1993. LNCS, vol. 803, pp. 1–45. Springer, Heidelberg (1994). https://doi.org/10.1007/3-540-58043-3_16
24. Kahn, G., MacQueen, D.B.: Coroutines and networks of parallel processes. In Gilchrist, B. (ed.) Information Processing, pp. 993–998. North-Holland Publishing Co. (1977)
25. Lee, E.A., Matsikoudis, E.: The semantics of dataflow with firing. In Huet, G., Plotkin, G., Lévy, J.J., Bertot, Y. (eds.): From Semantics to Computer Science: Essays in Memory of Gilles Kahn, Cambridge University Press (2009)
26. Eker, J., et al.: Taming heterogeneity–the Ptolemy approach. Proc. IEEE **91**(2), 127–144 (2003)
27. Ptolemaeus, C.: System Design, Modeling, and Simulation using Ptolemy II. Ptolemy.org, Berkeley (2014)
28. Zeigler, B.P., Praehofer, H., Kim, T.G.: Theory of Modeling and Simulation, 2nd edn. Academic Press, Cambridge (2000)
29. Arbab, F.: Reo: a channel-based coordination model for component composition. Math. Struct. Comput. Sci. **14**(3), 329–366 (2004)
30. Hoare, C.A.R.: Communicating sequential processes. Commun. ACM **21**(8), 666–677 (1978)
31. Tiller, M.M.: Introduction to Physical Modeling with Modelica. Kluwer Academic Publishers (2001)

32. Tripakis, S., Stergiou, C., Shaver, C., Lee, E.A.: A modular formal semantics for Ptolemy. Math. Struct. Comput. Sci. **23**(Special Issue 04), 834–881 (2013)
33. Ledeczi, A., et al.: The generic modeling environment. In: Workshop on Intelligent Signal Processing (2001)
34. Batchelor, G.K.: An Introduction to Fluid Dynamics. Cambridge University Press, Cambridge (1973)
35. Castagnari, C., de Berardinis, J., Forcina, G., Jafari, A., Sirjani, M.: Lightweight preprocessing for agent-based simulation of smart mobility initiatives. In: Cerone, A., Roveri, M. (eds.) SEFM 2017. LNCS, vol. 10729, pp. 541–557. Springer, Cham (2018). https://doi.org/10.1007/978-3-319-74781-1_36
36. Lee, E.A., Liu, J., Muliadi, L., Zheng, H.: Discrete-event models. In Ptolemaeus, C. (ed.) System Design, Modeling, and Simulation using Ptolemy II. Ptolemy.org, Berkeley (2014)
37. Khamespanah, E., Sirjani, M., Sabahi-Kaviani, Z., Khosravi, R., Izadi, M.: Timed Rebeca schedulability and deadlock freedom analysis using bounded floating time transition system. Sci. Comput. Program. **98**, 184–204 (2015)
38. Sirjani, M., Khamespanah, E.: On time actors. Theory and Practice of Formal Methods - Essays Dedicated to Frank de Boer on the Occasion of his 60th Birthday, pp. 373–392 (2016)
39. Reed, G.M., Roscoe, A.W.: A timed model for communicating sequential processes. Theor. Comput. Sci. **58**(1–3), 249–261 (1988)
40. Bagheri, M., et al.: Coordinated actor model of self-adaptive track-based traffic control systems. J. Syst. Softw. **143**, 116–139 (2018)
41. Cardoso, J., Lee, E.A., Liu, J., Zheng, H.: Continuous-time models. In Ptolemaeus, C. (ed.) System Design, Modeling, and Simulation using Ptolemy II. Ptolemy.org, Berkeley (2014)
42. Menon, P.K., Sweriduk, G.D., Bilimoria, K.: A new approach for modeling, analysis and control of air traffic flow. In: AIAA Conference on Guidance, Navigation, and Control (2004)
43. Baldwin, P., Kohli, S., Lee, E.A., Liu, X., Zhao, Y.: Modeling of sensor nets in Ptolemy II. In: Information Processing in Sensor Networks (IPSN) (2004)
44. Khakpour, N., Jalili, S., Sirjani, M., Goltz, U., Abolhasanzadeh, B.: HPobSAM for modeling and analyzing IT ecosystems - through a case study. J. Syst. Softw. **85**(12), 2770–2784 (2012)
45. Jayanthi Surendran Nair, J.: Modelling and analysing collaborating heavy machines. Master's thesis, Mälardalen University, School of Innovation, Design and Engineering (2017)
46. Castagnari, C., Corradini, F., Angelis, F.D., de Berardinis, J., Forcina, G., Polini, A.: Tangramob: an agent-based simulation framework for validating urban smart mobility solutions. CoRR abs/ arXiv:1805.10906 (2018)
47. Bayen, A.M., Raffard, R.L., Tomlin, C.J.: Eulerian network model of air traffic flow in congested areas. In: American Control Conference (2004)
48. Sun, D., Yang, S., Strub, I.S., Bayen, A.M., Sridhar, B., Sheth, K.: Eulerian trilogy. In: American Institute of Aeronautics and Astronautics (2006)
49. Chen, M., Hu, Q., Fisac, J.F., Akametalu, K., Mackin, C., Tomlin, C.J.: Reachability-based safety and goal satisfaction of unmanned aerial platoons on air highways. J. Guid. Control Dynam. **40**(6), 1360–1373 (2017)
50. Bayen, A., Raffard, R., Tomlin, C.: Lagrangian sensing: traffic estimation with mobile devices. In: American Control Conference (2009)

51. Andersson, J., de Lemos, R., Malek, S., Weyns, D.: Modeling dimensions of self-adaptive software systems. In: Software Engineering for Self-Adaptive Systems [outcome of a Dagstuhl Seminar], pp. 27–47 (2009)
52. Bagheri, M., et al.: Coordinated actors for reliable self-adaptive systems. In: Kouchnarenko, O., Khosravi, R. (eds.) FACS 2016. LNCS, vol. 10231, pp. 241–259. Springer, Cham (2017). https://doi.org/10.1007/978-3-319-57666-4_15
53. Bagheri, M., Khamespanah, E., Sirjani, M., Movaghar, A., Lee, E.A.: Runtime compositional analysis of track-based traffic control systems. SIGBED Rev. **14**(3), 38–39 (2017)
54. Khakpour, N., Jalili, S., Talcott, C.L., Sirjani, M., Mousavi, M.R.: PobSAM: Policy-based managing of actors in self-adaptive systems. Electr. Notes Theor. Comput. Sci. **263**, 129–143 (2010)
55. Claudel, C.G., Bayen, A.: Guaranteed bounds for traffic flow parameters estimation using mixed Lagrangian-Eulerian sensing. In: 2008 46th Annual Allerton Conference on Communication, Control, and Computing, pp. 636–645 (2008)

Regular Papers

Building Correct SDN Components from a Global Event-B Formal Model

J. Christian Attiogbé$^{(\boxtimes)}$ (iD)

LS2N - UMR CNRS 6004 - University of Nantes, Nantes, France
`Christian.Attiogbe@univ-nantes.fr`

Abstract. Software defined networking (SDN) brings flexibility in the construction and management of distributed applications by reducing the constraints imposed by physical networks and by moving the control of networks closer to the applications. However mastering SDN still poses numerous challenges among which the design of correct SDN components (more specifically controller and switches). In this work we use a formal stepwise approach to model and reason on SDN. Although formal approaches have already been used in this area, this contribution is the first state-based approach; it is based on the Event-B formal method, and it enables a correct-by-construction of SDN components. We provide the steps to build, using several refinements, a global formal model of a SDN system; correct SDN components are then systematically built from the global formal model satisfying the properties captured from the SDN description. Event-B is used to experiment with the approach.

Keywords: SDN · Correct design · Event-B · Refinement
Decomposition

1 Introduction

An essential constituent of distributed applications is the physical network behind them. Distributed applications very often build on existing middlewares which embody services provided at the network level. Thus the reliability of distributed applications depends not only on their own development but also on the reliability of the network. Due to the involvement of many physical devices, the network level has for many years been a source of severe complexities and constraints leading very often to the adoption of rigid solutions in the deployment of applications.

Fighting the lack of flexibility of physical networks resulted in the software-defined networking (SDN) initiative [1,15,17]. Software-defined networking provides the opportunity to go deeper in modelling and reasoning on networks, since it enables to define and manage more easily the networks at the software level. Indeed a software-defined network is made of a controller and switches which are abstractly defined before being implemented at software level. In this context an user application does not consider a physical network or a specific middleware but it is rather built on top of a virtual or open network.

© Springer Nature Switzerland AG 2018
K. Bae and P. C. Ölveczky (Eds.): FACS 2018, LNCS 11222, pp. 35–53, 2018.
https://doi.org/10.1007/978-3-030-02146-7_2

Even if software-defined networking makes it possible to control an entire network with software, through programs that tailor network behavior to suit specific applications and environments, programmers still have many difficulties to write correct SDN programs. This is due to the unpredictability of the SDN as a distributed asynchronous system, and the lack of correctly developed SDN frameworks or formally verified SDN frameworks. Much work have been undertaken around SDN; they address different aspects: building simulators and analysers for SDN, building SDN controllers, verifying the controller component of an software-defined network, etc.

However SDN deployment is still at its beginning and programmers or administrators still need trustworthy devices and frameworks. Such devices may be implemented from rigorously founded models and related reasoning and engineering tools. Besides, considering the keen interest and the demands for the deployment of SDN as a flexible infrastructure for specific applications, clouds applications, IoT, etc, which all require security, it is of tremendous importance to have at the disposal of developers trustworthy development, analysis and simulation frameworks. Formal models taking into account several of these aspects are then necessary. That are the challenges that motivate of our work.

The main contributions of this paper are: *(i)* capturing the SDN as a discrete-event system to foster its modelling with an event-based approach; *(ii)* a state-based core model for rigorous analysis, development and simulation frameworks dedicated to SDN applications; it is a global Event-B [2] model, designed as the basis of the stepwise construction of the various components of a SDN; *(iii)* the systematic derivation of correct components (SDN controller and switches) from the global model which is previously proved to have some required properties.

The article is organised as follows. Section 2 gives an overview of software-defined networking, related work and main issues. In Sect. 3 we introduce the main concepts for modelling SDN, an overview of Event-B method and then our approach to build the global abstract model by stepwise refinements. Section 4 shows how one can derive the construction of a correct SDN controller from the global formal model. Section 5 gives the first experimental results related to simulation and verification of global safety/liveness properties. We conclude in Sect. 6 and stress some challenges for future work.

2   Overview of SDN: Concepts and Architecture

The SDN architecture consists of three layers: user application, control, and data forwarding. Control and data are the most relevant ones when studying the SDN. Figure 1 depicts how the SDN is viewed from the user side as a single global switch which denotes an abstraction of an entire network. User applications can directly exploit an abstraction of the network. Network services are solicited directly from host machines linked to a physical device: a *switch* assumed to be under the SDN control.

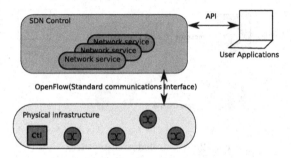

Fig. 1. The layered architecture of a SDN

In software-defined networking there is a physical separation between the *control-plane* (the management of the network and definition of rules to forward data packets) and the *data-plane* (how packets are forwarded according to control-plane) [15,17]. Indeed the network control (the high level or control-plane) is now separated from the packet forwarding (the low level or data-plane) activity and, physical devices inside the low level may be designed more easily; the network control is independent from device providers, the control is brought closer to software controllers and administrators. Traditional network services such as routing, access control, traffic engineering, security, etc can be implemented via various APIs provided by the SDN, instead of being vendor-dependent. The control and data levels are linked by an open communication interface. OpenFlow [1,9] is representative of such communication interfaces. OpenFlow is a standard communication interface, that moves the control of the network from the physical *switches* to logically centralized control software.

SDN has been used in variety of implementations, for example [16] is dedicated to the implementation of wireless networks, while in [5] the authors describe a tool, FlowChecker, which identifies any intra-switch misconfiguration within a Flow Table of a switch. RouteFlow [19] is a controller which implements virtualized IP routing over OpenFlow infrastructure.

2.1 Concepts and Components

We distinguish in Fig. 2 the main components of an SDN. Switches and controller are network devices that interact using packets and messages on data channel and message channel also called secure channel.

Switch. A switch is a device responsible of forwarding packets, to perform a hop-by-hop transfer of information through the network. A switch is configurable by the controller with which it interacts via a secure message channel. A switch interacts with other switches via a data channel.

Controller. A controller is a device responsible of controlling a whole network (a local or medium area network). It is used by the network administrator to dynamically configure, in an evolutive way, the switches with adequate forwarding information; it maintains the connectivity of the switches, etc. The controller

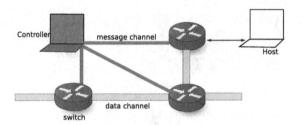

Fig. 2. A detailed architecture

initiates the switches behaviour, maintains them and instructs the switches with respect to specific actions. Packets not processed by the switches are sent to the controller via messages emitted on the message channel. The controller does not use the data channel.

Packet. A packet contains information related to various protocols (Ethernet, IP, etc). A packet has a header related to data and network layers and a body. Inside the header we have for instance: the destination and source addresses for each layer, the type of protocol, ...

Message. A message contains a control or management information addressed by the controller to a switch. The control information is for instance: which packet to drop, the indication of a port on which the switch may forward a data packet. A switch can also emit a message to a controller. In this case either the message contains a response to a control order (for instance the controller asked for the status of a switch) or a packet for which the switch does not have an entry in its table for forwarding the packet to its destination.

Flow Table. A flow table is a part of a switch. It describes the switch elementary behaviour. A flow table is made of several entries sent by the controller. Each entry has a header information and a body. The header may contain a message priority set by the controller. The body of the message can be a data packet, or a rule to process the incoming packets.

Interaction between switches and controller. A properly configured switch has routes to forward received packets coming from other network services. If the switch lacks of forwarding information, it sends the received packets to the controller. The controller is linked to the available switches and manages them directly with orders sent via messages on a *secure reliable channel*. These messages are used to configure and maintain the switches, defining for each one the rules to forward packets it receives. At this stage we have a simple interaction between application level, and the provided high level network services. But this interaction is more complex if we look at it in details. Consider for this purpose a detailed view depicted in Fig. 2, of the interaction with the SDN network.

2.2 OpenFlow: a Standard Interface

OpenFlow is a standard communications interface, supported by the Open Network Foundation [1, 9, 17]. OpenFlow has been precisely defined but not formally.

As such, OpenFlow provides a means for specifying data level or control-plane logics and also protocols. However there is no mandatory formal specification or formal requirements; accordingly the network systems resulting from OpenFlow may be incorrect or not satisfying safety conditions.

The OpenFlow semantics being informal, tool builders may assume particular behaviour and functioning for the network devices, leading to inconsistencies and incorrect behaviours; that is the case for the order in which packets are processed inside a switch.

2.3 Issues and Related Work

There is a keen interest for SDN, justifying several papers from both industry and academia. Important efforts are devoted to the implementation of SDN [16, 18, 19]. SDN provides flexible network systems and distributed systems development but there is no guarantee that these systems are safe or correct. SDN as an asynchronous system undergoes the impact of time passing and non-determinism or concurrency of events. Packets may be received and distributed in any order causing for instance inconsistent interpretation in the switches when a forwarding route arrives after the related packet is sent. One of the main issues in SDN is the inconsistent packet forwarding during a network update which results in an update inconsistency [8]. Update consistency requires that packets are either forwarded by an old version of the forwarding table or by the new version of the table (after an update), but not by an interleaving of the old and the new version.

These issues require efforts to build robust tools and protocols on the basis of thoroughly studied SDN models. Much work have been devoted to various aspects of SDN among which the modelling and reasoning on the SDN controller[10], the analysis of the SDN traffic [8, 14].

According to the state of the art [4, 6, 12, 15] most investigations address the implementation issue as an important challenge; some of the aspects taken into account in these papers are: scalability, performance, security, simulation. The correctness of the implementations has received less attention.

In [13] the authors address the challenge of building robust firewalls for protecting OpenFlow-based networks where network states and traffic are frequently changed. They propose the FlowGuard framework for the detection and the resolution of firewall policy violation. They use an algorithmic approach.

VeriFlow is a verification tool proposed in [14] for checking in real-time network invariants and policy correctness in OpenFlow networks. This work is based on direct implementation that monitors the update events occurring on the network; it uses an algorithmic approach for the forwarding rules.

SDNRacer [8] is a network analyzer which can ensure that a network is free of harmful errors such as data races or per-packet inconsistencies. The authors provide a formal semantics enriched with a happens-before model, to capture when events can happen concurrently.

The work in [10] is devoted to the verification of an SDN controller; the authors provide an operational model for OpenFlow and formalize it in the Coq proof assistant. This model is then used to develop a verified compiler and a run-time system for a high-level network programming language.

To sum up, the previous references are the preliminary steps towards making SDN networks more reliable; but much works remain to be done:

- making easier for developers the construction and verification of controllers from various existing well-researched models,
- enhancing machine-assisted configuration of controllers and OpenFlow-based switches,
- promoting the reuse of correct SDN components in the deployment of new SDN (that is interoperability).

The goal of our work is to serve these purposes by contributing with a global, extensible, refinable formal model. It is the first event-based one, making it easy to derive simulators and also to prove safety and liveness properties. It is provided as a reusable formal basis for any one interested, avoiding hence to repeat the efforts through the chains of work.

Unlike in the case dedicated to implementations, we follow an approach similar to those addressing modelling and reasoning on controllers, by defining for the SDN a global formal model from which the models of the components can be derived and then correctly implemented.

3   Stepwise Refinement-Based Modelling of SDN

We use Event-B [2] and adopt a correct-by-construction approach.

3.1   An Overview of Event-B

Event-B [2,11] is a modelling and development method where components are modelled as abstract machines which are composed and refined into concrete machines. An *abstract machine* describes a mathematical model of a system behaviour[1]. In an Event-B modelling process, abstract machines constitute the dynamic part whereas *contexts* are used to describe the static part. A *context* is seen by machines. It is made of carrier sets and constants. It may contain properties (defined on the sets and constants), axioms and theorems. A machine is described, using named clauses, by a state space made of typed variables and invariants, together with several *event* descriptions.

State Space of a Machine. The variables constrained by the invariant (typing predicate, properties) describe the state space of a machine. The change from one state to the other is due to the effect of the events of the machine. Specific

---

[1] A system behaviour is a discrete transition system.

properties required by the model may be included in the invariant. The predicate $I(x)$ denotes the invariant of machine, with x the state variables.

Events of an Abstract Machine. Within Event-B, an event is the description of a system transition. Events are spontaneous and show the way a system evolves. An event e is modelled as a *guarded substitution*: $e \cong eG \implies eB$ where eG is the event *guard* and eB is the event *body* or *action*. An event may occur only when its guard holds. The action of an event describes, with simultaneous generalised substitutions, how the system state evolves when this event occurs: disjoint state variables are updated simultaneously.

The effect of events are modelled with generalised logical substitution (S) using the global variables and constants. For instance a basic substitution x := e is logically equivalent to the predicate x' *such that* $x' = e$. This is symbolically written $x' : (x' = e)$ where x' corresponds to the state variable x after the substitution and e is an expression. In the rest of the paper, the variable x is generalised to the list of state variables.

Several events may have their guards held simultaneously; in this case, only one of them occurs. The system makes internally a nondeterministic choice. If no guard is true the abstract system is blocking (deadlock).

In Event-B *proof obligations* are defined to establish model consistency via invariant preservation. Specific properties (included in the invariant) of a system are also proved in the same way.

Refinement. An important feature of the Event-B method is the availability of refinement technique to design a concrete system from its abstract model by stepwise enrichment of the abstract model. During the refinement process new variables (y) are introduced; the invariant is strengthened without breaking the abstract invariant, and finally the events guards are strengthened. In the invariant $J(x, y)$ of the refinement, abstract variables (x) and concrete variables (y) are linked. The refinement is accompanied with proof obligations in order to prove their correctness with respect to the abstract model.

Rodin Tool. Rodin[2] is an open tool dedicated to building and reasoning on B models, using mainly provers and the ProB model-checker. Rodin is made of several modules (plug-ins) to work with B models and interact with related tools.

3.2 Abstractions for SDN Modelling

An SDN is made of a controller connected to several switches. The controller is linked to the switches via a secure message channel which conveys message flows between the controller and the switches. The switches are interconnected via a data channel which conveys data packets. Consequently, the elementary abstractions using the Event-B notations, are the basic sets that represent: the switches (SW_ID), the packets (PACKET), the messages (MESG), the

---

[2] http://wiki.event-b.org/index.php/Main_Page.

packet headers (HEADER), the states of a switch (SW_STATE). The messages have types and may contain packets[3]: $mesgType \in MESG \nrightarrow MESGTYPE$, $mesgPk \in MESG \nrightarrow PACKET$.

A packet has several headers (MAC source address, MAC destination address, MAC type, IP source address, IP destination address, IP protocol, transport source port, transport destination port), for simplification we consider only one of such header: $pHeader_i \in PACKET \nrightarrow HEADER$. In the model these headers are specified like the function $pHeader_i$. The previous sets and constants are gathered in a CONTEXT EnvCtx0 (see Fig. 3), seen by an abstract MACHINE which contains the variables and the typing predicate and properties in the VARIABLES and INVARIANT clauses. The context is then successively extended as the machines are refined.

CONTEXT EnvCtx0
SETS
    PACKET set of packets (exchanged between switches, controllers, hosts)
    MESG set of messages (exchanged between switches and controller)
    MESGTYPE message types
    ENTRY set of entries of the flow table
    HEADER header+Actions: set of actions applied by switch to match packets
    SW_ID switch ID
    SW_STATE Openflow switch state
CONSTANTS
    PKIn PKOut BarrierQ BarrierR FlowMd askStatus Status AddE DelE ModE
AXIOMS
    $MESGTYPE = \{PKIn, PKOut, BarrierQ, BarrierR, FlowMd, askStatus, Status,$
        $AddE, DelE, ModE\}$
END

Fig. 3. Event-B specification of the primary context

The SDN is a set of components that work concurrently in an asynchronous manner; we build a first global abstract model that simulates the functioning of this asynchronous system. The global abstract model will be the basis for the development of the components.

To structure this abstract model, we consider the data model and the discretisation of the behaviour (a set of observed events) of each of its components as a family of events. This is important for mastering the interaction between components and the forthcoming decomposition of the model.

Switches. Each switch has a flow table which contains the elementary behaviour of the switch according to the packets entering the switch. The behaviour of a switch is as follows: when it receives a message from the controller, it analyses the information inside the message and accordingly performs the instructions

---

[3] The symbol $\nrightarrow$ denotes a partial function; $\leftrightarrow$ denotes a relation.

of the controller, for example updating its table, delivering a packet to a given port indicated in the message, dropping a packet or buffering a packet contained in the message. When a switch receives a packet from another switch, either it forwards the packet to another switch according to the rules in its current table, or it forwards the packet to the controller if there is no rule matching the packet headers. Accordingly, we have a set of switches: $switches \subseteq SW\_ID$. Each switch has:

- a flow table which may be empty or made of several entries:
  $flowTable \in ENTRY \nrightarrow switches$.
  Each entry has several headers (similar as for packets); each one is specified as follows[4]:
  $eHeader_i \in ENTRY \nrightarrow HEADER$
  $dom(eHeader_i) = dom(flowTable)$
- a status: $swStatus \in SW\_ID \nrightarrow SW\_STATE \wedge dom(swStatus) = switches$
- a buffer $swIncomingMsg$ containing all messages received by the switches:
  $swIncomingMsg \subseteq MESG \times switches$
- a buffer $swIPk$ for all packets it receives, before treatment:
  $swIPk \in PACKET \leftrightarrow switches$; $swIncomingPk$ is the set of packets such that $swIncomingPk \subseteq PACKET$ and $swIncomingPk = dom(swIPk)$.
  Each packet has a header: $pHeader_i \in PACKET \nrightarrow HEADER$
- a buffer $swOMsg$ that contains messages to be sent to the controller:
  $swOMsg \in MESG \leftrightarrow switches$; $swOutgoingMsg$ is a set of messages such that $swOutgoingMsg \subseteq MESG \wedge swOutgoingMsg = dom(swOMsg)$
- a buffer $swOPk$ containing packets to be sent to other switches or to the controller: $swOPk \in PACKET \leftrightarrow switches$ and $swOutgoingPk$ the set of packets such that $swOutgoingPk \subseteq PACKET \wedge swOutgoingPk = dom(swOPk)$.

Behaviour of the switch. We capture the behaviour of the switch by considering how it is involved in the interaction with its environment. Each impact of the environment is considered as an event. The (re)actions of the switch are modelled as events that in turn impact or not the environment. We have then a set of events characterizing the switches; they are as follows.

sw_rcv_matchingPkt: the condition for the occurrence of this event is that there is in the incoming packets of a switch sw, a packet pkt, received from another switch via the data channel $((pkt \mapsto sw) \in dataChan)$, which header $(ahd = pHeader1(pkt))$ is pattern-matched with one entry of the flow table of sw: $(\exists ee.(((ee \in ENTRY) \wedge (ee \in dom(flowTable))) \wedge (eHeader1(ee) = ahd)))$; the effect of the event is that the packet should be forwarded to another switch: $swIPk := swIPk \cup \{pkt\}$
The Event-B specification of the event is given in the Fig. 4.

sw_rcv_unmatchingPkt: its occurs when a switch receives a packet (from another switch) which header does not match any entry of the flow table.

---

[4] dom denotes the domain of a relation; ran denotes the range.

sw_sndPk2ctrl: its occurs when a switch emits to the controller, a message containing an unmatched packet;

sw_sendPckt2sw: a switch sends a packet to another switch via the data channel;

sw_newFTentry: the occurrence of this event expresses that a new entry is added to the flow table. ···

---

event sw_rcv_matchingPkt // a switch receives a packet matching a flow table entry
ANY sw pkt ahd
WHERE   /* the guard */
    $sw \in switches \ \wedge \ pkt \in PACKET \ \wedge \ (pkt \mapsto sw) \in dataChan$
    $ahd \in HEADER \ \wedge \ pkt \in dom(pHeader1)$
    $ahd = pHeader1(pkt)$
    $\exists ee \cdot (((ee \in ENTRY) \wedge (ee \in dom(flowTable))) \wedge (eHeader1(ee) = ahd))$
    $sw \in dom(swIPk) \ \wedge \ sw \mapsto pkt \notin swIPk$
THEN   /* the substitution */
    $swIncomingPk := swIncomingPk \cup \{pkt\}$ // input buffer updated;
    $dataChan := dataChan \setminus \{pkt \mapsto sw\}$
    $swIPk := swIPk \cup \{sw \mapsto pkt\}$ // packet will be forwarded
END

Fig. 4. Event-B specification of the event sw_rcv_matchingPkt

Controller. A controller administrates the switches with control messages. It has buffers which contain messages or packets to be sent/received to/from switches: a buffer for incoming packets ($ctlIncomingPk \subseteq PACKET$); a buffer for outgoing packets ($ctlOutgoingPk \subseteq PACKET$).

The controller emits/receives messages on/from the message channel. These messages contain either data packets or instructions to control the switches. Among the control messages we have: the Add order to add an new entry into the table flow of a switch; Modf to modify an entry into the flow table of a switch; Del to delete an entry into the flow table of a switch.

Behaviour of the controller. As for the switch, the behaviour of the controller is captured and modelled as a set of events denoting how the controller interacts with its environment. Each impact of the environment is considered as an event; the (re)actions of the controller are modelled as events that in turn impact or not the environment.

As illustration, among the events of the controller we have the following:

ctl_emitPkt: this event occurs when the controller emits to a switch sw, through a message, one of its pending packets; the condition for this occurrence is that there is some pending packets in the dedicated buffer ($pkt \in ctlOutgoingPk$). The effect of the event is that a message containing the packet is added to the secure channel: $secureChan := secureChan \cup \{msg \mapsto sw\}$ and the buffer is updated: $ctlOutgoingPk := ctlOutgoingPk\backslash\{pkt\}$. Figure 5 gives the Event-B specification of the event; all the remaining events are specified in a similar way.

ctl_rcvPacketIn: this event occurs when the controller receives a packet from a switch which previously received it but does not have an entry matching it.

ctl_askBarrier: the occurrence of this event specifies when the controller asks for a barrier; that means the controller orders the switch to perform some control with urgency and to send a barrier acknowledgement.

---

event ctl_emitPkt // the controller emits a mesg conveying a packet
ANY sw pkt msg
WHERE   /* the guard */
    $sw \in switches$ // in destination to one of the switches
    $pkt \in PACKET$
    $pkt \in ctlOutgoingPk$ // one of the packet to be sent on the sw
    $msg \in MESG$ // a given message to convey the packet
    $(msg \mapsto PKOut) \in mesgType$ // a packet of type OUT
    $(msg \mapsto pkt) \in mesgPk$ // the message contains the packet
THEN   /* the substitution */
    $secureChan := secureChan \cup \{msg \mapsto sw\}$ //emission on the channel
    $ctlOutgoingPk := ctlOutgoingPk \setminus \{pkt\}$
END

Fig. 5. Event-B specification of the event ctl_emitPkt

The global abstract model comprises in an EVENT clause, all the events characterizing the switches and the controller; the occurrence of each event is due to some conditions of the SDN and this occurrence has effect on the SDN. In Event-B a *guard* captures each condition; an Event-B *substitution* describes the effect of the event.

Interaction between Controller and Switches. The interaction is based on communications via channels; we distinguish a data packet channel and a control message channel. The channels are modelled with sets. A switch or a controller writes/reads messages on/from the channels according to their behaviour.

$$secureChan \subseteq MESG \times switches$$
$$dataChan \subseteq PACKET \times switches$$

A first abstract Event-B model is obtained by gathering all these abstractions on data and behaviour.

3.3 Correctness Conditions of the Model

The correctness of the global model depends on the properties formulated in the invariant, enhanced and proved during the model construction. Such properties are carefully derived from the understanding and the structuring of the SDN (see Sect. 3.2).

For instance the model ensures that: *outgoing packets are sent by one of the switches or by the controller.*
This property (SP) is progressively built with the following parts of the invariant. The packets delivered by a switch to other switches according to routing information are called outgoing packets (see Sect. 3.2).

Each switch is equipped with a buffer of data packets it received ($swIPk$) and a buffer of data packets it forwarded ($swOPk$):
$$swIPk \in switches \leftrightarrow PACKET \quad \land \quad swOPk \in switches \leftrightarrow PACKET.$$

The packets forwarded by a switch to other switches should come from its proper buffer: $\forall sw.swOPk(sw) \subseteq swIPk(sw)$

The union of the packets to be delivered by the switches is denoted by $swOutgoingPk$: $swOutgoingPk \subseteq \mathrm{ran}(swOPk)$

The packets in transit through the switches are gathered in the $swSentPkts$ variable: $swSentPkts \subseteq PACKET$

In the same way all the packets sent by the controller are gathered in the $ctlSentPkts$ variable: $ctlSentPkts \subseteq PACKET$

Finally the property SP is expressed by:

$$swOutgoingPk \subseteq swSentPkts \cup ctlSentPkts$$

In a similar way, may properties among which the two following ones, are progressively formulated as parts of the invariant.

The packets in the data channel should be sent by the controller or by the switches.

$$\mathrm{dom}(dataChan) \subseteq swSentPkts \cup ctlSentPkts$$

The contents of the switches buffers ($swIncomingPk$) should come from the controller or other switches.

$$swIncomingPk \subseteq ctlSentPkts \cup swSentPkts$$

These properties are first stated in the abstract model and then refined along the development process according to the refinement of the state variables.

3.4   Model Construction Strategy: The Refinements

Despite the general development strategy in Event-B which consists in building an abstract global model of a system and then to use several refinements to make it precise, it is still challenging to determine the refinement steps according to the problem at hand. In this work we have considered as one of our targets, the main components of the SDN. That is, we tried to deal with details related to the targeted components (switches, controller). The questions are: what are the main features of the switches and how they impact their environments? what are the main features of the controller behaviour and how they impact its environment? By answering these questions we finished by introducing, for instance, that switches use various ports and they receive/emit messages on ports. Consequently the first abstract model of channels is impacted and then refined.

We focus on the architecture of the SDN, and then tried to list the details that will support actually the achievement of the network services (routing, access control, traffic engineering; see Sect. 2). We have listed, the detailed structure of packets, the structure of messages, the fine-grained processing of packets inside the switches. Then we order these details and tried to handle them one by one. It follows that we have to detail in the refinements: the structure of packets with various headers and body parts; the structure of messages, and accordingly the refinement of the abstract channels; the behaviour of the events that specify the behaviour of both switches and controller. This guided us to master the gradual modelling. From the methodological point of view this is a recipe for (Event-B) specifiers.

We also follow the basic recommendations of Event-B to consider small steps of refinement at time. Table 1 gives an overview of the refinement chains.

Table 1. The refinement steps

GblModel0	The first abstract model; all the events are specified at a high level; for instance we do not have yet information on ports, etc
GblModel0_1	Refinement. Ports and headers are introduced in the state space thus refined; the related events are refined
GblModel0_2	Refinement. Priorities are introduced in the state space; messages are sent from the controller with a priority in their header
GblModel0_3	Refinement. The events guard are refined according to priority rules

3.5 Data Refinement

The set of ports (PORTID) is introduced as data refinement details in the GblModel0_1 refined abstract model. Packets are sent on ports according to the actions defined in the entries of the flow table. One port (also called action) may be the destination of a set of packets.

$$actionsQueues \in PORTID \twoheadrightarrow \mathbb{P}(PACKET) \text{ // packets targeting a port}$$
$$actions \in ENTRY \twoheadrightarrow \mathbb{P}(ACTION) \text{ // ports concerned by an entry}$$
$$\text{dom}(actions) = \text{dom}(flowTable) \text{ // all entries have target ports}$$

An entry may specify several actions or ports. The various fields in SDN packets are also introduced as data refinement with the functions: $macSrc$, $macDst$, $IpSrc$, $IpDst$, $IpProto$, $TpSrc$, $TpDst$, $TpSrcPt$, $TpDstPt$.

3.6 Behavioural Refinement

Explicit priority. The controller (via a human administrator) can introduce *priorities* as an information contained in the messages. Priorities are comparable, they are numbers. Consequently, we introduced this refinement level where the messages are refined by adding to them a field which represents their priority. In Event-B, this is a function giving the priority of each message:

$msgPriority \in MESG \nrightarrow MSG\_PRIORITY$ where $MSG\_PRIORITY$ is the set of priorities (a subset of naturals).

Accordingly, the event ctl_emitPkt for instance, is now refined in the model (GblModel0_2); its substitution sets the priority of the message which is sent.

Implicit priority. We introduced implicit priorities via a partial order on messages to be sent; in the sequel the symbol $\prec$ denotes this partial order.

To avoid inconsistencies in the behaviour of switches, the messages they sent should be reordered. In practice, when for instance the flow table is modified by an instruction coming from the controller, the outgoing packet in a switch may be forwarded in a wrong destination due to the modification. Besides, the controller can use the barrier to impose a quick modification.

Accordingly the modification messages coming from the switch should have lower priority compared with the forwarding messages. A priority rule which reorder the events, is that: the add control messages are processed after the forwarding of all data packets. The involved events in the model are: sw_newFTentry, sw_sendPckt2sw, sw_sendPk2Ctrl. Therefore we have the following ordering:

sw_newFTentry $\prec$ sw_sendPckt2sw
sw_sendPk2ctrl $\prec$ sw_sendPckt2sw
sw_sendPk2ctrl $\prec$ sw_newFTentry

As far as the Del order is concerned, as lost packets in the network can be claimed, we use this hypothesis to consider that the Del order has priority on the forward packet. For the Add order, this does not present an inconsistency risk for outgoing packets. For this reason the Add order can be processed in any order. Barrier messages coming from the controller are the most priority ones. Unmatched packets to be returned to the controller are lower priority than the packet to be forwarded to other switches: a rule is that packets to the controller are sent if there is no packet to be forwarded to other switches.

These priorities have been implemented (in GblModel0_3) as a refinement of our model. The guards of the involved events have been strengthen with these rules.

4   Deriving Correct Controller and Switch Components

The purpose is to derive SDN components from the global model resulting from the chain of refinements; such derivation is enabled with Event-B via the use of *model decomposition* techniques: the Abrial-style decomposition (called the A-style decomposition) [3] based on shared variables, and the Butler-style decomposition (called the B-style decomposition) [7, 20] based on shared events. Indeed when decomposing into sub-models a model where events use state variables, either the decomposition is based on the partition of the state variables (and some events may need variables in different sub-models; these are shared events) or the decomposition is based on the partition of events in which case some variables may be needed by events in different sub-models, these are shared variables). In the A-style decomposition, which we have used, events are first partitioned between Event-B sub-components. Then, according to shared variables only modified by one of the sub-components, the events which modify the variables in one component, are introduced as *external events* in the sub-components which do not modify the variables. These external events simulate the behaviour of the events which modify the variables, in the components where the variables are not modified. To avoid inconsistency, external events should not be refined. In the B-style decomposition, variables are first partitioned between the sub-components and then shared events (which use the variables of both sub-components) are split between the sub-components according to the used variables. We used the A-style decomposition because it is more relevant when we consider that the events describe the behaviour of each specific component (controller, switch) of the SDN.

Decomposition into a Controller and Switches

According to our modelling approach (see Sect. 3.2) where events are gathered by family, it is straightforward to list the events that describe the behaviour of the controller in order to separate them from the events related to the switches. The controller component is made of all the events, already introduced as such and prefixed with ctrl, which simulate the behaviour of the controller (see Sect. 3.2): ctl_emitPkt, ctl_rcvPacketIn, ctl_askBarrier, etc. Formally, the decomposition is as if a model $\mathcal{M}_\Sigma$ composed of components $\mathcal{S}_{\sigma_1}$ and $\mathcal{C}_{\sigma_2}$, such that[5] $\mathcal{M}_\Sigma \vDash P$, is split into sub-models $\mathcal{S}_{\sigma_1}$ and $\mathcal{C}_{\sigma_2}$ such that $\mathcal{S}_{\sigma_1} \vDash P$ and $\mathcal{C}_{\sigma_2} \vDash P$, with $\Sigma = \sigma_1 \cup \sigma_2$ the alphabet of $\mathcal{M}_\Sigma$ and σ_1 (resp. σ_2) the alphabet of $\mathcal{S}_{\sigma_1}$ (resp. $\mathcal{C}_{\sigma_2}$).

We experimented with the decomposition plugin of the Rodin toolkit using the A-Style decomposition approach.

A challenging issue here is the question of partitioning a set of identical behaviours; for instance if we would like to decompose the behaviours of the switches as a partition. This question is out of the scope of the existing decomposition techniques because of the non-determinism of data and event modelling.

5   Experimentations and Assessment

The global abstract model has been incrementally worked out by combining invariant verification, refinements and simulation. This is done with the Rodin platform[6]. In Table 2 we give the statistics of the performed proofs

---

[5] The symbol $\vDash$ denotes the logical satisfaction.
[6] http://wiki.event-b.org/index.php.

on the abstract model and its refinements; the Rodin platform generates consistency proof obligations and refinement proof obligations for the submitted models (see Sect. 3.1). These proof obligations were mostly automatically discharged by the Rodin prover; the remaining are interactively proved. The complete model is available at http://pagesperso.ls2n.fr/~attiogbe-c/mespages/nabla/sdn/SDN-WP2.pdf

The model of the last refinement level has been decomposed into a controller component and switches which preserve all the proved properties. One benefit of deriving components from a global formal model is the ability to study required properties involving the components and their environ-

Table 2. Proof statistics

Elt Name	Total	Auto	Manual	Undischarged
SDN-WP2	210	202	8	0
GlModel0	97	94	3	0
GlModel0_1	63	59	4	0
GlModel0_1_1	2	2	0	0
GblModel0_2	2	2	0	0
GblModel0_3	0	0	0	0

ment. We have illustrated this study with a few properties expected from SDN. Both safety and liveness properties have been considered. This can be extended to other specific properties, following a similar approach.

We have expressed and proved several global properties on the model before its decomposition into components. For instance: *The data packets received by any switch are sent by the controller or by the other switches.*

Proof. Assume *ctlSentPkts* be the set of packets sent by the controller; we have to prove that $\forall sw.(sw : switches \Rightarrow swIPs[\{sw\}] \subseteq ctlSentPks)$. If *swIncomingPks* is the union of the buffers of the switches, then it suffices to establish that $swIncomingPks \subseteq ctlSentPkts$. □

Several such safety properties (e.g. Table 3 and Sect. 3.3) have been expressed as invariants in the Event-B model and proved using the Rodin prover.

Table 3. A part of the considered safety properties

SP_a	Any packet in the data channel was sent by the controller or the switches
SP_b	Any packet in the switches buffers was sent by the controller or the switches
SP_c	The packets sent via the message channel are contained in *ctl_sentPkts*

Similarly, liveness properties study is undertaken using stepwise checking of basic properties. For instance, we prove that, the data packets generated by the controller, are finally emitted by this later. The formula LP_{deliv} (see Table 4) expresses this property. Literally it describes that after the occurrence of the event ctl_havePacket we will finally (F) observe the occurrence of ctl_emitPkt. The other formula in Table 4 are similar; the X symbol stands for the next operator. Event-B provides, via the ProB tool integrated in the Rodin, the facilities to state and prove liveness properties. ProB supports LTL, its extension LTL[e] and CTL properties with the standard modal and temporal operators.

Table 4. A part of the liveness properties in LTL/ProB

$\mathbf{LP}_{OKstatus}$	$e(ctl\_askStatusMsg) \Rightarrow F(e(ctl\_rcvStatus))$
$\mathbf{LP}_{deliv}$	$e(ctl\_havePacket) \Rightarrow F(e(ctl\_emitPkt))$
$\mathbf{LP}_{OKMach}$	$e(ctl\_emitPkt) \Rightarrow X(e(sw\_rcv\_machingPkt))$

6   Conclusion

We have shown how to build correct controller and switches components from the refinement of a global formal Event-B model of an SDN system. The correctness was established according to the properties captured and formulated as invariants from the SDN system requirements. The global model was first built by a systematic construction using refinements and then decomposed into the target components. The construction of the abstract model itself was achieved so as to be reusable as a recipe for Event-B developers, following the steps we had identified. We overcame the challenging modelling in Event-B, of an SDN system, viewing it as a discrete events system, and thus as an interaction between its main components. We evaluated our model and components for their conformance to the properties required for SDN systems. We experimented with the various aspects related to property proving and simulation, using the Rodin tool. As far as we know, among the related work using formal approaches, this study is the first one proposing an event-based approach for studying SDN systems.

We provided a core event-based model to set the foundation of frameworks dedicated to the development, analysis and simulation of SDN-based applications.

As future work, instead of a one-shot derivation of a specific code for the controller, we are investigating a parametric environment to enable the construction of specific controllers targeting various languages. The same idea is relevant for the switches. In light-weight distributed applications requiring the deployment of ad-hoc SDN, it is desirable to build various specific SDN switches from a single abstract model. Consequently, a process of generic refinement into code will be beneficial.

Acknowledgment. We thank the reviewers for helping to improve the paper.

References

1. Software-Defined Networking: The New Norm for Networks. ONF White paper (2012)
2. Abrial, J.-R.: Modeling in Event-B: System and Software Engineering. Cambridge University Press, Cambridge (2010)
3. Abrial, J.-R., Hallerstede, S.: Refinement, decomposition, and instantiation of discrete models: application to Event-B. Fundam. Inform. **77**(1–2), 1–28 (2007)
4. Akhunzada, A., Gani, A., Anuar, N.B., Abdelaziz, A., Khan, M.K., Hayat, A., Khan, S.U.: Secure and dependable software defined networks. J. Netw. Comput. Appl. **61**, 199–221 (2016)
5. Al-Shaer, E., Al-Haj, S.: FlowChecker: configuration analysis and verification of federated openflow infrastructures. In: Proceedings of 3rd ACM Workshop on Assurable and Usable Security Configuration, SafeConfig '10, USA, pp. 37–44. ACM (2010)
6. Alsmadi, I., Xu, D.: Security of software defined networks: a survey. Comput. Secur. **53**, 79–108 (2015)
7. Butler, M.: Decomposition structures for Event-B. In: Leuschel, M., Wehrheim, H. (eds.) IFM 2009. LNCS, vol. 5423, pp. 20–38. Springer, Heidelberg (2009). https://doi.org/10.1007/978-3-642-00255-7_2
8. El-Hassany, A., Miserez, J., Bielik, P., Vanbever, L., Vechev, M.: SDNRacer: concurrency analysis for software-defined networks. In: Proceedings of 37th ACM SIGPLAN Conference on Programming Language Design and Implementation, PLDI'16, USA, pp. 402–415 (2016)
9. Foundation, O.W.: Openflow switch specification. ONF **TS-006**(Version 1.3.0), 1–106 (2012)
10. Guha, A., Reitblatt, M., Foster, N.: Machine-verified network controllers. In: Proceedings of 34th ACM SIGPLAN Conference on Programming Language Design and Implementation, PLDI '13, USA, pp. 483–494. ACM (2013)
11. Hoang, T.S., Kuruma, H., Basin, D.A., Abrial, J.-R.: Developing topology discovery in Event-B. Sci. Comput. Program. **74**(11–12), 879–899 (2009)
12. Horvath, R., Nedbal, D., Stieninger, M.: A literature review on challenges and effects of software defined networking. Procedia Comput. Sci. **64**, 552–561 (2015); In: Conference on ENTERprise Information Systems/International Conference on Project MANagement/Conference on Health and Social Care Information Systems and Technologies, CENTERIS/ProjMAN/HCist (2015). Accessed 7–9 Oct 2015
13. Hu, H., Han, W., Ahn, G.-J., Zhao, Z.: FLOWGUARD: building robust firewalls for software-defined networks. In: Proceedings of 3rd Workshop on Hot Topics in Software Defined Networking, HotSDN '14, USA, pp. 97–102. ACM (2014)
14. Khurshid, A., Zou, X., Zhou, W., Caesar, M., Godfrey, P.B.: VeriFlow: verifying network-wide invariants in real time. In: Proceedings of 10th USENIX Conference on Networked Systems Design and Implementation, NSDI'13, USA, pp. 15–28. USENIX Association (2013)
15. Kreutz, D., Ramos, F.M.V., Verssimo, P.E., Rothenberg, C.E., Azodolmolky, S., Uhlig, S.: Software-defined networking: a comprehensive survey. Proc. IEEE **103**(1), 14–76 (2015)
16. Mahmud, A., Rahmani, R.: Exploitation of openflow in wireless sensor networks. In: Proceedings of 2011 International Conference on Computer Science and Network Technology, vol. 1, pp. 594–600 (2011)
17. OpenNetworkFoundation. SDN Architecture Overview. (V1.0) (2013)

18. Raza, M.H., Sivakumar, S.C., Nafarieh, A., Robertson, B.: A comparison of software defined network (SDN) implementation strategies. Procedia Comput. Sci. **32**, 1050–1055 (2014); In: The 5th International Conference on Ambient Systems, Networks and Technologies (ANT-2014), the 4th International Conference on Sustainable Energy Information Technology (SEIT-2014)
19. Rothenberg, C.E., Chua, R., Bailey, J., Winter, M., Corra, C.N.A., de Lucena, S.C., Salvador, M.R., Nadeau, T.D.: When open source meets network control planes. Computer **47**(11), 46–54 (2014)
20. Silva, R., Butler, M.: Shared event composition/decomposition in Event-B. In: Aichernig, B.K., de Boer, F.S., Bonsangue, M.M. (eds.) FMCO 2010. LNCS, vol. 6957, pp. 122–141. Springer, Heidelberg (2011). https://doi.org/10.1007/978-3-642-25271-6_7

Event-B Formalization of a Variability-Aware Component Model Patterns Framework

Jean-Paul Bodeveix[1]([✉]), Arnaud Dieumegard[2,3], and Mamoun Filali[4]

[1] IRIT-UPS, 118 Route de Narbonne, 31062 Toulouse, France
`Jean-Paul.Bodeveix@irit.fr`
[2] IRT Saint Exupéry, 3 Rue Tarfaya, 31400 Toulouse, France
`Anaud.Dieumegard@irit.fr`
[3] ONERA, 2 Avenue Edouard Belin, 31055 Toulouse, France
[4] IRIT-CNRS, 118 Route de Narbonne, 31062 Toulouse, France
`Mamoun.Filali@irit.fr`

Abstract. In the domain of model driven engineering, patterns have emerged as an ubiquitous structuring mechanism. Actually, patterns are used for instance at the requirement analysis level, during system design, and during the deployment and code generation phases. In this paper, we are interested in making precise the use of such a notion during system design. More precisely, our ultimate goal is to provide a semantic framework to support correct by construction architectures, i.e., the structural correctness of the architectures obtained through the application of patterns. For this purpose, we propose an Event-B modeling scheme for hierarchical component models. This model is built incrementally through horizontal refinements which introduce components, ports and lastly connectors. Patterns with variability are defined, instantiated and applied to user models. We show that these operations preserve the structural properties of the component model.

Keywords: Design patterns · Formal refinement · Variability
System engineering · Critical systems

1 Introduction

In the domain of model driven engineering, patterns have emerged as an ubiquitous structuring mechanism. Patterns are used for instance to express and structure requirements and to ease their analysis [8]. During the process of system development, during deployment, or for code generation activities, they ensure knowledge capitalization, and production homogeneity. Patterns may take various form and are specifically structured: textual patterns expressed as sentences, structural patterns for describing components combinations, code patterns for

---

This work was done while working on the MOISE project at IRT Saint Exupery.

© Springer Nature Switzerland AG 2018
K. Bae and P. C. Ölveczky (Eds.): FACS 2018, LNCS 11222, pp. 54–74, 2018.
https://doi.org/10.1007/978-3-030-02146-7_3

code generation ... We focus here on the development of system architectures that shall be refined until they can be used for equipment level refinement. The work we present here results from exchanges with safety system engineers who practice patterns for solving identified safety issues. We specifically focus here on automatically instantiated safety refinement patterns. The patterns we rely on are based on the ones detailed in [22].

We are1 interested in making precise the use of such a notion in the system development process. More precisely, our ultimate goal is to provide a semantic framework to support correct by construction architectures, i.e., the structural correctness of the architectures obtained through the application of patterns. For this purpose, we propose to use Event-B as the support platform to define the notion of hierarchical component. This Event-B model is built incrementally through horizontal refinements which introduce components, ports and lastly connectors. Patterns with variability are then defined, instantiated so that variable elements are fixed. Lastly we define pattern application on user models. We show that this transformation preserves the structural properties of the component model. We remark that Event-B is mainly used to assess the correctness of the patterns that engineers apply to given architectures.

We remark that achieving the production of structurally correct component models may be reached using different approaches. The *translation validation* approach [23] consists of verifying each individual translation whereas *transformation verification* [7] consists of verifying once and for all the generator itself. In this paper, we adopt the transformation verification approach. The specification of the transformation and its verification are done incrementally through successive refinements as supported by the Event-B method [2].

Section 2 motivates our proposal by means of a small case study and presents our pattern model. In Sect. 3, we describe how patterns are applied to component models. Section 4 introduces our formal modeling framework based on Event-B. Section 5 details within this formal setting the steps followed to apply a pattern to a model. Section 6 discusses some related works. Section 7 concludes and suggests some future works.

2 Motivating Example

We describe here an example that will be used first to clarify what we mean by a pattern and by pattern application. The next paragraph features a very simple component model. We then showcase the transformation of this model to replicate one of its components. Focus will be on the N-Version programming pattern as described in [22]. This pattern is proposed in the context of architecture safety in order to enhance system robustness. We detail its structure and content, the solution that is provided by the application of such a pattern, and its complexity from the scope of its variability.

2.1   Component Models

In our work, we consider hierarchical components models as an abstraction of the classical "boxes and arrows" modeling formalism used to model: systems as for example Capella [27], SysML [21] or AADL [14]; software as for example BIP [6], UML [25], Scade [4]; or hardware as for example VHDL [16]. In each of these formalisms, components are connected through arrows (and sometimes ports or interfaces).

We provide in Fig. 1 an example of a very simple component model. This model features the Sub1 component with 2 input ports and 1 output port. Each port of the component is connected to another component through links. In addition to the structural description of our simple model, we have attached

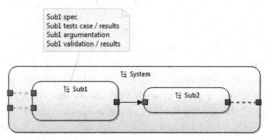

Fig. 1. A simple component model

to the Sub1 component one comment (yellow box) representing the association of a component with its specification, its verification or its validation artifacts or any other information of interest related to the component.

2.2   Replicating a Component

In the use case depicted in this paper, we propose to take the example that some analysis of the system leads to the need to provide different implementations of the Sub1 component in order to make the system fault tolerant. This mechanism is in this context referred to as replication of a component.

An example of our simple system where the Sub1 component has been replicated is provided in Fig. 2. In this new version of the model, we have three versions (Sub1_X) ($X \in \{1, 2, 3\}$) whose inputs are taken from the original inputs of the Sub1 component and dispatched using specific duplication (dupl_Y) ($Y \in \{1, 2\}$) components whose purpose are to replicate their inputs on each one of their outputs (the specification of these components is provided in the dupl spec comments). Then, the outputs of the replicated Sub1_X components are connected to a new component (vote_1) in charge of taking the decision of which one of the Sub1_X component output shall be relied on and sent to the outputs of the original Sub1 component.

One may remark that applying such a replication not only preserves the original structure of the model (the interface of the Sub1 component is the same), but also duplicates elements of the original model (the new Sub1_X components) and introduces new elements such as replication specifications (Diverse implementation of Sub1_1, Sub1_2, Sub1_3, Vote spec, and dupl spec).

2.3   Pattern Model

The previously depicted model modifications are considered in our setting as an example of the application of a design pattern. The model of Fig. 1 is the source model, and the model of Fig. 2 is the target or destination model where the pattern have been applied. What remains to be defined is what is the model of the pattern itself.

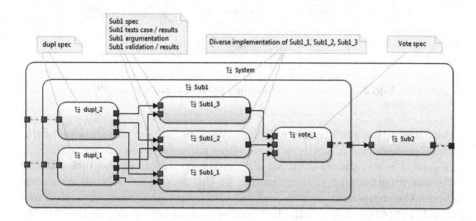

Fig. 2. A component model where a component is replicated twice

Many design pattern description formats have been defined in the litera-ture. We decided to rely on the classical pattern description format proposed by Coplien [9]. This comprises many information among which are the name of the pattern, its context of use and the problem solved by the pattern, the strength and weaknesses of the pattern, a graphical model representation and many other information. We also rely on the work of Preschern et al. [22] where a set of archi-tectural safety patterns are proposed for high level architecture definition. These patterns are connected to IEC 61508 standard methods for achieving safety and are extended with formal argumentation models. A simple example of such a pattern is provided in Fig. 3.

While this representation of a pattern is very interesting, it is nevertheless restrictive on the structural description of the pattern. It may be interesting to explicitly express the parameters of the pattern and its variability. In the context of the N-Version Programming pattern, N is a parameter meaning the number of times the software is developed. This parameter also impacts the implementation of the voting algorithm (Voter block). In addition to these, the links between the blocks described in the Solution section of Fig. 3 are a simplification of the actual possible links between blocks as there may be multiple links between these blocks: the N version of the block all have the same number of input values and output values. Both of these numbers are also parameters

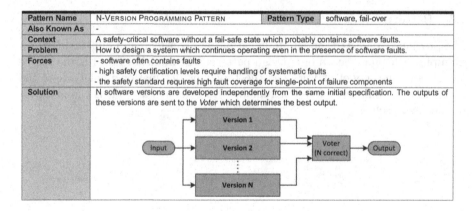

Pattern Name	N-VERSION PROGRAMMING PATTERN	Pattern Type	software, fail-over
Also Known As	-		
Context	A safety-critical software without a fail-safe state which probably contains software faults.		
Problem	How to design a system which continues operating even in the presence of software faults.		
Forces	- software often contains faults - high safety certification levels require handling of systematic faults - the safety standard requires high fault coverage for single-point of failure components		
Solution	N software versions are developed independently from the same initial specification. The outputs of these versions are sent to the *Voter* which determines the best output.		

Fig. 3. N-Version Programming pattern extract from [22]

of the pattern that shall be made explicit. We thus propose an extension of this model representation of patterns where these parameters are made explicit.

Figure 4 is our proposal for an alternative graphical representation of the N-Version programming pattern model. In this model, we rely on structural elements like components, ports, and links between components through ports, and `multiplicity` objects attached to components and ports. `multiplicity` objects are represented as small grey boxes in the figure. In this pattern model, three different multiplicity elements are defined: `nb_comp`, `nb_in`, and `nb_out`. They respectively stand for the number of times the component is replicated, and the number of input and output ports of the replicated component.

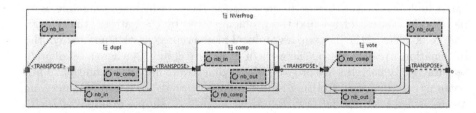

Fig. 4. The N-Version programming pattern model

By selecting the model element to be replicated (`Sub1` in Fig. 1), the last two `multiplicity` objects values are set (respectively to 2 and 1). The user shall then provide the value for `nb_comp` which is set to 3 in this case. Based on the user selection and provided values, the pattern model is instantiated: (1) its root component will have two input ports and one output port; (2) the root component of the pattern will be renamed as `Sub1`; (3) the `comp` component will be replicated `nb_comp` times as copies of the `Sub1` component with `nb_in` input ports and `nb_out` output ports; (4) the `dupl` component will be instantiated

nb_in times with one input port and nb_comp output ports; (5) the vote component will be instantiated nb_out times with nb_comp input ports and one output
port; (6) links between components are elaborated depending on their connection
pattern (detailed in the following section); Here, we use the *Transpose* pattern
to connect port i of component j to port j of component i; (7) finally, the original Sub1 model element is replaced with the newly produced Sub1 component
and its content. Figure 5 shows two instances of our N-Version-Programming
pattern, the first one with (nb_in=2 nb_out=1 nb_comp=3) and the second one
with (nb_in=2 nb_out=2 nb_comp=3).

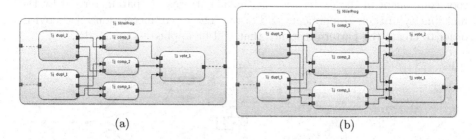

(a)   (b)

Fig. 5. (a) shows a first instance of the pattern. (b) shows a second instance.

In our setting, a pattern model is thus a family (in the product line [18] terminology) of models. Each combination of multiplicities allows for the definition
of a *pattern instance*. The production of design pattern instances and the application of the produced pattern instance on a model shall thus be implemented.

The object of the Event-B model proposed in this paper is first to formally
define the previously presented structure of a pattern, and second to propose
a formal definition of the pattern instantiation and application algorithms. We
have also produced a formalization of the structure of component models and
pattern models as Ecore[1] metamodels that is a de-facto standard formalism for
the specification of graph grammars[2]. This second formalization is used in order
to easily produce tools for the creation, edition and display of model instances
used throughout this paper. We do not detail these elements here.

3   Pattern Application

Our starting point is a parameterized pattern of which parameters are the multiplicities attached to pattern elements (components and ports). This pattern
is to be applied to a model. We distinguish three steps for pattern application:
initialization, elaboration, and application of patterns as depicted in Fig. 6.

---

[1] https://www.eclipse.org/modeling/emf/.
[2] Unlike abstract syntax which usually describe trees.

Fig. 6. Pattern application process

3.1 Pattern Initialization

During the initialization step, some of the pattern parameters are set and the root component of the pattern is identified. Patterns are parameterized by the multiplicity of their components and ports. These parameters must be fixed in order to create the pattern instance that will be applied to the model.

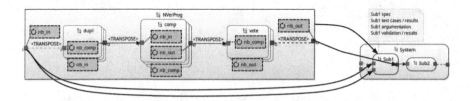

Fig. 7. Pattern (Fig. 1) to model (Fig. 4) mapping

Parameters of the pattern interface are defined through the mapping (Fig. 7) of pattern elements to model elements. This mapping constrains the multiplicity of some elements ($\mathtt{nb\_in} = 2$, $\mathtt{nb\_out} = 1$ in the figure). The $\mathtt{nb\_comp}$ multiplicity should be set by the user.

3.2 Pattern Instance Elaboration

The goal of the second step is to "elaborate" the pattern. This elaboration leads to a pattern instance where multiplicities have been suppressed and which can be directly applied to a given model. The elaboration of a pattern is a complex operation since a pattern can be considered as recursive along two dimensions: horizontally due to the multiplicities and vertically due to the nesting of components. This leads to the fact that the number of instances of a sub-component is the product of the multiplicities of all its ancestors including itself. When a component is replicated its contained ports are also replicated.

Links between ports are unfolded depending on their semantics which specify how the multiple instances of the source and destination port in the pattern should be connected. It is illustrated in Fig. 8 where components s and t have respective multiplicities m_s and m_t and are linked through ports of respective multiplicities m_p and m_q. We note that these link semantics are called *connection patterns* in AADL [14]. Also, frameworks like BIP [6] and

Fig. 8. Pattern link

Reo [5] provide expressive ways to define connectors between given components. However, our work is more concerned by the *application* of a pattern to an initial design.

Table 1 gives for each connection pattern the constraints on its elements multiplicities, and its textual and graphical mapping schemes.

Table 1. Connection patterns

Name	Multiplicities constraints	Source to target mapping scheme	Graphical mapping scheme
One_To_One	$m_p = m_q \wedge m_s = m_t$	$s_{i,j} \to t_{i,j}$	s_1 $\ldots s_i \ldots$ s_{n_2} ; t_1 $\ldots t_i \ldots$ t_{n_4}
First	$(m_p = 1 \vee m_q = 1) \wedge$ $m_s = m_t$	$s_{i,1} \to t_{i,1}$ $(m_p = 1$ case$)$	s_1 $\ldots s_i \ldots$ s_{n_2} ; t_1 $\ldots t_j \ldots$ t_{n_4}
	$m_p = m_q \wedge$ $(m_s = 1 \vee m_t = 1)$	$s_{1,i} \to t_{1,i}$ $(m_s = 1$ case$)$	s_1 ; t_1 $\ldots t_j \ldots$ t_{n_4}
Last	$(m_p = 1 \vee m_q = 1) \wedge$ $m_s = m_t$	$s_{i,1} \to t_{i,n}$ $(m_p = 1$ case$)$	s_1 $\ldots s_i \ldots$ s_{n_2} ; t_1 $\ldots t_j \ldots$ t_{n_4}
	$m_p = m_q \wedge$ $(m_s = 1 \vee m_t = 1)$	$s_{1,i} \to t_{n,i}$ $(m_s = 1$ case$)$	s_1 ; t_1 $\ldots t_j \ldots$ t_{n_4}
Rotate	$m_p = m_q \wedge m_s = m_t$	$s_{i,j} \to t_{(i+1)\% n_2, j}$	s_1 $\ldots s_{n_2 - 1}$ s_{n_2} ; t_1 t_2 $\ldots$ t_{n_4}
Transpose	$m_p = m_t \wedge m_s = m_q$	$s_{i,j} \to t_{j,i}$	s_1 $\ldots s_i \ldots$ s_{n_2} ; t_1 $\ldots t_j \ldots$ t_{n_4}

This table can be extended to support additional connection patterns. For example, variants of `Rotate` could be parameterized by the number of shifts, shifting could be applied to ports or components or both...

3.3   Pattern Instance Application

In the final step, the unfolded pattern instance can be applied to the model. Applying a pattern instance comes to merging instance model elements into the user model while keeping mapped elements identical. In category theory, this operation can be seen as a pushout where mapped elements are identified.

4   Formal Framework and Component Model

Our formal framework is modeled in Event-B which supports powerful data modelling capacities inherited from set theory and offers events as the unique control structure to define data evolution. After an overview of Event-B, we describe our methodology and our component model in an incremental way.

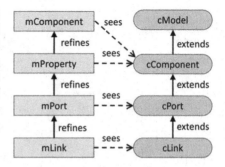

Fig. 9. Event-B model structure

4.1   A Brief Overview of Event-B

The Event-B method allows the development of correct by construction systems and software [2]. It supports a formal development process based on a refinement mechanism with mathematical proofs. We take as example the framework we have developed to illustrate the structure of an Event-B project (Fig. 9). In this figure, boxes represent Event-B machines, rounded boxes contexts, and arrows relations between these elements. Static data models are introduced incrementally through a chain of context extensions (here, with `cModel` as root). Dynamic data updated by events are introduced in machines (here, with `mComponent` as root) and subsequently refined. Each machine can access context data through the `sees` link. Contexts define abstract data types through sets, constants and axioms while machines define symbolic labelled transition systems. The state of a transition system is defined as the value of machine variables. Labelled transitions are defined by events specifying the new value of variables while preserving invariants. Moreover, the **theorem** clause expresses facts that should be satisfied. Proof obligations for wellformedness, invariant preservation and theorems are automatically generated by the Rodin tool [26]. They can be discharged thanks to automatic proof engines (CVC4, Z3 ...) or through assisted proofs.

Notations. For the most part, Event B uses standard set theory and its usual set notation. Some notations are specific to Event B:

- **pair construction:** pairs are constructed using the maplet operator $\mapsto$. A pair is thus denoted $a \mapsto b$ instead of (a, b). The set of pairs $a \mapsto b$ where $a \in A$ and $b \in B$ is denoted $A \times B$.
- A subset of $A \times B$ is a *relation*. The set of relations from A to B is denoted $A \leftrightarrow B = \mathcal{P}(A \times B)$. A relation $r \in A \leftrightarrow B$ has a domain: $\mathbf{dom}(r)$ and a codomain: $\mathbf{ran}(r)$. When a relation r relates an element of $\mathbf{dom}(r)$ with at most one element, it is called a function. The set of partial functions from A to B is denoted $A \nrightarrow B$, the set of total functions is denoted $A \rightarrow B$. The image of a set A by a relation r is denoted $r[A]$.
- The relation composition of two relations $r_1 \in A \leftrightarrow B$ and $r_2 \in B \leftrightarrow C$ is denoted as $r_1; r_2$.
- The **direct product** $r_1 \otimes r_2$ of relations $r_1 \in A \leftrightarrow B_1$ and $r_2 \in A \leftrightarrow B_2$ is the relation containing the pairs $(x \mapsto (y_1 \mapsto y_2))$ where $x \mapsto y_1 \in r_1$ and $x \mapsto y_2 \in r_2$.
- **domain restriction:** $D \lhd r = \{x \mapsto y \mid (x \mapsto y) \in r \wedge x \in D\}$
- **range restriction:** $r \rhd D = \{x \mapsto y \mid (x \mapsto y) \in r \wedge y \in D\}$
- **overwrite:** $f \oplus g = ((\mathbf{dom}(f) \backslash \mathbf{dom}(g)) \lhd f) \cup g$. For instance, such a notation is used to denote a new array obtained by changing the element of an array a at index i: $a \oplus \{i \mapsto e'\}$.

As already said, Event-B machines specify symbolic transitions through events. An event has three optional parts: parameters (**any** p1 ... pn), guards (**where** ...) specifying constraints to be satisfied by parameters and state variables, and actions (**then** ...) specifying state variables updates. Guards are defined in set-based predicate logic.

4.2   Methodology

The aim of our work is to provide a formal semantics to the application of patterns with multiplicities. This formal semantics is obtained through horizontal refinements [2]. We first elaborate an initial machine dealing with our basic components. Then, through refinements, we introduce new machines dealing successively with components having properties, ports and links. The last machine can be considered as the specification of a pattern application and the starting point for code generation through vertical refinements [1]. In the following, we first give a global overview of the considered development, then, we detail the Event-B machines underlying this development.

4.3   Incremental Description of the Component Model

Since our focus is on system engineering, our basic entity is a model denoted by the set Model. Each model has its *own* components which belong to the set Component. Patterns are introduced as a subset of Model. Except for these base sets, modeling elements are introduced through machine variables as we intend to build and update models. These modeling elements will be introduced incrementally using a horizontal refinement-based approach. At first, we introduce components in the machine mComponent. A model is related to a finite set of components. Each component belongs to at most one model. Furthermore, components associated to patterns have a multiplicity which will be used to parameterize the elaboration of pattern instances (c.f. Listing 1.1[3]).

We adopt a hierarchical *component* model. We formalize the hierarchy property over the components of each model. The partial function container returns the parent of a component, if any.

Listing 1.1. Models and components

```
@comp components ∈ Model ↔ Component
@comp_finite ∀m·finite(components[{m}])
@comp_not_shared components⁻¹ Component ⤔ Model
@c_mult c_multiplicity ∈ components[Pattern] → ℕ
```

In order to be well defined, containment should be acyclic. To ensure this property, we assume the existence of an irreflexive superset of the transitive closure of the container function: it is represented by the existentially quantified relation f [12]. Note that Event-B does not provide a transitive closure operator and even if it was available, using a superset is sufficient and leads to simpler proof obligations (c.f. Listing 1.2).

Listing 1.2. Hierarchy of components

```
@cont_ty container ∈ ran(components) ⤔ ran(components)
@cont_ctr components;container;components⁻¹ ⊆ id
@acycl ∃f· f ∈ Component ↔ Component ∧ container ⊆ f ∧ f;f ⊆ f ∧ id ∩ f = ∅
```

In order to support modular descriptions, a component defines a set of input or output *ports* (c.f. Listings 1.3 and 1.4). A base set Port, partitioned into input and output ports (IPort and OPort) is introduced in an extension cPort of the context cComponent.

Listing 1.3. Ports context

```
context cPort extends cComponent
sets Port
constants IPort OPort
axioms
  @part partition (Port, IPort, OPort)
end
```

Listing 1.4. Port invariants

```
@port_ty ports ∈ ran(components) ↔ Port
@port_finite ∀c·finite(ports[{c}])
@port_not_shared ports⁻¹ ∈ Port ⤔ Component
@p_mult p_multiplicity ∈ (components;ports)[Pattern] → ℕ
```

---

[3] In Event-B, proposition labels are introduced by the @ symbol.

Modeling elements related to ports are declared in a refinement, named mPort, of the root machine. A port belongs to at most one component. Ports of pattern components have a multiplicity. A base set Link is added in the context cLink. Our component model is refined (machine mLink) to add *links* between pairs of ports. A link is also defined through its source and destination ports. For this purpose, we introduce the src and dst functions (Listing 1.5).

The direction of links must be compatible with the one of its source and destination ports. A link can connect a component port and a sub-component port or two sub-component ports, which

Listing 1.5. Links

```
@link_ty   links ∈ ran(components) ↔ Link
@link_finite  ∀c· finite( links [{c}])
@src_ty   src ∈ ran(links) → ran(ports)
@dst_ty   dst ∈ ran(links) → ran(ports)
```

leads to four cases (graphically pictured in Fig. 10 and formalized in Listing 1.6). For example, if an input port is connected to an output port (case (1)), these ports belong to the same component. Thus, the source and destination ports, supposed to be an input and an output, are ports of the component to which the link is attached. In the same way, case (2) can be read as follows: if a link of a given component connects an input to an input, its source is a port of this component and its destination is a port of a direct sub-component.

Listing 1.6. Connection constraints

```
@link_cio  links ; (( src ⊗ dst) ▷ (IPort × OPort)) ⊆ ports ⊗ ports
@link_cii  links ; (( src ⊗ dst) ▷ (IPort × IPort)) ⊆ ports ⊗ (container⁻¹; ports)
@link_coi  links ; (( src ⊗ dst) ▷ (OPort × IPort)) ⊆ (container⁻¹; ports) ⊗ (container⁻¹; ports)
@link_coo  links ; (( src ⊗ dst) ▷ (OPort × OPort)) ⊆ (container⁻¹; ports) ⊗ ports
```

We comment these constraints by expanding the formula labelled link_cio[4]

$$\forall\ c\ p_1\ p_2.$$

$$\overbrace{\phantom{\text{src}}}^{p_1 = \text{src}(l)} \quad \overbrace{\phantom{\text{dst}}}^{p_2 = \text{dst}(l)}$$

$$(\exists l.c \mapsto l \in \text{links} \wedge l \mapsto p_1 \in \text{src} \wedge l \mapsto p_2 \in \text{dst} \wedge p_1 \in \text{IPort} \wedge p_2 \in \text{OPort})$$
$$\Rightarrow c \mapsto (p_1 \mapsto p_2) \in \text{ports} \otimes \text{ports}$$
$$\forall\ c\ l.\ c \mapsto l \in \text{links} \wedge \text{src}(l) \in \text{IPort} \wedge \text{dst}(l) \in \text{OPort}$$
$$\Rightarrow c \mapsto \text{src}(l) \in \text{ports} \wedge c \mapsto \text{dst}(l) \in \text{ports}$$

which can be read as the source and destination ports belong to the same c component.

The presence of links between components and ports with multiplicities impose constraints on these multiplicities. Multiplicities are attached to ports and components of the subset Pattern of Model. Pattern links must be coherent with these multiplicities and depend on the nature of the link.

---

[4] The equations over braces are deduced from the functionality of src and dst (Listing 1.5).

We only consider here (Listing 1.7) *Transpose* links which should connect instance port number i of instance component number j to instance port number j of instance component number i where i and j are in the range of pattern port and component mul-

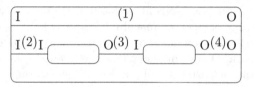

Fig. 10. Component (I/O) ports links

tiplicities. In order to make unfolding possible, the multiplicity of the source port should be equal to the multiplicity of the target component, and conversely.

Listing 1.7. Multiplicity constraints

```
@tsrc ∀l·l∈ (components;links)[{Pat}]∩Transpose ⇒ p_multiplicity (src(l))= c_multiplicity (ports⁻¹(dst(l)))
@tdst ∀l·l∈ (components;links)[{Pat}]∩Transpose ⇒ p_multiplicity (dst(l))= c_multiplicity (ports⁻¹(src(l)))
```

Properties (e.g. requirements, tests, constraints...) may be associated to components, ports and links. We thus have defined the `Property` set, the elements of which are attached to components through the `cProperties` relation. We have only considered here properties attached to components.

The invariant properties we have introduced apply either to specific models (patterns when multiplicities are concerned) or to any model. The events we will present now let patterns unchanged, but create instances and update user models. They should thus establish or preserve these wellformedness properties. Three identifiers are introduced to designate these models: `Pat` for a pattern, `Inst` for a pattern instance and `Mdl` for a user model. These identifiers are declared as constants but they designate models defined through the variables introduced by the successive refinements, which allow them to evolve.

5   Pattern Application in Event-B

We study the application of domain specific design patterns to produce refinements of architecture models and ensure that the produced model including the instantiated pattern is a structurally correct refinement. We present the successive steps, illustrated by Fig. 11, needed to perform pattern application in an iterative way. In this figure, loops express the repeated firing of events during the top down traversal of the pattern structure.

5.1   Pattern Initialization Step

The `initialize_pattern` event instantiates the parameters of the pattern and identifies the root components of the pattern. This event is enriched in each refinement:

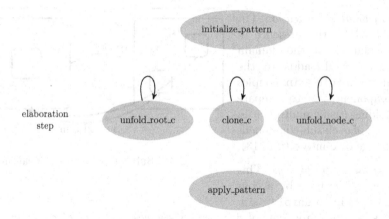

Fig. 11. Pattern application steps

Component and ports level Component (resp. ports) mapping between the pattern and the source model are provided. They allow for the extraction of components (resp. ports) multiplicities based on the number of source model elements mapped to the considered pattern element. Additional explicit pattern components (resp. ports) multiplicities are also provided by the user.

Link level. Finally at the link level, link mappings are provided and multiplicity constraints are checked depending on the link semantics (c.f. multiplicity constraints provided in Table 1).

5.2 Instance Elaboration Step

This step is initiated by the `unfold_root_c` which marks root components to be unfolded. Then, the events `unfold_node_c` and `clone_c` express the elaboration of a pattern along these two dimensions. Actually, these two events operate in a mutually recursive way. Auxiliary events and state variables are introduced to make the replication process iterative. These events are enriched in each refinement:

Component level

Root components unfolding. The instantiation event sets the variable `to_unfold_c` with the set of pattern components without containers. The `unfold_root_c` event takes one such component c, creates the associated instance components. The number of the created component is the multiplicity of c. The event stores the couples (instance, c) in the function `to_clone_c` used as a temporary variable to fire the next step. Links between instance and pattern components are stored in `i2p_c` (Fig. 12).

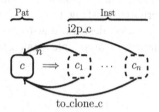

Fig. 12. Unfolding roots

Sub-component identification. This step is fired by the presence of a component c in the domain of to_clone_c. It adds to the relation to_unfold_c_in couples (sub-component, c) to prepare the unfolding (using multiplicities n_1 and n_2) of each sub-component of the image of c into c (Fig. 13).

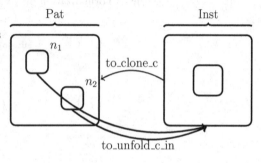

Fig. 13. Sub-component identification

Sub-component unfolding. This step (Fig. 14) is fired by a couple (c, dest) in to_unfold_c_in. It creates as sub-components of dest new instances $c_1, \ldots, c_n$ of c, the number of which corresponding to its multiplicity. The new sub-components are mapped to c in to_clone_c to pursue the unfolding process.

Port level. The sub-component identification step is enriched by storing in to_unfold_p_in ports to be unfolded with their destination component. A new event is added to unfold ports. It is fired by the presence of a pattern port in the relation to_unfold_p_in. Ports are created with the same direction as the pattern port and

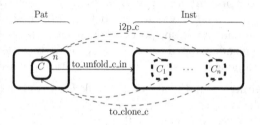

Fig. 14. Sub-components unfolding

linked to the instance component. The variable i2p_p is used to store mappings between instance and pattern ports.

Link level. We fire link creation within a given instance component c after its sub-components unfolding. For this purpose, four injective mappings, indexed by multiplicities, are declared from pattern source and destination components and ports to sub-components of c and their input or output ports. As a consequence, we only consider here links between two sub-components, not redirection links between a component and a sub-component, or cross-links from an input to an output of a component. In the Event-B model, we only consider *transpose* links. The corresponding multiplicity constraint is added and the array of links is created (Listing 1.8). We can see the four mappings (sci, spi, dci, dpi) to source (s) then destinations (d) components (c) and ports (p) instances (i) and the newly created links (new_l).

Listing 1.8. Link Unfolding

```
@links links := links ∪ ({c} × ran(new_l))
@nsrc src := src ∪ {ip,ic· ip ↦ ic ∈ dom(new_l) | new_l(ip↦ic) ↦ spi(sci(ic))(ip)}
@ndst dst := dst ∪ {ip,ic· ip ↦ ic ∈ dom(new_l) | new_l(ip↦ic) ↦ dpi(dci(ip))(ic)}
```

Properties. When elements (components, ports or links) are duplicated, their associated properties are also duplicated. This is done in the mProperty machine where the unfolding events are refined. An example of such a refinement for the unfold_root_c event is provided in Listing 1.9[5]. A similar refinement is applied for the replication of properties for ports and links in the respective events.

Listing 1.9. Properties replication for components

```
event unfold_root_c extends unfold_root_c
   then
      @prop cProperties := cProperties ∪ (ran(new_c)×cProperties[{c}])
end
```

Instantiation properties. Properties of pattern instantiation are stated as invariants. We have already expressed that the instance model (as well as any model) is well structured. We have added additional properties stating that pattern and instance models seen as labelled graphs are bisimilar with respect to the component-to-component relation container, the component-to-port relation ports, the link-to-port relations src and dst and specified the semantics of transpose links:

```
@inst2pat_cont inst2pat_c;container = container;inst2pat_c
@inst2pat_comp inst2pat_p;ports⁻¹ = ports⁻¹;inst2pat_c
@inst2pat_l_src inst2pat_l;src = src;inst2pat_p
@inst2pat_l_dst inst2pat_l;dst = dst;inst2pat_p
@transp_correct1 ∀l·l ∈ (components;links)[{Inst}] ∩ Transpose ⇒
      p_index(src(l)) = c_index(ports⁻¹(dst(l)))
@transp_correct2 ∀l·l ∈ (components;links)[{Inst}] ∩ Transpose ⇒
      p_index(dst(l)) = c_index(ports⁻¹(src(l)))
```

5.3 Instantiated Pattern Application Step

Pattern application is specified by the event apply_pattern initially defined for component-only models and then incrementally specified to support ports and links. This event applies the pattern instance obtained through the preceding step to the user-supplied model. This event is enriched in each refinement:

Component level. Pattern instance application (Listing 1.10) is fired by providing a mapping inst_components from instance components to model components.

---

[5] In Event-B, event action labels are introduced by the @ symbol.

Listing 1.10. Instance application at Component level

```
event apply_pattern // transformation du mod\'{e}le
  any inst_components // instance mapping
     new_components
  where
    @ic inst_components ∈ components[{Inst}] ⤖ components[{Mdl}]
    @nc new_components ∈ components[{Inst}] \ dom(inst_components) ↣ Component \ ran(components)
    @acycl_inst_components dom(inst_components) ◁ container;inst_components ⊆ inst_components;container
    @acycl_container container[dom(inst_components)] ⊆ dom(inst_components)
  then
    @m components := components ∪ ({Mdl}×ran(new_components))
    @f container := container ∪ ((inst_components ∪ new_components)⁻¹;container;
                     (inst_components ∪ new_components))
end
```

Listing 1.11. Updated superset of the model containment relation

```
new_components⁻¹; f; inst_components; f0 ∪
(new_components⁻¹; f; (new_components ∪ inst_components)) ∪ f0
```

Unmapped components (not belonging to the interface), designated by the **new_components** identifier, will be created and inserted to the set of components of the model. The container function of the model is updated to take into account containment coming from the pattern instance (Fig. 15).

The main point is to show that invariant properties are preserved, one of them being the

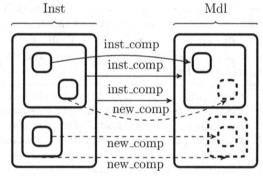

Fig. 15. Pattern application

acyclicity of the containment relationship. Some hypotheses (**@acycl_inst** and **@acycl_container**) are needed to avoid merging a graph and its inverse: if an instance component is mapped to a model component and has a container, this container should be mapped to the container of the model component. The acyclicity proof is then quite automatic once the superset of the transitive closure of the new container function has been provided. Given supersets **f** and **f0** of the pattern instance (resp. user model) containment function supposed to be closed for composition. The relation of Listing 1.11 contains the updated (after pattern application) model containment relation, it is closed for composition and is irreflexive. The added hypotheses ensure that the pattern instance is inserted as a subtree of the user model. Thus the two containment relations need not be interleaved.

Listing 1.12. Instance application at Property level

```
event apply_pattern extends apply_pattern
  any inst_props
  where
    @inst_prop inst_props ∈ Property ⇸ Property // pattern properties to model properties
  then
    @prop cProperties := cProperties ∪
      ((inst_components ∪ new_components)⁻¹;cProperties; (id ◁ inst_props))
```

Properties. Properties attached to pattern components are transferred to their corresponding model components (Listing 1.12). However, if pattern properties are instanciated by model properties, these ones are used instead.

Port and link levels. Instance pattern application is extended to ports using the same code schema as for components. Container update is replaced by port-to-component update. Furthermore port mapping and new ports should preserve port direction. In the same way, links are considered and link to port attachments are made consistent.

6   Related Works

A refinement pattern is a transformation rule that constructs a model refinement. The generation of correct-by-construction B/Event-B refinements has already been studied. They either propose a dedicated language for the expression of patterns ([24] for B, [17] for Event-B), or a pattern is seen as a usual Event-B machine that is mapped on the Event-B machine to be refined [15].

However, rather than focusing on patterns applied on Event-B models, our objective is the formalization using Event-B of the instantiation and the application of patterns for system architectures expressed using component models. Let us remark that a pioneering work advocating a formal approach, especially for architectural design patterns, is [3,11]. Behavioral semantics of the patterns is considered thanks to TLA: the Temporal Logic of Actions [19] and the behavioral correctness of the composition with respect to safety and fairness properties is proven. To the best of our knowledge, this work has not been mechanized.

We have chosen Event-B as a meta-level framework and used it to express a semantics for components models usually adopted by Model Based System Engineering frameworks [13,28]. Using this framework, we have defined a semantics for the definition, the instantiation and the application of patterns. As in [13], patterns are defined by adding multiplicities to target models and a pattern application algorithm is proposed. However, we consider component models, not argumentation models and our formalization is incremental (horizontal refinement) and its dynamics has been formalized through Event-B events. Thus, pattern elaboration and application are not monolithic algorithms and can easily be extended through refinement. As a consequence, correctness proofs can also be of finer grain.

As we said in the introduction, patterns are used in many stages of the development process. Temporal patterns have been proposed by [10] to promote the use of temporal logics for behavioural specifications. Also, in a context closer to ours, with respect to the underlying component model, [20] consider dynamic properties of patterns. However, their approach is based on model checking and consequently follows a translation validation approach whereas we follow a transformation verification approach. It should be interesting to investigate how such dynamic properties could be combined with the static properties presented in this paper and evaluate well suited verification approaches.

7   Conclusion

As said in the introduction, the work presented here results from exchanges with safety system engineers. Safety concerns lead to applying some design patterns selected among those solving the identified safety issues. In order to make the pattern library reusable, we provide a limited form of variability management through pattern model element multiplicities. We have presented an Event-B specification of two main operations needed to support the process: pattern instantiation taking into account variability and pattern instance application to the user model. These operations are modeled in an incremental way based on horizontal refinements and are shown to preserve basic structural properties of the component model.

Additional work may also be done in order to prove relevant properties on the pattern instantiation and application algorithms especially regarding the correctness of the application of the pattern. Such correctness shall be defined properly in terms of preservation of replicated model elements properties. Extensions of the pattern instantiation/application mechanisms may allow the mapping of sets of components/ports/links to a single pattern model element. This leads to a more powerful instantiation mechanism allowing in our example to replicate the chain of components used as input of the replicated component. As said in the introduction, we have used Event-B mainly to assess the correctness of pattern application. We believe that this "correct by construction" approach is interesting for the elaboration of frameworks dedicated to, e.g. safety, engineers.

References

1. Abrial, J.-R.: The B-book: Assigning Programs to Meanings. Cambridge University Press, New York (1996)
2. Abrial, J.-R.: Modeling in Event-B: System and Software Engineering, 1st edn. Cambridge University Press, New York (2010)
3. Alencar, P.S.C., Cowan, D.D., Lucena, C.J.P.: A formal approach to architectural design patterns. In: Gaudel, M.-C., Woodcock, J. (eds.) FME 1996. LNCS, vol. 1051, pp. 576–594. Springer, Heidelberg (1996). https://doi.org/10.1007/3-540-60973-3_108

4. Abdulla, P.A., Deneux, J., Stålmarck, G., Ågren, H., Åkerlund, O.: Designing safe, reliable systems using scade. In: Margaria, T., Steffen, B. (eds.) ISoLA 2004. LNCS, vol. 4313, pp. 115–129. Springer, Heidelberg (2006). https://doi.org/10.1007/11925040_8

5. Arbab, F.: Reo: a channel-based coordination model for component composition. Math. Struct. Comput. Sci. **14**(3), 329–366 (2004)

6. Basu, A., Bensalem, S., Bozga, M., Combaz, J., Jaber, M., Nguyen, T.-H., Sifakis, J.: Rigorous component-based system design using the BIP framework. IEEE Softw. **28**(3), 41–48 (2011)

7. Blazy, S., Leroy, X.: Mechanized semantics for the clight subset of the C language. J. Autom. Reason. **43**(3), 263–288 (2009)

8. Carson, R.S.: Implementing structured requirements to improve requirements quality. In: INCOSE International Symposium, vol. 25, pp. 54–67. Wiley Online Library (2015)

9. Coplien, J.O.: Software Patterns. SIGS Management Briefings. SIGS books & multimedia, New York (1996)

10. Dwyer, M.B., Avrunin, G.S., Corbett, J.C.: Patterns in property specifications for finite-state verification. In: Proceedings of the ICSE' 99, Los Angeles, CA, USA, May 16–22, pp. 411–420 (1999)

11. Dong, J., Alencar, P.S.C., Cowan, D.D., Yang, S.: Composing pattern-based components and verifying correctness. J. Syst. Softw. **80**(11), 1755–1769 (2007)

12. Damchoom, K., Butler, M., Abrial, J.-R.: Modelling and proof of a tree-structured file system in event-b and rodin. In: Liu, S., Maibaum, T., Araki, K. (eds.) ICFEM 2008. LNCS, vol. 5256, pp. 25–44. Springer, Heidelberg (2008). https://doi.org/10.1007/978-3-540-88194-0_5

13. Denney, E., Pai, G., Whiteside, I.: Model-driven development of safety architectures. In: 20th ACM/IEEE International Conference on Model Driven Engineering Languages and Systems, MODELS 2017, Austin, TX, USA, September 17–22, 2017, pp. 156–166. IEEE Computer Society (2017)

14. Feiler, P.H., Gluch, D.P.: Model-Based Engineering with AADL - An Introduction to the SAE Architecture Analysis and Design Language. SEI Series in Software Engineering. Addison-Wesley, Upper Saddle River (2012)

15. Hoang, T.S., Fürst, A., Abrial, J.-R.: Event-B patterns and their tool support. Softw. Syst. Model. **12**(2), 229–244 (2013)

16. Heinkel, U., Glauert, W., Wahl, M.: The VHDL Reference: A Practical Guide to Computer-Aided Integrated Circuit Design (Including VHDL-AMS) with Other. Wiley, New York (2000)

17. Iliasov, A., Troubitsyna, E., Laibinis, L., Romanovsky, A.: Patterns for refinement automation. In: de Boer, F.S., Bonsangue, M.M., Hallerstede, S., Leuschel, M. (eds.) FMCO 2009. LNCS, vol. 6286, pp. 70–88. Springer, Heidelberg (2010). https://doi.org/10.1007/978-3-642-17071-3_4

18. Kang, K., Cohen, S., Hess, J., Novak, W., Peterson, A.: Feature-oriented domain analysis (foda) feasibility study. Technical Report CMU/SEI-90-TR-021, Software Engineering Institute, Carnegie Mellon University, Pittsburgh, PA (1990)

19. Lamport, L.: Specifying Systems: The TLA+ Language and Tools for Hardware and Software Engineers. Addison-Wesley, Boston (2002)

20. Marmsoler, D., Degenhardt, S.: Verifying patterns of dynamic architectures using model checking. In: Kofron, J., Tumova, J. (eds.) Proceedings International Workshop on Formal Engineering approaches to Software Components and Architectures, FESCA@ETAPS 2017, Uppsala, Sweden, 22nd April 2017, vol. 245 of EPTCS, pp. 16–30 (2017)

21. OMG. OMG Systems Modeling Language (OMG SysML), Version 1.3 (2012)
22. Preschern, C., Kajtazovic, N., Kreiner, C.: Building a safety architecture pattern system. In: Proceedings of the 18th European Conference on Pattern Languages of Program, EuroPLoP '13, pp. 17:1–17:55, ACM, New York, NY, USA (2015)
23. Pnueli, A., Siegel, M., Singerman, E.: Translation validation. In: Steffen, B. (ed.) TACAS 1998. LNCS, vol. 1384, pp. 151–166. Springer, Heidelberg (1998). https://doi.org/10.1007/BFb0054170
24. Requet, A.: BART: a tool for automatic refinement. In: Börger, E., Butler, M., Bowen, J.P., Boca, P. (eds.) ABZ 2008. LNCS, vol. 5238, pp. 345–345. Springer, Heidelberg (2008). https://doi.org/10.1007/978-3-540-87603-8_33
25. Rumbaugh, J., Jacobson, I., Booch, G.: Unified Modeling Language Reference Manual, 2nd edn. Pearson Higher Education (2004)
26. http://www.event-b.org/
27. Sango, M., Vallée, F., Vié, A.-C., Voirin, J.-L., Leroux, X., Normand, V.: MBSE and MBSA with Capella and safety architect tools. In: Fanmuy, G., Goubault, E., Krob, D., Stephan, F. (eds.) CSDM 2016, p. 239. Springer, Cham (2016). https://doi.org/10.1007/978-3-319-49103-5_22
28. Voirin, J.L.: Model-based System and Architecture Engineering with the Arcadia Method. Elsevier Science (2017)

A Logical Characterization of Differential Privacy via Behavioral Metrics

Valentina Castiglioni[1]([✉]), Konstantinos Chatzikokolakis[2],
and Catuscia Palamidessi[3]

[1] INRIA Saclay - Ilê de France, Palaiseau, France
valentina.castiglioni@inria.fr
[2] CNRS and LIX Ecole Polytechnique, Palaiseau, France
[3] INRIA Saclay - Ilê de France and LIX Ecole Polytechnique, Palaiseau, France

Abstract. *Differential privacy* is a formal definition of privacy ensuring that sensitive information relative to individuals cannot be inferred by querying a database. In this paper, we exploit a modeling of this framework via labeled Markov Chains (LMCs) to provide a *logical characterization of differential privacy*: we consider a probabilistic variant of the Hennessy-Milner logic and we define a *syntactical distance* on formulae in it measuring their syntactic disparities. Then, we define a *trace distance* on LMCs in terms of the syntactic distance between the sets of formulae satisfied by them. We prove that such distance *corresponds* to the *level of privacy* of the LMCs. Moreover, we use the distance on formulae to define a real-valued semantics for them, from which we obtain a *logical characterization of weak anonymity*: the level of anonymity is measured in terms of the smallest formula distinguishing the considered LMCs. Then, we focus on *bisimulation semantics* on nondeterministic probabilistic processes and we provide a *logical characterization of generalized bisimulation metrics*, namely those defined via the *generalized* Kantorovich lifting. Our characterization is based on the notion of *mimicking formula of a process* and the *syntactic distance* on formulae, where the former captures the observable behavior of the corresponding process and allows us to characterize bisimilarity. We show that the generalized bisimulation distance on processes is equal to the syntactic distance on their mimicking formulae. Moreover, we use the distance on mimicking formulae to obtain *bounds* on differential privacy.

1 Introduction

With the ever-increasing use of internet-connected devices, such as computers, IoT appliances and GPS-enabled equipment, personal data are collected in larger and larger amounts, and then stored and manipulated for the most diverse purposes. The exposure of personal data raises all kinds of privacy threats, and it has motivated researchers to develop theories and techniques to protect users from these risks.

The state of the art in privacy research is represented by *differential privacy* (DP) [21], a framework originally proposed for protecting the privacy of

© Springer Nature Switzerland AG 2018
K. Bae and P. C. Ölveczky (Eds.): FACS 2018, LNCS 11222, pp. 75–96, 2018.
https://doi.org/10.1007/978-3-030-02146-7_4

participants in statistical databases, and now applied to geolocation [34], social networks [35] and many other domains. DP is based on the idea of obfuscating the link between the answers to queries and the personal data by adding controlled (probabilistic) noise to the answers. One of the main advantages of DP with respect to previous approaches is its compositionality. Namely, if we combine the information that we obtain by querying two differentially-private mechanisms, the resulting mechanism is also differentially-private.

Recently, a distributed variant of DP has emerged, *called local differential privacy* (LDP) [20]. In this variant, users obfuscate their personal data by themselves, before sending them to the data collector. In this way, the data collector can only see, stock and analyze the obfuscated data. LDP, like DP, is compositional, and furthermore it has the further advantages that it does not need to trust the data collector. LDP is having a considerable impact, specially after large companies such as Apple and Google have started to adopt it for collecting the data of their users for statistical purposes [22].

In this paper, we consider $d_{\mathcal{X}}$-privacy [11], a metric-based generalization of differential privacy that subsumes both DP and LDP by exploiting a metric in the domain of secrets to capture the desired privacy protection semantics. We study $d_{\mathcal{X}}$-privacy in the context of probabilistic transition systems (PTSs) and labeled Markov chains (LMCs), aiming at importing the rich concepts and techniques that have been developed in the area of Concurrency Theory. In particular, we focus on *behavioral metrics* and on their logical counterparts, exploring their use to specify privacy properties.

Behavioral metrics [1,8,12,13,17,25,31,32,39] represent the quantitative analogue of behavioral equivalences and preorders measuring the disparities in the behavior of processes. Here, we consider a probabilistic extension $\mathbb{L}$ of the Hennessy-Milner logic (HML) [28] and we propose a notion of *trace metric* defined via a *syntactic distance* over formulae in $\mathbb{L}$, namely a pseudometric on formulae measuring their syntactic disparities. Informally, we consider formulae expressing probabilistic linear properties and we define the trace metric between two processes as the Hausdorff lifting of the syntactic distance over the sets of formulae satisfied by them. Such trace metric will allow us to obtain the first *logical characterization of $d_{\mathcal{X}}$-privacy*.

Although $d_{\mathcal{X}}$-privacy is defined in terms of a *multiplicative* variant of the *total variation* distance, one could also define privacy properties based on the standard total variation, as in the case of *weak anonymity* from [16]. We exploit the distance on formulae to define a real-valued semantics for them, from which we obtain a *logical characterization of weak anonymity*.

Then we switch from trace to bisimulation semantics and we provide a *logical bound* on $d_{\mathcal{X}}$-privacy. We consider the generalized notion of Kantorovich lifting [12], which allows to define distances suitable to deal with privacy and security properties. We provide a *logical characterization* of the *generalized bisimulation metrics* from [12], using the syntactic distance over formulae in the probabilistic extension $\mathcal{L}$ of HML [14], and the notion of *mimicking formula of a process* [9]. The latter is a special formula in $\mathcal{L}$ that captures the observable behavior of a process and allows us to characterize bisimilarity. We show that the generalized bisimulation distance between two processes is equal to the (generalized) distance between their mimicking formulae, called *logical distance*. Moreover, we show that we can exploit the logical distance to obtain bounds on d_χ-privacy. Notice that dealing with bisimulation semantics instead of traces would allow us to develop efficient algorithms for the evaluation of the logical distance (following, e.g., [4]), and thus of approximations on d_χ-privacy. Furthermore, we could exploit the *non-expansiveness* results obtained in [12] to favor compositional reasoning over d_χ-privacy.

Related work. As already mentioned, this paper builds on the work of [9, 12]. The main novelty is that we develop a technique for characterizing privacy properties, and that we deal with d_χ-privacy rather than DP.

Verification of differential privacy has been itself an active area of research. Prominent approaches based on formal methods are those based on type systems [23,36] and logical formulations [5]. Earlier papers [40,41] defined bisimulation metrics suitable for proving DP, however they suffered from the fact that the respective kernel relations do not fully characterize probabilistic bisimilarity.

Contribution. Summarizing, the main contributions of this paper are:

1. We define a trace metric over LMCs in terms of a syntactic distance on formulae in $\mathbb{L}$, a probabilistic refinement of HML.
2. We show that such trace metric allows us to obtain a logical characterization of d_χ-privacy.
3. We exploit the syntactic distance on formulae to define a real-valued semantics for them, from which we get a logical characterization of weak anonymity.
4. We provide a logical characterization of the generalized bisimilarity metric by using the syntactic distance over $\mathcal{L}$ and the notion of mimicking formulae of processes in a PTS.
5. We exploit the characterization of the bisimilarity metric to obtain bounds on d_χ-privacy.

2   Background

The PTS model. PTSs [37] combine LTSs [30] and discrete time Markov chains [27], to model reactive behavior, nondeterminism and probability. The state space is a set $\mathcal{S}$ of *processes*, ranged over by $s, t, \ldots$ and transition steps take processes to *probability distributions* over $\mathcal{S}$, namely mappings $\pi \colon \mathcal{S} \to [0, 1]$ with $\sum_{s \in \mathcal{S}} \pi(s) = 1$. By $\Delta(\mathcal{S})$ we denote the set of all distributions over $\mathcal{S}$, ranged over by $\pi, \pi', \ldots$ The support of $\pi \in \Delta(\mathcal{S})$ is the set $\mathsf{supp}(\pi) = \{s \in \mathcal{S} \mid \pi(s) > 0\}$. We consider only distributions with *finite* support. For $s \in \mathcal{S}$ we denote by δ_s the *Dirac distribution* defined by $\delta_s(s) = 1$ and $\delta_s(t) = 0$ for $s \neq t$.

Definition 1 (PTS, [37]). *A nondeterministic probabilistic labeled transition system (PTS) is a triple $(\mathcal{S}, \mathcal{A}, \to)$, where: $\mathcal{S}$ is a countable set of processes, $\mathcal{A}$ is a countable set of actions, and $\to \subseteq \mathcal{S} \times \mathcal{A} \times \Delta(\mathcal{S})$ is a transition relation.*

We write $s \xrightarrow{a} \pi$ for $(s,a,\pi) \in \rightarrow$, $s \xrightarrow{a}$ if there is a distribution $\pi \in \Delta(\mathcal{S})$ with $s \xrightarrow{a} \pi$, and $s \xnrightarrow{a}$ otherwise. Let $\mathrm{init}(s) = \{a \in \mathcal{A} \mid s \xrightarrow{a}\}$ denote the set of the actions that can be performed by s. Let $\mathrm{der}(s,a) = \{\pi \in \Delta(\mathcal{S}) \mid s \xrightarrow{a} \pi\}$ denote the set of the distributions reachable from s through action a. We say that a process $s \in \mathcal{S}$ is *image-finite* if for all actions $a \in \mathrm{init}(s)$ the set $\mathrm{der}(s,a)$ is finite [29]. We consider only image-finite processes.

Labeled Markov Chains. We call *trace* any finite sequence of action labels in $\mathcal{A}^\star$, ranged over by $\alpha, \alpha', \ldots$, and we use $\mathfrak{e}$ to denote the empty trace.

A *labeled Markov chain* (LMC) is a fully probabilistic PTS, namely a PTS in which for each process we have at most one available transition. In a LMC, a process s induces a probability measure over traces $\mathrm{Pr}(s, \cdot)$, defined for each trace α recursively as follows:

$$\mathrm{Pr}(s, \alpha) = \begin{cases} 1 & \text{if } \alpha = \mathfrak{e} \\ 0 & \text{if } \alpha = a\alpha' \text{ and } s \xnrightarrow{a} \\ \displaystyle\sum_{s' \in \mathrm{supp}(\pi)} \pi(s')\mathrm{Pr}(s', \alpha') & \text{if } \alpha = a\alpha' \text{ and } s \xrightarrow{a} \pi. \end{cases}$$

We can express the *observable behavior* of processes in a LMC in terms of the *linear properties* that they satisfy, or equivalently in terms of the traces that they can perform. Hence, it is natural to compare process behavior in LMCs by means of *trace semantics* (see for instance [4]).

Definition 2 (Trace equivalence on LMCs). *Assume a LMC $(\mathcal{S}, \mathcal{A}, \rightarrow)$. Processes $s, t \in \mathcal{S}$ are trace equivalent, written $s \sim_{\mathrm{Tr}} t$, if for all traces $\alpha \in \mathcal{A}^\star$ it holds that $\mathrm{Pr}(s, \alpha) = \mathrm{Pr}(t, \alpha)$.*

Pseudometric spaces. For a countable set X, a non-negative function $d \colon X \times X \to \mathbb{R}^+$ is a *metric* on X whenever it satisfies: (i) $d(x,y) = 0$ iff $x = y$, for all $x, y \in X$; (ii) $d(x,y) = d(y,x)$, for all $x, y \in X$; (iii) $d(x,y) \leq d(x,z) + d(z,y)$, for all $x, y, z \in X$. By relaxing the first axiom to (i)' $d(x,x) = 0$ for all $x \in X$, we obtain the notion of *pseudometric*. We say that d is an *extended* (pseudo)metric if we allow its value to be $+\infty$, notation $d \colon X \times X \to [0, +\infty]$. Given a (pseudo)metric d on X, the pair (X, d) is called *(pseudo)metric space*. The *kernel* of a (pseudo)metric d on X is the set $\mathrm{ker}(d) = \{(x,y) \in X \times X \mid d(x,y) = 0\}$. Given two (pseudo)metric spaces $(X, d_X), (Y, d_Y)$, the function $f \colon X \to Y$ is *1-Lipschitz* w.r.t. d_X, d_Y iff $d_Y(f(x), f(x')) \leq d_X(x, x')$ for all $x, x' \in X$. We denote by $1\text{-}\mathrm{Lip}[(X, d_X), (Y, d_Y)]$ the set of such functions. Given any (pseudo)metric space (X, d), the *diameter* of X w.r.t. d, denoted by $\oslash_d(X)$, is the maximal distance of two elements in X, namely $\oslash_d(X) = \sup_{x, y \in X} d(x, y)$.

The Hausdorff lifting allows us to lift a (pseudo)metric over elements in a set X to a (pseudo)metric over the power set of X, denoted by $\mathcal{P}(X)$.

Definition 3 (Hausdorff metric). *Let $d \colon X \times X \to [0, +\infty]$ be a pseudometric. The Hausdorff lifting of d is the pseudometric $\mathbf{H}(d) \colon \mathcal{P}(X) \times \mathcal{P}(X) \to$*

$[0, +\infty]$ *defined for all sets* $X_1, X_2 \subseteq X$ *by*

$$\mathbf{H}(d)(X_1, X_2) = \max \left\{ \sup_{x_1 \in X_1} \inf_{x_2 \in X_2} d(x_1, x_2), \sup_{x_2 \in X_2} \inf_{x_1 \in X_1} d(x_2, x_1) \right\}$$

with, by convention $\sup_\emptyset = 0$ *and* $\inf_\emptyset = \oslash_d(X)$.

3 Logical Characterization of Differential Privacy: A Trace Metric Approach

In this section we present the first logical characterization for $d_{\mathcal{X}}$-privacy.

We recall briefly the definitions. The interested reader can find more details in [11]. Let $\mathcal{X}$ be an arbitrary set of *secrets* provided with distance $d_{\mathcal{X}}$. Let $\mathcal{Z}$ be a set of *observables*, and let M be a randomized mechanism from $\mathcal{X}$ to $\mathcal{Z}$, namely a function that assigns to every element of $\mathcal{X}$ a probability distribution on $\mathcal{Z}$. We say that M is $\varepsilon \cdot d_{\mathcal{X}}$-privateif for any two secrets $\mathbf{x}, \mathbf{x}' \in \mathcal{X}$ and any measurable subset Z of $\mathcal{Z}$, we have $M(\mathbf{x})(Z)/M(\mathbf{x}')(Z) \leq e^{\varepsilon \cdot d_{\mathcal{X}}(\mathbf{x}, \mathbf{x}')}$. The idea is that $d_{\mathcal{X}}(\mathbf{x}, \mathbf{x}')$ represents a *distinguishability level* between $\mathbf{x}$ and $\mathbf{x}'$: the more we want to confuse them, the more similar the probabilities of producing the same answers in the randomization process should be. Notice that $d_{\mathcal{X}}$-privacy subsumes standard DP, by setting $\mathcal{X}$ to be the set of databases, and $d_{\mathcal{X}}$ the Hamming distance between databases: $d_{\mathcal{X}}(\mathbf{x}, \mathbf{x}')$ is the number of records in which $\mathbf{x}$ and $\mathbf{x}'$ differ. The resulting property is, by transitivity, equivalent to say that for all $\mathbf{x}$ and $\mathbf{x}'$ which are adjacent (i.e., $d_{\mathcal{X}}(\mathbf{x}, \mathbf{x}') = 1$), $M(\mathbf{x})(Z)/M(\mathbf{x}')(Z) \leq e^{\varepsilon}$. Note that we consider here an equivalent definition of DP in which the adjacency relation is defined as differing in the value of one record. The standard definition, in which $\mathbf{x}$ and $\mathbf{x}'$ are adjacent if $\mathbf{x}'$ is obtained from $\mathbf{x}$ by adding or removing one record, can be specified by using an extra value to indicate absence of the record.

Furthermore, $d_{\mathcal{X}}$-privacy subsumes LDP as well, by setting $d_{\mathcal{X}}$ to be the discrete distance, i.e., $d_{\mathcal{X}}(\mathbf{x}, \mathbf{x}') = 0$ if $\mathbf{x} = \mathbf{x}'$ and $d_{\mathcal{X}}(\mathbf{x}, \mathbf{x}') = 1$ otherwise.

To formalize $d_{\mathcal{X}}$-privacy, we will exploit the *multiplicative variant of the total variation distance* on probability distributions.

Definition 4 (Multiplicative total variation distance, [38]). *Let X be a set. The* multiplicative *variant of the* total variation distance *on $\Delta(X)$ is the function* $tv_\otimes \colon \Delta(X) \times \Delta(X) \to [0, +\infty]$ *defined, for all* $\pi, \pi' \in \Delta(X)$, *as* $tv_\otimes(\pi, \pi') = \sup_{x \in X} |\ln(\pi(x)) - \ln(\pi'(x))|$.

For $\mathcal{X}$ set of secrets and $\mathcal{Z}$ set of observables, $d_{\mathcal{X}}$-privacy is defined as follows.

Definition 5 ($d_{\mathcal{X}}$-privacy, [11]). *Let $\varepsilon > 0$ and $d_{\mathcal{X}}$ be any distance on $\mathcal{X}$. A randomized mechanism* $M \colon \mathcal{X} \to \Delta(\mathcal{Z})$ *is* $\varepsilon \cdot d_{\mathcal{X}}$-private *iff*

$$tv_\otimes(M(\mathbf{x}), M(\mathbf{x}')) \leq \varepsilon \cdot d_{\mathcal{X}}(\mathbf{x}, \mathbf{x}') \ \forall \, \mathbf{x}, \mathbf{x}' \in \mathcal{X}.$$

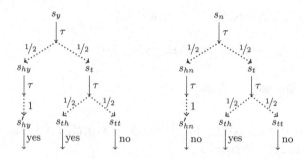

Fig. 1. The mechanism 'Randomized responses' as a LMC. For simplicity, an arrow $u \xrightarrow{a}$ with no target models the evolution of process u to the Dirac distribution δ_{nil}, with nil process that can execute no action, via the execution of a

Interestingly, each randomized mechanisms can be modeled as a LMC. Each secret $\mathbf{x}$ is mapped to a state $s_{\mathbf{x}}$ in the LMC and the observable result of the mechanism applied to $\mathbf{x}$ is modeled by the traces executable by $s_{\mathbf{x}}$ in the LMC. The randomized mechanism M on $\mathbf{x}$ is then modeled as the trace distribution induced by $s_{\mathbf{x}}$. More formally, we consider $\mathcal{Z} = \mathcal{A}^{\star}$ and we define $M(\mathbf{x})(\alpha) = \Pr(s_{\mathbf{x}}, \alpha)$ for each $\alpha \in \mathcal{A}^{\star}$.

We give an example based on local differential privacy. The mechanism is called "Randomized responses" and is a simplified instance of the system RAP-POR used by Google to protect the privacy of their users [22].

Example 1 (Randomized responses). Suppose that we want to collect the answers to some embarrassing question (for instance "Have you ever cheated on your partner?") for some statistic purpose. To persuade people to answer truly, we allow them to report the true answer with probability 3/4, and the opposite answer with probability 1/4. In this way, the privacy of the user will be protected in the sense that the answers collector will not know for sure whether the person has cheated or not. In fact, the system is $\log 3$-locally differentially private. At the same time, if the population is large enough, the collector will be able to obtain a good statistical approximation of the real percentage of cheaters.

To implement the system, we can use a (fair) coin: the person tosses the coin twice, and if the first result is head, he answers truly, otherwise he answers "yes" or "no" depending on whether the second result is, resp., head or tail. The results of the coin tossings, of course, has to be invisible to the data collector, and thus we represent it as an internal action τ.

The LMCs s_y and s_n in Fig. 1 represent the mechanism applied to two individuals: s_y that has cheated and s_n has not. s_y will toss the coin and make a transition τ. Then, depending on the result, will go in a state s_h or s_t with even probability. From s_h it will toss a coin again, and then make a transition *yes* to a final state. From s_t it will toss the coin and go in states s_{th} and s_{tt} with even probability. From s_{th} and s_{tt} it will then make transitions *yes* and *no*, resp., and then terminate. The system s_n is analogous, with *yes* and *no* inverted.

To obtain the logical characterization of d_χ-privacy we can investigate the semantics of the so obtained LMCs. In particular, we will exploit a notion of *trace metric* evaluated on *modal formulae* expressing linear properties of processes in LMCs. Informally, we will consider a simple probabilistic variant of the modal logic capturing the trace semantics in the fully nondeterministic case to define a *probabilistic trace semantics* for processes. Then, we will define a metric for such a semantics in terms of a syntactic distance over the formulae in the considered logic and we will use such a distance to characterize d_χ-privacy. Interestingly, although the considered trace semantics is based on a quite limited observation power, it will allow us to obtain the first *logical characterization* of d_χ-privacy (Thoerem 2): we will show that the trace metrics so defined on LMCs coincides with the multiplicative variant of the total variation distance (Proposition 2).

3.1   Trace Metrics on LMCs

Probabilistic trace semantics compares the behavior of processes w.r.t. the probabilities that they assign to the same linear properties, namely to the same traces. In the literature we can find several notions of probabilistic trace equivalence, of which $\sim_{\mathrm{Tr}}$ given in Definition 2 is an example, and we refer the interested reader to [6] for a survey. Such a wealth of notions derives from the interplay of nondeterminism and probability that we can witness in quantitative systems and the different interpretations that researchers have given to it. We can also find several proposals of behavioral distances measuring the disparities of processes w.r.t. the same linear properties, that is their differences in the probabilities of executing the same traces (see, e.g., [1,4,39]).

As the focus of this paper is on d_χ-privacy, we adopt a different approach, w.r.t. to those referenced, to the definition of a trace metric on LMCs. In fact, we hark back to the seminal work [17] on bisimulation metrics and: (i) We provide a logical characterization of $\sim_{\mathrm{Tr}}$ by means of a simple modal logic $\mathbb{L}$ that allows us to express traces and their probability of being executed, so that s and t are trace equivalent if they satisfy the same formulae in $\mathbb{L}$. (ii) We quantify the trace metric on processes in terms to the formulae distinguishing them. Informally, in [17] this is obtained by transforming formulae into functional expressions and by interpreting the satisfaction relation as integration. Then, the distance on processes is defined on the so obtained *real-valued* logic by considering the maximal disparity between the images of processes through all functional expressions. Here, we propose a much simpler approach based on the *boolean-valued* logic $\mathbb{L}$: we introduce a (family of generalized) *syntactic distance* on formulae in $\mathbb{L}$ and we define the *trace metric* on processes as the Hausdorff lifting of the syntactic distance to the sets of formulae satisfied by processes.

The logic $\mathbb{L}$ extends the one used in the nondeterministic case to express trace semantics [7] (and corresponding to the subclass of *linear formulae*) with a probabilistic modality expressing the execution probabilities of traces.

Definition 6 (Modal logic $\mathbb{L}$). *The logic* $\mathbb{L} = \mathbb{L}^l \cup \mathbb{L}^p$ *is given by the classes of* linear formulae $\mathbb{L}^l$ *and of* probabilistic formulae $\mathbb{L}^p$ *over* $\mathcal{A}$, *defined by:*

$$\mathbb{L}^l: \quad \Phi ::= \quad \top \mid \langle a \rangle \Phi \qquad\qquad \mathbb{L}^p: \quad \Psi ::= \quad r\Phi$$

where: (i) Φ *ranges over* $\mathbb{L}^l$, *(ii)* Ψ *ranges over* $\mathbb{L}^p$, *(iii)* $a \in \mathcal{A}$; *(iv)* $r \in [0, 1]$.

We say that a trace α is compatible with the linear formula Φ, notation $\alpha = \mathrm{Tr}(\Phi)$, if the sequence of action labels in α is exactly the same sequence of labels of the diamond modalities in Φ, i.e., $\alpha = \mathrm{Tr}(\langle a_1 \rangle \ldots \langle a_n \rangle \top)$ iff $\alpha = a_1 \ldots a_n$.

Definition 7 (Semantics of $\mathbb{L}$). *For any* $s \in \mathcal{S}$, *the satisfaction relation* $\models \subseteq \mathcal{S} \times \mathbb{L}^l \cup \mathbb{L}^p$ *is defined by structural induction over formulae in* $\mathbb{L}^l \cup \mathbb{L}^p$ *by*

- $s \models \top$ *always;*
- $s \models \langle a \rangle \Phi$ *iff* $s \xrightarrow{a} \pi$ *for some* π *such that* $s' \models \Phi$ *for some* $s' \in \mathsf{supp}(\pi)$;
- $s \models r\Phi$ *iff* $s \models \Phi$ *and* $\mathrm{Pr}(s, \mathrm{Tr}(\Phi)) = r$.

For each process $s \in \mathcal{S}$, *we let* $\mathbb{L}(s) = \{\Psi \in \mathbb{L}^p \mid s \models \Psi\}$.

Example 2 (Randomized responses II). Consider processes s_y, s_n in Fig. 1. One can easily check that

$$\mathbb{L}(s_y) = \{1\langle\tau\rangle\top, 1\langle\tau\rangle\langle\tau\rangle\top, 3/4\langle\tau\rangle\langle\tau\rangle\langle yes\rangle\top, 1/4\langle\tau\rangle\langle\tau\rangle\langle no\rangle\top\}$$
$$\mathbb{L}(s_n) = \{1\langle\tau\rangle\top, 1\langle\tau\rangle\langle\tau\rangle\top, 1/4\langle\tau\rangle\langle\tau\rangle\langle yes\rangle\top, 3/4\langle\tau\rangle\langle\tau\rangle\langle no\rangle\top\}$$

By means of $\mathbb{L}$ we can provide a logical characterization of $\sim_{\mathrm{Tr}}$: two processes are trace equivalent if and only if they satisfy the same formulae in $\mathbb{L}$.

Theorem 1. *Assume an LMC* $(\mathcal{S}, \mathcal{A}, \rightarrow)$. *Then for all processes* $s, t \in \mathcal{S}$ *we have that* $s \sim_{\mathrm{Tr}} t$ *iff* $\mathbb{L}(s) = \mathbb{L}(t)$.

We can now proceed to the definition of the *trace metric*. The definition of the *syntactic distance* on formulae in $\mathbb{L}$ is parametric w.r.t. a generic metric $\mathcal{D}$ on $[0, 1]$ that plays the role of a ground distance on the weights of probabilistic formulae, to which a syntactic distance could not be applied. For this reason we shall sometimes speak of *generalized* syntactic distance and trace metric.

Definition 8 (Distance on $\mathbb{L}$). *Let* $([0, 1], \mathcal{D})$ *be a metric space. The function* $\mathbf{dm}_{\oslash_{\mathcal{D}}} \colon \mathbb{L}^l \times \mathbb{L}^l \to \{0, \oslash_{\mathcal{D}}([0, 1])\}$ *is defined as the discrete metric over* $\mathbb{L}^l$, *namely* $\mathbf{dm}_{\oslash_{\mathcal{D}}}(\Phi_1, \Phi_2) = 0$ *if* $\Phi_1 = \Phi_2$ *and* $\mathbf{dm}_{\oslash_{\mathcal{D}}}(\Phi_1, \Phi_2) = \oslash_{\mathcal{D}}([0, 1])$ *otherwise. The function* $\mathfrak{d}^{\mathrm{p}}_{\mathcal{D}} \colon \mathbb{L}^p \times \mathbb{L}^p \to [0, \oslash_{\mathcal{D}}([0, 1])]$ *is defined over* $\mathbb{L}^p$ *as follows:*

$$\mathfrak{d}^{\mathrm{p}}_{\mathcal{D}}(r_1\Phi_1, r_2\Phi_2) = \begin{cases} \mathcal{D}(r_1, r_2) & \text{if } \mathbf{dm}_{\oslash_{\mathcal{D}}}(\Phi_1, \Phi_2) = 0 \\ \oslash_{\mathcal{D}}([0, 1]) & \text{otherwise.} \end{cases}$$

Definition 9 (Trace metric). *Let* $([0, 1], \mathcal{D})$ *be a metric space. The* trace metric *over processes* $\mathbf{d}^T_{\mathcal{D}} \colon \mathcal{S} \times \mathcal{S} \to [0, \oslash_{\mathcal{D}}([0, 1])]$ *is defined for all* $s, t \in \mathcal{S}$ *by*

$$\mathbf{d}^T_{\mathcal{D}}(s, t) = \mathbf{H}(\mathfrak{d}^{\mathrm{p}}_{\mathcal{D}})(\mathbb{L}(s), \mathbb{L}(t)).$$

The kernel of each generalized trace metric corresponds to $\sim_{\mathrm{Tr}}$.

Proposition 1. *For all possible choices of the metric* $\mathcal{D}$, *trace equivalence is the kernel of the trace metric, namely* $\sim_{\mathrm{Tr}} = \ker(\mathbf{d}^T_{\mathcal{D}})$.

3.2 Logical Characterization of $d_{\mathcal{X}}$-privacy

We can now present the logical characterization result for $d_{\mathcal{X}}$-privacy. As the $d_{\mathcal{X}}$-privacy property is basically a measure of the level of privacy of a system, a logical characterization for it should be interpreted as a logical characterization of a behavioral metric, in the sense of [9,10,17], rather than in the sense of behavioral equivalences. Roughly speaking, we evaluate the $d_{\mathcal{X}}$-privacy property by exploiting the linear properties of the mechanism as expressed by our trace metric, and thus by the logic $\mathbb{L}$. More formally, we let $\mathbf{d}_{\otimes}^{T}$ denote the multiplicative variant of our trace metric, i.e., the one with $\mathcal{D}(r_1, r_2) = |\ln(r_1) - \ln(r_2)|$. Then, we prove that $\mathbf{d}_{\otimes}^{T}$ coincides with the multiplicative total variation distance on the trace distributions induced by processes.

Proposition 2. *For any $s \in \mathcal{S}$ let $\mu_s = \Pr(s, \cdot)$. Then $\mathbf{d}_{\otimes}^{T}(s, t) = tv_{\otimes}(\mu_s, \mu_t)$.*

We can then formalize our logical characterization of $d_{\mathcal{X}}$-privacy.

Theorem 2 (Logical characterization of $d_{\mathcal{X}}$-privacy). *Let M be a randomized mechanism defined by $M(\mathbf{x})(\alpha) = \Pr(s_{\mathbf{x}}, \alpha)$ for all $\mathbf{x} \in \mathcal{X}$, $\alpha \in \mathcal{A}^{\star}$. Then, given $\varepsilon > 0$, M is $\varepsilon \cdot d_{\mathcal{X}}$-private if $\mathbf{d}_{\otimes}^{T}(s_{\mathbf{x}}, s_{\mathbf{x}'}) \leq \varepsilon \cdot d_{\mathcal{X}}(\mathbf{x}, \mathbf{x}') \,\forall\, \mathbf{x}, \mathbf{x}' \in \mathcal{X}$.*

Example 3 (Randomized responses, III). We can show that the mechanism 'Randomized responses' described in Example 1 is $\log 3$-locally differentially private by evaluating the trace distance between processes s_y and s_n in Fig. 1. By comparing the sets of formulae $\mathbb{L}(s_y)$ and $\mathbb{L}(s_n)$ given in Example 2, we can infer that

$$\mathbf{d}_{\otimes}^{T}(s_y, s_n) = \max \left\{ \begin{array}{l} \partial_{\otimes}^{p}(3/4\langle\tau\rangle\langle\tau\rangle\langle yes\rangle\top, 1/4\langle\tau\rangle\langle\tau\rangle\langle yes\rangle\top) \\ \partial_{\otimes}^{p}(1/4\langle\tau\rangle\langle\tau\rangle\langle no\rangle\top, 3/4\langle\tau\rangle\langle\tau\rangle\langle no\rangle\top) \end{array} \right\}$$
$$= |\ln(3/4) - \ln(1/4)| = \ln(3).$$

3.3 Logical Characterization of Weak Anonymity: From Boolean to Real Semantics

So far, we have seen how we can express the $d_{\mathcal{X}}$-privacy property as a syntactic distance over modal formulae capturing trace semantics. However, in the literature, when behavioral metrics are considered, logics equipped with a real-valued semantics are usually used for the characterization, which is then expressed as

$$d(s, t) = \sup_{\phi \in L} |[\![\phi]\!](s) - [\![\phi]\!](t)| \tag{1}$$

where d is the behavioral metric of interest, L is the considered logic and $[\![\phi]\!](s)$ denotes the value of the formula ϕ in process s accordingly to the real-valued semantics (see eg. [1,3,17–19]). In this Section, we exploit the syntactic distance on $\mathbb{L}$ to provide a real valued semantics for formulae and thus a characterization of *weak probabilistic anonymity* expressed accordingly to classic schema in (1).

  Weak probabilistic anonymity [16] uses the *additive* total variation distance tv to measure the degree of protection of the identity of a user while performing a particular task. Hence, the set of secrets $\mathcal{X}$ is now the set of users' identities and a randomized mechanism $M \colon \mathcal{X} \to \Delta(\mathcal{Z})$ has to introduce some noise so that from the 'performed tasks' in $\mathcal{Z}$ an adversary cannot discover the identity of the user that actually performed them. Finally, we recall that the total variation distance is defined by $tv(\mu, \mu') = \sup_{Z \in \mathcal{Z}} |\mu(Z) - \mu'(Z)|$ for all $\mu, \mu' \in \Delta(\mathcal{Z})$.

Definition 10 (Weak probabilistic anonymity [16]**).** *Let M be a randomized mechanism defined by $M(\mathbf{x})(\alpha) = \Pr(s_{\mathbf{x}}, \alpha)$ for all $\mathbf{x} \in \mathcal{X}$, $\alpha \in \mathcal{A}^\star$. Then, given $\varepsilon > 0$, M satisfies ε-weak anonymity if $tv(M(\mathbf{x}), M(\mathbf{x}')) \leq \varepsilon \; \forall \, \mathbf{x}, \mathbf{x}' \in \mathcal{X}$.*

So, we consider all metric spaces $([0, 1], \mathcal{D})$ with $\oslash_{\mathcal{D}}([0, 1]) < \infty$ and: 1. We use the syntactic distance over formulae in $\mathbb{L}$ to define a (generalized) real valued semantics for those modal formulae. 2. We show that the total variation distance satisfies the general schema in (1) w.r.t. such real semantics. 3. We express the ε-weak anonymity property as an upper bound to the total variation distance on the values of formulae in the processes of the LMCs.

Equipping modal formulae with a real-valued semantics means assigning to each formula ϕ a real number in $[0, 1]$ expressing *how much* a given process s satisfies ϕ; value 1 stands for $s \models \phi$. We exploit our distance over formulae to define such a semantics. Informally, let L be the class of formulae of interest, let $D_{\mathcal{D}}$ be any generalized syntactic distance defined on L (like, eg., the distance $\partial_{\mathcal{D}}^{\mathsf{P}}$ for the logic $\mathbb{L}$) and for each process s let $L(s)$ denote the set of formulae in L satisfied by s. To quantify how much the formula $\phi \in L$ is satisfied by process s, we evaluate first how far ϕ is from being satisfied by s. This corresponds to the minimal distance between ϕ and a formula satisfied by s, namely to $\inf_{\phi' \in L(s)} D_{\mathcal{D}}(\phi, \phi')$. Then we simply notice that being $D_{\mathcal{D}}(\phi, \phi')$ far from s is equivalent to be $\oslash_{\mathcal{D}}([0, 1]) - D_{\mathcal{D}}(\phi, \phi')$ close to it (notice that $\oslash_{\mathcal{D}}([0, 1])$ has to be finite in order to obtain a meaningful value). Thus, we assign to ϕ the value $\oslash_{\mathcal{D}}([0,1]) - \inf_{\phi' \in L(s)} D_{\mathcal{D}}(\phi, \phi') / \oslash_{\mathcal{D}}([0,1])$ in s, where the normalization w.r.t. $\oslash_{\mathcal{D}}([0, 1])$ ensures that this value is in $[0, 1]$.

Definition 11 (Real valued semantics). *Let $([0, 1], \mathcal{D})$ be a metric space with $\oslash_{\mathcal{D}}([0, 1]) < \infty$. Assume any class of formulae L, let $D_{\mathcal{D}}$ be any generalized syntactic distance over L. We define the* value of $\phi \in L$ in process $s \in \mathcal{S}$ *as*

$$[\![\phi]\!]_{\mathcal{D}}(s) = 1 - \frac{\inf_{\phi' \in L(s)} D_{\mathcal{D}}(\phi, \phi')}{\oslash_{\mathcal{D}}([0, 1])}$$

Example 4. Consider s_y in Fig. 1 and $\mathcal{D}(r_1, r_2) = |r_1 - r_2|$ for all $r_1, r_2 \in [0, 1]$. Notice that $\oslash_{\mathcal{D}}([0, 1]) = 1$. For any $r \in [0, 1]$, consider the formula $\varphi_r = r\langle\tau\rangle\langle\tau\rangle\langle yes\rangle\top$. Then $\inf_{\varphi \in \mathbb{L}(s_y)} \partial_{\mathcal{D}}^{\mathsf{P}}(\varphi_r, \varphi) = \partial_{\mathcal{D}}^{\mathsf{P}}(\varphi_r, 3/4\langle\tau\rangle\langle\tau\rangle\langle yes\rangle\top) = |r - 3/4|$. Hence, the value of φ_r in s_y is given by $[\![\varphi_r]\!]_{\mathcal{D}}(s_y) = 1 - |r - 3/4|$.

Before proceeding to the characterization, notice that for each class of formulae L equipped with a generalized syntactical distance $D_{\mathcal{D}}$ we can provide an equivalent reformulation of the Hausdorff metric as in the following Proposition.

Proposition 3. *Let* $([0,1], \mathcal{D})$ *be a metric space. Assume a class of formulae* L *and let* $D_{\mathcal{D}}$ *be any generalized syntactic distance over* L. *For any* $L_1, L_2 \subseteq L$ *we have that* $\mathbf{H}(D_{\mathcal{D}})(L_1, L_2) = \sup_{\phi \in L} |\inf_{\phi_1 \in L_1} D_{\mathcal{D}}(\phi, \phi_1) - \inf_{\phi_2 \in L_2} D_{\mathcal{D}}(\phi, \phi_2)|$.

If we focus on the class of formulae $\mathbb{L}$, from Proposition 3 we can immediately derive the characterization of trace metrics in terms of real-valued formulae.

Lemma 1. *Let* $([0,1], \mathcal{D})$ *be a metric space with* $\oslash_{\mathcal{D}}([0,1]) < \infty$. *For all processes* $s, t \in \mathcal{S}$ *it holds that* $\mathbf{d}_{\mathcal{D}}^T(s,t) = \sup_{\Psi \in \mathbb{L}^{\mathrm{P}}} |[\![\Psi]\!]_{\mathcal{D}}(s) - [\![\Psi]\!]_{\mathcal{D}}(t)|$.

By abuse of notation, for any linear formula $\Phi \in \mathbb{L}^1$, we write $[\![\Phi]\!]_{\mathcal{D}}(s)$ in place of $[\![1\Phi]\!]_{\mathcal{D}}(s)$. Moreover, we write the 'generalized' metrics defined on the metric space $([0,1], \mathcal{D})$, with $\mathcal{D}(x,y) = |x-y|$, with no $\mathcal{D}$ subscripts. Then, the following characterization of the total variation distance holds.

Proposition 4. *Let* $([0,1], \mathcal{D})$ *be a metric space with* $\oslash_{\mathcal{D}}([0,1]) < \infty$. *For any* $s \in \mathcal{S}$ *define* $\mu_s = \Pr(s, \cdot)$. *Then,* $tv_{\mathcal{D}}(\mu_s, \mu_t) = \sup_{\Phi \in \mathbb{L}^1} |[\![\Phi]\!]_{\mathcal{D}}(s) - [\![\Phi]\!]_{\mathcal{D}}(t)|$. *In particular, we have* $tv(\mu_s, \mu_t) = \sup_{\Phi \in \mathbb{L}^1} |[\![\Phi]\!](s) - [\![\Phi]\!](t)|$.

Finally, we can express ε-weak anonymity property as an upper bound to the total variation distance on the values of formulae in the processes of the LMCs, accordingly to the general schema in (1).

Theorem 3 (Logical characterization of weak anonymity). *Let* M *be a randomized mechanism defined by* $M(\mathbf{x})(\alpha) = \Pr(s_{\mathbf{x}}, \alpha)$ *for all* $\mathbf{x} \in \mathcal{X}$, $\alpha \in \mathcal{A}^*$. *Then, given* $\varepsilon > 0$, M *satisfies* ε-*weak anonymity if* $\sup_{\Phi \in \mathbb{L}^1} |[\![\Phi]\!](s_{\mathbf{x}}) - [\![\Phi]\!](s_{\mathbf{x}'})| \leq \varepsilon \; \forall \, \mathbf{x}, \mathbf{x}' \in \mathcal{X}$.

4   A Logical Bound on $d_{\mathcal{X}}$-privacy: From Traces to Bisimulations

So far we have shown how it is possible to obtain a characterization of $d_{\mathcal{X}}$-privacy by exploiting trace semantics and a notion of syntactic distance on modal formulae. However, one could argue that there are no efficient algorithms to evaluate the trace metric, and therefore the $d_{\mathcal{X}}$-privacy property, especially if the state space of the LMC is infinite. In [4] it is proved that we can obtain upper bounds on the evaluation of trace metrics by exploiting bisimulation-like distances, for which polynomial-time algorithms can be provided. Here, we follow a similar reasoning: we switch from LMCs to the more general semantic model of *PTSs*, we consider the *generalized bisimulation metrics* introduced in [12] and we provide a *logical characterization* for them. This is based on the notion of syntactic distance on formulae and the notion of *mimicking formula* of a process from [9,10]. As in previous Sect. 3.1, the former is a pseudometric on a probabilistic version of HML $\mathcal{L}$ that extends $\mathbb{L}$ with modalities allowing us to express the interplay of nondeterminism and probability typical of PTSs (Sect. 4.2). The latter is a special formula in $\mathcal{L}$ that alone expresses the observable behavior w.r.t. bisimulation semantics of the process to which it is related and allows us to characterize bisimilarity (Sect. 4.3). Then we show that the syntactic distance between the mimicking formulae of processes equals their bisimulation distance (Sect. 4.4) and that, when we focus on LMCs, it gives an upper bound on $d_\mathcal{X}$-privacy properties of mechanisms (Sect. 4.5).

As a final remark, note that using bisimulation metrics and their characterization would allow us to apply the compositional results obtained for them in [12] also to $d_\mathcal{X}$-privacy properties. Due to space limitations, we leave their formal development as future work. Now, we proceed to recall some base notions on bisimulation semantics and generalized bisimulation metrics.

4.1   Generalized Bisimilarity Metric

Probabilistic (bi)simulations. A probabilistic bisimulation is an equivalence relation over $\mathcal{S}$ that equates processes $s, t \in \mathcal{S}$ if they can mimic each other's transitions and evolve to distributions that are in turn related by the same bisimulation. To formalize this, we need to lift relations over processes to relations over distributions. Informally, given a relation $\mathcal{R}$ on processes we say that two distributions $\pi, \pi' \in \Delta(\mathcal{S})$ are related by the lifting of $\mathcal{R}$, denoted by $\mathcal{R}^\dagger$, iff they assign the same probabilistic weights to the same equivalence classes in $\mathcal{R}$.

Definition 12 (Relation lifting, [15]). *Let X be a set. The lifting of a relation $\mathcal{R} \subseteq X \times X$ is the relation $\mathcal{R}^\dagger \subseteq \Delta(X) \times \Delta(X)$ with $\pi \, \mathcal{R}^\dagger \, \pi'$ whenever there is a set of indexes I s.t.*

$$(i) \ \pi = \sum_{i \in I} p_i \delta_{x_i}, \quad (ii) \ \pi' = \sum_{i \in I} p_i \delta_{y_i}, \quad and \quad (iii) \ x_i \, \mathcal{R} \, y_i \ for \ all \ i \in I.$$

Definition 13 (Probabilistic bisimulation, [33]). *Assume a PTS. A binary relation $\mathcal{R} \subseteq \mathcal{S} \times \mathcal{S}$ is a* probabilistic bisimulation *if whenever $s \, \mathcal{R} \, t$*

- *if $s \xrightarrow{a} \pi_s$ then there is a transition $t \xrightarrow{a} \pi_t$ such that $\pi_s \, \mathcal{R}^\dagger \, \pi_t$;*
- *if $t \xrightarrow{a} \pi_t$ then there is a transition $s \xrightarrow{a} \pi_s$ such that $\pi_t \, \mathcal{R}^\dagger \, \pi_s$;*

The union of all probabilistic bisimulations is the greatest probabilistic bisimulation, denoted by $\sim$ and called bisimilarity, *and is an equivalence.*

Generalized bisimulation metrics. For our purposes, we need to lift a pseudometric over processes to a pseudometric over distributions over processes. We follow the approach of [12], that considers the *generalized Kantorovich lifting*. Take a generic metric space (V, d_V), with $V \subseteq \mathbb{R}$ is a convex subset of the reals. A function $f \colon X \to V$ can be lifted to a function $\hat{f} \colon \Delta(X) \to V$ by taking its expected value, i.e., $\hat{f}(\pi) = \sum_{x \in X} \pi(x) f(x)$ (requiring V to be convex ensures that $\hat{f}(\pi) \in V$). Then, for each V, we define the lifting of a pseudometric d_X over X to a pseudometric over $\Delta(X)$ via the *generalized Kantorovich metric* $\mathbf{K}_V$.

Definition 14 (Generalized Kantorovich lifting, [12]). *For a pseudometric space (X, d_X) and a metric space (V, d_V) with $V \subseteq \mathbb{R}$ convex, the generalized Kantorovich lifting of d_X w.r.t. (V, d_V) is the pseudometric $\mathbf{K}_V \colon \Delta(X) \times \Delta(X) \to [0, +\infty]$ defined, for all $\pi, \pi' \in \Delta(X)$ by*

$$\mathbf{K}_V(d_X)(\pi, \pi') = \sup \left\{ d_V(\hat{f}(\pi), \hat{f}(\pi')) \mid f \in 1\text{-}Lip[(X, d_X), (V, d_V)] \right\}.$$

Bisimulations answer the question of whether two processes behave precisely the same way or not. Bisimulation metrics answer the more general question of how far the behavior of two processes is. They are defined as the least fixed points of a suitable functional on the following structure. Let (V, d_V) be a metric space and let $\mathbf{D}$ be the set of pseudometrics d on $\mathcal{S}$ such that $\oslash_d(\mathcal{S}) \leq \oslash_{d_V}(V)$. Then $(\mathbf{D}, \preceq)$ with $d_1 \preceq d_2$ iff $d_1(s, t) \leq d_2(s, t)$ for all processes $s, t \in \mathcal{S}$, is a complete lattice. In detail, for each set $D \subseteq \mathbf{D}$ the supremum and infimum are $\sup(D)(s, t) = \sup_{d \in D} d(s, t)$ and $\inf(D)(s, t) = \inf_{d \in D} d(s, t)$ for all $s, t \in \mathcal{S}$. The bottom element is function $\mathbf{0}$ with $\mathbf{0}(s, t) = 0$ for all $s, t \in \mathcal{S}$, and the top element is function $\mathbf{1}$ with $\mathbf{1}(s, t) = \oslash_{d_V}(V)$ if $s \neq t$, and $\mathbf{1}(s, t) = 0$ otherwise.

The quantitative analogue of bisimulation is defined by means of a functional $\mathbf{B}_V$ over the lattice $(\mathbf{D}, \preceq)$. By means of a *discount factor* $\lambda \in (0, 1]$, $\mathbf{B}_V$ allows us to specify how much the behavioral distance of future transitions is taken into account to determine the distance between two processes [2,17]. $\lambda = 1$ expresses no discount, so that the differences in the behavior of s and t are considered irrespective of after how many steps can be observed.

Definition 15 (Generalized bisimulation metric functional, [12]). *Let (V, d_V) be a metric space, with $V \subseteq \mathbb{R}$ convex. Let $\mathbf{B}_V : \mathbf{D} \to \mathbf{D}$ be the function defined for all $d \in \mathbf{D}$ and $s, t \in \mathcal{S}$ by*

$$\mathbf{B}_V(d)(s, t) = \sup_{a \in \mathcal{A}} \mathbf{H}(\lambda \cdot \mathbf{K}_V(d))(\operatorname{der}(s, a), \operatorname{der}(t, a)).$$

Remark 1. It is easy to show that for any pseudometric d the lifting $\mathbf{K}_V(d)$ is an extended pseudometric for any choice of (V, d_V). However, in general the lifting does not preserve the boundedness properties of d. To guarantee $\mathbf{K}_V(d)$ to be bounded we need to assume that the metric d_V is *ball-convex*, namely the open balls in the generated topology are convex sets. This is not an issue for this paper, since all the considered metrics satisfy the ball-convex property. Thus, henceforth, whenever we consider a metric space (V, d_V) with $V \subseteq \mathbb{R}$ convex, we subsume also the ball-convex property for the metric d_V.

We can show that $\mathbf{B}_V$ is monotone [12]. Then, as $(\mathbf{D}, \preceq)$ is a complete lattice, by the Tarski theorem $\mathbf{B}_V$ has the least fixed point. Bisimulation metrics are the pseudometrics being prefixed points of $\mathbf{B}_V$ and the *bisimilarity metric* $\mathbf{d}_{\lambda, V}$ is the least fixed point of $\mathbf{B}_V$ and its kernel is probabilistic bisimilarity [12].

Definition 16 (Generalized bisimulation metric, [12]). *A pseudometric $d : \mathcal{S} \times \mathcal{S} \to [0, +\infty]$ is a bisimulation metric iff $\mathbf{B}_V(d) \preceq d$. The least fixed point of $\mathbf{B}_V$ is denoted by $\mathbf{d}_{\lambda, V}$ and called the bisimilarity metric.*

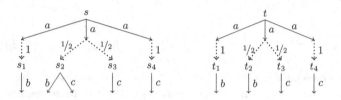

Fig. 2. The classic bisimilarity distance between s, t is $\mathbf{d}_\lambda(s, t) = 1/2 \cdot \lambda$

4.2   The Modal Logic $\mathcal{L}$

We introduce the *modal logic* $\mathcal{L}$ of [14], which extends HML [28] with a probabilistic choice modality that allows us to express the behavior of probability distributions over processes.

Definition 17 (Modal logic $\mathcal{L}$, [14]). *The logic* $\mathcal{L} = \mathcal{L}^{\mathrm{s}} \cup \mathcal{L}^{\mathrm{d}}$ *is given by the classes of* state formulae $\mathcal{L}^{\mathrm{s}}$ *and* distribution formulae $\mathcal{L}^{\mathrm{d}}$ *over* $\mathcal{A}$ *defined by:*

$$\mathcal{L}^{\mathrm{s}}: \quad \varphi ::= \top \mid \neg\varphi \mid \bigwedge_{j \in J} \varphi_j \mid \langle a \rangle \psi \qquad\qquad \mathcal{L}^{\mathrm{d}}: \quad \psi ::= \bigoplus_{i \in I} r_i \varphi_i$$

where: (i) φ *ranges over* $\mathcal{L}^{\mathrm{s}}$, *(ii)* ψ *ranges over* $\mathcal{L}^{\mathrm{d}}$, *(iii)* $a \in \mathcal{A}$, *(iv)* $J \neq \emptyset$ *is a countable set of indexes, (v)* $I \neq \emptyset$ *is a finite set of indexes and (vi)* $r_i \in (0, 1]$ *for all* $i \in I$ *and* $\sum_{i \in I} r_i = 1$.

We shall write $\varphi_1 \wedge \varphi_2$ for $\bigwedge_{j \in J} \varphi_j$ with $J = \{1, 2\}$, and $\langle a \rangle \varphi$ for $\langle a \rangle \bigoplus_{i \in I} r_i \varphi_i$ with $I = \{i\}$, $r_i = 1$ and $\varphi_i = \varphi$. We use $\top$ instead of $\bigwedge_\emptyset$ to improve readability.

Formulae are interpreted over a PTS. A distribution π satisfies the formula $\bigoplus_{i \in I} r_i \varphi_i$ if, for each $i \in I$, π assigns probability (at least) r_i to processes satisfying the formula φ_i. This is formalized by requiring that π can be rewritten as a convex combination of distributions π_i, using the r_i as weights, such that all the processes in $\mathsf{supp}(\pi_i)$ satisfy the formula φ_i.

Definition 18 (Semantics of $\mathcal{L}$, [14]). *The satisfaction relation* $\models \subseteq (\mathcal{S} \times \mathcal{L}^{\mathrm{s}}) \cup (\Delta(\mathcal{S}) \times \mathcal{L}^{\mathrm{d}})$ *is defined by structural induction on formulae in* $\mathcal{L}$ *by*

- $s \models \top$ *always;*
- $s \models \neg\varphi$ *iff* $s \models \varphi$ *does not hold;*
- $s \models \bigwedge_{j \in J} \varphi_j$ *iff* $s \models \varphi_j$ *for all* $j \in J$;
- $s \models \langle a \rangle \psi$ *iff* $s \xrightarrow{a} \pi$ *for a distribution* $\pi \in \Delta(\mathcal{S})$ *with* $\pi \models \psi$,
- $\pi \models \bigoplus_{i \in I} r_i \varphi_i$ *iff* $\pi = \sum_{i \in I} r_i \pi_i$ *for some distributions* $\pi_i \in \Delta(\mathcal{S})$ *such that for all* $i \in I$ *we have* $s \models \varphi_i$ *for all states* $s \in \mathsf{supp}(\pi_i)$.

We introduce the relation of $\mathcal{L}$-*equivalence* over formulae in $\mathcal{L}$, which identifies formulae that are indistinguishable by their syntactic structure. Such an equivalence is obtained as the greatest fixed point of a proper transformation E of relations on state formulae.

Definition 19 ([9]). *Let* $\mathcal{R} \subseteq \mathcal{L}^s \times \mathcal{L}^s$ *be any equivalence relation on* $\mathcal{L}^s$. *The transformation* $E \colon \mathcal{L}^s \times \mathcal{L}^s \to \mathcal{L}^s \times \mathcal{L}^s$ *is defined as:* $(\varphi, \varphi') \in E(\mathcal{R})$ *iff*

- $\varphi = \varphi'$;
- $\varphi = \bigwedge_{j \in J} \varphi_j$, $\varphi' = \bigwedge_{j \in (J \setminus \{h\}) \cup I} \varphi_j$ *and* $(\varphi_h, \bigwedge_{i \in I} \varphi_i) \in \mathcal{R}$, *for* $I \cap J = \emptyset$;
- $\varphi = \bigwedge_{j \in J} \varphi_j$, $\varphi' = \bigwedge_{j \in (J \setminus \{i\})} \varphi_j$ *and* $(\varphi_i, \bigwedge_{j \in I} \varphi_j) \in \mathcal{R}$, *for* $I \subseteq J \setminus \{i\}$;
- $\varphi = \bigwedge_{j \in J} \varphi_j$, $\varphi' = \bigwedge_{i \in I} \varphi_i$ *and there is a bijection* $f \colon J \to I$ *with* $(\varphi_j, \varphi_{f(j)}) \in \mathcal{R}$, $\forall j \in J$;
- $\varphi = \neg \varphi_1$, $\varphi' = \neg \varphi_2$ *and* $(\varphi_1, \varphi_2) \in \mathcal{R}$;
- $\varphi = \langle a \rangle \psi$, $\varphi' = \langle a \rangle \psi'$ *and* $(\psi, \psi') \in \mathcal{R}^\dagger$.

It is easy to check that the transformation E is monotone on the complete lattice $(\mathcal{L}^s \times \mathcal{L}^s, \subseteq)$ and hence, by Tarski's theorem E has a greatest fixed point. We define the $\mathcal{L}$-equivalence of formulae as such a greatest fixed point.

Definition 20 ($\mathcal{L}$-equivalence).   *The* $\mathcal{L}$-*equivalence of formulae* $\equiv_{\mathcal{L}} \subseteq$ $\mathcal{L}^s \times \mathcal{L}^s$ *is defined as* $\equiv_{\mathcal{L}} = \max\{\mathcal{R} \subseteq \mathcal{L}^s \times \mathcal{L}^s \mid \mathcal{R} \subseteq E(\mathcal{R})\}$.

4.3   The Mimicking Formulae

In [14] it was proved that the logic $\mathcal{L}$ is *adequate* for bisimilarity, i.e., two processes are bisimilar iff they satisfy the same formulae in $\mathcal{L}$. The drawback of this valuable result is in that to verify the equivalence we would need to test all the formulae definable in the logic, that is infinitely many formulae. As an alternative, in [15] a characterization of bisimilarity was given in terms of *characteristic formulae* [26] of processes, i.e., particular formulae that alone capture the entire equivalence class of the related process: if ϕ_s is the characteristic formula of process s for bisimilarity, then $s \sim t$ iff $t \models \phi_s$. This is the so called *expressive* characterization of an equivalence and allows us to establish process equivalence by testing a single formula. Unfortunately, also in this case there is a little drawback: to guarantee the possibility of constructing the characteristic formulae we need a very rich logic. For instance, [15] uses the probabilistic μ-calculus which, differently from $\mathcal{L}$, allows for arbitrary formulae to occur after the diamond modality and includes fixpoint operators.

Recently, [9,10] proposed a different technique for the characterization. When we compare the behavior of two processes, we compare those properties that are observable for them w.r.t. the considered semantics. The idea is to introduce a special formula, called *mimicking formula*, for each process expressing all and only its observable properties. In a broader sense, the mimicking formula of a process can be regarded as its specification. [9,10] showed that semantic equivalence of processes holds iff their mimicking formulae are syntactically equivalent (Theorem 4 below). Hence, to establish process equivalence we need only two formulae. Moreover, the logic on which the mimicking formulae are constructed is always *minimal* w.r.t. the chosen semantics, i.e., it only includes the operators necessary to express the observable properties w.r.t. that semantics.

Here, we recall the definition of mimicking formula and the *weak expressive* characterization of bisimilarity from [9]. Mimicking formulae are defined inductively over the depth of formulae as *up-to-k mimicking formulae*. Intuitively, the *up-to-k mimicking formula* of process s, denoted by φ_s^k, characterizes the branching structure of the first k-steps of s by specifying which transitions are enabled for s as well as all the actions that it cannot perform.

Definition 21 (Mimicking formula, [9]). *For a process $s \in S$ and $k \in \mathbb{N}$, the* up-to-k mimicking formula of s, *notation φ_s^k, is defined inductively by*

$$\varphi_s^0 = \top$$

$$\varphi_s^k = \bigwedge_{(s,a,\pi)\in\to} \langle a \rangle \bigoplus_{t\in\mathrm{supp}(\pi)} \pi(t)\varphi_t^{k-1} \wedge \bigwedge_{b\notin\mathrm{init}(s)} \neg\langle b \rangle\top$$

Then, the mimicking formula *of s, notation φ_s, is defined as $\varphi_s = \lim_{k\to\infty} \varphi_s^k$.*

Example 5. Consider s in Fig. 2 and assume that $\mathcal{A} = \{a, b, c\}$. We aim to construct the mimicking formula of s. We have

$$\varphi_{\mathrm{nil}} = \neg\langle a \rangle\top \wedge \neg\langle b \rangle\top \wedge \neg\langle c \rangle\top \qquad \varphi_{s_1} = \langle b \rangle\varphi_{\mathrm{nil}} \wedge \neg\langle a \rangle\top \wedge \neg\langle c \rangle\top$$

$$\varphi_{s_2} = \langle b \rangle\varphi_{\mathrm{nil}} \wedge \langle c \rangle\varphi_{\mathrm{nil}} \wedge \neg\langle a \rangle\top \qquad \varphi_{s_3} = \langle c \rangle\varphi_{\mathrm{nil}} \wedge \neg\langle a \rangle\top \wedge \neg\langle b \rangle\top$$

$$\varphi_{s_3} = \varphi_{s_4}$$

$$\varphi_s = \langle a \rangle\varphi_{s_1} \wedge \langle a \rangle(1/2\varphi_{s_2} \oplus 1/2\varphi_{s_3}) \wedge \langle a \rangle\varphi_{s_4} \wedge \neg\langle b \rangle\top \wedge \neg\langle c \rangle\top.$$

Mimicking formulae allow us to characterize probabilistic bisimilarity.

Theorem 4 ([9]). *Given any $s, t \in S$ we have that $\varphi_s \equiv_{\mathcal{L}} \varphi_t$ iff $s \sim t$.*

4.4 $\mathcal{L}$-Characterization of a Family of Bisimilarity Metrics

In this Section we exploit the relation between the semantic properties of a process and the syntactic structure of its mimicking formula to provide a logical characterization of the family of bisimilarity metrics introduced in Sect. 4.1. The idea follows that of [9,10]: 1. Firstly we transform the logic $\mathcal{L}$ into a family of metric spaces by defining a suitable *syntactic distance* over formulae. Intuitively, since distribution formulae are defined as probability distributions over state formulae, we can exploit the generalized Kantorovich metric to lift the distance over state formulae to a distance over distribution formulae. 2. Then we lift these syntactic distances to a family of pseudometrics over processes, called *logical distances*. Briefly, the logical distance $\ell_{\lambda,V}$ between two processes is defined as the syntactic distance between their mimicking formulae. 3. We show that the logical distance $\ell_{\lambda,V}$ coincides with the bisimilarity metric $\mathbf{d}_{\lambda,V}$ (Theorem 5 below).

The family of syntactic distances over formulae is defined inductively over the depth of formulae and their structure.

Definition 22 (Up-to-k distance on $\mathcal{L}$). *Let* $\lambda \in (0,1]$ *and let* (V, d_V) *be a metric space with* $V \subseteq \mathbb{R}$ *convex. For* $k \in \mathbb{N}$*, the* up-to-k *distance on state formulae is the mapping* $\mathfrak{d}_{\lambda,V}^k \colon \mathcal{L}^s \times \mathcal{L}^s \to [0, +\infty]$ *defined by:*

$$\mathfrak{d}_{\lambda,V}^0(\varphi_1, \varphi_2) = 0 \text{ for all } \varphi_1, \varphi_2 \in \mathcal{L}^s$$

$$\mathfrak{d}_{\lambda,V}^k(\varphi_1, \varphi_2) = \begin{cases} 0 & \text{if } \varphi_1 = \top, \varphi_2 = \top \\ \mathfrak{d}_{\lambda,V}^k(\varphi_1', \varphi_2') & \text{if } \varphi_1 = \neg\varphi_1', \varphi_2 = \neg\varphi_2' \\ \lambda \cdot \mathbf{K}_V(\mathfrak{d}_{\lambda,V}^{k-1})(\psi_1, \psi_2) & \text{if } \varphi_1 = \langle a \rangle \psi_1, \varphi_2 = \langle a \rangle \psi_2 \\ \mathbf{H}(\mathfrak{d}_{\lambda,V}^k)(\{\varphi_j\}_{j \in J}, \{\varphi_i\}_{i \in I}) & \text{if } \varphi_1 = \bigwedge_{j \in J} \varphi_j, \varphi_2 = \bigwedge_{i \in I} \varphi_i \\ \oslash_{d_V}(V) & \text{otherwise.} \end{cases}$$

Clearly, the mapping $\mathfrak{d}_{\lambda,V}^k$ is a pseudometric and it is bounded whenever $\mathbf{K}_V$ is bounded. The discount factor $\lambda \in (0,1]$ allows us to specify how much the distance between state formulae at the same depth is taken into account. For this reason, the discount factor λ is introduced in the evaluation of the distance between equally labeled diamond modalities.

We define the family of *syntactic distances over formulae*, denoted by $\mathfrak{d}_{\lambda,V}$, as the limit of their up-to-k distances. Since we consider only the metric spaces (V, d_V) for which $\mathbf{K}_V$ is bounded (cf. Remark 1), the existence of such a limit is ensured by the following two results.

Lemma 2. *For each* $k \in \mathbb{N}$ *and for all* $\varphi, \varphi' \in \mathcal{L}^s$*,* $\mathfrak{d}_{\lambda,V}^{k+1}(\varphi, \varphi') \geq \mathfrak{d}_{\lambda,V}^k(\varphi, \varphi')$.

Proposition 5. *The mapping* $\mathfrak{d}_{\lambda,V} \colon \mathcal{L}^s \times \mathcal{L}^s \to [0, +\infty]$ *defined, for all* $\varphi, \varphi' \in \mathcal{L}^s$*, by* $\mathfrak{d}_{\lambda,V}(\varphi, \varphi') = \lim_{k \to \infty} \mathfrak{d}_{\lambda,V}^k(\varphi, \varphi')$ *is well-defined.*

We are now ready to lift the metric on $\mathcal{L}$ to a metric on $\mathcal{S}$. To this aim, we exploit the close relation between processes and their own mimicking formulae.

Definition 23 (Logical distance). *For any* $k \in \mathbb{N}$*, the* up-to-k *logical distance* $\ell_{\lambda,V}^k \colon \mathcal{S} \times \mathcal{S} \to [0, +\infty]$ *over processes is defined for all* $s, t \in \mathcal{S}$ *by* $\ell_{\lambda,V}^k(s, t) = \mathfrak{d}_{\lambda,V}^k(\varphi_s^k, \varphi_t^k)$*. Then, the* logical distance $\ell_\lambda \colon \mathcal{S} \times \mathcal{S} \to [0, +\infty]$ *over processes is defined, for all* $s, t \in \mathcal{S}$ *by* $\ell_{\lambda,V}(s, t) = \mathfrak{d}_{\lambda,V}(\varphi_s, \varphi_t)$.

The next Theorem gives us the logical characterization of the generalized bisimilarity metrics in terms of the logical distances over processes.

Theorem 5. *Let* $\lambda \in (0,1]$*. For any* $s, t \in \mathcal{S}$ *we have* $\ell_{\lambda,V}(s, t) = \mathbf{d}_{\lambda,V}(s, t)$.

4.5 A Logical Bound on $d_{\mathcal{X}}$-privacy: The Logical Distance

We exploit the *multiplicative variant* of the logical distance over processes to obtain a *logical bound* on $d_{\mathcal{X}}$-privacy. In detail, we model randomized mechanisms as LMCs and then: 1. We show that the multiplicative variant of the logical distance on the states of the LMC is an upper bound to the multiplicative total variation distance on the trace distributions induced by them. 2. We rephrase the $d_\mathcal{X}$-privacy property as an upper bound on the logical distance between states corresponding to the considered secrets.

We remark that since we will use traces as a mere representation of the information on secrets, the actual length of the trace should play no role in the evaluation of the distances. More precisely, the depth of the mimicking formula of the process that induces those traces in the LMC should not interfere in the evaluation of the distance as we are not interested in keeping track of the number of computation steps performed by a process, but, rather, in the possibility of executing them and the related execution probability. Hence, in the remaining of this Section we assume the discount factor $\lambda = 1$ and we omit it.

As shown in [12], we can express the multiplicative total variation distance in terms of the multiplicative variant of the Kantorovich lifting $\mathbf{K}_\otimes$ of the discrete metric over traces. More precisely, we let $\mathbf{dm}_{\oslash_V}$ be the $\oslash_{d_V}(V)$-valued discrete metric over $\mathcal{A}^*$ which is defined as $\mathbf{dm}_{\oslash_V}(\alpha, \alpha') = 0$ if $\alpha = \alpha'$ and $\mathbf{dm}_{\oslash_V}(\alpha, \alpha') = \oslash_{d_V}(V)$ otherwise. To define $\mathbf{K}_\otimes$, we need to consider $V = [0,1]$ and $d_\otimes(x,y) = |\ln(x) - \ln(y)|$. In [12] it has been proved that for $\oslash_{d_\otimes}([0,1]) = +\infty$ it holds $tv_\otimes = \mathbf{K}_\otimes(\mathbf{dm}_{\oslash_\otimes})$. Hence, from $\mathbf{d}_{\lambda,\otimes} \geq \mathbf{K}_\otimes(\mathbf{dm}_{\oslash_\otimes})$ (cf. [12]) and Theorem 5 we obtain the following result.

Proposition 6. *Assume a LMC and let s,t be two processes in it. Let $\pi_s = \Pr(s,\cdot)$ and $\pi_t = \Pr(t,\cdot)$. Then $tv_\otimes(\pi_s, \pi_t) \leq \ell_\otimes(s,t)$.*

We remark that Proposition 2, Theorem 5 and Proposition 6 imply that $\mathbf{d}_\otimes^T \preceq \mathbf{d}_\otimes$.

We can then restate Definition 5 in terms of an upper bound on the multiplicative logical distance, thus obtaining the logical bound on $d_\mathcal{X}$-privacy.

Theorem 6 (Logical bound on $d_\mathcal{X}$-privacy). *Let M be a randomized mechanism defined by $M(\mathbf{x})(\alpha) = \Pr(s_\mathbf{x}, \alpha)$ for all $\mathbf{x} \in \mathcal{X}$, $\alpha \in \mathcal{A}^*$. Then, given $\varepsilon > 0$, M is $\varepsilon \cdot d_\mathcal{X}$-private if $\ell_\otimes(s_\mathbf{x}, s_{\mathbf{x}'}) \leq \varepsilon \cdot d_\mathcal{X}(\mathbf{x}, \mathbf{x}') \,\forall\, \mathbf{x}, \mathbf{x}' \in \mathcal{X}$.*

The following example illustrates a case of standard differential privacy.

Example 6. Consider two medical databases x and x', both of size n,[1] and assume that they are adjacent, i.e. that they differ only for one individual record. Assume that we ask a counting query of the form $a = $"How many people in the database have the disease d_a?". Assume that, to sanitize the answer, we use a geometric mechanism [24], namely a probabilistic function that reports as answer the integer j with a probability distribution of the form $p_a(j) = c\,e^{-|i-j|\varepsilon}$, where i is the true answer, ε is the desired privacy level, and c is a normalization factor. In order to obtain a finite support, we can truncate the mechanism in the interval $[0,n]$, namely accumulate on 0 all the probability mass of the interval $(-\infty, 0]$, and on n all the probability mass of the interval $[n, +\infty)$. It is well known that the resulting mechanism is ε-differentially private. Consider now a

---

[1] We recall that we are using a notion of privacy in which all databases have the same number of records n, and the absence of a record is represented by a special value.

new counting query of the form b = "How many people in the database have the disease d_b ?", and again, assume that the answer is sanitized by a truncated geometric mechanism of the same form, with probability distribution p_b.

From the differential privacy literature we know that the combination of both mechanisms, in which the second query is asked after having obtained the answer from the first one, is 2ε-differentially private. However, we can obtain a better bound by looking at the various situations. To this purpose, let us consider the systems s and s' corresponding to the two databases x and x' respectively, and let p_a, p_b, p'_a and p'_b the probability distributions for the queries a and b in x and x' respectively. We can completely describe them by the mimicking formulae (which in this case are also characteristic formulae) φ and φ' defined as (for simplicity we omit the negative parts and the probabilities when they are 1):

$$\varphi_s = \langle a \rangle \bigoplus_{j \in [0,n]} p_a(j)\langle j \rangle \langle b \rangle \bigoplus_{m \in [0,n]} p_b(m)\langle m \rangle \top$$

$$\varphi_{s'} = \langle a \rangle \bigoplus_{j \in [0,n]} p'_a(j)\langle j \rangle \langle b \rangle \bigoplus_{m \in [0,n]} p'_b(m)\langle m \rangle \top$$

Consider now the four scenarios obtained by combining the various cases that the individual corresponding to the new record in x' has or does not have the diseases d_a and d_b.

- If he does not have either of them, then p_a coincides with p'_a and p_b coincides with p'_b, which means that the distance between φ_s and $\varphi_{s'}$ is 0: the two systems are indistinguishable (0-differentially private).
- If he has d_a but not d_b, or vice versa, then either p_a coincides p'_a and the ratio between p_b and p'_b is bound by ε, or vice versa. The distance between φ_s and $\varphi_{s'}$ is ε: the two systems are ε-differentially private.
- If he has both d_a and d_b, then the ratio between p_a and p'_a, and that between p_b and p'_b, are bound by ε. The distance between φ_s and $\varphi_{s'}$ is 2ε: the two systems are 2ε-differentially private.

5 Conclusions

We have provided a logical characterization of generalized bisimulation metrics, based on the notions of mimicking formulae, i.e., formulae capturing the observable behavior of a particular process, and distance on formulae, i.e., a pseudometric on formulae measuring their syntactic disparities. Moreover, we have used the distance on formulae to obtain logical bounds on differential privacy properties. Then we have applied the same method to a simpler class of formulae expressing the trace semantics, thus obtaining a logical characterization of differential privacy and a classic logical characterization of weak anonymity.

As future work, we will further investigate the relation between the distance on formulae and real valued semantics on richer classes of formulae, by providing a thorough comparison with the real-valued semantics proposed in [17,18] for the characterization of bisimulation semantics. Moreover, we aim at using the metrics and logical properties explored in this paper to reason about privacy in concurrent systems. This will require to deal with nondeterminism, which is already considered in the present paper, but probably we will need to reason explicitly about the scheduler and to restrict its capabilities, in order to avoid the problem of the "omniscient scheduler", which could break any privacy defense. Finally, we aim at developing quantitative analysis techniques and tools for proving privacy properties.

References

1. de Alfaro, L., Faella, M., Stoelinga, M.: Linear and branching system metrics. IEEE Trans. Softw. Eng. **35**(2), 258–273 (2009)
2. de Alfaro, L., Henzinger, T.A., Majumdar, R.: Discounting the future in systems theory. In: Baeten, J.C.M., Lenstra, J.K., Parrow, J., Woeginger, G.J. (eds.) ICALP 2003. LNCS, vol. 2719, pp. 1022–1037. Springer, Heidelberg (2003). https://doi.org/10.1007/3-540-45061-0_79
3. de Alfaro, L., Majumdar, R., Raman, V., Stoelinga, M.: Game refinement relations and metrics. Log. Methods Comput. Sci. 4(3) (2008)
4. Bacci, G., Bacci, G., Larsen, K.G., Mardare, R.: Converging from branching to linear metrics on Markov chains. In: Leucker, M., Rueda, C., Valencia, F.D. (eds.) ICTAC 2015. LNCS, vol. 9399, pp. 349–367. Springer, Cham (2015). https://doi.org/10.1007/978-3-319-25150-9_21
5. Barthe, G., Köpf, B., Olmedo, F., Béguelin, S.Z.: Probabilistic relational reasoning for differential privacy. In: Proceedings of POPL. ACM (2012)
6. Bernardo, M., De Nicola, R., Loreti, M.: Revisiting trace and testing equivalences for nondeterministic and probabilistic processes. Log. Methods Comput. Sci. 10(1) (2014)
7. Bloom, B., Fokkink, W.J., van Glabbeek, R.J.: Precongruence formats for decorated trace semantics. ACM Trans. Comput. Log. **5**(1), 26–78 (2004)
8. van Breugel, F., Worrell, J.: A behavioural pseudometric for probabilistic transition systems. Theor. Comput. Sci. **331**(1), 115–142 (2005)
9. Castiglioni, V., Gebler, D., Tini, S.: Logical characterization of bisimulation metrics. In: Proceedings of QAPL'16. EPTCS **227**, 44–62 (2016)
10. Castiglioni, V., Tini, S.: Logical characterization of trace metrics. In: Proceedings of QAPL@ETAPS 2017. EPTCS **250**, 39–74 (2017)
11. Chatzikokolakis, K., Andrés, M.E., Bordenabe, N.E., Palamidessi, C.: Broadening the scope of differential privacy using metrics. In: De Cristofaro, E., Wright, M. (eds.) PETS 2013. LNCS, vol. 7981, pp. 82–102. Springer, Heidelberg (2013). https://doi.org/10.1007/978-3-642-39077-7_5
12. Chatzikokolakis, K., Gebler, D., Palamidessi, C., Xu, L.: Generalized bisimulation metrics. In: Baldan, P., Gorla, D. (eds.) CONCUR 2014. LNCS, vol. 8704, pp. 32–46. Springer, Heidelberg (2014). https://doi.org/10.1007/978-3-662-44584-6_4
13. Deng, Y., Chothia, T., Palamidessi, C., Pang, J.: Metrics for action-labelled quantitative transition systems. Electr. Notes Theor. Comput. Sci. **153**(2), 79–96 (2006)
14. Deng, Y., Du, W.: Logical, metric, and algorithmic characterisations of probabilistic bisimulation. CoRR abs/ arXiv:1103.4577 (2011)
15. Deng, Y., van Glabbeek, R.J.: Characterising probabilistic processes logically - (extended abstract). In: Proceedings of LPAR-17, pp. 278–293 (2010)

16. Deng, Y., Palamidessi, C., Pang, J.: Weak probabilistic anonymity. ENTCS **180**(1), 55–76 (2007)
17. Desharnais, J., Gupta, V., Jagadeesan, R., Panangaden, P.: Metrics for labelled Markov processes. Theor. Comput. Sci. **318**(3), 323–354 (2004)
18. Desharnais, J., Jagadeesan, R., Gupta, V., Panangaden, P.: The metric analogue of weak bisimulation for probabilistic processes. Proc. LICS **2002**, 413–422 (2002)
19. Du, W., Deng, Y., Gebler, D.: Behavioural pseudometrics for nondeterministic probabilistic systems. In: Fränzle, M., Kapur, D., Zhan, N. (eds.) SETTA 2016. LNCS, vol. 9984, pp. 67–84. Springer, Cham (2016). https://doi.org/10.1007/978-3-319-47677-3_5
20. Duchi, J.C., Jordan, M.I., Wainwright, M.J.: Local privacy and statistical minimax rates. In: Proceedings of the 54th Annual IEEE Symposium on Foundations of Computer Science (FOCS), pp. 429–438. IEEE Computer Society (2013)
21. Dwork, C.: Differential privacy. In: Bugliesi, M., Preneel, B., Sassone, V., Wegener, I. (eds.) ICALP 2006. LNCS, vol. 4052, pp. 1–12. Springer, Heidelberg (2006). https://doi.org/10.1007/11787006_1
22. Erlingsson, Ú., Pihur, V., Korolova, A.: RAPPOR: randomized aggregatable privacy-preserving ordinal response. In: Ahn, G., Yung, M., Li, N. (eds.) Proceedings of the 2014 ACM SIGSAC Conference on Computer and Communications Security (CCS), pp. 1054–1067. ACM (2014)
23. Gaboardi, M., Haeberlen, A., Hsu, J., Narayan, A., Pierce, B.C.: Linear dependent types for differential privacy. In: POPL, pp. 357–370 (2013)
24. Ghosh, A., Roughgarden, T., Sundararajan, M.: Universally utility-maximizing privacy mechanisms. In: Proceedings of the 41st Annual ACM Symposium on Theory of Computing (STOC), pp. 351–360. ACM (2009)
25. Giacalone, A., Jou, C.C., Smolka, S.A.: Algebraic reasoning for probabilistic concurrent systems. In: Proceedings of IFIP Work, Conference on Programming, Concepts and Methods, pp. 443–458 (1990)
26. Graf, S., Sifakis, J.: A modal characterization of observational congruence on finite terms of CCS. Inf. Control **68**(1–3), 125–145 (1986)
27. Hansson, H., Jonsson, B.: A logic for reasoning about time and reliability. FAC **6**(5), 512–535 (1994)
28. Hennessy, M., Milner, R.: Algebraic laws for nondeterminism and concurrency. J. Assoc. Comput. Mach. **32**, 137–161 (1985)
29. Hermanns, H., Parma, A., Segala, R., Wachter, B., Zhang, L.: Probabilistic logical characterization. Inf. Comput. **209**(2), 154–172 (2011)
30. Keller, R.M.: Formal verification of parallel programs. Commun. ACM **19**(7), 371–384 (1976)
31. Kwiatkowska, M., Norman, G.: Probabilistic metric semantics for a simple language with recursion. In: Penczek, W., Szałas, A. (eds.) MFCS 1996. LNCS, vol. 1113, pp. 419–430. Springer, Heidelberg (1996). https://doi.org/10.1007/3-540-61550-4_167
32. Larsen, K.G., Mardare, R., Panangaden, P.: Taking it to the limit: approximate reasoning for Markov processes. In: Rovan, B., Sassone, V., Widmayer, P. (eds.) MFCS 2012. LNCS, vol. 7464, pp. 681–692. Springer, Heidelberg (2012). https://doi.org/10.1007/978-3-642-32589-2_59
33. Larsen, K.G., Skou, A.: Bisimulation through probabilistic testing. Inf. Comput. **94**(1), 1–28 (1991)
34. Machanavajjhala, A., Kifer, D., Abowd, J.M., Gehrke, J., Vilhuber, L.: Privacy: theory meets practice on the map. Proc. ICDE **2008**, 277–286 (2008)
35. Narayanan, A., Shmatikov, V.: De-anonymizing social networks. In: Proceedings of S&P 2009, pp. 173–187 (2009)

36. Reed, J., Pierce, B.C.: Distance makes the types grow stronger: a calculus for differential privacy. In: Proceedings of ICFP, pp. 157–168. ACM (2010)
37. Segala, R.: Modeling and Verification of Randomized Distributed Real-Time Systems. Ph.D. thesis, MIT (1995)
38. Smith, A.D.: Efficient, differentially private point estimators. CoRR abs/ arXiv:0809.4794 (2008)
39. Song, L., Deng, Y., Cai, X.: Towards automatic measurement of probabilistic processes. Proc. QSIC **2007**, 50–59 (2007)
40. Tschantz, M.C., Kaynar, D., Datta, A.: Formal verification of differential privacy for interactive systems (extended abstract). ENTCS 276, 61–79 (2011)
41. Xu, L., Chatzikokolakis, K., Lin, H.: Metrics for differential privacy in concurrent systems. In: Ábrahám, E., Palamidessi, C. (eds.) FORTE 2014. LNCS, vol. 8461, pp. 199–215. Springer, Heidelberg (2014). https://doi.org/10.1007/978-3-662-43613-4_13

Incremental Computation of Synthesis Rules for Free-Choice Petri Nets

Prabhakar M. Dixit[1]([⊠]), H. M. W. Verbeek[1], and Wil M. P. van der Aalst[2]

[1] Eindhoven University of Technology, Eindhoven, The Netherlands
{p.m.dixit,h.m.w.verbeek}@tue.nl
[2] Rheinisch-Westflische Technische Hochschule, (RWTH), Aachen, Germany
wvdaalst@pads.rwth-aachen.de

Abstract. In this paper, we propose a novel approach that calculates all the possible applications of synthesis rules, for well-formed free-choice Petri nets [8], in a speedy way to enable an interactive editing system. The proposed approach uses a so-called *incremental synthesis structure*, which can be used to extract all the synthesis rules, corresponding to a given net. Furthermore, this structure is updated incrementally, i.e. after usage of a synthesis rule, to obtain the incremental synthesis structure of the newly synthesized net. We prove that the proposed approach is correct and complete in order to synthesize any well-formed free-choice Petri net, starting with an initial well-formed atomic net and the corresponding incremental synthesis structure. A variant of the proposed approach has been implemented that allows interactive modeling (discovery) of sound business processes (from event logs). Experimental results show that the proposed approach is fast, and outperforms the baseline, and hence is well-suited for enabling interactive synthesis of very large nets.

Keywords: Free-choice Petri nets · Interactive system
Incremental synthesis rules computation

1 Introduction

Petri nets serve as an effective tool for modeling the control flow of asynchronous concurrent systems. In order to be useful, in application areas such as business process management, it is imperative that the Petri nets representing the business processes adhere to certain properties, e.g. soundness [1]. In this paper, we propose an approach that allows interactive editing of free-choice Petri nets from smaller nets by preserving certain properties (such as well-formedness). We show that the proposed approach is fast, and thus has negligible waiting times and thereby well-suited for enabling an interactive editing system. Moreover, using the guarantees from [8], we show that the approach can be used to synthesize any well-formed free-choice Petri net. A sub-class of such nets can also be used to model sound business processes, and is also applicable in the field of process mining.

© Springer Nature Switzerland AG 2018
K. Bae and P. C. Ölveczky (Eds.): FACS 2018, LNCS 11222, pp. 97–117, 2018.
https://doi.org/10.1007/978-3-030-02146-7_5

Petri net synthesis techniques allow synthesizing bigger Petri nets from smaller Petri nets. In many cases, the synthesized net guarantees certain structural and behavioral properties, depending on the net it was synthesized from. The technique of synthesizing Petri nets from smaller nets is not new, and has been well-researched for over two decades [2,7,12]. Synthesis rules are basically reverse applications of *reduction rules*, which are well researched in the literature [3–5,13,14] for a variety of different applications [11,16]. The work in [6] provides a way of interactively synthesizing Petri nets using a knitting technique. However, the completeness and correctness of these rules is not guaranteed. In our case, we refer to the synthesis techniques that allow Petri net expansion, one transition and/or place at a time. We use such rules to enable a user interactive well-formed free-choice Petri net editing system. Compared to the approaches from the literature, our main focus is not to suggest new synthesis rules, but to develop an approach that allows speedy computation of all possible applications of synthesis rules to enable an interactive system for editing/modeling of well-formed free-choice Petri nets.

In our approach, we use the synthesis rule kit from [8], which are mainly derived from [5], that allow synthesis of any well-formed free-choice Petri net, starting with an initial well-formed atomic net. The synthesis rule kit consists of three rules which allow (i) addition of a transition, (ii) addition of a place, or (iii) addition of a transition and a place to a Petri net. Thus these rules could be used as the building blocks for enabling interactive free-choice Petri net editing/modeling, which guarantee well-formedness. To enable interactive modeling, it is ideal to pre-populate all the possible applications of synthesis rules for any given net. However, computing all the synthesis operations in a brute-force way for any given net can be computationally expensive and hence very slow, especially for the first two rules, which require solving a system of linear equations to check the applicability of the rule. This is clearly not feasible as the size of the net grows, as the number of applications of synthesis rules would grow too.

In this paper, we address the issue of computing all the applications of synthesis rules for a given well-formed free choice net in a speedy way to allow interactive editing. We propose an approach based on an *incremental synthesis structure*, that can be used to calculate all the possible applications of synthesis rules, for a given well-formed net. This meta-structure is updated after application of any rule, to contain information to extract all the possible applications of synthesis rules corresponding to the newly synthesized net. We show that by starting with a correct and complete incremental synthesis structure for the initial net, we can calculate the incremental synthesis structure of any synthesized net, and thereby calculate all the possible applications of synthesis rules in an incremental way.

The remainder of the paper is structured as follows. We review the preliminaries in Sect. 2. In Sects. 3 and 4 we discuss the approach for calculating the synthesis rules in an incremental fashion, as well as discuss the correctness and completeness of the proposed approach. In Sect. 5, we briefly discuss the implementation and application of the approach to business processes. We evaluate the proposed approach in Sect. 6, followed by the conclusions and future research directions in Sect. 7.

2 Preliminaries

This section introduces some basic definitions and background of the concepts used in this paper.

A bag over some set S is a function from S to the natural numbers that assigns only a finite number of elements from S a positive value. For a bag B over set S and $s \in S$, $B(s)$ denotes the number of occurrences of s in B, often called the cardinality of s in B. Note that a finite set of elements of S is also a bag over S, namely the function yielding 1 for every element in the set and 0 otherwise. The set of all bags over set S is denoted $\mathcal{B}(S)$. We use brackets to explicitly enumerate a bag and superscripts to denote cardinalities. For example $[a^2, b^3, c]$ denotes a bag in which the elements a, b and c are contained 2, 3 and 1 times resp. Bag B is a subbag of bag B', denoted $B \leq B'$, iff, for all $s \in S$, $B(s) \leq B'(s)$. The standard operators can be extended to bag, e.g., $[a^2] + [a^2, b^3, c] = [a^4, b^3, c]$. Furthermore, we also allow addition or subtraction of bags with sets, e.g., $[a^2, b^3, c] - \{a\} = [a, b^3, c]$.

A relation $R \subseteq X \times Y$ is a set of pairs, where $\pi_1(R) = \{x \mid (x, y) \in R\}$ denotes the domain of R, $\pi_2(R) = \{y \mid (x, y) \in R\}$ denotes the range of R, and $\omega(R) = \pi_1(R) \cup \pi_2(R)$ denotes the elements of R. For example, $\omega(\{(a, b), (b, c)\}) = \{a, b, c\}$. $f : X \nrightarrow Y$ denotes a partial function with domain $dom(f) \subseteq X$ and range $rng(f) = \{f(x) \mid x \in X\} \subseteq Y$. $f : X \to Y$ denotes a total function, i.e., $dom(f) = X$. Given a finite set $A = \{a_1, \ldots, a_k\}$, every mapping $\mathbf{X}$ from A to $\mathbb{Q}$, denoted $\mathbf{X} : A \to \mathbb{Q}$ can be represented by the vector $(\mathbf{X}(a_1) \ldots \mathbf{X}(a_k))$. We do not distinguish between the mapping $\mathbf{X}$ and the vector $(\mathbf{X}(a_1) \ldots \mathbf{X}(a_k))$. $\mathbf{X} \cdot \mathbf{Y}$ denotes the scalar product of two vectors. Similarly, if $\mathbf{C}$ is a matrix, then $\mathbf{X} \cdot \mathbf{C}$ and $\mathbf{C} \cdot \mathbf{X}$ denote the left and right products of $\mathbf{X}$ and $\mathbf{C}$. We do not use different symbols for row and column vectors. For e.g., if we write $\mathbf{X} = (\mathbf{X}(a_1) \ldots \mathbf{X}(a_k))$, it serves as a column vector in $\mathbf{C} \cdot \mathbf{X}$.

Definition 1 (Petri net). *A Petri net N is a tuple (P, T, F) such that:*

- *P is a finite set of places,*
- *T is a finite set of transitions such that $P \cap T = \emptyset$, and*
- *$F \subseteq (P \times T) \cup (T \times P)$ is the set of arcs, also called the flow relation.*

For a Petri net $N = (P, T, F)$, and a node $n \in P \cup T$, the *preset* of n in N, denoted $\overset{N}{\bullet} n$, is the set of all nodes that have an arc to n, that is, $\overset{N}{\bullet} n = \{n' \mid (n', n) \in F\}$. Likewise, the *postset* of n in N, denoted $n \overset{N}{\bullet}$,

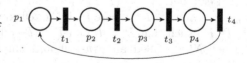

Fig. 1. An example well-formed free-choice Petri net (N_3).

is the set of all nodes that have an arc from n, that is, $n \overset{N}{\bullet} = \{n' | (n, n') \in F\}$. In case the net N is clear from the context, we typically omit it from these notations and use $\bullet n$ instead of $\overset{N}{\bullet} n$ etc. A Petri net $N = (P, T, F)$ is called a free-choice (or FC) net if for $r, u \in T$, it holds that $\bullet r \cap \bullet u = \emptyset$ or $\bullet r = \bullet u$. Figure 1 is also a FC net. The nodes of a Petri net can be used to populate a so-called incidence matrix.

Definition 2 (Incidence matrix). *Let* $N = (P, T, F)$ *be a Petri net. The incidence matrix* $\mathbf{N} : (P \times T) \to \{1, 0, -1\}$ *of N is defined by*

$$
\mathbf{N}(s, r) = \begin{cases} -1, & \text{if } (s, r) \in F \text{ and } (r, s) \notin F; \\ 1, & \text{if } (s, r) \notin F \text{ and}(r, s) \in F; \\ 0, & \text{otherwise}. \end{cases}
$$

Table 1 shows the incidence matrix corresponding to the Petri net from Fig. 1. The column vector of $\mathbf{N}$ is associated to a transition t is denoted by $\mathbf{t}$ and given as $\mathbf{t} : P \to \{-1, 0, 1\}$. Similarly, the row vector associated to a place p is $\mathbf{p} : T \to \{-1, 0, 1\}$. $\mathbf{t}(s)$ denotes the value corresponding to the place s, e.g., $\mathbf{t_2}(p_2) = -1$.

Table 1. Incidence matrix $\mathbf{N_3}$ of Fig. 1.

	t_1	t_2	t_3	t_4
p_1	-1	0	0	1
p_2	1	-1	0	0
p_3	0	1	-1	0
p_4	0	0	1	-1

A marking M of a Petri net $N = (P, T, F)$ is a bag over the places of N, that is, $M \in \mathcal{B}(P)$. A marking M is typically represented as a collection $M(s)$ of *tokens* for every place s. Removing a token from s then corresponds to removing one occurrence of s from M, and adding a token to s corresponds to adding one occurrence of s to M.

Let $N = (P, T, F)$ be a Petri net, let M be a marking of N, and let $r \in T$ be a transition of N. Transition r is *enabled* in M, denoted $M \overset{r}{\to}$, if and only if $\bullet r \leq M$. An enabled transition may *fire*, which leads to a new marking M', where $M' = M - \bullet r + r \bullet$, that is, in the new marking, a token is first removed from every place in the preset of r and a token is then added to every place in the postset of r. This firing is denoted as $M \overset{r}{\to} M'$.

Let $\sigma = \langle t_1, t_2 ..., t_n \rangle \in T^*$ be a sequence of transitions. $M \overset{\sigma}{\to} M'$ denotes that there is a set of markings $M_0, M_1, ..., M_n$ such that $M_0 = M$, $M_n = M'$, and $M_i \overset{t_{i+1}}{\to} M_{i+1}$ for $0 \leq i < n$. A marking M' is *reachable* from M if there exists a σ such that $M \overset{\sigma}{\to} M'$.

We use $R(N, M)$ to denote the set of markings reachable from marking M in Petri net N, i.e. $R(N, M) = \{M' | M' \in \mathcal{B}(P) \wedge M \overset{\sigma}{\to} M' \text{ for some } \sigma \in T^*\}$.

A Petri net $N = (P, T, F)$ is called *strongly connected* if and only if $\forall_{n, n' \in P \cup T} (n, n') \in F^*$, where F^* is the reflexive transitive closure of F. Let $N' = (P', T', F')$ such that $P' \subseteq P$ and $T' \subseteq T$ and $F' = F \cap ((P' \times T') \cup (T' \times P'))$. The net N' is called an *S-net* if and only if for all $r \in T'$ it holds that

$| \overset{N'}{\bullet} r | = 1 = | r \overset{N'}{\bullet} |$, that is, every transition has a single place in its pre-set and a single place in its postset. The S-net N' is called an *S-component* of net N if and only if N' is strongly connected and for all $s \in P'$ it holds that $\overset{N}{\bullet} s \cup s \overset{N}{\bullet} \subseteq T'$. The net N is called *S-coverable* if and only if for every place $s \in P$ there exists an S-component that contains s. Similarly, we can define *T-components*.

A transition r belonging to a Petri net N with an initial marking M is called *live*, if and only if for every $M' \in R(N, M)$ there exists an $M'' \in R(N, M')$ that enables the transition r. The net N is called *live* in M if and only if all its transition are live in M. Furthermore, N is *deadlock-free* in M if and only if every reachable marking enables at least one transition.

A place s in a Petri net N with the initial marking M is called *k-bounded* (where k is a natural number), if and only if the place s never holds more than k tokens in any reachable marking, i.e. $\forall_{M' \in R(N, M)} : M'(s) \leq k$. A place p is called bounded in M if and only if it is k-bounded in M for some k. The net N is called *bounded* in M if and only if all its places are bounded in M, it is called *unbounded* in M otherwise. A Petri net net N is called well-formed, if and only if there exists a marking M, such that N is live and bounded in M [8].

2.1 Synthesis Rules

The starting net used in our app-roach is a strongly connected atomic net containing one place and one transition, as shown in Fig. 2. The synthesis rules described in [8] are valid for *all* well-formed FC nets. We

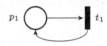

Fig. 2. Initial atomic net N_0.

first discuss the two linearly dependent synthesis rules. A linearly dependent rule allows for an introduction of a new place *or* a new transition in a net. We begin by introducing linearly dependency, which is then used to define the linear dependency rules.

Definition 3 (Linear dependency). *Let $\mathbf{M}$ be an $m \times n$ matrix and let $\mathbb{Q}$ be the set of all rational numbers. An n-dimensional vector $\mathbf{A}$ is linearly dependent on the rows of $\mathbf{M}$ iff there exists an m-dimensional vector $\lambda : \{1 \cdots m\} \to \mathbb{Q}$, s.t., $\lambda \cdot \mathbf{M} = \mathbf{A}$. Similarly, an m-dimensional vector $\mathbf{B}$ is linearly dependent on the columns of $\mathbf{M}$ iff there exists an n-dimensional vector $\mu : \{1 \cdots n\} \to \mathbb{Q}$, s.t. $\mathbf{M} \cdot \mu = \mathbf{B}$.*

Following the definition of linear dependency, we now discuss the two linearly dependent rules from [8].

Definition 4 (Linearly Dependent Place Rule ψ_P (derived from [8])).
*Let $N = (P, T, F)$ and $N' = (P', T', F')$ be two FC nets. N' is synthesized from
N, i.e. $(N, N') \in \psi_P$ if and only if:*

1. $T' = T$
2. $P' \setminus P = \{p\}$
3. $F' = F \cup \tilde{F}$, where $\tilde{F} \subseteq (((\{p\} \times T) \cup (T \times \{p\}))$
4. **p** *is linearly dependent on the rows of* **N**
5. $\overset{N'}{\bullet} p \cup p \overset{N'}{\bullet} \neq \emptyset$

Figure 3a shows the application of ψ_P rule on the net N_3 from Fig. 1. It can
easily be seen that $\mathbf{p_5} = (1, 0, 0, -1)$, where $\mathbf{p_5}(t_1) = 1$, $\mathbf{p_5}(t_2) = 0$ and so on, is
linearly dependent on the rows of $\mathbf{N_3}$ (Table 1), such that $\mathbf{p_5} = \mathbf{p_2} + \mathbf{p_3} + \mathbf{p_4}$.
Similarly, we can define the linearly dependent transition rule as follows:

**Definition 5 (Linearly Dependent Transition Rule ψ_T (derived from
[8])).** *Let $N = (P, T, F)$ and $N' = (P', T', F')$ be two FC nets. N' is synthesized
from N, i.e. $(N, N') \in \psi_T$ if and only if:*

1. $P' = P$
2. $T' \setminus T = \{t\}$
3. $F' = F \cup \tilde{F}$, where $\tilde{F} \subseteq ((P \times \{t\}) \cup (\{t\} \times P))$
4. **t** *is linearly dependent on the columns of* **N**
5. $\overset{N'}{\bullet} t \cup t \overset{N'}{\bullet} \neq \emptyset$

Figure 3b shows the application of ψ_T rule on the net N_4 from Fig. 3a. Having defined the linear dependency rules, we now define the final rule, i.e. the
abstraction rule, which allows expansion of a net by adding a new place *and* a
new transition. The abstraction rule can be formally defined as:

Definition 6 (Abstraction Rule ψ_A [8]). *Let $N = (P, T, F)$ and $N' =
(P', T', F')$ be two FC nets. N' is synthesized from N, i.e. $(N, N') \in \psi_A$ if
and only if there exists a non-empty set of transitions $R \subseteq T$ and a non-empty
set of places $S \subseteq P$ such that:*

1. $P' \setminus P = \{p\}$
2. $T' \setminus T = \{t\}$
3. $R \times S \subseteq F \cap (T \times P)$
4. $F' = (F \setminus (R \times S)) \cup ((R \times \{p\}) \cup (\{p\} \times \{t\}) \cup (\{t\} \times S))$

We can get to the net N_3 from Fig. 1, by using three applications of the ψ_A
rule on the initial net N_0 from Fig. 2. An important property of these synthesis
rules is that they preserve well-formedness for FC nets [8]. That is, if $(N, N') \in
\psi_A \cup \psi_T \cup \psi_P$, then N' is well-formed iff N is well-formed. Furthermore, it has

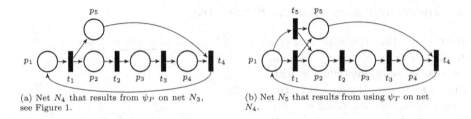

(a) Net N_4 that results from ψ_P on net N_3, see Figure 1.

(b) Net N_5 that results from using ψ_T on net N_4.

Fig. 3. Applications of linear dependency synthesis rules.

been shown that these rules are complete to synthesize any well-formed FC net, starting with the initial atomic net of Fig. 2.

3 Synthesis Space

In this section, we use the synthesis rules for FC nets from [8], in order to discuss the concept of synthesis space. The synthesis space contains all the applications of ψ_A, ψ_P and ψ_T rules on a well-formed FC net by adding a new transition and/or a new place. Formally, the synthesis space is defined as:

Definition 7 (Synthesis Space SS). *Let $N = (P, T, F)$ be a well-formed FC net, and let F_N be the universe of well-formed FC nets. The synthesis space $SS(N) = SS_A(N) \cup SS_P(N) \cup SS_T(N)$, where: $SS_A(N) = \{N' = (P', T', F') \in F_N \mid (N, N') \in \psi_A \wedge \{t\} = T' \backslash T \wedge \{p\} = P' \backslash P\}$, $SS_T(N) = \{N' = (P', T', F') \in F_N \mid (N, N') \in \psi_T \wedge \{t\} = T' \backslash T\}$, and $SS_P(N) = \{N' = (P', T', F') \in F_N \mid (N, N') \in \psi_P \wedge \{p\} = P' \backslash P\}$.*

$SS_A(N)$, $SS_P(N)$ and $SS_T(N)$ are all disjoint for a well-formed FC net N, because ψ_A results in addition of a new transition t *and* a new place p, whereas ψ_P or ψ_T results in addition of a new place p *or* a new transition t resp. In essence, the newly added place p or transition t can be renamed as any place s or r resp. Thus, using [8], we argue that the synthesis space contains all the possible applications of synthesis rules, for a given well-formed FC net N. After N' is selected from $SS(N)$, the synthesis space $SS(N')$ corresponding to N' needs to be recomputed. Calculating the synthesis space would thus require exploring all the possible ways in which ψ_A, ψ_P or ψ_T can be applied.

The two linearly dependent rules require solving a system of linear equations in order to check their applicability. Contrary to this, the ψ_A rule can be checked *locally*, i.e. by checking the existence of arcs between pre transitions R and post places S. Hence, it is trivial to calculate all the possible applications of ψ_A rule, however for ψ_P and ψ_T rules this is not the case. In order to overcome this, we introduce an incremental way of calculating the synthesis space for linear dependency rules, discussed in the following section.

4   Incremental Synthesis Structure

As recomputing the synthesis space from scratch is computationally expensive especially while calculating the linear dependency rules, we introduce an intermediary structure, called the *incremental synthesis structure (ISS)*, which is used to extract the synthesis space for non-local rules. After choosing any net from the synthesis space, the incremental synthesis structure is updated to contain information required to extract the synthesis space corresponding to the new net.

Figure 4 provides an overview of our approach. As we cater only to the applications of linear dependency rules (ψ_T or ψ_P), the incremental

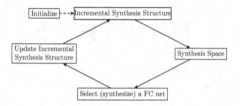

Fig. 4. The incremental synthesis structure (ISS) corresponding to the initial net is calculated in a brute force way. ISS contains all the possible linear dependencies that could be added to a net resulting in well-formed FC nets, among others. The linear dependencies that result in well-formed FC nets are extracted to populate the synthesis space. Upon selecting a net from the synthesis space, the ISS is updated corresponding to the net selected.

synthesis structure contains only column and row vectors, from which candidates can be derived for linearly dependent transitions or places. A (non-existing) candidate transition can be identified by two sets of (existing) places: the set P_I of input places for the candidate transition and the set P_O of output places for the candidate transition. Likewise, a candidate place can be identified by a set T_I of input transitions and a set T_O of output transitions. Using these nodes as input and output, a new place (transition) can be added to the net. We now define, how we can derive these sets of input and output nodes from a vector.

Definition 8 (Input/output sets from a vector). *Let $N = (P, T, F)$ be a FC Petri net, and let $\mathbf{tt} : P \to \{-1, 0, 1\}$ be a $|P|$-dimensional vector. Let $P^i(\mathbf{tt}) = \{s \in P \mid \mathbf{tt}(s) = i\}$. Then the set of input/output places for $\mathbf{tt}$, denoted as $\mathfrak{N}(\mathbf{tt})$, is defined as follows:*
$\mathfrak{N}(\mathbf{tt}) = \{(P_I, P_O) \mid P_I = P^{-1}(\mathbf{tt}) \cup X \wedge P_O = P^1(\mathbf{tt}) \cup X \wedge X \subseteq P^0(\mathbf{tt}) \wedge P_I \cup P_O \neq \emptyset\}.$

Similarly, let $\mathbf{pp} : T \to \{-1, 0, 1\}$ be a $|T|$-dimensional vector. Let $T^i(\mathbf{pp}) = \{r \in T \mid \mathbf{pp}(r) = i\}$. Then the sets of input/output transitions for $\mathbf{pp}$, denoted as $\mathfrak{N}(\mathbf{pp})$, is defined as follows:
$\mathfrak{N}(\mathbf{pp}) = \{(T_I, T_O) \mid T_I = T^1(\mathbf{pp}) \cup X \wedge T_O = T^{-1}(\mathbf{pp}) \cup X \wedge X \subseteq T^0(\mathbf{pp}) \wedge T_I \cup T_O \neq \emptyset\}.$

A single vector can result in multiple pairs of input and output nodes. For example, consider a vector $\mathbf{tt_1} = (1, -1, 0, 0, -1)$ corresponding to the net N_4 from Fig. 3a, where $\mathbf{tt_1}(p_1) = 1$, $\mathbf{tt_1}(p_2) = -1$ and so on. Then $\mathfrak{N}(\mathbf{tt_1}) = \{(\{p_2, p_3, p_5\}, \{p_1, p_3\}), (\{p_2, p_4, p_5\}, \{p_1, p_4\}), (\{p_2, p_3, p_4, p_5\}, \{p_1, p_3, p_4\}), (\{p_2, p_5\}, \{p_1\})\}$. Having linked vectors to possible input and output nodes, we now define a so-called *valid ISS vector*.

Definition 9 (Valid ISS vector). *Let* $N = (P, T, F)$ *be a well-formed FC net. A* $|P|$-*dimensional vector* $\mathbf{tt} : P \to \mathbb{Z}$ *is called a valid ISS column vector in* N *iff*

1. $\mathbf{tt} : P \to \{-1, 0, 1\}$ *and* $\mathbf{tt}$ *is linearly dependent on the columns of* $\mathbf{N}$,
2. $\exists (P_I, P_O) \in \mathfrak{N}(\mathbf{tt})$, *such that either*
   (a) $\exists_{r \in T} \bullet r = P_I$, *or*
   (b) $\exists_{R \subseteq T} R \times P_I \subseteq F \wedge R \neq \emptyset$

Similarly, a $|T|$-*dimensional vector* $\mathbf{pp} : T \to \mathbb{Z}$ *is called a valid ISS row vector in* N, *iff*

1. $\mathbf{pp} : T \to \{-1, 0, 1\}$ *and* $\mathbf{pp}$ *is linearly dependent on the rows of* $\mathbf{N}$,
2. $\exists (T_I, T_O) \in \mathfrak{N}(\mathbf{pp})$, *such that either*
   (a) $\exists_{s \in P} s \bullet = T_O$, *or*
   (b) $\exists_{S \subseteq P} T_O \times S \subseteq F \wedge S \neq \emptyset$

Again, consider the vector $\mathbf{tt_1} = (1, -1, 0, 0, -1)$ corresponding to the net N_5 from Fig. 3b, where $\mathbf{tt_1}(p_1) = 1$, $\mathbf{tt_1}(p_2) = -1$ and so on. This vector is linearly dependent on the columns of the incidence matrix $\mathbf{N_4}$ (see Table 2), as $\mathbf{tt_1} = \mathbf{t_2} + \mathbf{t_3} + \mathbf{t_4}$. Hence $\mathbf{tt_1}$ satisfies condition (1) from Definition 9.

Furthermore we have $\mathfrak{N}(\mathbf{tt_1}) = \{(\{p_2, p_3, p_5\}, \{p_1, p_3\}),$ $(\{p_2, p_4, p_5\}, \{p_1, p_4\}), (\{p_2, p_3, p_4, p_5\}, \{p_1, p_3, p_4\}), (\{p_2, p_5\},$ $\{p_1\})\}$. The first three pairs do not satisfy either of the conditions, i.e. (2)(a) or (2)(b), from Definition 9. However, the fourth pair satisfies condition (2)(b), which states that $\exists_{R \in T} R \times P_I \subseteq F$, in this particular case, $R = \{t_1\}$, and $P_I = \{p_2, p_5\}$. Hence, as $\mathbf{tt_1}$ satisfies condition (1) and (2)(b) of Definition 9, it is a valid ISS column vector. Having defined *valid ISS vectors*, we now define the incremental synthesis structure, as follows.

Table 2. Incidence matrix $\mathbf{N_4}$ of Fig. 3a.

	t_1	t_2	t_3	t_4
p_1	-1	0	0	1
p_2	1	-1	0	0
p_3	0	1	-1	0
p_4	0	0	1	-1
p_5	1	0	0	-1

Definition 10 (Incremental Synthesis Structure (ISS)). *Let* $N = (P, T, F)$ *be a well-formed FC net. The incremental synthesis structure is a tuple* $ISS(N) = (\mathbf{TT}, \mathbf{PP})$, *where:*

1. $\mathbf{TT}$ *is a non-empty set of vectors, s.t.* $\mathbf{tt} \in \mathbf{TT}$ *iff* $\mathbf{tt}$ *is a valid ISS column vector in* N.
2. $\mathbf{PP}$ *is a non-empty set of vectors, s.t.* $\mathbf{pp} \in \mathbf{PP}$ *iff* $\mathbf{pp}$ *is a valid ISS row vector in* N.

If a valid ISS vector satisfies conditions (1) and (2)(a) in Definition 9, then it can be used to apply ψ_T (or ψ_P), as shown in Lemma 1.

Lemma 1. *Let* $N = (P, T, F)$ *be a well-formed FC net, let* $\mathbf{tt}$ *be a valid ISS column vector, let* $(P_I, P_O) \in \mathfrak{N}(\mathbf{tt})$, *and let* $r \in T$ *such that* $\overset{N}{\bullet} r = P_I$. *Then, we can use* ψ_T *to add a new transition* t *in* N *to get* $N' = (P', T', F')$, *i.e.* $(N, N') \in \psi_T$, *where* $\{t\} = T' \setminus T$ *and* $\overset{N'}{\bullet} t = P_I \wedge t \overset{N'}{\bullet} = P_O$.

Proof. The fact that $\exists_{r \in T} \overset{N}{\bullet} r = P_I$ ensures that the net N remains a FC net after adding t. The fact that $\mathbf{tt}$ is a valid ISS column vector ensures that $P_I \cup P_O \neq \emptyset$, and that $\mathbf{t} \, (= \mathbf{tt})$ is linearly dependent on the columns of $\mathbf{N}$. Hence, it follows from Definition 5 that a vector following conditions (1) and (2)(a) can be used to apply ψ_T. A similar argument can be made for ψ_P.

Consider a vector $\mathbf{tt_2} = (-1, 1, 0, 0, 1)$ corresponding to the net from Fig. 3a, such that $\mathbf{tt_2}(p_1) = -1$, $\mathbf{tt_2}(p_2) = 1$, $\mathbf{tt_2}(p_3) = 0$ and so on. Clearly, $\mathbf{tt_2}$ satisfies condition (1) of Definition 9, as $\mathbf{tt_2} = \mathbf{t_1}$ (see Table 2). We can obtain a pair $(\{p_1\}, \{p_2, p_5\}) \in \mathfrak{N}(\mathbf{tt_2})$. This pair is valid according to condition (2)(a) of Definition 9, as $\bullet \, t_1 = \{p_1\}$. Hence according to Lemma 1, we can use $\mathbf{tt_2}$ to add a new linearly dependent transition with $\{p_1\}$ as the input and $\{p_2, p_4\}$ as the output. Figure 3b is indeed a demonstration of adding this transition. In contrast, the second condition of valid ISS vector is in place to deduce linear dependencies that may come into effect in future, as will become evident in sections to follow.

Lemma 2. *Synthesis space for linear dependency rules can be extracted using* **TT** *and* **PP**.

Proof. For every $\mathbf{tt} \in \mathbf{TT}$, we can extract a set of pair of places $(P_I, P_O) \in \mathfrak{N}(\mathbf{tt})$. From Lemma 1, we know that if a valid ISS vector is valid according to conditions (1) and (2)(a), then we can use ψ_T. If ISS is complete, i.e. contains all the possible valid ISS vectors, then it is clear that we can extract all the possible pairs that result in valid constructions of well-formed nets by adding transitions using Lemma 1. By definition, **TT** (and **PP**) is complete and contains all the valid ISS vectors. It should be noted that the newly added node can be named as desired. Therefore, using the definition of Definition 5 (and Definition 4) it can be said that **TT** (and **PP**) contains complete information to extract all the pairs which could be used to apply ψ_T (and ψ_P).

The synthesis space for ψ_P and ψ_T rules can be extracted using the incremental synthesis structure. It should be noted that a single valid ISS vector can result in multiple valid candidate nodes in the net, and hence can result in multiple applications of a rule.

We argue that ISS can be incrementally updated which can then be used to obtain the synthesis space. The ISS corresponding to the initial atomic net N_0 from Fig. 2 is: $\mathbf{TT_0} = \{(0)\}$, and $\mathbf{PP_0} = \{(0)\}$.

It should be noted that $\mathbf{TT_0}$ and $\mathbf{PP_0}$ contain symmetrical elements. Since there is only one place (transition), the mapping between vector and places (transitions) of $\mathbf{TT_0}$ ($\mathbf{PP_0}$)is evident. In the following sections we discuss the changes to ISS after the selection of a net (application of a rule) from the synthesis space. Furthermore, we prove that the changes made are necessary and sufficient to derive the new ISS corresponding to the new net. We know that the synthesis of a net leads to addition of a transition and/or place. Since the incidence matrix is extended after the application of a synthesis rule, we need to

extend the corresponding vectors from the ISS with one dimension corresponding to the newly added node. In order to do so, we first define extending a vector
as follows.

Definition 11 (Vector extension $\mathbf{v}^{\frown e \mapsto k}$). *Let* $\mathbf{v} : A \rightarrow \mathbb{Q}$ *be an n-
dimensional vector, such that* $e \notin A \wedge |A| = n$. *Then* $\mathbf{v}^{\frown e \mapsto k} : A \cup \{e\} \rightarrow \mathbb{Q}$
is an $n + 1$-dimensional vector such that:

$$\mathbf{v}^{\frown e \mapsto k}(a) = \begin{cases} \mathbf{v}(a), \text{ if } a \in A; \\ k, \text{ otherwise (i.e. } a = e) \end{cases}$$

We now discuss the updates to the ISS, after application of each type of synthesis rule. We argue that starting with $ISS(N_0)$, we can incrementally update
the ISS corresponding to any synthesized net. Furthermore, by maintaining the
ISS corresponding to each synthesized net, we can always deduce the synthesis
space using Lemma 2.

4.1   ISS Updates After Application of ψ_P and ψ_T

In this section, we discuss the updates in the incremental synthesis structure
after the usage of linear dependency rules.

Theorem 1 (Extracting ISS after ψ_P). *Let* $N = (P, T, F)$ *and* $N' =
(P', T', F')$ *be two well-formed FC nets, where* $(N, N') \in \psi_P$ *and* $\{p\} = P' \setminus P$.
Let λ *be such that* $\lambda \cdot \mathbf{N} = \mathbf{p}$. *As* $(N, N') \in \psi_P$, *such a* λ *exists. Let* $ISS(N)
= (\mathbf{TT}, \mathbf{PP})$ *be the incremental synthesis structure of N. Then we can extract*
$\mathbf{PP'}$ *and* $\mathbf{TT'}$:

- $\mathbf{PP'} = \mathbf{PP}$
- $\mathbf{TT'} = \bigcup_{\mathbf{tt} \in \mathbf{TT}} f_t(\mathbf{tt})$ *where,*

$$f_t(\mathbf{tt}) = \begin{cases} \{\mathbf{tt}^{\frown p \mapsto \lambda \cdot \mathbf{tt}}\}, \text{ if } \mathbf{tt}^{\frown p \mapsto \lambda \cdot \mathbf{tt}} \text{ is a valid ISS vector in } N' \\ \emptyset, \text{ otherwise} \end{cases}$$

s.t. $ISS(N') = (\mathbf{TT'}, \mathbf{PP'})$ *is the incremental synthesis structure of N'.*

Proof We show that Theorem 1 is correct and complete separately for $\mathbf{PP'}$ and
$\mathbf{TT'}$.

$\mathbf{PP'}$ Since $\mathbf{p}$ is linearly dependent on the rows of $\mathbf{N}$, the ranks of $\mathbf{N}$ and $\mathbf{N'}$
   are the same. Since the rank is unchanged, there cannot be any new linear
   combinations possible. Since, there are no new transitions added, it can be
   trivially verified that all the elements of $\mathbf{PP}$ are valid as-is in the new net N',
   i.e. $\mathbf{PP} = \mathbf{PP'}$.
$\mathbf{TT'}$ As $\mathbf{p}$ is linearly dependent on the rows of $\mathbf{N}$, the rank is not changed,
   and no new linear combinations are possible. However, since there is a newly
   added row, all the vectors from $\mathbf{TT}$ need to be extended corresponding to the
   row of the newly added place p. In Theorem 1, for a vector $\mathbf{tt}$ this value

is chosen to be $\lambda \cdot \mathbf{tt}$. We now show that this is indeed the correct value. Without loss of generality, lets assume $\mathbf{p}$ is the last row of $\mathbf{N'}$:

$$\mathbf{N'} = \begin{pmatrix} \mathbf{N} \\ \lambda \cdot \mathbf{N} \end{pmatrix} \quad as \ \mathbf{p} = \lambda \cdot \mathbf{N} \tag{1}$$

Let $\mathbf{tt} \in \mathbf{TT}$. We know that $\mathbf{tt}$ is linearly dependent on the columns of $\mathbf{N}$, i.e. for some μ it holds that $\mathbf{tt} = \mathbf{N} \cdot \mu$ We can obtain a corresponding vector which is linearly dependent on the columns of $\mathbf{N'}$ as: $\mathbf{N'} \cdot \mu$. If we extend $\mathbf{N'}$ with such a vector as the last column, then we get $(\mathbf{N'} \ \mathbf{N'} \cdot \mu)$. From Eq. 1, we have

$$\begin{pmatrix} \mathbf{N} & \mathbf{N} \cdot \mu \\ \lambda \cdot \mathbf{N} & \lambda \cdot \mathbf{N} \cdot \mu \end{pmatrix} = \begin{pmatrix} \mathbf{N} & \mathbf{tt} \\ \lambda \cdot \mathbf{N} & \lambda \cdot \mathbf{tt} \end{pmatrix}, \ as \ we \ know \ that \ \mathbf{N} \cdot \mu = \mathbf{tt}$$

Therefore, for $\mathbf{tt}$ to be linearly dependent in $\mathbf{N'}$ the value of the row corresponding to the newly added place should be $\lambda \cdot \mathbf{tt}$. This is exactly whats done in Theorem 1. This is irrespective of the λ chosen. Consider two vectors λ_1 and λ_2 such that $\lambda_1 \cdot \mathbf{N} = \mathbf{p} = \lambda_2 \cdot \mathbf{N} \wedge \lambda_1 \neq \lambda_2$. Then $\lambda_1 \cdot \mathbf{tt} = \lambda_2 \cdot \mathbf{tt} : \lambda_1 \cdot \mathbf{tt} = \lambda_1 \cdot \mathbf{N} \cdot \mu = \mathbf{p} \cdot \mu = \lambda_2 \cdot \mathbf{N} \cdot \mu = \lambda_2 \cdot \mathbf{tt}$.

Let's re-visit the running example from Fig. 1, and the usage of ψ_P as shown in Fig. 3a. The incidence matrices of the nets before and after the usage of ψ_P are shown in Fig. 5, which also contains three valid ISS column vectors and the changes to those vectors using Theorem 1. It is clear that all the three derived vectors satisfy condition (1) of Definition 9 in the derived net. $(\{p_2, p_5\}, \{p_1\}) \in \mathfrak{N}(\mathbf{tt_1})$, and hence $(\{p_2, p_5\}, \{p_1\})$ satisfies condition (2)(b) of Definition 9 in the derived net. Hence $\mathbf{tt_1}$ is a valid ISS column vector in the new net too. $(\{p_1\}, \{p_2, p_5\}) \in \mathfrak{N}(\mathbf{tt_2})$, which satisfies condition (2)(a) according to Definition 9. Hence $\mathbf{tt_2}$ is a valid ISS column vector in the new net too. However, there is no pair in $\mathfrak{N}(\mathbf{tt_3})$ which satisfies either condition (2)(a) or (2)(b) of Definition 9, hence $\mathbf{tt_3}$ is not a valid ISS vector in the new net, and hence its removed according to Theorem 1.

	t_1	t_2	t_3	t_4
p_1	-1	0	0	1
p_2	1	-1	0	0
p_3	0	1	-1	0
p_4	0	0	1	-1

	$\mathbf{tt_1}$	$\mathbf{tt_2}$	$\mathbf{tt_3}$
	1	-1	1
	-1	1	0
	0	0	-1
	0	0	0

	t_1	t_2	t_3	t_4
p_1	-1	0	0	1
p_2	1	-1	0	0
p_3	0	1	-1	0
p_4	0	0	1	-1
p_5	1	0	0	-1

	$\mathbf{tt_1}$	$\mathbf{tt_2}$	$\mathbf{tt_3}$
	1	-1	1
	-1	1	0
	0	0	-1
	0	0	0
	-1	1	-1

(a) Incidence matrix $\mathbf{N_3}$ and valid ISS column vectors corresponding to the net N_3 from Figure 1 ($\mathbf{tt_1} = \mathbf{t_2} + \mathbf{t_3} + \mathbf{t_4}$, $\mathbf{tt_2} = \mathbf{t_1}$ and $\mathbf{tt_3} = \mathbf{t_3} + \mathbf{t_4}$).

(b) Incidence matrix $\mathbf{N_4}$ and the updated vectors corresponding to the net N_4 from Figure 3a (after using ψ_P).

Fig. 5. Example showing the usage of Theorem 1.

Similarly, the incremental synthesis structure can be updated after the usage of ψ_T, as follows.

Theorem 2 (Extracting ISS after ψ_T). *Let $N = (P,T,F)$ and $N' = (P',T',F')$ be two well-formed FC nets, where $(N,N') \in \psi_T$, where $\{t\} = T' \backslash T$. Let μ be such that $\mathbf{N} \cdot \mu = \mathbf{t}$. As $(N,N') \in \psi_T$, such a μ exists. Let $ISS(W) = (\mathbf{TT}, \mathbf{PP})$ be the incremental synthesis structure corresponding to the net N. Then we can extract $\mathbf{PP'}$ and $\mathbf{TT'}$:*

- $\mathbf{TT'} = \mathbf{TT}$
- $\mathbf{PP'} = \bigcup_{\mathbf{pp} \in \mathbf{PP}} f_p(\mathbf{pp})$ *where,*

$$f_p(\mathbf{pp}) = \begin{cases} \mathbf{pp}^{\frown t \mapsto \mathbf{pp} \cdot \mu}, & \text{if } \mathbf{pp}^{\frown t \mapsto \mathbf{pp} \cdot \mu} \text{ is a valid ISS vector in } N' \\ \emptyset, & \text{otherwise} \end{cases}$$

s.t. $ISS(N') = (\mathbf{TT'}, \mathbf{PP'})$ is the incremental synthesis structure of N'.

The proof of Theorem 2 is symmetrical to the proof of Theorem 1.

4.2 ISS Updates for ψ_A

Following the updates to the incremental synthesis structure after the usage of ψ_P and ψ_T, we now discuss the approach used for extracting the incremental synthesis structure after the usage of ψ_A. Before that, we discuss a couple of lemmata, which are used to support the theorem for extracting incremental synthesis structure after the usage of ψ_A.

Lemma 3 *Let $N = (P,T,F)$ and $N' = (P',T',F')$ be two well-formed FC nets, such that $(N,N') \in \psi_A, p = P' \backslash P$ and $t = T' \backslash T$. Let a vector $\mathbf{tt'}$ be linearly dependent on the columns of $\mathbf{N'}$, such that $\mathbf{tt'}(p) = 0$. Consider a vector $\mathbf{tt}$, such that $\mathbf{tt'} = \mathbf{tt}^{\frown p \mapsto 0}$. Then $\mathbf{tt}$ is linearly dependent on the columns of $\mathbf{N}$ iff $\mathbf{tt'}$ is linearly dependent on the columns of $\mathbf{N'}$.*

Proof. Without loss of generality, if we assume that the last row of $\mathbf{N'}$ corresponds to p and the last column of $\mathbf{N'}$ corresponds to t, then from [8] (pg. 139), $\mathbf{N'}$ can be decomposed such that: $\mathbf{N'} = \tilde{\mathbf{N}} \cdot A^{-1}$ where

$$\tilde{\mathbf{N}} = \begin{pmatrix} \mathbf{N} & B \\ 0 \ldots 0 & -1 \end{pmatrix} \text{ where } \begin{pmatrix} B \\ -1 \end{pmatrix} \text{ is the last column of } \mathbf{N'}$$

and A^{-1} is a $T \times T$ matrix, s.t.: $A^{-1}[u,v] = \begin{cases} 1 & \text{if } u = v \\ -1 & \text{if } u = t \wedge v \in \overset{N'}{\bullet} p \\ 0 & \text{otherwise} \end{cases}$

$\Rightarrow$ If $\mathbf{tt'}$ is linearly dependent, we have $\mathbf{tt'} = \mathbf{N'} \cdot \mu$. Therefore, $\mathbf{tt'} = \tilde{\mathbf{N}} \cdot A^{-1} \cdot \mu = \tilde{\mathbf{N}} \cdot \gamma$, where $\gamma = A^{-1} \cdot \mu$. We can re-write this as:

$$\begin{pmatrix} \mathbf{tt''} \\ 0 \end{pmatrix} = \begin{pmatrix} \mathbf{N} & B \\ 0 \ldots 0 & -1 \end{pmatrix} \cdot \begin{pmatrix} Y \\ \gamma(p) \end{pmatrix} \text{ where } \gamma = \begin{pmatrix} Y \\ \gamma(p) \end{pmatrix} \wedge \mathbf{tt'} = \begin{pmatrix} \mathbf{tt''} \\ 0 \end{pmatrix}$$

From above, we have $\gamma(p) = 0$. Since $\gamma(p) = 0$ and $\mathbf{tt'}(p) = 0$ we have:

$$\mathbf{tt''} = \mathbf{N} \cdot Y$$

Hence, the vector $\mathbf{tt''} = \mathbf{tt}$ is linearly dependent on the columns of $\mathbf{N}$.

<= Similarly, by following the steps above in reverse, we can show that if $\mathbf{tt}$ is linearly dependent on the columns of $\mathbf{N}$, then $\mathbf{tt}^{\frown p \mapsto 0}$ is linearly dependent on the columns of $\mathbf{N'}$.

Lemma 4 *Let N be a well-formed FC net, let $\mathbf{tt}$ be a valid ISS vector in N satisfying condition (1), let $(P_I, P_O) \in \mathfrak{N}(\mathbf{tt})$, and let $R \subseteq T$ be such that $R \times P_I \subseteq F \wedge R \neq \emptyset$. Let $(N, N') \in \psi_A$, s.t. $t = T' \setminus T \wedge p = P' \setminus P \wedge t\overset{N'}{\bullet} = P_I$. Then $\mathbf{tt}^{\frown p \mapsto 0} + \mathbf{t}$ is a valid ISS vector in N', and there exists a pair $(\{p\}, P_O) \in \mathfrak{N}(\mathbf{tt}^{\frown p \mapsto 0} + \mathbf{t})$ that satisfies condition (2)(a) of Definition 9.*

Proof. By construction of ψ_A, we know the values of the column vector corresponding to t in $\mathbf{N'}$ are: $\mathbf{t}(s) = \begin{cases} -1, & \text{if } s = p \\ 1, & \text{if } s \in P_I \\ 0, & \text{otherwise} \end{cases}$

As $\mathbf{tt}$ is linearly dependent on the columns of $\mathbf{N}$, from Lemma 3, we know that a vector $\mathbf{tt}^{\frown p \mapsto 0}$ is linearly dependent on the columns of $\mathbf{N'}$, and hence a vector $\mathbf{tt'} = \mathbf{tt}^{\frown p \mapsto 0} + \mathbf{t}$ is linearly dependent on columns of $\mathbf{N'}$ too. The values of such a vector $\mathbf{tt'}$ are as follows:

$$\mathbf{tt'}(s) = \begin{cases} 0, & \text{when } s \in P_I \setminus P_O & \text{as } \mathbf{tt}^{\frown P \mapsto 0}(s) = -1 \wedge \mathbf{t}(s) = 1 \\ 1, & \text{when } s \in P_O \setminus P_I & \text{as } \mathbf{tt}^{\frown P \mapsto 0}(s) = 1 \quad \wedge \mathbf{t}(s) = 0 \\ 1, & \text{when } s \in P_I \cap P_O & \text{as } \mathbf{tt}^{\frown P \mapsto 0}(s) = 0 \quad \wedge \mathbf{t}(s) = 1 \\ -1, & \text{when } s = p & \text{as } \mathbf{tt}^{\frown P \mapsto 0}(s) = 0 \quad \wedge \mathbf{t}(s) = -1 \\ 0, & \text{otherwise} & \text{as } \mathbf{tt}^{\frown P \mapsto 0}(s) = 0 \quad \wedge \mathbf{t}(s) = 0 \end{cases}$$

As $\mathbf{tt'} : P' \to \{-1, 0, 1\}$ and $\mathbf{tt'}$ is linearly dependent on the columns of $\mathbf{N'}$, it satisfies condition (1) from Definition 9. We have a pair $(\tilde{P}_I, \tilde{P}_O) \in \mathfrak{N}(\mathbf{tt'})$, such that $\tilde{P}_I = \{p\} \wedge \tilde{P}_O = P_O$. Since $\overset{N'}{\bullet} t = \tilde{P}_I$, $\mathbf{tt'}$ is valid according to condition (2)(a) of Definition 9 for the pair $(\{p\}, P_O)$.

A similar argument can be made about a row vector which is valid according to condition (2)(b) of Definition 9.

Lemma 5 *Let $N = (P, T, F)$ be a well-formed FC net. Let $(N, N') \in \psi_A$ s.t. $\{p\} = P' \setminus P \wedge \{t\} = T' \setminus T$, and let $\overset{N'}{\bullet} p = R \wedge t \overset{N'}{\bullet} = S$. Let $\mathbf{tt'}$ be a valid ISS column vector in the net N'. Let $(P_I, P_O) \in \mathfrak{N}(\mathbf{tt'})$ which satisfies either condition (2)(a) or (2)(b) of Definition 9. Then, $p \in P_I \implies S \cap P_I = \emptyset$, and $p \in P_O \implies S \cap P_O = \emptyset$.*

Proof. The crux of this proof lies in the fact that well-formedness implies S-coverability. As a result, all synthesis rules preserve S-coverability. For both condition (2)(a) and condition (2)(b) (with Lemma 4) it can be shown that any S-component covering a place $s \in S$ also has to cover the place p. Adding a transition which would have s and p both as inputs (outputs), would necessarily break all S-components for place s, leaving s uncovered. As a result, if p is an input (output) of a transition to add, then s can not be an input (output) of this transition as well (see Fig. 6). Using T-coverability, we can prove a similar theorem on R and t.

Having discussed lemmata and theorem related to the usage of ψ_A , we now discuss the theorem for updating the prior elements and creating new elements in the incremental synthesis structure after the usage of ψ_A.

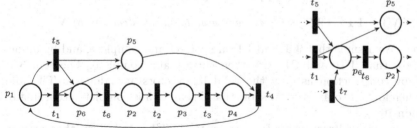

(a) Net N_6 obtained from net N_5 of Figure 3b after using ψ_A rule with $R = \{t_1, t_5\} \wedge S = \{p_2\}$.

(b) Fragment of N_6 after using ψ_T rule to add t_7 with some input P_I and output $\{p_2, p_6\}$. No S-component covers p_2.

Fig. 6. Example demonstrating Lemma 5.

Table 3. Values corresponding to an arbitrary place s.

$s = p$	$s \in \tilde{P}_I$	$s \in \tilde{P}_O$	$s \in S$	t	$\mathbf{tt'_1}$	$\mathbf{tt'_2}$	$\mathbf{tt'_3}$	$\mathbf{tt'_4}$
✓	✗	✗	✗	-1	0	-1	1	0
✗	✗	✗	✓	1	0	0	0	0
✗	✗	✓	✗	0	1	1	1	1
✗	✓	✗	✗	0	-1	-1	-1	-1
✗	✗	✓	✓	0	-	1	-	1
✗	✓	✗	✓	0	-	-	-1	-1
✗	✓	✓	✗	0	0	0	0	0
✗	✓	✓	✓	0	-	-	-	0
✗	✗	✗	✗	0	0	0	0	0

Theorem 3 *(Extracting ISS after usage of ψ_A) Let $N = (P, T, F)$ be a well-formed FC net and let $ISS(N) = (\mathbf{TT}, \mathbf{PP})$ be its incremental synthesis structure. Let $N' = (P', T', F')$, such that $(N, N') \in \psi_A$. Note that, $\{p\} = P' \setminus P \wedge \{t\} = T' \setminus T$. Let $\overset{N'}{\bullet} p = R \wedge t \overset{N'}{\bullet} = S$. Then we can extract* $\mathbf{PP'}$ *and* $\mathbf{TT'}$:

– $\mathbf{TT'} = \bigcup_{\mathbf{tt} \in \mathbf{TT}} f_a(\mathbf{tt})$ *where,*

$$f_a(\mathbf{tt}) = \begin{matrix} \{\mathbf{tt}^{\frown p \mapsto 0} & \mid \mathbf{tt}^{\frown p \mapsto 0} \text{ is a valid ISS vector in } N' & \} \cup \\ \{\mathbf{tt}^{\frown p \mapsto 0} + \mathbf{t} & \mid \mathbf{tt}^{\frown p \mapsto 0} + \mathbf{t} \text{ is a valid ISS vector in } N' & \} \cup \\ \{\mathbf{tt}^{\frown p \mapsto 0} - \mathbf{t} & \mid \mathbf{tt}^{\frown p \mapsto 0} - \mathbf{t} \text{ is a valid ISS vector in } N' & \} \end{matrix}$$

– $\mathbf{PP'} = \bigcup_{\mathbf{pp} \in \mathbf{PP}} f_a(\mathbf{pp})$ *where,*

$$f_a(\mathbf{pp}) = \begin{cases} \{\mathbf{pp}^{\wedge t \mapsto 0} & | \ \mathbf{pp}^{\wedge t \mapsto 0} \ \textit{is a valid ISS vector in } N' \ \} \ \cup \\ \{\mathbf{pp}^{\wedge t \mapsto 0} + \mathbf{p} \ | \ \mathbf{pp}^{\wedge t \mapsto 0} + \mathbf{p} \ \textit{is a valid ISS vector in } N' \ \} \ \cup \\ \{\mathbf{pp}^{\wedge t \mapsto 0} - \mathbf{p} \ | \ \mathbf{pp}^{\wedge t \mapsto 0} - \mathbf{p} \ \textit{is a valid ISS vector in } N' \ \} \end{cases}$$

s.t. $ISS(N') = (\mathbf{PP'}, \mathbf{TT'})$ *is the incremental synthesis structure of* N'.

Proof. We assume that $\mathbf{TT}$ and $\mathbf{PP}$ are correct and complete, and by induction, show that $\mathbf{TT'}$ and $\mathbf{PP'}$ are then correct and complete. Theorem 3 is correct by construction as only the valid ISS vectors are added to $\mathbf{TT'}$ and $\mathbf{PP'}$. Therefore, we only need to show that Theorem 3 is complete according to Definition 10.

We take an arbitrary valid ISS vector $\mathbf{tt'} \in \mathbf{TT'}$, and show that we can obtain it from some vector $\mathbf{tt} \in \mathbf{TT}$. Since $\mathbf{tt'}$ is a valid ISS vector in N', we know that there exists a pair $(P_I, P_O) \in \mathfrak{N}(\mathbf{tt'})$, which satisfies either condition (2)(a) or condition (2)(b) of Definition 9. We prove the completeness based on the presence (or absence) of newly added place p in P_I and P_O. We can have four cases: *(i)* $p \in P_I \wedge p \in P_O$, in this case we refer to the vector as $\mathbf{tt'_1}$, *(ii)* $p \in P_I \wedge p \notin P_O$, in this case we refer to the vector as $\mathbf{tt'_2}$, *(iii)* $p \notin P_I \wedge p \in P_O$, in this case refer to the vector as $\mathbf{tt'_3}$, and *(iv)* $p \notin P_I \wedge p \notin P_O$, in this case refer to the vector as $\mathbf{tt'_4}$.

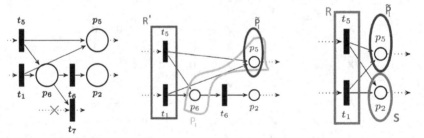

(a) Fragment of net N_6 from Figure 6a. Transition t_7 is extracted from a pair which satisfies condition (2)(a) of Definition 9. If $p_6 \in P_I$, then $P_I = \{p_6\}$.

(b) Fragment of N_6. A pair (P_I, P_O) that satisfies condition (2)(b) or Definition 9, such that $R' = \{t_1, t_5\} \wedge P_I = \{p_5, p_6\}$.

(c) Fragment from Figure 3b, corresponding to net N_5, such that $R = R' \wedge S = \{p_2\} \wedge \tilde{P}_I = \{p_5\}$.

Fig. 7. Demonstration of Theorem 3 using well-formed FC Petri net fragments.

Let $\tilde{P}_I = P_I \setminus \{p\}$ and $\tilde{P}_O = P_O \setminus \{p\}$. The value corresponding to an arbitrary place s in the vectors $\mathbf{tt'_1}, \mathbf{tt'_2}, \mathbf{tt'_3}, \mathbf{tt'_4}$ and $\mathbf{t}$ is shown in Table 3. For example, for a place s, such that $s \neq p \wedge s \in \tilde{P}_I, S \wedge s \notin \tilde{P}_O$ the value of $\mathbf{tt'_3}(s)$ is -1, according to Table 3. The values for some of the elements are left blank. These are the impossible cases which would otherwise violate Lemma 5. For example, for $\mathbf{tt'_2}$, the value corresponding to $s \neq p \wedge s \in \tilde{P}_I, S \wedge s \notin \tilde{P}_O$ is empty. This is because in the case (ii) corresponding to $\mathbf{tt'_2}$, $p \in P_I$. Hence $S \cap \tilde{P}_I = \emptyset$. We now show the proof of completeness for case (i) above, i.e. when *(i)* $p \in P_I \wedge p \in P_O$ $(\mathbf{tt}'_1)$. The proof for completeness of the other cases is similar.

(i) $p \in P_I \wedge p \in P_O$ $(\mathbf{tt}'_1)$ Consider a vector $\mathbf{tt}$, such that $\mathbf{tt}'_1 = \mathbf{tt}^{\neg p \mapsto 0}$. Using Lemma 3, we can say that $\mathbf{tt}$ satisfies the condition (1) of Definition 9 in N. For all places except p, $\mathbf{tt}$ has the same values as $\mathbf{tt}'_1$. Hence from Table 3, we know that $(S \cup \tilde{P}_I, S \cup \tilde{P}_O) \in \mathfrak{N}(\mathbf{tt})$ in N. We show that this pair satisfies the condition (2)(b) of Definition 9 in N, and thus using $\mathbf{tt}$ we can get $\mathbf{tt}'_1$. Since $\mathbf{tt}'_1$ is a valid ISS vector, we have two cases:

$\mathbf{tt}'_1$ **satisfies condition (2)(a)** Assume $r \in T'$ such that $\overset{N'}{\bullet} r = P_I$. From the construction of ψ_A, we know that $\overset{N'}{\bullet} t = \{p\}$. As $p \in P_I$ and the net is free-choice, we conclude that $P_I = \{p\}$. Hence, we have $\tilde{P}_I = \emptyset$ (see Fig. 7a). Hence the set of input places is only S. However, by construction of ψ_A, $R \times S \subseteq F$ in N. Hence $(S \cup \tilde{P}_I, S \cup \tilde{P}_O)$ satisfies condition (2)(b) of Definition 9 in the net N.

$\mathbf{tt}'_1$ **satisfies condition (2)(b)** Assume $R' \subseteq T'$ such that $R' \times P_I \subseteq F'$, i.e. $R' \times (\{p\} \cup \tilde{P}_I) \subseteq F'$. As $R' \times \{p\} \subseteq F'$, we know that $R' \subseteq R$. Hence, by construction of ψ_A, we know that in the net N, $R' \times (\tilde{P}_I \cup S) \subseteq F$ (see Fig. 7b and Fig. 7c). Hence $(S \cup \tilde{P}_I, S \cup \tilde{P}_O)$ satisfies condition (2)(b) of Definition 9 in the net N.

The proof of correctness and completeness for **PP** is symmetrical.

5   Implementation and Application

A variant of the proposed approach has also been implemented in the "InteractiveProcessMining" package of the process mining toolkit ProM [15], that serves as the basis for enabling interactive process discovery/modeling of sound business processes. The extraction from well-formed free-choice nets to business processes is outside the scope of this paper, but is straightforward and is well established in the literature [1]. For example, Fig. 8 shows the snapshot of a business process built using the implementation from ProM. The business process from Fig. 8 is indeed the net from Fig. 1 obtained by removing the arc from t_4 to p_1 and adding a new place and an arc from t_4 to the newly added place. Further, the transitions t_2 and t_3 are labeled as workflow activities *Patient enters* and *Get medicines* respectively. Such an editor can be used as a stand-alone business process editor or can be combined with the information from the event logs recorded

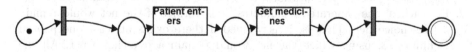

Fig. 8. Snapshot of the implementation from ProM for modeling/discovering business processes using the incremental synthesis structure as the basis.

in the information systems to enable interactive process discovery. The editor allows only those edit operations that are allowed by the synthesis rules, thus guaranteeing the soundness of modeled/discovered process models. [9,10] show the applications of such an editor to discover process models and repair event logs, in the context of process mining. Moreover, calculating the synthesis rules in an incremental way prevents long waiting times, as shown in Sect. 6.

6   Evaluation

In this section, the time taken to compute the synthesis space by using the incremental synthesis structure (ISS) approach is compared with the Brute force (BF) approach, under the same conditions and by using the same solver. In order to do so, starting with the initial net N_0, a random net was synthesized by using a random synthesis rule. Another random synthesis rule was applied on the synthesized net, to obtain a new random net. This was repeated until the application of 250 random synthesis rules. At any point, each of the three synthesis rules (ψ_A, ψ_P, ψ_T) have equal chance of being chosen. This essentially relates to choosing a random net from the synthesis space of Sect. 2.1. Figure 9 shows the experimental set-up. After applying a synthesis rule, the time taken for computing the synthesis space using the BF approach and the ISS approach were recorded. In an interactive setting, for e.g. for editing business process models, the waiting times for user should be as short as possible. Hence the synthesis space calculation was aborted if the time taken to compute the synthesis space exceeded 5000 milliseconds. This experiment was repeated 30 times in total. That is, starting with the initial net, random synthesis rules were applied 250 times, for a total of 30 times.

The average time taken to compute the synthesis space using the BF approach and the ISS approach at each synthesis iteration is plotted in Fig. 10a. It should be noted that the time scale is logarithmic in nature. In order to compare the BF approach and the ISS approach effectively, only time averages below 1000 ms are plotted. For the BF approach, the time taken to compute synthesis space rises quickly and exponentially. Just after 10 synthesis iterations, the average time taken to compute synthesis space using BF approach is more than 5000 milliseconds. The high computation times for BF approach can be attributed to the following factors:

1. As the number of nodes grows with each synthesis iteration, the number of possible permutations grows exponentially. In the BF approach, calculation of all the possible applications of ψ_T and ψ_P rules requires exploration of all the possible vector permutations, to generate the possible candidates.
2. For each of the generated candidates, it is verified if the net would remain a free-choice net. That is, it is verified if there exists at least one pair in Definition 8, using which the net would remain a free-choice net. All the candidates that violate this condition are removed.
3. For all the remaining candidates, it is verified if it is linearly dependent on the incidence matrix of the net.

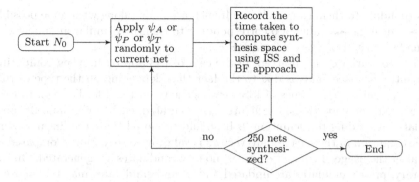

Fig. 9. The experimental setup to test the the performance of Incremental Synthesis Structure (ISS) vs Brute Force (BF) approach (repeated 30 times in total).

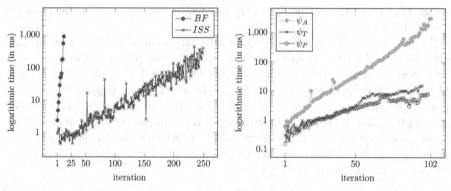

(a) Average time taken for brute force (BF) vs incremental synthesis structure (ISS) approach after 250 random synthesis iterations (repeated 30 times). BF computation was stopped after 10 synthesis iterations as it took longer than 5000 ms.

(b) Average computation times for incremental synthesis structure after usage of ψ_P, ψ_T and ψ_A rules resp.

Fig. 10. Performance evaluation of the proposed approach.

Clearly, as the number of nodes grows, the number of permutations grows too. Moreover, validating the linear dependence of multiple vectors becomes inefficient rather quickly. Compared to this, in the ISS approach proposed in this paper, the growth seems rather gradual. This can be attributed to the fact that, unlike the BF approach, we do not have to compute all the possible permutations for any given net. More importantly, the third step of verification of linear dependence is not required for our approach. This is due to the fact that, ISS only results in linearly dependent vectors after usage of ψ_A, ψ_P and ψ_T rules. Therefore, our approach mainly deals only with the non-expensive step 2, when compared to the BF approach. Extraction of all the valid ψ_T and ψ_P rules from ISS is rather trivial. Practically, for any non-zero ISS column vector in **TT** to result in ψ_T; it can be quickly verified if the places that have a value of -1

corresponding to them can result in a free-choice node (along with some possible places which have a value of 0 corresponding to them). A similar argument can be made for the row vectors from **PP**.

A lot of variation is observed, in the case of ISS approach, when computing the synthesis space. This is due to the fact that depending on the type of rule used, the computation times of ISS vary, as shown in Fig. 10b. For e.g., if a ψ_A rule is used, then additional candidates are generated, each of which needs to be validated according to Definition 9. It should be noted that, the linear dependence condition of these candidate vectors is valid by construction. Compared to ψ_A, after the usage of ψ_P and ψ_T rules, no new candidates are generated. On the contrary, prior candidates are updated and invalid candidates may be removed. Hence, the computation of synthesis space after usage of ψ_P and ψ_T rules is much faster compared to the computation of synthesis rules after the usage of ψ_A rule. It should be noted that in Fig. 10b we plot the averages corresponding to each type of synthesis rule. Contrary to this, in Fig. 10a we plot the averages across all the rules.

As evident, the time taken for computing the synthesis space grows exponentially with the BF approach. The time taken to compute the synthesis space using ISS also grows exponentially, however this growth is gradual and acceptable in practical circumstances. For e.g., while synthesizing larger nets, the ISS approach took, on an average, less than 1 second even after 250 iterations, i.e. after applying 250 synthesis rules starting with the initial net N_0. It is clear that the proposed approach is much faster and outperforms the BF approach, and hence is suited for synthesizing very large free-choice Petri nets in an interactive way (i.e. by having short waiting times).

7   Conclusion and Future Work

In order to enable interactive editing of well-formed free-choice Petri nets, we presented a robust approach to incrementally calculate all the possible applications of synthesis rules to deduce well-formed free-choice Petri nets. After fixing the incremental synthesis structure of the initial atomic net, we have shown that the incremental synthesis structure can be correctly and completely calculated after the usage of each synthesis rule. As shown in the evaluation, the proposed approach outperforms the brute force approach in terms of speed, without losing on accuracy of the results. Moreover, by using the guarantees of [8], we can conclude that we can use this incremental approach to calculate any well-formed free-choice Petri net, starting with a well-formed initial atomic net. The proposed approach also served as the basis of the winning entry for discovering process models in the process discovery challenge of at the BPM 2017 conference, which also demonstrates very well the applicability of this approach in the field of business process mining. In the future, we would like to explore the possibilities of extending such an incremental synthesis approach in the context of non-free-choice constructs.

References

1. van der Aalst, W.M.P., van Hee, K.M., ter Hofstede, A.H.M., Sidorova, N., Verbeek, H.M.W., Voorhoeve, M., Wynn, M.T.: Soundness of workflow nets: classification, decidability, and analysis. Formal Asp. Comput. **23**(3), 333–363 (2011)
2. Badouel, E., Bernardinello, L., Darondeau, P.: Process Discovery, pp. 283–300. Springer, Berlin (2015)
3. Bergenthum, Robin, Desel, Jörg, Lorenz, Robert, Mauser, Sebastian: synthesis of petri nets from scenarios with VipTool. In: van Hee, Kees M., Valk, Rüdiger (eds.) PETRI NETS 2008. LNCS, vol. 5062, pp. 388–398. Springer, Heidelberg (2008). https://doi.org/10.1007/978-3-540-68746-7_25
4. Berthelot, G.: Transformations and decompositions of nets. In: Brauer, W., Reisig, W., Rozenberg, G. (eds.) Petri Nets: Central Models and Their Properties, pp. 359–376. Springer, Berlin (1987)
5. Berthelot, G.: Lri-Iie: checking properties of nets using transformations. In: Rozenberg, G. (ed.) Advances in Petri Nets 1985, pp. 19–40. Springer, Berlin (1986)
6. Chao, D.Y., Wang, D.T.: Petri net synthesis and synchronization using knitting technique. In: Proceedings of IEEE International Conference on Systems, Man and Cybernetics. vol. 1, pp. 652–657 (1994)
7. Datta, A., Ghosh, S.: Synthesis of a class of deadlock-free Petri nets. J. ACM (JACM) **31**(3), 486–506 (1984)
8. Desel, J., Esparza, J.: Free Choice Petri Nets, vol. 40. Cambridge University Press, Cambridge (2005)
9. Dixit, P.M., Buijs, J.C.A.M., van der Aalst, W.M.P.: Prodigy : Human-in-the-loop process discovery. In: 2018 12th International Conference on Research Challenges in Information Science (RCIS), pp. 1–12 (2018)
10. Dixit, P.M., et al.: Detection and interactive repair of event ordering imperfection in process logs. In: Krogstie, J., Reijers, H.A. (eds.) Advanced Information Systems Engineering, pp. 274–290. Springer International Publishing, Cham (2018)
11. van Dongen, B.F., van der Aalst, W.M.P., Verbeek, H.M.W.: Verification of epcs: Using reduction rules and petri nets. In: Pastor, O., Falcão e Cunha, J. (eds.) Advanced Information Systems Engineering: 17th International Conference, CAiSE 2005, Porto, Portugal, June 13–17, 2005. Proceedings, pp. 372–386. Springer, Berlin (2005)
12. Esparza, J.: Synthesis rules for Petri nets, and how they lead to new results. In: International Conference on Concurrency Theory, pp. 182–198. Springer, Berlin (1990)
13. Esparza, Javier, Hoffmann, Philipp: Reduction rules for colored workflow nets. In: Stevens, Perdita, Wąsowski, Andrzej (eds.) FASE 2016. LNCS, vol. 9633, pp. 342–358. Springer, Heidelberg (2016). https://doi.org/10.1007/978-3-662-49665-7_20
14. Murata, T.: Petri nets: properties, analysis and applications. Proc. IEEE **77**(4), 541–580 (1989)
15. van Dongen, B.F., de Medeiros, A.K.A., Verbeek, H.M.W., Weijters, A.J.M.M., van der Aalst, W.M.P.: The ProM framework: a new era in process mining tool support. In: Ciardo, Gianfranco, Darondeau, Philippe (eds.) ICATPN 2005. LNCS, vol. 3536, pp. 444–454. Springer, Heidelberg (2005). https://doi.org/10.1007/11494744_25
16. Verbeek, H.M.W., van der Aalst, W.M.P.: Woflan 2.0 a petri-net-based workflow diagnosis tool. In: Nielsen, M., Simpson, D. (eds.) International Conference on Applications and Theory of Petri Nets, pp. 475–484. Springer, Berlin (2000)

Programming Dynamic Reconfigurable Systems

Rim El Ballouli$^{(\boxtimes)}$, Saddek Bensalem, Marius Bozga$^{(\boxtimes)}$,
and Joseph Sifakis

University Grenoble Alpes, CNRS, Grenoble, INP, 38000 Grenoble, France
`rim.el-ballouli@uni-grenoble-alpes.fr` ,
`marius.bozga@univ-grenoble-alpes.fr`

Abstract. DR-BIP is an extension of the BIP component framework intended for programming reconfigurable systems encompassing various aspects of dynamism. It relies on architectural motifs to structure the architecture of a system and to coordinate its reconfiguration at runtime. An architectural motif defines a set of interacting components that evolve according to reconfiguration rules. With DR-BIP, the dynamism can be captured as the interplay of dynamic changes in three independent directions (1) the organization of interactions between instances of components in a given configuration; (2) the reconfiguration mechanisms allowing creation/deletion of components and management of their interaction according to a given architectural motif; (3) the migration of components between predefined architectural motifs which characterizes dynamic execution environments. The paper lays down the formal foundation of DR-BIP, illustrates its expressiveness on few examples and discusses avenues for dynamic reconfigurable system design.

Keywords: Architectural motifs · Components
Reconfigurable systems

1 Introduction

Modern computing systems exhibit dynamic and reconfigurable behavior. They evolve in uncertain environments and have to continuously adapt to changing internal or external conditions. This is essential to efficiently use system resources e.g. reconfiguring the way resources are accessed and released in order to adapt the system behavior in case of mishaps such as faults, and to provide the adequate functionality when the external environment changes dynamically as in mobile systems. In particular, mobile systems are becoming important in many application areas including transport, telecommunications and robotics.

Institute of Engineering Univ. Grenoble Alpes.

The research leading to these results has received funding from the European Union Horizon 2020 research and innovation programme under grant agreement no. 700665 CITADEL (Critical Infrastructure Protection using Adaptive MILS).

K. Bae and P. C. Ölveczky (Eds.): FACS 2018, LNCS 11222, pp. 118–136, 2018.
https://doi.org/10.1007/978-3-030-02146-7_6

There exist two complementary approaches for the expression of dynamic coordination rules. One respects a strict separation between component behavior and its coordination. Coordination is exogenous in the form of an architecture that describes global coordination rules between the coordinated components. This approach is adopted by numerous Architecture Description Languages (ADL) (see [7] for a survey). The other approach is based on endogenous coordination by using explicitly primitives in the code describing the behavior of components. Most programming models use internalized coordination mechanisms. Components usually have interfaces that specify their capabilities to coordinate with other components. Composing components boils down to composing interfaces. This approach is in particularly adopted by formalisms based on π-calculus and process algebra, such as [1,9–11]. The obvious advantage of endogenous coordination is that programmers do not have to build explicitly a global coordination model. Consequently, the absence of such a model makes the validation of coordination mechanisms and the study of their underlying properties much harder. Exogenous coordination is advocated for enabling the study of the coordination mechanisms and their properties. It motivated numerous publications and the development of 100+ ADLs [15].

There exists a huge literature on architecture modeling reviewed in detailed surveys classifying the various approaches and outlining new trends and needs [7,8,14,15,18,19]. Despite the impressive amount of work on this topic there is no clear understanding about how different aspects of architecture dynamism can be characterized.

We consider that the degree of dynamism of a system can be captured as the interplay of dynamic change in three independent aspects. The first aspect requires the ability to describe parametric system coordination for arbitrary number of instances component types. For example, systems with m Producers and n Consumers or Rings formed from n identical components. The second aspect requires the ability to add/delete components and manage their interaction rules depending on dynamically changing conditions. This is needed for a reconfigurable ring of n components e.g. removing a component which self-detects a failure and adding the removed component after recovery. So adding/deleting components implies the dynamic application of specific interaction rules depending on their type. This is also needed for mobile components which are subject to dynamic interaction rules depending on the state of their neighborhood. The third aspect is currently the most challenging. It meets in particular, the vision of "fluid architectures" [19] which allows components/services to seamlessly roam and continue their activities on any available device or computer. Applications and objects live in an environment which is conceptually an architecture motif. They can be dynamically transported from one motif to another. Supporting dynamic migration of components allows a disciplined and easy-to-implement management of dynamically changing coordination rules. For instance, self-organizing systems may adopt different coordination motifs to adapt their behavior so as to meet a global property.

The paper proposes *Dynamic Reconfigurable* BIP (DR-BIP) component framework, an extension of BIP [2,3] which encompasses all these three aspects of dynamism. DR-BIP represents one step further in the research work which lead previously to DyBIP [6] for BIP with dynamic interactions and more recently to FunctionalBIP [12] and JavaBIP [17] for BIP with dynamic components and interactions. As such, DR-BIP follows an exogenous approach respecting the strict separation between behavior and architecture. It directly encompasses multiparty interaction [4] and is rooted in formal operational semantics allowing a rigorous implementation. DR-BIP privileges an imperative and exogenous style characterizing dynamic architecture as a set of interaction rules implemented by connectors and a set of configuration rules.

Although it does not allow adhoc dynamism, it directly encompasses all kinds of dynamism at run time [7]: programmed dynamism and in addition adaptive dynamism, and self-organizing dynamism. It provides support for component creation and removal at run time. Moreover, DR-BIP directly supports component migration from one motif to another. It supports programmed reconfiguration and triggered reconfiguration in particular [8]. The big advantage from using motifs is that when a component is created, its type defines the interaction with other components. So, a motif is a "world" where components live and from which they can migrate to join other "worlds" [19].

The paper is organized as follows. Section 2 provides a brief overview of the DR-BIP and major design principles. Section 3 briefly recalls the key concepts of BIP and its operational semantics. Section 4 introduces the motif concept and its semantics. Section 5 introduces motif-based systems. Section 6 presents an example with results using the DR-BIP implementation. Finally, Sect. 7 presents conclusions and future work directions.

2   DR-BIP Overview

The DR-BIP framework relies on the key concept of *architectural motif* as the elementary unit of description of dynamic architectures. A motif encapsulates (i) behavior, as a set of components, (ii) interaction rules between components and (iii) reconfiguration rules about creating/deleting or moving components.

Systems are constructed as a superposition of several motifs, possibly sharing their components and evolving altogether.

Figure 1 provides an overall view of the structure and evolution of a motif-based system. The initial configuration consists of six interacting components organized in

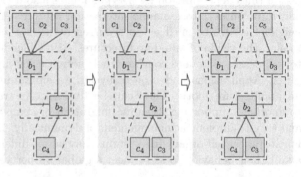

Fig. 1. An example: system reconfigurations

three motifs (indicated with dashed lines). The central motif contains components b_1 and b_2 connected in a ring. The upper motif contains components b_1, c_1, c_2, c_3, with b_1 being connected to all others. The lower motif contains connected components b_2, c_4. The second system configuration (in the middle) shows the evolution following a reconfiguration step. Component c_3 *migrated* from the upper motif to the lower motif, by disconnecting from b_1 and connecting to b_2. The central motif is not impacted by the move. The third system configuration (right) shows one more reconfiguration step. Two new components have been created b_3 and c_5. The central motif now contains one additional component b_3, interconnected along b_1 and b_2 forming a larger ring. In addition a new motif is created containing b_3 and c_5.

The example above contains actually two types of motifs: ring motif and star motif. Types of motifs may be defined separately by giving the types of hosted components and their parametric interactions and reconfiguration rules. Then, systems are described by superposing a number of such motifs on a set of components. In this manner, the overall system architecture captures specific architectural/functional properties by design.

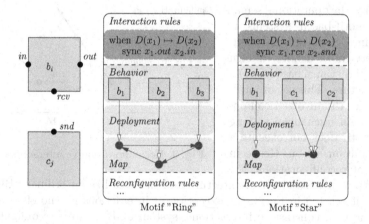

Fig. 2. An example: motifs definition

Figure 2 depicts the principle of motif definition in DR-BIP. Motifs are structurally organized as the deployment of component instances on a logical map. Maps are graph-like structures consisting of interconnected positions. Deployments relate components to positions on the map. The definition of the motif is completed by two sets of rules, defining respectively interactions and reconfiguration actions. Both sets of rules are interpreted on the current motif configuration. The first defines a set of interactions between components. The second defines reconfiguration actions to update the content of the motif, that is, the components, map and deployment.

The "Ring" motif illustrated in Fig. 2 (left) defines the first type of motif used in the previous example. Three components b_1, b_2, b_3 are deployed into a three-position circular map. Given some deployment function D, the interaction rule reads as follows: for components x_1, x_2 deployed on adjacent nodes $D(x_1) \mapsto D(x_2)$ connect their ports $x_1.out$ and $x_2.in$. The rule *defines* three interactions between the b's components namely $b_1.out\ b_3.in$, $b_3.out\ b_2.in$, $b_2.out\ b_1.in$ that correspond to the ring shown in Fig. 1 (right). The "Star" motif illustrated in Fig. 2 (right) defines the second type. Here, three components are deployed into a two-position map. The interaction rule reads as follows: for components x_1, x_2 deployed on adjacent nodes $D(x_1) \mapsto D(x_2)$ connect their ports $x_1.rcv$ and $x_2.snd$. The rule *defines* two interactions, namely $b_1.rcv\ c_1.snd$ and $b_1.rcv\ c_2.snd$, also illustrated in Fig. 1 (middle, right).

The reasons for choosing maps and deployments as a mean for structuring motifs are their simplicity. On one hand, maps and deployments are common concepts, easy to understand, manipulate and formalize. On the other hand, they adequately support the definition of arbitrarily complex sets of interactions over components by relating them to connectivity properties (neighborhood, reachability, etc). Moreover, maps and deployments are orthogonal to behavior. Therefore they can be manipulated/updated independently and provide also a very convenient way to express various forms of reconfiguration.

Finally, the operational semantics of motif-based systems is defined in a compositional manner. Every motif defines its own set of interactions based on its local structure. This set of interactions and the involved components remain unchanged as long as the motif does not execute a reconfiguration action. Hence in absence of reconfigurations, the

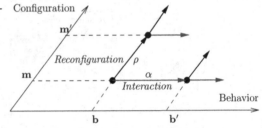

Fig. 3. Reconfiguration vs interaction steps

system keeps a fixed static architecture and behaves like an ordinary BIP system. As illustrated in Fig. 3, the execution of interactions has no effect on the architecture. In contrast to interactions, system and/or motif reconfigurations rules are used to define explicit changes to the architecture. Nonetheless, these changes have no impact on components, i.e. all running components preserve their state although components may be created/deleted.

3   Component-Based Systems

BIP [2,3] is the underlying component-based framework for programming dynamic systems (DR-BIP). In BIP, systems are constructed from atomic components, which are finite state automata, extended with data and ports. Communication between components is by multiparty interactions with data transfer. BIP systems are static in the sense that components and interactions are fixed at design time and do not change during system execution. We briefly recall the key BIP concepts and their operational semantics.

3.1 Component Types and Instances

A component type B^t is an extended labeled transition system (L, P, V, T), where L is a finite set of control locations, P is a finite set of ports, V is a finite set of data variables and $T \subseteq L \times P \times \mathcal{G}(V) \times \mathcal{F}(V) \times L$ is a finite set of labeled transitions, where $\mathcal{G}(V)$ and $\mathcal{F}(V)$ are respectively Boolean guards and update functions defined over variables V. Every transition $\tau = (\ell, p, g, f, \ell') \in T$ is equivalently denoted as $\tau = \ell \xrightarrow{p\,g\,f} \ell' \in T$. For every port $p \in P$, we associate a subset of variables $V_p \subseteq V$ exported and available for interaction through p.

For a component type $B^t = (L, P, V, T)$, its set of states is $Q = L \times \mathbf{V}$ where $\mathbf{V}$ is the set of all valuations defined on V. A valuation of a set of variables V is a function $\mathbf{v} : V \to \mathcal{D}$, where $\mathcal{D}$ is an underlying domain of data values. The semantics of a component type B^t is defined as the labeled transition system $[\![B^t]\!] = (Q, \Sigma, \to)$ where the set of labels $\Sigma = \{p(\mathbf{v}_p) \mid \mathbf{v}_p \in \mathbf{V}_p\}$ and transitions $\to \subseteq Q \times \Sigma \times Q$ are defined by the rule:

$$\frac{\tau = \ell \xrightarrow{p\,g\,f} \ell' \in T \qquad g(\mathbf{v}) \qquad \mathbf{v}_p'' \in \mathbf{V}_p \qquad \mathbf{v}' = f(\mathbf{v}[\mathbf{v}_p''/V_p])}{B^t \;:\; (\ell, \mathbf{v}) \xrightarrow{p(\mathbf{v}_p'')} (\ell', \mathbf{v}')}$$

That is, $(\ell', \mathbf{v}')$ is a successor of $(\ell, \mathbf{v})$ labeled by $p(\mathbf{v}_p'')$ iff (1) $\tau = \ell \xrightarrow{p\,g\,f} \ell'$ is a transition of T, (2) the guard g holds on the current state valuation $\mathbf{v}$, (3) $\mathbf{v}_p''$ is a valuation of exported variables V_p and (4) $\mathbf{v}' = f(\mathbf{v}[\mathbf{v}_p''/V_p])$ that is, the next-state valuation $\mathbf{v}'$ is obtained by applying f on $\mathbf{v}$ previously updated according to $\mathbf{v}_p''$. Whenever a p-labeled successor exists in a state, we say that p is *enabled* in that state.

We consider a finite set of component types, fixed a priori. A component instance b is a couple (B^t, k) for some $k \in \mathbb{N}$. We denote respectively by $ports(b)$, $states(b)$, $labels(b)$ the set of ports, states and labels associated to the instance b according to its type.

Example 1. Figure 4 (left) illustrates graphically a component type. The component has three ports (*in*, *out*, *rcv*) attached with variables (respectively u, v, w). It has two control locations (*idle*, *busy*) and three transitions labeled by the ports. For example, the transition labeled by *in* changes control location from *idle* to *busy* while performing the computation $v := u + w$.

3.2 Systems of Components

Systems of components $\Gamma(B)$ are obtained by composing a finite set of component instances $B = \{b_1, ..., b_n\}$ using a finite set of multiparty interactions Γ. A multiparty *interaction* a is a triple (P_a, G_a, F_a), where $P_a \subseteq \bigcup_{i=1}^{n} ports(b_i)$ is a set of ports, G_a is a Boolean guard, and F_a is an update function. By definition, P_a must use at most one port of every component in B, that is, $|P_i \cap P_a| \le 1$ for all

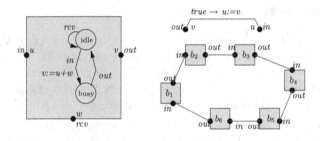

Fig. 4. Component types, interactions and systems in BIP

$i \in \{1..n\}$. Therefore, we simply denote $P_a = \{b_i.p_i\}_{i \in I}$, where $I \subseteq \{1..n\}$ contains the indices of the components involved in a and for all $i \in I, p_i \in ports(b_i)$. G_a and F_a are defined on the variables exported by ports in P_a (i.e., $\bigcup_{p \in P_a} V_p$).

The semantics of a system $S = \Gamma(B)$ is defined as the labeled transition system $[\![S]\!] = (Q, \Sigma, \rightarrow)$ where the set of states $Q = \langle b \mapsto q \mid b \in B, q \in states(b) \rangle$, the set of labels $\Sigma \subseteq \mathcal{P}(ports(B) \times \mathcal{P}(\mathbf{V}))$ contains the ports and sets of values exchanged on interactions and transitions $\rightarrow$ are defined by the rule:

$$\frac{a = (\{b_i.p_i\}_{i \in I}, G_a, F_a) \in \Gamma \quad G_a(\{\mathbf{v}_{p_i}\}_{i \in I}) \quad \{\mathbf{v}_{p_i}''\}_{i \in I} = F_a(\{\mathbf{v}_{p_i}\}_{i \in I}) \quad \forall i \in I. \left(B_i^t : (\ell_i, \mathbf{v}_i) \xrightarrow{p_i(\mathbf{v}_{p_i}'')} (\ell_i', \mathbf{v}_i')\right) \quad \forall i \notin I. (\ell_i, \mathbf{v}_i) = (\ell_i', \mathbf{v}_i')}{\Gamma(B) : \langle b_1 \mapsto (\ell_1, \mathbf{v}_1), \dots, b_n \mapsto (\ell_n, \mathbf{v}_n) \rangle \xrightarrow{\{b_i.p_i(\mathbf{v}_{p_i}'')\}_{i \in I}} \langle b_1 \mapsto (\ell_1', \mathbf{v}_1'), \dots, b_n \mapsto (\ell_n', \mathbf{v}_n') \rangle}$$

For each $i \in I$, $\mathbf{v}_{p_i}$ above denotes the valuation $\mathbf{v}_i$ restricted to variables of V_{p_i}. The rule expresses that S can execute an interaction $a \in \Gamma$ *enabled* in state $((\ell_1, \mathbf{v}_1), \dots, (\ell_n, \mathbf{v}_n))$, iff (1) for each $p_i \in P_a$, the corresponding component instance b_i can execute a transition labeled by p_i, and (2) the guard G_a of the interaction holds on the current valuation $\mathbf{v}_{p_i}$ of exported variables on ports in a. Execution of a triggers first the update function F_a which modifies exported variables V_{p_i}. The new values obtained, encoded in the valuation $\mathbf{v}_{p_i}''$, are then used by the components' transitions. The states of components that do not participate in the interaction remain unchanged.

Example 2. Figure 4 (right) illustrates a system obtained by composing six b_i instances with six *out in* interactions in a ring structure. It shows a binary interaction between two ports *out*, *in*, having guard *true* and update function $u := v$. That is, whenever the interaction is executed, the data is transferred from the *out* port to the *in* port.

4   Motifs for Dynamic Architectures

Motifs are dynamic structures composed of interacting components. Their structure is expressed as a combination of three concepts namely, behavior, map and deployment. The behavior consists of a set of components. The map is an underlying logical structure (backbone) used to organize the interaction of components. The deployment provides the association between the components and the map. The components within a motif run in parallel and synchronize using multiparty interactions. The set of multiparty interactions is defined by interaction rules evaluated on the structure of the motif. Finally, the motif structure is also evolving. Any of the three constituents can be modified i.e., components can be added/removed to/from the motif, the map and/or the deployment can change. The motif evolution is expressed using reconfiguration rules, which evaluate and update the motif structure accordingly. The following section introduces formally all the motif-related concepts.

4.1   Maps and Deployments

Maps and deployments are abstract concepts used to organize the motifs. Maps denote arbitrary dynamic collections of inter-connected nodes (positions). They are defined as particular instances of generic map types H^t characterized by (i) an underlying domain $N(H^t)$ of nodes, (ii) a set of primitives $\Omega(H^t)$ to update/access the map content and (iii) a logic $\mathcal{L}(H^t)$ to express constraints on the map content.

We use maps as dynamic data structures (objects). For a map H, its set of nodes is denoted by $dom(H)$. For any primitive $op \in \Omega(H^t)$ we will use the dotted notation $H.op(\cdots)$ to denote the update and/or access to the map H according to op. Moreover, for any $\psi \in \mathcal{L}(H^t)$ we will use $H \models \psi$ to denote that the constraint ψ is satisfied on H.

Example 3. Map types can be directed graphs (V, E) where vertices V denote the positions and edges $E \subseteq V \times V$ expressing the connectivity between these positions. Such a map type (i) has the domain V, (ii) can be manipulated explicitly using primitives such as addVertex, remVertex, addEdge, remEdge and (iii) has predicate constraints such as edge constraints $\cdot \mapsto \cdot$, path constraints $\cdot \mapsto^* \cdot$), etc, with the usual meaning.

Example 4. In the "Ring" example from Fig. 5 the map type is a specific type of graph, that is, a cyclic graph, whose (i) vertices compose the domain and (ii) primitives include initialize, extend, remove to respectively initialize, extend by one vertex and remove one vertex from it.

Deployments are partial mappings of a set B of component instances to the nodes of a map H, formally $D : B \to dom(H) \cup \{\bot\}$. As for maps, deployments are dynamic data structures defined as particular instances of a generic deployment types D^t. We consider a set of primitives $\Omega(D^t)$ to update and/or access the deployment as well as a logic $\mathcal{L}(D^t)$ to express constraints on it.

4.2   Motif Types

Definition 1. *A motif type M^t is a tuple $((\mathcal{B}, \mathcal{H}, \mathcal{D}), \mathcal{IR}, \mathcal{RR})$ where:*

- *the triple* $(\mathcal{B}, \mathcal{H}, \mathcal{D})$ *are motif meta-variables used to maintain respectively the set of component instances, the map and the deployment of component instances to the map,*
- $\mathcal{IR}$ *is a set of motif interaction rules of the form* $(\mathcal{Z}, \Psi, P_I, G_I, F_I)$ *where* $\mathcal{Z}$ *is a set of rule parameters,* Ψ *is a rule constraint, and* (P_I, G_I, F_I) *is the interaction specification, namely the set of ports of involved components, the guard and the data transfer.*
- $\mathcal{RR}$ *is a set of motif reconfiguration rules of the form* $(\mathcal{Z}, \Psi, G_R, \mathcal{Z}_L, A_R)$ *where as before* $\mathcal{Z}$ *is a set of rule parameters,* Ψ *is a rule constraint,* G_R *is a reconfiguration guard,* $\mathcal{Z}_L$ *are local rule parameters, and* A_R *is a (sequence of) reconfiguration action(s).*

The motif configuration is defined by a consistent valuation of meta-variables $\mathcal{B}$, $\mathcal{H}$, $\mathcal{D}$ respectively as B, a set of components instances, H a map, and $D :$ $B \to dom(H) \cup \{\perp\}$ a deployment. The configuration can dynamically change as the meta-variables are being updated when reconfiguration rules are executed. The meaning of the rules is explained in the next subsections.

Example 5. Figure 5 (left) provides the formal definition of the "Ring" motif type presented in Sect. 2. The motif type contains one interaction rule denoted as sync-inout and three reconfiguration rules denoted respectively do-init, do-insert and do-remove. Figure 5 (right) provides one motif configuration defined by the set of six component instances $B = \{b_i\}_{i=1,6}$, the map H defined as the cyclic graph of six nodes $\{n_i\}_{i=1,6}$, and the deployment $D = \{b_i \mapsto n_i\}_{i=1,6}$.

sync-inout(x_1: C, x_2 : C) $\equiv$ <u>when</u> D(x_1) $\mapsto$ D(x_2)
    sync x_1.out x_2.in / true $\to$ x_2.u := x_1.v
do-init() $\equiv$ <u>when</u> B = $\emptyset$
    <u>do</u> x_1 := B.create(C, busy),
        x_2 := B.create(C, idle), H.init(),
        n_1 := H.extend(), D(x_1) := n_1
        n_2 := H.extend(), D(x_2) := n_2
do-insert() $\equiv$ <u>do</u> x := B.create(C, idle),
    n := H.extend(), D(x) := n
do-remove(x : C) $\equiv$ <u>when</u> |B| $\geq$ 3 $\wedge$ x.idle
    <u>do</u> n := D(x), B.delete(x), H.remove(n)

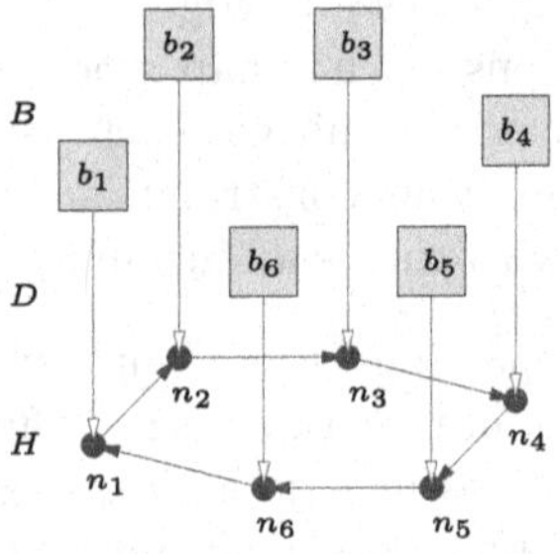

Fig. 5. The "Ring" motif type

4.3   Rule Constraints

The motif behavior is defined by interaction and reconfiguration rules. Rule parameters $\mathcal{Z}$ include typed symbols denoting (sets of) component instances or map nodes and interpreted as (subsets) elements of B or $dom(H)$ respectively.

Rule constraints Ψ are boolean combinations of map, deployment and basic constraints built using parameters in $\mathcal{Z}$ and meta-variables $\mathcal{B}, \mathcal{H}, \mathcal{D}$:

$$\Psi :: = \psi^0 \mid \psi^{\mathcal{H}} \mid \psi^{\mathcal{D}} \mid \Psi_1 \wedge \Psi_2 \mid \neg \Psi$$

In the above, Ψ^0 denotes any basic constraint using equality and/or cardinality constraints on parameters, $\Psi^{\mathcal{H}}$ denotes a constraint on the map (conforming to the map logic $\mathcal{L}(H^t)$) and $\Psi^{\mathcal{H}}$ denotes a constraint on the deployment (conforming to the deployment logic $\mathcal{L}(D^t)$).

For fixed motif content in terms of B, H, D, for given interpretation ζ of parameters, the constraint satisfaction $B, H, D, \zeta \models \Psi$ is defined recursively on the structure of Ψ as follows:

$$B, H, D, \zeta \models \psi^0 \text{ iff } \zeta \cup [B/\mathcal{B}, H/\mathcal{H}, D/\mathcal{D}] \models \psi^0$$
$$B, H, D, \zeta \models \psi^{\mathcal{H}} \text{ iff } H, \zeta \cup [B/\mathcal{B}, D/\mathcal{D}] \models \psi^{\mathcal{H}}$$
$$B, H, D, \zeta \models \psi^{\mathcal{D}} \text{ iff } D, \zeta \cup [B/\mathcal{B}, H/\mathcal{H}] \models \psi^{\mathcal{D}}$$
$$B, H, D, \zeta \models \Psi_1 \wedge \Psi_2 \text{ iff } B, H, D, \zeta \models \Psi_1 \text{ and } B, H, D, \zeta \models \Psi_2$$
$$B, H, D, \zeta \models \neg\Psi \text{ iff } B, H, D, \zeta \not\models \Psi$$

That means, equality/inequality constraints are evaluated in the usual way on the context ζ extended with the current valuation for meta-variables $\mathcal{B}, \mathcal{H}, \mathcal{D}$. Map constraints are evaluated as defined by their underlying logic $\mathcal{L}(H^t)$ on the map H and the context ζ extended with the valuation for meta-variables $\mathcal{B}, \mathcal{D}$. The evaluation of deployment constraints is similar.

4.4   Interactions Rules

Interaction rules are used to define multiparty interactions on the components instances within the motif. The syntax of the interaction specification part is as follows:

$$\text{ports: } P_I :: = x.p \mid X.p \mid P_I \; P_I$$
$$\text{guard: } G_I :: = \textbf{true} \mid e_I \mid G_I \wedge G_I \mid \neg G_I$$
$$\text{action: } F_I :: = \epsilon \mid x.v := e_I \mid X.v := e_I \mid a_I, a_I$$
$$\text{expression: } e_I :: = x.v \mid X.v \mid op(e_I, \cdots, e_I)$$

The symbols x, X are rule parameters denoting respectively component instances or sets of component instances. Moreover, p is a component port, v is a component (exported) data variable and op is an operation on data values. A rule is syntactically well-formed iff all parameter names used in expressions (part of the guard or data transfer) are also used as part of the interacting port specification. That is, only data from components participating in the interaction can be used.

For given B, H and D in a motif, the set of multiparty interactions $\Gamma(r)$ corresponding to an interaction rule $r = (\mathcal{Z}, \Psi, P_I, G_I, F_I)$ is defined as:

$$\Gamma(r) = \left\{ (P_a, G_a, F_a) \;\middle|\; \begin{array}{l} B, H, D, \zeta \models \Psi \\ P_a = P_I(\zeta), \; G_a = G_I(\zeta), \; F_a = F_I(\zeta) \\ (P_a, G_a, F_a) \; well \; formed \end{array} \right\}$$

The triple P_a, G_a, F_a is considered well formed iff it conforms to the definition of multiparty interactions, namely if P_a does not contain replicated or multiple ports of the same components, as well as if G_a and F_a use and update only variables exported on ports in P_a.

Example 6. The ring motif illustrated in Fig. 5 has a unique interaction rule denoted *sync-inout.* The rule connects the *out* port of a component x_1 to the *in* port of the component x_2 deployed next to it on the map. The resulting interactions are depicted in the right part of Fig. 4.

4.5   Reconfiguration Rules

Reconfiguration rules are used to define actions impacting the content / organization of the motif. These actions essentially include creating/deleting component instances, updating the map structure and/or the deployment of component instances to the map. They are expressed as specific updates on the corresponding $\mathcal{B}$, $\mathcal{H}$, $\mathcal{D}$ meta-variables. For enhanced expressiveness, reconfiguration rules might use additional local parameters (that is, the local context $\mathcal{Z}_L$) with arbitrary types (data, component instances, map nodes, etc). The local context is updated using standard assignments.

The syntax of reconfiguration guards and actions is as follows:

$$\text{guard: } G_R :: = G_I$$
$$\text{action: } A_R :: = \epsilon \mid x := \mathcal{B}.create(B^t, q) \mid \mathcal{B}.delete(x) \mid$$
$$\mathcal{H}.op_1(...) \mid \mathcal{D}.op_2(...) \mid z := e \mid A_R, A_R$$

The symbol x denotes a rule parameter interpreted as component instance, z is an arbitrary local rule parameter and e is an arbitrary expression built on parameters and available operators. The intuitive meaning of reconfiguration actions is as follows. The action ϵ denotes an empty action with no effect. The action $x := \mathcal{B}.create(B^t, q)$ denotes the creation of a new component instance of type B^t. The newly created instance is x and is added to the set of components instances B. The parameter q denotes the initial state for the instance. The action $\mathcal{B}.delete(x)$ denotes the deletion of the component x from the motif, that is, the removal of the component instance x from the set B. The action $\mathcal{H}.op_1(...)$ denotes an update of the map according to an operator op_1 from $\Omega(H^t)$ and specific parameters. Similarly, the action $\mathcal{D}.op_2(...)$ denotes an update of the deployment according to an operator op_2 from $\Omega(D^t)$. Finally, the action $z := e$ denotes an update of a rule parameter according to the expression e.

Formally, the semantics $[\![A_R]\!]$ of a reconfiguration action A_R is defined as a function[1] updating the motif content (B, H, D), the set of component

---

[1] Up to the choice of fresh component instance.

configurations ($\mathbf{b}$) and the parameter interpretation (ζ):

$$\llbracket \epsilon \rrbracket (B, H, D, \mathbf{b}, \zeta) = (B, H, D, \mathbf{b}, \zeta)$$
$$\llbracket x := \mathcal{B}.create(B^t, q) \rrbracket (B, H, D, \mathbf{b}, \zeta) = (B \cup \{b\}, H, D', \mathbf{b}', \zeta')$$
$$\text{where } b = (B^t, k) \text{ fresh}, D' = D[b \mapsto \bot], \mathbf{b}' = \mathbf{b}[b \mapsto q], \zeta' = \zeta[x \mapsto b]$$
$$\llbracket \mathcal{B}.delete(x) \rrbracket (B, H, D, \mathbf{b}, \zeta) = (B \setminus \{b\}, H, D_{|B \setminus \{b\}}, \mathbf{b}, \zeta) \text{ where } b = \zeta(x) \in B$$
$$\llbracket \mathcal{H}.op_1(...) \rrbracket (B, H, D, \mathbf{b}, \zeta) = (U, H', D_{|H'}, \mathbf{b}, \zeta) \text{ where } H' = H.op_1(...)$$
$$\llbracket \mathcal{D}.op_2(...) \rrbracket (B, H, D, \mathbf{b}, \zeta) = (B, H, D', \mathbf{b}, \zeta) \text{ where } D' = D.op_2(...)$$
$$\llbracket z := e \rrbracket (B, H, D, \mathbf{b}, \zeta) = (B, H, D, \mathbf{b}, \zeta[z \mapsto e(\zeta \cup (B/\mathcal{B}, H/\mathcal{H}, D/\mathcal{D}))])$$
$$\llbracket A_{R1}, A_{R2} \rrbracket (B, H, D, \mathbf{b}, \zeta) = (\llbracket A_{R2} \rrbracket \circ \llbracket A_{R1} \rrbracket)(B, H, D, \mathbf{b}, \zeta)$$

Example 7. The ring motif illustrated in Fig. 5 contains three reconfiguration rules. The rule *do-init* initializes the motif with a ring of two components. The rule *do-create* creates a new component in the ring. The rule *do-remove(x)* removes an idle component x from the ring, provided it contains more than 3 components.

4.6 Operational Semantics

A motif evolves by performing two categories of steps, namely interactions and reconfigurations. Interactions are defined from interaction rules and are executed by motif components. Reconfiguration are defined by reconfiguration rules.

Formally, the semantics of a motif type $M^t = ((\mathcal{B}, \mathcal{H}, \mathcal{D}), \mathcal{IR}, \mathcal{RR})$ is defined as the labeled transition system $\llbracket M^t \rrbracket = (Q, \Sigma, \rightarrow)$ where

- the states of set Q correspond to motif configurations B, H, D consistently extended with configurations for all component instances $\mathbf{b} = \langle b \mapsto q \mid b \in B, q \in states(b) \rangle$,
- the labels of Σ correspond to valid interactions α constructed on components and reconfiguration actions ρ,
- the transitions $\rightarrow = \underset{I}{\rightarrow} \cup \underset{R}{\rightarrow}$ correspond to execution of respectively multi-party interactions as defined by interaction rules ($\underset{I}{\rightarrow}$) and reconfiguration actions, as defined by reconfiguration rules ($\underset{R}{\rightarrow}$), formally

$$(\text{Mot-I}) \quad \frac{\Gamma = \cup_{r \in \mathcal{IR}} \Gamma(r) \qquad \Gamma(B) : \mathbf{b} \xrightarrow{\alpha} \mathbf{b}'}{M^t : (B, H, D, \mathbf{b}) \xrightarrow[I]{\alpha} (B, H, D, \mathbf{b}')}$$

$$(\text{Mot-R}) \quad \frac{(\mathcal{Z}, \Psi, G_R, \mathcal{Z}_L, A_R) \in \mathcal{RR} \qquad B, H, D, \zeta \models \Psi}{\frac{G_R(\zeta)(\mathbf{b}) = true \qquad \llbracket A_R \rrbracket (B, H, D, \mathbf{b}, \zeta) = (B', H', D', \mathbf{b}', \zeta')}{M^t : (B, H, D, \mathbf{b}) \xrightarrow[R]{\rho} (B', H', D', \mathbf{b}')}}$$

The rule (Mot-I) says that the motif executes a multiparty interaction α and change the configurations of components instances from $\mathbf{b}$ to $\mathbf{b}'$ iff (1) α belongs to the set of valid interactions Γ defined from the interaction rules and (2) a valid step labeled by α is indeed allowed between $\mathbf{b}$ and $\mathbf{b}'$ according to the component-based semantics. The rule (MOT-R) says that the motif executes a reconfiguration if (1) some reconfiguration rule is enabled at the current motif configuration, when both its constraint Ψ and guards G_R are satisfied for the given interpretation of parameter ζ and configurations of component instances $\mathbf{b}$ and (2) the current and next motif configuration are related according to the semantics of the action A_R. The dichotomy between interaction and recon-figuration steps ensures separation of concerns for execution within a motif as previously discussed in Sect. 2 and illustrated in Fig. 3.

5 Motif-Based Systems

We consider systems defined as collections of motifs sharing a set of components. In such systems, every motif can evolve independently of the others, depending on its internal structure and associated rules. In addition, several motifs can also synchronize altogether and perform a joint reconfiguration over the system.

Two ways of coordination between motifs are therefore possible: implicit coor-dination, by means of shared components and explicit coordination, by means of inter-motif reconfiguration rules.

This section introduces formally inter-motif reconfiguration and defines the operational semantics of motif-based systems. We consider a finite set of motif types. A motif instance m is a couple (M^t, k) for some $k \in \mathbb{N}$.

5.1 Inter-motif Reconfiguration Rules

The rules for inter-motif reconfiguration allow joint reconfiguration of several motif instances. In addition to the application of local reconfiguration actions, these rules allow two additional types of actions, respectively creation and dele-tion of motif instances, and exchanging component instances between motifs.

Inter-motif reconfiguration rules are defined as tuples $(\mathcal{Z}^\star, \Psi^\star, G^\star, \mathcal{Z}_L^\star, A_R^\star)$ similar to local reconfiguration rules. The set of rule parameter $\mathcal{Z}^\star$ might include additional symbols denoting motif instances (y). The constraints $\Psi^\star$ are defined by the grammar:

$$\Psi^\star ::= \Psi^{0\star} \mid \langle y : \Psi \rangle \mid \Psi_1^\star \wedge \Psi_2^\star \mid \neg \Psi^\star$$

In the above, $\Psi^{0\star}$ denotes some basic equality/inequality constraint expressed on context parameters, $\langle y : \Psi \rangle$ denotes a local constraint Ψ to be checked in the context of the motif instance y.

These constraints are evaluated on motif configurations extended with con-text parameters. Motif configurations are tuples $(M, \mathbf{m})$ where M is a set of motif instances and $\mathbf{m} = \langle m \mapsto (B, H, D) \mid m \in M \rangle$ provides the structure of these instances in terms of behavior, map and deployment. The constraints are evaluated as follows:

$$M, \mathbf{m}, \zeta \models \Psi^{0\star} \text{ iff } \zeta_\mathbf{m} \models \Psi^{0\star}$$
$$M, \mathbf{m}, \zeta \models \langle y : \Psi \rangle \text{ iff } B, H, D, \zeta_\mathbf{m} \models \Psi \text{ where } m \mapsto (B, H, D) \in \mathbf{m}, \zeta(y) = m$$
$$M, \mathbf{m}, \zeta \models \Psi_1^\star \wedge \Psi_2^\star \text{ iff } M, \mathbf{m}, \zeta \models \Psi_1^\star \text{ and } M, \mathbf{m}, \zeta \models \Psi_2^\star$$
$$M, \mathbf{m}, \zeta \models \neg \Psi^\star \text{ iff } M, \mathbf{m}, \zeta \not\models \Psi^\star$$

In the above, $\zeta_{\mathbf{m}}$ denotes an extended context, including valuations for all meta-variables $\mathcal{B}$, $\mathcal{H}$, $\mathcal{D}$ accessed using parameters y of ζ:

$$\zeta_{\mathbf{m}} = \zeta \cup \langle y.\mathcal{B} \mapsto B, y.\mathcal{H} \mapsto H, y.\mathcal{D} \mapsto D \mid \zeta(y) = m, \ m \mapsto (B, H, D) \in \mathbf{m}\rangle$$

Inter-motif reconfiguration guards and actions are defined by:

$$\text{guard: } G_R^* ::= G_I$$
$$\text{action: } A_R^* ::= \epsilon \mid y := \mathcal{M}.create(M^t, (e_B, e_H, e_D)) \mid \mathcal{M}.delete(y) \mid$$
$$y.\mathcal{B}.migrate(x) \mid \langle y : A_R\rangle \mid z := e \mid A_R^*, A_R^*$$

That is, guards are the same as for interaction rules. The action $y := \mathcal{M}.create(M^t, (e_B, e_H, e_D))$ denotes the creation of a new motif instance y of type M^t, with initial structure defined by the valuation of e_B, e_H, e_D. The action $\mathcal{M}.delete(y)$ denotes the deletion of the motif instance y, that is, its removal from the set of motif instances. The action $y.\mathcal{B}.migrate(x)$ denotes the insertion of an existing component instance x within the set of component instances of the motif y. Finally, the action $\langle y : A_R\rangle$ denotes any local reconfiguration action to be executed in the context of the motif instance y.

Formally, the semantics $[\![A_R^*]\!]$ of inter-motif reconfiguration actions is defined as a function updating motif configurations $(M, \mathbf{m})$, component configurations $(B, \mathbf{b})$ and context parameters (ζ), as follows:

$$[\![y := \mathcal{M}.create(M^t, (e_B, e_H, e_D))]\!](M, \mathbf{m}, B, \mathbf{b}, \zeta) = (M \cup \{m\}, \mathbf{m}', B, \mathbf{b}, \zeta')$$
$$\text{where } m = (M^t, k) \text{ fresh}, \ \mathbf{m}' = \mathbf{m} \cup \langle m \mapsto (e_B, e_H, e_D)(\zeta_{\mathbf{m}})\rangle, \zeta' = \zeta[y \mapsto m]$$

$$[\![\mathcal{M}.delete(y)]\!](M, \mathbf{m}, B, \mathbf{b}, \zeta) = (M \setminus \{m\}, \mathbf{m}_{|M \setminus \{m\}}, B, \mathbf{b}, \zeta)$$
$$\text{where } m = \zeta(y) \in M$$
$$[\![y.\mathcal{B}.migrate(x)]\!](M, \mathbf{m}, B, \mathbf{b}, \zeta) = (M, \mathbf{m}', B, \mathbf{b}, \zeta)$$
$$\text{where } m = \zeta(y) \in M, m \mapsto (B_1, H, D) \in \mathbf{m}, \ \zeta(x) \mapsto b \in B,$$
$$\mathbf{m}' = \mathbf{m}[m \mapsto (B_1 \cup \{b\}, H, D[b \mapsto \bot])]$$
$$[\![\langle y : A_R\rangle]\!](M, \mathbf{m}, B, \mathbf{b}, \zeta) = (M, \mathbf{m}', B', \mathbf{b}', \zeta')$$
$$\text{where } m = \zeta(y) \in M, m \mapsto (B_1, H, D) \in \mathbf{m},$$
$$[\![A_R]\!](B_1, H, D, \mathbf{b}, \zeta) = (B_1', H', D', \mathbf{b}', \zeta')$$
$$\text{where } \mathbf{m}' = \mathbf{m}[m \mapsto (B_1', H', D')], B' = B \cup B_1'$$
$$[\![z := e]\!](M, \mathbf{m}, B, \mathbf{b}, \zeta) = (M, \mathbf{m}, B, \mathbf{b}, \zeta[z \mapsto \zeta_{\mathbf{m}}(e)])$$
$$[\![A_{R1}^*, A_{R2}^*]\!](M, \mathbf{m}, B, \mathbf{b}, \zeta) = ([\![A_{R2}^*]\!] \circ [\![A_{R1}^*]\!])(M, \mathbf{m}, B, \mathbf{b}, \zeta)$$

Example 8. Consider an inter-motif reconfiguration rule for two "Ring" motifs:

do-merge(y_1, y_2 : Ring) $\equiv$
    when $y_1.\mathsf{B} \cap y_2.\mathsf{B} = \emptyset$ and $|y_1.\mathsf{B}| + |y_2.\mathsf{B}| \leq 10$
    do B = $y_1.\mathsf{B} \cup y_2.\mathsf{B}$, D = $y_1.\mathsf{D} \cup y_2.\mathsf{D}$, H = merge-cycle($y_1.\mathsf{H}$, $y_2.\mathsf{H}$),
        M.create(Ring, (B, H, D)), M.delete(y_1), M.delete(y_2)

The rule allows merging two Ring motif instances y_1, y_2 into a single one, whenever their sets of component instances are disjoint and altogether their number does not exceed 10. The new motif is created by taking the union of component instances, the union of deployments and the merging of the two underlying cyclic maps. The original motifs y_1 and y_2 are deleted.

5.2 Operational Semantics

A motif-based system $\mathcal{S}$ is defined as a tuple $((B_i^t)_i, (M_j^t)_j, \mathcal{RR}^*))$ consisting of a set of component types $(B_i^t)_i$, a set of motif types $(M_j^t)_j$ and a set of inter-motif reconfiguration rules $\mathcal{RR}^*$.

A motif-based system evolves either by executing interactions and/or reconfiguration within any of the motifs, or by executing some inter-motif reconfiguration. Formally, the semantics of motif-based systems $\mathcal{S}$ is defined as the labeled transition system $[\![\mathcal{S}]\!] = (Q, \Sigma, \rightarrow)$ where:

- the set Q of system configuration contains tuples $(M, \mathbf{m}, B, \mathbf{b})$ where $M = \{m_1, m_2, ...\}$ is a set of motif instances, $\mathbf{m} = \langle m_j \mapsto (B_j, H_j, D_j) \mid m_j \in M, B_j \subseteq B \rangle$ are the motif configurations, B is the set of components instances, and $\mathbf{b} = \langle b \mapsto q \mid b \in B, q \in states(b) \rangle$ are the component configurations,
- the set of labels Σ correspond to valid interactions α on component instances, local reconfiguration actions ρ and inter-motif reconfiguration actions ρ^*,
- the set of transitions $\rightarrow = \underset{I}{\rightarrow} \cup \underset{R}{\rightarrow} \cup \underset{R^*}{\longrightarrow}$ correspond to execution of respectively multiparty interactions as defined by interaction rules $(\underset{I}{\rightarrow})$, local reconfiguration as defined by local reconfiguration rules $(\underset{R}{\rightarrow})$ and global reconfiguration actions $(\underset{R^*}{\longrightarrow})$, formally

$$
\text{(M-I)} \quad \frac{\begin{array}{cc} m_j \mapsto (B_j, H_j, D_j) \in \mathbf{m} & M_j^t \; : \; (B_j, H_j, D_j, \mathbf{b}_j) \xrightarrow{\alpha}{}_I (B_j, H_j, D_j, \mathbf{b}_j') \\ \multicolumn{2}{c}{\mathbf{b}' = \mathbf{b}[B_j \mapsto \mathbf{b}_j']} \end{array}}{\mathcal{S} \; : \; (M, \mathbf{m}, B, \mathbf{b}) \xrightarrow{\alpha}{}_I (M, \mathbf{m}, B, \mathbf{b}')}
$$

$$
\text{(M-R1)} \quad \frac{\begin{array}{ccc} m_j \mapsto (B_j, H_j, D_j) \in \mathbf{m} & M_j^t : (B_j, H_j, D_j, \mathbf{b}_j) \xrightarrow{\rho}{}_R (B_j', H_j', D_j', \mathbf{b}_j') \\ \mathbf{m}' = \mathbf{m}[(B_j', H_j', D_j')/m_j] & B' = B \cup B_j' & \mathbf{b}' = \mathbf{b}[\mathbf{b}_j'/B_j'] \end{array}}{\mathcal{S} \; : \; (M, \mathbf{m}, B, \mathbf{b}) \xrightarrow{\rho}{}_R (M, \mathbf{m}', B', \mathbf{b}')}
$$

$$
\text{(M-R2)} \quad \frac{\begin{array}{ccc} (\mathcal{Z}^*, \Psi^*, G^*, \mathcal{Z}_L^*, A_R^*) \in \mathcal{RR}^* & M, \mathbf{m}, \zeta \models \Psi^* & G^*(\zeta)(\mathbf{b}) = true \\ \multicolumn{3}{c}{[\![A_R^*]\!](M, \mathbf{m}, B, \mathbf{b}, \zeta) = (M', \mathbf{m}', B', \mathbf{b}', \zeta')} \end{array}}{\mathcal{S} \; : \; (M, \mathbf{m}, B, \mathbf{b}) \xrightarrow{\rho^*}{}_{R^*} (M', \mathbf{m}', B', \mathbf{b}')}
$$

Rules (M-I) and (M-R1) lift the transitions (steps) allowed within the motifs at the level of the system, respectively for interactions and reconfigurations. The rule (M-R2) handles inter-motif reconfiguration. These transitions are allowed if (1) some inter-motif reconfiguration rule is enabled and (2) the current and next system configurations are related by the semantics of A_R^*.

6   Implementation and Experiments

We have developed a prototype implementation of DR-BIP including a concrete language to describe motif-based systems and an interpreter (implemented in JAVA) for the operational semantics. The language provides syntactic constructs for describing component and motif types, with some restrictions on the maps and deployments allowed[2]. The interpreter allows the computation of enabled interactions and (inter-motif)reconfiguration rules on system configurations, and their execution according to predefined policies (interactive, random, etc).

We have effectively used DR-BIP for programming reconfigurable systems in different application domains [13]. For better illustration of DR-BIP concepts, we reconsider hereafter the exercise on dynamic task management for a multicore platform proposed in [13]. A *multicore task system* consists of a fixed $n \times n$ grid of interconnected homogeneous cores, each executing a finite number of tasks. Every

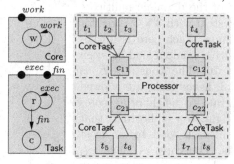

Fig. 6. Multicore task system

task is either running or completed; running tasks may execute on the associated cores and get eventually completed. The load of a core is defined as the number of its associated tasks, both running and completed. A multicore task system is *dynamic* if the overall number of tasks and their allocation to cores may change over time. More specifically, new running tasks may enter the system at the core c_{11} and completed tasks may be withdrawn from the system at the core c_{nn}. Moreover, any task is allowed to migrate from its core to any of the neighboring cores (left, right, top or bottom) in the grid, provided the load of the receiving core is smaller (K).

Figure 6 presents the overall structure of the motif-based system for four cores. We distinguish two types of atomic components, namely Task and Core. Multiple cores are interconnected together in a motif of type Processor. The interconnecting topology reflects the platform architecture (e.g., a 2×2 grid in the figure) and is enforced using a similar grid-like map and deployment. An additional CoreTask motif type is used to represent every core with its assigned tasks. The interactions in the system are defined within the CoreTask motif. The execution of a task by the core and resp. the task completion are represented by the rules:

sync-coretask-exec(x_1 : Core, x_2 : Task) $\equiv$ sync x_1.work x_2.exec
sync-coretask-fin(x : Task) $\equiv$ sync x.fin

The migration of a task from one core to another is modeled using an inter-motif reconfiguration rule which involves three distinct motifs. A task x_3 migrates from

---

[2] Maps are restricted to simple graphs e.g., chain, cyclic, star.

motif y_1 (of type CoreTask) to motif y_2 (of type CoreTask) if the core x_1 of y_1 is connected to the core x_2 of y_2 (according to the processor motif Processor) and if the number of tasks in y_1 exceeds the number of tasks in y_2 by constant K:

do-migrate$(y_1, y_2$: CoreTask, y_3 : Processor, x_1, x_2 : Core, x_3 : Task$) \equiv$
    <u>when</u> $\langle\ y_1 : x_1 \in \mathsf{B}\ \rangle \wedge \langle\ y_2 : x_2 \in \mathsf{B}\ \rangle \wedge \langle\ y_3 : \mathsf{D}(x_1) \mapsto \mathsf{D}(x_2)\ \rangle \wedge$
        $|y_1.\mathsf{B}| > |y_2.\mathsf{B}| + \mathsf{K} \wedge x_3 \in y_1.\mathsf{B}$
    <u>do</u> y_2.migrate(x_3), y_1.delete(x_3)

Figure 7 illustrates the execution of the dynamic multicore task system with 3×3 cores for 3000 steps. Each core is initialized with a random load between 1 and 20. The constant K is set to 3, hence tasks are allowed to migrate to neighboring cores (left, right, top or bottom) that differ in task load by at least 3 tasks. The cores c_{11}, and c_{33} are used to respectively create new tasks and withdraw completed tasks. These two cores retain the maximum and minimum load. As tasks migrate, the task load of cores converges and balances along the execution having at most a difference of 3 tasks between neighboring cores. For example, in core c_{21} the task load increased from 6 to 14. As expected the cores (c_{21}, and c_{12}) closest to c_{11} maintain a high load and as we move away from c_{11} the core's load gradually decreases.

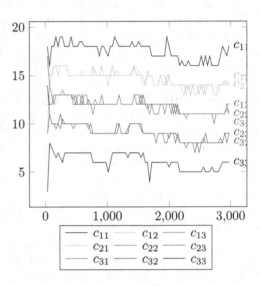

Fig. 7. Task load across 3000 steps

7   Discussion

The DR-BIP framework for programming dynamic reconfigurable systems has been designed to encompass three complementary structuring aspects of component-based coordination. Architecture motifs are environments where live instances of components of predefined types subject to specific parametric interaction and reconfiguration rules. Reconfiguration within a motif supports in addition to creation/deletion of components, the dynamic change of maps and the mobility of components. Maps are a common reference structure that proves to be very useful for both the parametrization of interactions and the mobility of components. It is important to note that a map can have either a purely logical interpretation, or a geographical one or a combination of both. For instance, a purely logical map is needed to describe the functional organization of the coordination in a ring or a pipeline. To describe mobility rules of cars on a highway a map is needed representing at some abstraction level their external environment e.g. the structure of the highway with fixed and mobile obstacles. Finally a map with both logical and geographic connectivity relations may be used for cars on a highway to express their coordination rules. These depend not only on the physical environment but also on the communication features available.

Structuring a system as a set of loosely coordinated motifs confers the advantage that when components are created or migrate, we do not need to specify associated coordination rules; depending on their type, components are subject to predefined coordination rules of motifs. Clearly these results are too recent and there are many open avenues to be explored. One is how we make sure that the modeled systems meet given properties. The proposed structuring principle allows a separation of concerns between interaction and reconfiguration aspects. To verify correctness of the parametric interacting system of a motif we extend the approach adopted for static BIP: assuming that dynamic connectors correctly enforce the sought coordination, it remains to show that restricting the behavior of deadlock-free components does not introduce deadlocks. We have recently shown this approach can be extended for parametric systems [5].

To verify the correctness of reconfiguration operations a different approach is taken. If we have already proven correctness of the parametric interacting system of a motif, it is enough to prove that its architecture style is preserved by statements changing the number of components, move components and modify maps and their connectivity. In other words the architecture style is an invariant of the coordination structure. This can be proven by structural induction. The architecture style of a motif can be characterized by a formula of configuration logic ϕ [16]. We have to prove that if a model m of the system satisfies ϕ then after the application of a reconfiguration operation the resulting model m' satisfies ϕ.

References

1. Allen, R., Douence, R., Garlan, D.: Specifying and analyzing dynamic software architectures. In: Astesiano, E. (ed.) FASE 1998. LNCS, vol. 1382, pp. 21–37. Springer, Heidelberg (1998). https://doi.org/10.1007/BFb0053581
2. Basu, A., et al.: Rigorous component-based system design using the BIP framework. IEEE Softw. **28**(3), 41–48 (2011)
3. Basu, A., Bozga, M., Sifakis, J.: Modeling heterogeneous real-time systems in BIP. In: SEFM'06 Proceedings, pp. 3–12. IEEE Computer Society Press (2006)
4. Bliudze, S., Sifakis, J.: The algebra of connectors structuring interaction in BIP. IEEE Trans. Comput. **57**(10), 1315–1330 (2008)
5. Bozga, M., Iosif, R., Sifakis, J.: Checking deadlock-freedom of parametric component-based systems. arXiv preprint arXiv:1805.10073 (2018)
6. Bozga, M., Jaber, M., Maris, N., Sifakis, J.: Modeling dynamic architectures using Dy-BIP. In: Gschwind, T., De Paoli, F., Gruhn, V., Book, M. (eds.) SC 2012. LNCS, vol. 7306, pp. 1–16. Springer, Heidelberg (2012). https://doi.org/10.1007/978-3-642-30564-1_1
7. Bradbury, J.: Organizing definitions and formalisms for dynamic software architectures. Technical Report 2004–477, Software Technology Laboratory, School of Computing, Queen's University (2004)

8. Butting, A., Heim, R., Kautz, O., Ringert, J.O., Rumpe, B., Wortmann, A.: A classification of dynamic reconfiguration in component and connector architecture description languages. In: 4th International Workshop on Interplay of Model-Driven and Component-Based Software Engineering (ModComp'17) (2017)

9. Canal, C., Pimentel, E., Troya, J.M.: Specification and refinement of dynamic software architectures. In: Donohoe, P. (ed.) Software Architecture. ITIFIP, vol. 12, pp. 107–125. Springer, Boston, MA (1999). https://doi.org/10.1007/978-0-387-35563-4_7

10. Cuesta, C., de la Fuente, P., Barrio-Solárzano, M.: Dynamic coordination architecture through the use of reflection. In: Proceedings of the 2001 ACM Symposium on Applied Computing, pp. 134–140. ACM (2001)

11. De Nicola, R., Loreti, M., Pugliese, R., Tiezzi, F.: A formal approach to autonomic systems programming: the SCEL language. TAAS $9(2)$, 7:1–7:29 (2014)

12. Edelmann, R., Bliudze, S., Sifakis, J.: Functional BIP: embedding connectors in functional programming languages. J. Log.Al Algebr. Methods Program. 92, 19–44 (2017)

13. El Ballouli, R., Bensalem, S., Bozga, M., Sifakis, J.: Four exercises in programming dynamic reconfigurable systems: methodology and solution in DR-BIP. In: Leveraging Applications of Formal Methods, Verification and Validation: Foundational Techniques - 8th International Symposium, ISoLA 2018 (2018), to appear

14. Garlan, D.: Software architecture: a travelogue. In: Future of Software Engineering (FOSE'14), pp. 29–39. ACM (2014)

15. Malavolta, I., Lago, P., Muccini, H., Pelliccione, P., Tang, A.: What industry needs from architectural languages: a survey. IEEE Trans. Softw. Eng. $39(6)$, 756–779 (2006)

16. Mavridou, A., Baranov, E., Bliudze, S., Sifakis, J.: Configuration logics: modeling architecture styles. J. Log. Algebr. Methods Program $86(1)$, 2–29 (2017)

17. Mavridou, A., Rutz, V., Bliudze, S.: Coordination of dynamic software components with JavaBIP. In: International Conference on Formal Aspects of Component Software, pp. 39–57. Springer (2017)

18. Oreizy, P.: Issues in modeling and analyzing dynamic software architectures. In: International Workshop on the Role of Software Architecture in Testing and Analysis, pp. 54–57 (1998)

19. Taivalsaari, A., Mikkonen, T., Syst, K.: Liquid software manifesto: The era of multiple device ownership and its implications for software architecture. In: IEEE 38th Annual Computer Software and Applications Conference (COMPSAC'14) (2014)

Automating Verification of State Machines with Reactive Designs and Isabelle/UTP

Simon Foster$^{(\boxtimes)}$ ⓘ, James Baxter, Ana Cavalcanti, Alvaro Miyazawa,
and Jim Woodcock

University of York, York, UK
simon.foster@york.ac.uk

Abstract. State-machine based notations are ubiquitous in the description of component systems, particularly in the robotic domain. To ensure these systems are safe and predictable, formal verification techniques are important, and can be cost-effective if they are both automated and scalable. In this paper, we present a verification approach for a diagrammatic state machine language that utilises theorem proving and a denotational semantics based on Unifying Theories of Programming (UTP). We provide the necessary theory to underpin state machines (including induction theorems for iterative processes), mechanise an action language for states and transitions, and use these to formalise the semantics. We then describe the verification approach, which supports infinite state systems, and exemplify it with a fully automated deadlock-freedom check. The work has been mechanised in our proof tool, Isabelle/UTP, and so also illustrates the use of UTP to build practical verification tools.

1 Introduction

The recent drive for adoption of autonomous robots into situations where they interact closely with humans means that such systems have become safety critical. To ensure that they are both predictable and safe within their applied context, it is important to adequately prototype them in a variety of scenarios. Whilst physical prototyping is valuable, there is a limit to the breadth of scenarios that can be considered. Thus, techniques that allow virtual prototyping, based on mathematically principled models, can greatly enhance the engineering process. In particular, formal verification techniques like model checking and theorem proving can enable exhaustive coverage of the state space.

Diagrammatic notations are widely applied in component modelling, and particularly the modelling of robotic controllers via state machines. Standards like UML[1] and SysML[2] provide languages for description of component interfaces, the system architecture, and the behaviour of individual components. These

---

[1] Unified Modelling Language. http://www.uml.org/.

[2] Systems Modelling Language. http://www.omgsysml.org/.

ⓒ Springer Nature Switzerland AG 2018
K. Bae and P. C. Ölveczky (Eds.): FACS 2018, LNCS 11222, pp. 137–155, 2018.
https://doi.org/10.1007/978-3-030-02146-7_7

notations have proved popular due to a combination of accessibility and precise modelling techniques. In order to leverage formal verification in this context, there is a need for formal semantics and automated tools. Since UML is highly extensible, a specific challenge is to provide scalable semantic models that support extensions like real-time, hybrid computation, and probability.

RoboChart [1,2] is a diagrammatic language for the description of robotic controllers with a formal semantics based on Hoare and He's *Unifying Theories of Programming* [3] (UTP). The core of RoboChart is a formalised state machine notation that can be considered a subset of UML/SysML state machine diagrams enriched with time and probability constructs. Each state machine has a well defined interface describing the events that are externally visible. The behaviour of states and transitions is described using a formal action language that corresponds to a subset of the **Circus** modelling language [4]. The notation supports real-time constraints, through delays, timeouts and deadlines, and also probabilistic choices, to express uncertainty. The use of UTP, crucially, enables us to provide various semantic models for state machines that account for different computational paradigms, and yet are linked through a common foundation.

In previous work [1], model checking facilities for RoboChart have been developed and applied in verification. This provides a valuable automated technique for model development, which allows detection of problems during the early development stages. However, explicit state model checking is limited to checking finite state models. In practice this means that data types must be abstracted with a small number of elements. In order to exhaustively check the potentially very large or infinite state space of many robotic applications, symbolic techniques, like theorem proving, are required. For theorem proving to be practically applicable, like model checking, automation is highly desirable.

In this paper we present an automated verification technique for a subset of RoboChart state machines in Isabelle/HOL [5]. With it, state machines can be verified against properties formalised in a refinement statement, such as deadlock freedom. We mechanise the state machine meta-model, including its data types, well-formedness constraints, and validation support. We use a UTP theory of reactive designs [6,7] to provide a dynamic semantics, based guarded iteration [8]. We also engineer automated proof support in our UTP implementation, Isabelle/UTP [9]. The semantics can, therefore, be used to perform verification of infinite-state systems by theorem proving, with the help of a verified induction theorem, and Isabelle/HOL's automated proof facilities [10]. Our denotational approach, like UML, is extensible, and further mechanised UTP theories can account for real-time [11], probability [12], and other paradigms [13]. Our work also serves as a template for building verification tools with Isabelle/UTP.

In Sect. 2 we outline background material for our work. In Sect. 3 we begin our contributions by extending reactive designs with guarded iteration and an induction theorem for proving invariants. In Sect. 4 we mechanise reactive programs in Isabelle/UTP, based on the reactive-design theory, and provide symbolic evaluation theorems. In Sect. 5 we mechanise a static semantics of state machines. In Sect. 6 we provide the dynamic semantics, utilising the result from Sect. 3, and prove a specialised induction law. In Sect. 7 we outline our verification technique, show how to automatically prove deadlock freedom for an example state machine. Finally, in Sect. 8 we conclude and highlight related work.

2 Preliminaries

2.1 RoboChart

RoboChart [1] describes robotic systems in terms of a number of controllers that communicate using shared channels. Each controller has a well defined interface, and its behaviour is described by one or more state machines. A machine has local state variables and constants, and consists of nodes and transitions, with behaviour specified using a formal action language [4]. Advanced features such as hierarchy, shared variables, real-time constraints, and probability are supported.

A machine, **GasAnalysis**, is shown in Fig. 1; we use it as a running example. It models a component of a chemical detector robot [14] that searches for dangerous chemicals using its spectrometer device, and drops flags at such locations. **GasAnalysis** is the component that decides how to respond to a sensor reading. If gas is detected, then an analysis is performed to see whether the gas is above or below a given threshold. If it is below, then the robot attempts to triangulate a position for the source location and turns toward it, and if it is above, it stops.

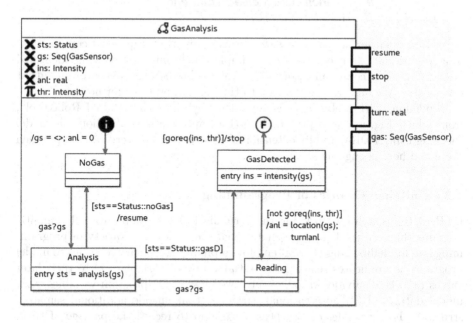

Fig. 1. GasAnalysis state machine in RoboChart

The interface consists of four events. The event *gas* is used to receive sensor readings, and *turn* is used to communicate a change of direction. The remaining events, *resume* and *stop* carry no data, and are used to communicate that the robot should resume its searching activities, or stop. The state machine uses four state variables: *sts* to store the gas analysis status, *gs* to store the present reading, *ins* to store the reading intensity, and *anl* to store the angle the robot is pointing. It also has a constant *thr* for the gas intensity threshold. RoboChart provides basic types for variables and constants, including integers, real numbers, sets, and sequences (*Seq(t)*). The user can also define additional types, that can be records, enumerations, or entirely abstract. For example, the type *Status* is an enumerated type with constructors *gasD* and *noGas*.

The behaviour is described by 6 nodes, including an initial node (i); a final node (F); and four states: *NoGas*, *Analysis*, *GasDetected*, and *Reading*. The transitions are decorated with expressions of the form *trigger*[*condition*]/*statement*. When the event *trigger* happens and the guard *condition* is true, then *statement* is executed, before transitioning to the next state. All three parts can optionally be omitted. RoboChart also permits states to have entry, during, and exit actions. In our example, both *Analysis* and *GasDetected* have entry actions.

The syntax of actions is given below, which assumes a context where event and state variable identifiers have been specified using the nonterminal *ID*.

Definition 2.1 (Action Language Syntax).

$$Action \ := \ Event \mid \textbf{skip} \mid ID := Expr \mid Action \ ; \ Action \mid$$
$$\textbf{if } Expr \textbf{ then } Action \textbf{ else } Action \textbf{ end}$$
$$Event \ := \ ID \mid ID\,\textbf{?}\,ID \mid ID\,\textbf{!}\,Expr$$

An action is either an event, a **skip**, an assignment, a sequential composition, or a conditional. An event is either a simple synchronisation on some identified event e, an input communication ($e?x$) that populates a variable x, or an output event ($e!v$). We omit actions related to time and operations for now.

Modelling with RoboChart is supported by the Eclipse-based RoboTool[3], from which Fig. 1 was captured. RoboTool automates verification via model checking using FDR4, and its extension to incorporate the verification approach presented here is ongoing work.

2.2 Unifying Theories of Programming

UTP [3,15] is a framework for the formalisation of computational semantic domains that are used to give denotational semantics to a variety of programming and modelling languages. It employs alphabetised binary relations to model programs as predicates relating the initial values of variables (x) to their later values (x'). UTP divides variables into two classes: (1) program variables, that model data, and (2) observational variables, that encode additional semantic structure. For example, *clock* : $\mathbb{N}$ is a variable to record the passage of time. Unlike a program variable, it makes no sense to assign values to *clock*, as this would model arbitrary time travel. Therefore, observational variables are constrained using healthiness conditions, which are encoded as idempotent functions

---

[3] https://www.cs.york.ac.uk/circus/RoboCalc/robotool/.

on predicates. For example, application of $\boldsymbol{HT}(P) \triangleq (P \wedge clock \leq clock')$ results in a healthy predicate that specifies there is no reverse time travel.

The observational variables and healthiness conditions give rise to a subset of the alphabetised relations called a *UTP theory*, which can be used to justify the fundamental theorems of a computational paradigm. A UTP theory is the set of fixed points of the healthiness condition: $[\![\boldsymbol{H}]\!] \triangleq \{P \mid \boldsymbol{H}(P) = P\}$. A set of signature operators can then be defined, under which the theory's healthiness conditions are closed, and are thus guaranteed to construct programs that satisfy these theorems. UTP theories allow us to model a variety of paradigms beyond simple imperative programs, such as concurrency [3,4], real-time [11], object orientation [16], hybrid [13,17], and probabilistic systems [12].

The use of relational calculus means that the UTP lends itself to automated program verification using refinement $S \sqsubseteq P$: program P satisfies specification S. Since both S and P are specified in formal logic, and refinement equates to reverse implication, we can utilise interactive and automated theorem proving technology for verification. This allows application of tools like Isabelle/HOL to program verification, which is the goal of our tool, Isabelle/UTP [9].

2.3 Isabelle/HOL and Isabelle/UTP

Isabelle/HOL [5] consists of the Pure meta-logic, and the HOL object logic. Pure provides a term language, polymorphic type system, syntax translation framework for extensible parsing and pretty printing, and an inference engine. The jEdit-based IDE allows LATEX-like term rendering using Unicode. An Isabelle theory consists of type declarations, definitions, and theorems, which are usually proved by composition of existing theorems. Theorems have the form of $[\![P_1; \cdots ; P_n]\!] \Longrightarrow Q$, where P_i is an assumption, and Q is the conclusion. The simplifier tactic, **simp**, rewrites terms using theorems of the form $f(x_1 \cdots x_n) \equiv y$.

HOL implements an ML-like functional programming language founded on an axiomatic set theory similar to ZFC. HOL is purely definitional: mathematical libraries are constructed purely by application of the foundational axioms, which provides a highly principled framework. HOL provides inductive datatypes, recursive functions, and records. Several basic types are provided, including sets, functions, numbers, and lists. Parametric types are written by precomposing the type name, τ, with the type variables $[a_1, \cdots, a_n]\tau$, for example $[nat]list$[4].

Isabelle/UTP [9,18] is a semantic embedding of UTP into HOL, including a formalisation of the relational calculus, fundamental laws, proof tactics, and facilities for UTP theory engineering. The relational calculus is constructed such that properties can be recast as HOL predicates, and then automated tactics, such as **auto**, and **sledgehammer** [10], can be applied. This strategy is employed by our workhorse tactic, **rel-auto**, which automates proof of relational conjectures.

Proof automation is facilitated by encoding variables as lenses [9]. A lens $x::\tau \Longrightarrow \alpha$ characterises a τ-shaped region of the type α using two functions:

---

[4] The square brackets are not used in Isabelle; we add them for readability.

$get_x::\alpha \rightarrow \tau$ and $put_x::\alpha \rightarrow \tau \rightarrow \alpha$, that query and update the region, respectively. Intuitively, x is a variable of type τ within the alphabet type α. Alphabet types can be encoded using the **alphabet** $r = f_1::\tau_1 \cdots f_n::\tau_n$ command, that constructs a new record type r with n fields, and a lens for each field. Lenses can be independent, meaning they cover disjoint regions, written $x \bowtie y$, or contained within another, written $x \preceq y$. These allow us to express meta-logical style properties without actually needing a meta-logic [9].

The core UTP types include predicates $[\alpha]upred$, and (homogeneous) relations $[\alpha]hrel$. Operators are denoted using lenses and lifted HOL functions. An important operator is substitution, $\sigma \dagger P$, which applies a state update function $\sigma::\alpha \rightarrow \alpha$ to an expression, and replaces variables in a similar way to syntactic substitution. Substitutions can be built using lens updates $\sigma(x \mapsto v)$, for $x::\tau \Longrightarrow \alpha$ and $v::[\tau, \alpha]uexpr$, and we use the notation $(\!|x_1 \mapsto v_1, \cdots, x_n \mapsto v_n|\!)$ for a substitution in n variables. Substitution theorems can be applied with the simplifier to perform symbolic evaluation of an expression.

All the theorems and results that we present in this paper have been mechanically validated in Isabelle/UTP, and the proofs can be found in our repository[5].

2.4 Stateful-Failure Reactive Designs

RoboChart is a reactive language, where controllers exchange events with one another and the robotic platform or the environment. Reactive programs can make decisions both internally, based on the evaluation of their own state, and externally, by offering several events. Consequently, they pause at particular quiescent points during execution, when awaiting a communication. Unlike sequential programs, they need not terminate but may run indefinitely.

The UTP theory of stateful-failure reactive designs [7,19] exists to give denotational semantics to reactive programming languages, such as CSP [3], *Circus* [4], and rCOS [20]. It is a relational version of the stable failures-divergences semantic model, as originally defined in the UTP book [3,15] using event traces and refusal sets, but extended with state variables. Its healthiness condition, **NCSP**, which we previously mechanised [7], characterises relations that extend the trace, update variables, and refuse certain events in quiescent phases. The signature includes unbounded nondeterministic choice ($\bigsqcap_{i \in I} P(i)$), conditional ($P \lhd b \rhd Q$), and sequential composition ($P \, \fatsemi \, Q$). $[\![\textbf{NCSP}]\!]$ forms a complete lattice under $\sqsubseteq$, with top element **miracle** and bottom **chaos**, and also a Kleene algebra [7], which allows reasoning about iterative reactive programs.

The signature also contains several specialised operators. Event action, $do(e)$, describes the execution of an event expression e, that ranges over state variables. When activated, it waits for e to occur, and then it terminates. Generalised assignment ($\langle \sigma \rangle_a$) uses a substitution σ to update the state, following Back [21]. Basic assignment can be defined as $(x := v) \triangleq \langle (\!|x \mapsto v|\!) \rangle_a$, and a unit as **skip** $\triangleq \langle id \rangle_a$. External choice, $\square \, i \in A \bullet P(i)$ indexed by set A, as in CSP, permits one of the branches to resolve either by an event, or by termination. A

---

[5] https://github.com/isabelle-utp/utp-main/tree/master/robochart/untimed.

binary choice $P \square Q$ is denoted by $\square X \in \{P, Q\} \bullet X$. A guard, $b \,\&\, P$, executes P when b is true, and is otherwise equivalent to **stop**, the deadlocked action. These operators obey several algebraic laws [7]; a small selection is below.

Theorem 2.2. *If P is **NCSP**-healthy, then the following identities hold:*

$$\textbf{\textit{miracle}} \mathbin{\raisebox{0.3ex}{\tiny\,;}} P = \textbf{\textit{miracle}} \tag{1}$$

$$\langle \sigma \rangle_a \mathbin{\raisebox{0.3ex}{\tiny\,;}} P = \sigma \dagger P \tag{2}$$

$$(\textbf{\textit{do}}(a) \square \textbf{\textit{do}}(b)) \mathbin{\raisebox{0.3ex}{\tiny\,;}} P = \textbf{\textit{do}}(a) \mathbin{\raisebox{0.3ex}{\tiny\,;}} P \square \textbf{\textit{do}}(b) \mathbin{\raisebox{0.3ex}{\tiny\,;}} P \tag{3}$$

(1) states that miracle is a left annihilator for sequential composition. (2) allows us to push an assignment into a successor program by inserting a substitution. (3) allows us to left distribute through an external choice of events.

Our theory supports specifications using reactive contracts: $[P \vdash Q \mid R]$. It consists of three relations over the state variables, trace variable (**tt**), and refusal set variable (**ref**). P characterises assumptions of the initial state and trace, Q characterises quiescent behaviours, and R characterises terminating behaviours. Our previous result [7] shows that any reactive program can be denoted using a reactive contract, which can be calculated by equational laws. This enables a verification strategy that checks refinements between a specification and implementation contract, and has been implemented in a tactic called **rdes-refine** [6], that can be used to check for deadlock [7], and which we employ in this paper.

3 Foundations for State Diagrams

In this section we extend the theory of reactive designs with constructs necessary to denote state machines, and prove several theorems, notably an induction law for iterative programs. Although these programming constructs are rather standard, we consider their semantics in the reactive programming paradigm, rather than in the standard sequential programming setting. It is a pleasing aspect of our approach that standard laws hold in this much richer context.

State machines describe how to transition from one node to another. The main construct we use to denote them is a reactive version of Dijkstra's guarded iteration statement [8] **do** $i \in I \bullet b(i) \twoheadrightarrow P(i)$ **od**, which repeatedly selects an indexed statement $P(i)$, based on whether its respective guard $b(i)$ is true. I is an index set, which when finite gives rise to the more programmatic form of **do** $b_1 \twoheadrightarrow P_1 \mid \cdots \mid b_n \twoheadrightarrow P_n$ **od**. We begin by defining Dijkstra's alternation construct, **if** $i \in I \bullet b(i) \twoheadrightarrow P(i)$ **fi** [8], which underlies iteration.

Definition 3.1 (Guarded Commands, Assumptions, and Alternation).

$$b \twoheadrightarrow P \triangleq P \lhd b \rhd \textbf{\textit{miracle}}$$

$$[b] \triangleq b \twoheadrightarrow \textbf{\textit{skip}}$$

$$\textbf{\textit{if}}\, i \in I \bullet b(i) \twoheadrightarrow P(i)\, \textbf{\textit{fi}} \triangleq \left(\bigsqcap_{i \in I} b(i) \twoheadrightarrow P(i) \right) \sqcap \left(\left(\neg \bigvee_{i \in I} b(i) \right) \twoheadrightarrow \textbf{\textit{chaos}} \right)$$

$b \rightarrow P$ is a "naked" guarded command [22]. Its behaviour is P when b is true, and miraculous otherwise, meaning it is impossible to execute. By Theorem 2.2, **miracle** is a left annihilator for sequential composition, and so any following behaviour is excluded when b is false. An assumption $[b]$ guards **skip** with b, and thus holds all variables constant when b is true, and is otherwise miraculous. $[\![NCSP]\!]$ is closed under both these operators since they are defined only in terms of healthy elements $\lhd \cdot \rhd$, **miracle**, and **skip**.

Alternation is a nondeterministic choice of guarded commands. When $b(i)$ is true for $i \in I$, $P(i)$ can be executed. Any command which has $b(i)$ false evaluates to **miracle** and thus is eliminated. If no $b(i)$ is true, then its behaviour is **chaos**. If multiple $b(i)$ are true then one of the corresponding $P(i)$ is nondeterministically selected. $[\![NCSP]\!]$ is closed under alternation since it comprises only healthy elements. From this definition we can prove a number of characteristic laws.

Theorem 3.2. *If,* $\forall i \bullet P(i)$ *is* **NCSP**, *then the following identities hold:*

$$\textbf{if}\, i \in \emptyset \bullet b(i) \twoheadrightarrow P(i)\, \textbf{fi} = \textbf{chaos} \tag{1}$$

$$\textbf{if}\, i \in \{k\} \bullet b(i) \twoheadrightarrow P(i)\, \textbf{fi} = P(k) \lhd b(k) \rhd \textbf{chaos} \tag{2}$$

$$\left[\bigvee_{i \in I} b(i)\right] \, \mathring{,}\, \textbf{if}\, i \in I \bullet b(i) \twoheadrightarrow P(i)\, \textbf{fi} = \left(\bigsqcap_{i \in I} b(i) \twoheadrightarrow P(i)\right) \tag{3}$$

In words, (1) shows that alternation over an empty set presents no options, and so is equivalent to **chaos**; (2) shows that a singleton alternation can be rewritten as a binary conditional; (3) shows that, if we assume that one of its branches is true, then an alternation degenerates to a nondeterministic choice.

We now define guarded iteration as the iteration of the corresponding alternation whilst at least one of the guards remains true.

Definition 3.3 (*Guarded Iteration*).

$$\textbf{do}\, i{\in}I \bullet b(i) \twoheadrightarrow P(i)\, \textbf{od} \triangleq \left(\bigvee_{i \in I} b(i)\right) \circledast (\textbf{if}\, i{\in}I \bullet b(i) \twoheadrightarrow P(i)\, \textbf{fi})$$

We use the reactive while loop $(b \circledast P)$ to encode the operator, and can thus utilise our previous results [7] to reason about it. In keeping with the reactive programming paradigm, this while loop can pause during execution to await interaction, and it also need not terminate. However, in order to ensure that the underlying fixed point can be calculated, we assume that for all $i \in I$, $P(i)$ is productive [17]: that is, it produces at least one event whenever it terminates. This ensures that divergence caused by an infinite loop is avoided. Iteration is closed under $[\![NCSP]\!]$, since the while loop and alternation both are.

We can now prove the following fundamental refinement law for iteration.

Theorem 3.4 (Iteration Induction). *If,* $\forall i \bullet P(i)$ *is* **NCSP**, *then:*

$$\frac{\forall i \in A \bullet P(i)\ is\ Productive \quad S \sqsubseteq I \, \mathring{,}\, [\bigwedge_{i \in A}(\neg b(i))]}{\forall i \in A \bullet S \sqsubseteq I \, \mathring{,}\, [b(i)] \, \mathring{,}\, P(i) \quad \forall i \in A \bullet S \sqsubseteq S \, \mathring{,}\, [b(i)] \, \mathring{,}\, P(i)}{S \sqsubseteq I \, \mathring{,}\, \textbf{do}\, i \in A \bullet b(i) \twoheadrightarrow P(i)\, \textbf{od}}$$

The law states the provisos under which an iteration, with initialiser I, preserves invariant S. These are: (1) every branch is productive; (2) if I causes the iteration to exit immediately then S is satisfied; (3) for any $i \in A$ if I holds initially, $b(i)$ is true, and $P(i)$ executes, then S is satisfied (base case); and (4) for any $i \in A$ if $b(i)$ is true, and $P(i)$ executes, then S is satisfied (inductive case). This law forms the basis for our verification strategy.

4   Mechanised Reactive Programs

In this section we turn our reactive design theory into an Isabelle/HOL type, so that we can use the type system to ensure well-formedness of reactive programs, which supports our verification strategy. The type allows efficient proof and use of the simplifier to perform rewriting and also symbolic evaluation so that assignments can be pushed forward and substitutions applied. We use it to encode both state machine actions in Sect. 5, and the dynamic semantics in Sect. 6. We first describe a general result for mechanising programs, apply it to reactive programs, and also introduce a novel operator to express frame extension.

In UTP, all programs are unified by encoding them in the alphabetised relational calculus. Programs in different languages of various paradigms therefore have a common mathematical form, and can be both compared and semantically integrated. This idea is retained in Isabelle/UTP by having all programs occupy the type $[\alpha]hrel$, with a suitably specialised alphabet type α [18].

In Isabelle/UTP, we characterise a theory by (1) an alphabet type T, which may be parametric; and (2) a healthiness function, $\boldsymbol{H}::[T]hrel \to [T]hrel$. The theory signature consists of operators with the form $f_i::([T]hrel)^k \to [T]hrel$, each of which is accompanied by a proven closure theorem

$$f\text{-}H\text{-}closed : [\![P_1 \ is \ \boldsymbol{H}; \ \cdots \ ; \ P_k \ is \ \boldsymbol{H}]\!] \Longrightarrow f(P_1, \cdots, P_k) \ is \ \boldsymbol{H}$$

which ensures that the operator constructs healthy elements, provided its parameters are all healthy. For example, the reactive design theory has a theorem $[\![P \ is \ \boldsymbol{NCSP}; \ Q \ is \ \boldsymbol{NCSP}]\!] \Longrightarrow (P \ \fatsemi \ Q) \ is \ \boldsymbol{NCSP}$, which demonstrates that sequential composition is in the signature. Theories also typically have algebraic laws, like those in Theorem 2.2, which can be applied to reasoning about programs and thence to produce verification tools [6,7].

This approach has several advantages for theory engineering [3,15]. There is a unified notion of refinement that can be applied across semantic domains. Operators like nondeterministic choice ($\sqcap$) and sequential composition ($\fatsemi$) can occupy several theories, which facilitates generality and semantic integration. General algebraic laws can be proved, and then directly reused in more specialised UTP theories. The UTP approach means that theories can be both combined and extended for a wide variety of computational paradigms and languages.

However, there is a practical downside, which is that the programming theorems, such as those in Theorem 2.2, require healthiness of the constituent parameters, and therefore it is necessary to first invoke the closure theorems. In the context of verification, constantly proving closure can be very inefficient, particularly for larger programs. This is because Isabelle's simplifier works best when invoked with pure equations $f(x_1, \cdots, x_n) \equiv y$ with minimal provisos.

Our solution uses the Isabelle type system to shoulder the burden of closure proof. We use the **typedef** mechanism, which creates a new type T from a non-empty subset $A :: \mathbb{P}(U)$ of existing type U. For a UTP theory, we create a type with $A = [\![H]\!]$, which is a subset of the UTP relations. This then allows optimised proof for a particular UTP theory, but at the cost of generality and semantic extensibility which are more suited to the UTP relational domain.

In order to obtain the signature for the new type, we utilise the lifting package [23], whose objective is to define operators on T in terms of operators on U, provided that A is closed under each operator. Specifically, if f is a signature operator in k arguments, then we can create a lifted operator $\widehat{f} :: T^k \to T$ using Isabelle's **lift-definition** command [23]. This raises a proof obligation that $f \in [\![H]\!]^k \to [\![H]\!]$, which can be discharged by the corresponding closure theorem. Programs constructed from the lifted operators are well-formed by construction.

Finally, to lift the algebraic theorems for each lifted operator $\widehat{f}$, we use the *transfer* tactic [23]. It allows us to prove theorems like $\widehat{f}(P_1, \cdots, P_k) = \widehat{g}(P_1, \cdots, P_k)$, where $P_i :: T$ is a free variable, by converting it to a theorem of the form $[\![Q_1 \text{ is } H; \ \cdots; \ Q_k \text{ is } H]\!] \implies f(Q_1, \cdots, Q_k) = g(Q_1, \cdots, Q_k)$. This means the closure properties of each parameter Q_i can be utilised in discharging provisos of the corresponding UTP theorems, but the lifted theorems do not require them. We will now use this technique for our reactive program type.

The reactive designs alphabet is $[s, e]st\text{-}csp$, for state space s and event type e. **NCSP** [7], of type $[[s, e]st\text{-}csp]hrel \to [[s, e]st\text{-}csp]hrel$, characterises the theory. We use it to define the reactive program type, $[s, e]Action$ and lift each theory operator from Sects. 2 and 3. For example, guard is a function $(b \ \& \ P) :: [s, e]Action$, for $b :: [s]upred$ and $P :: [s, e]Action$. For the action language, we define basic events $e \triangleq do(e)$, send $e!v \triangleq do(e.v)$, and receive $e?x \triangleq \Box v \bullet do(e.v) \ \fatsemi \ x := v$. From these lifted definitions, and using the *transfer* tactic, all the laws in Theorems 2.2 and 3.4 can be recast for the new operators, but without closure conditions. We then prove substitution laws for $\sigma \dagger P$, where $\sigma :: s \to s$ and $P :: [s, e]Action$, which can be used for symbolic evaluation.

Theorem 4.1 (Symbolic Evaluation Laws).

$$\sigma \dagger [b] = [\sigma \dagger b] \ \fatsemi \ \langle \sigma \rangle_a \quad \sigma \dagger (P \ \Box \ Q) = (\sigma \dagger P) \ \Box \ (\sigma \dagger Q)$$
$$\sigma \dagger (P \ \fatsemi \ Q) = (\sigma \dagger P) \ \fatsemi \ Q \quad \sigma \dagger (b \ \& \ P) = (\sigma \dagger b) \ \& \ (\sigma \dagger P)$$
$$\sigma \dagger \langle \rho \rangle_a = \langle \rho \circ \sigma \rangle_a \quad \sigma \dagger e!v = e!(\sigma \dagger v) \ \fatsemi \ \langle \sigma \rangle_a$$

These laws show how substitution applies and distributes through the operators. In combination with the assignment law of Theorem 2.2 (2), they can be used to apply state updates. For example, one can automatically prove that

$$(x := 2 \ \fatsemi \ y := (3 * x) \ \fatsemi \ e!(x + y)) = (e!8 \ \fatsemi \ \langle x \mapsto 2, y \mapsto 6 \rangle_a)$$

since we can combine the assignments and push them through the send event.

To denote state machines, we need a special variable ($actv$) to record the currently active node. This is semantic machinery, and no action is permitted access to it. We impose this constraint via frame extension: $a\!:\![P]^+\!::\![s_1, e]Action$, for $a\!::\!s_2 \Longrightarrow s_1$ and $P\!::\![s_2, e]Action$, that extends the alphabet of P. It is similar to a frame in refinement calculus [22], which prevents modification of variables, but also uses the type system to statically prevent access to them. Lens a identifies a subregion α of the larger alphabet β, that P acts upon. Intuitively, α is the set of state machine variables, and β this set extended with $actv$. P can only modify variables within α, and others are held constant. We prove laws for this operator, which are also be used in calculating the semantics.

Theorem 4.2 (Frame Extension Laws).

$$a\!:\![P\,\fatsemi\,Q]^+ \;=\; a\!:\![P]^+\,\fatsemi\,a\!:\![Q]^+ \quad a\!:\![e?x]^+ \;=\; e?(a\!:\!x) \quad a\!:\![x := v]^+ \;=\; a\!:\!x := v$$

Frame extension distributes through sequential composition. For operators like event receive and assignment, the variable is extended by the lens a, which is like a namespace operator ($a\!:\!x$). Specifically, it manipulates the region characterised by x within the region of a. This completes the mechanised reactive language.

5   Static Semantics

In this section we formalise a state machine meta-model in Isabelle/HOL, which describes the variables, transitions, and nodes. The meta-model, presented below, is based on the untimed subset of RoboChart, but note that our use of UTP ensures that our work is extensible to more advanced semantic domains [11,12,17]. For now we omit constructs concerned with interfaces, operations, shared variables, during actions, and hierarchy, and focus on basic machines.

Definition 5.1 (State Machine Meta-Model).
$StMach :=$ **statemachine** ID
$\qquad\qquad$ **vars** $NameDecl^*$ **events** $NameDecl^*$ **states** $NodeDecl^*$
$\qquad\qquad$ **initial** ID **finals** ID^* **transitions** $TransDecl^*$
$NameDecl := ID\ [:\ Type]$
$NodeDecl := ID$ **entry** $Action$ **exit** $Action$
$TransDecl := ID$ **from** ID **to** ID **trigger** $Event$ **condition** $Expr$ **action** $Action$

A state machine is composed of an identifier, variable declarations, event declarations, state declarations, an initial state identifier, final state identifiers, and transition declarations. Each variable and event consists of a name and a type. A state declaration consists of an identifier, entry action, and exit action. A transition declaration consists of an identifier, two state identifiers for the source and target nodes, a trigger event, a condition, and a body action. Whilst we do not directly consider hierarchy, this can be treated by flattening out substates.

We implement the meta-model syntax using Isabelle's parser, and implement record types $[s, e] Node$ and $[s, e] Transition$, that correspond to the *NodeDecl* and *TransDecl* syntactic categories. They are both parametric over the state-space s and event types e. *Node* has fields $nname::string$, $nentry::[s, e] Action$, and $nexit::[s, e] Action$, that contain the name, entry action, and exit action. *Transition* has fields $src::string$, $tgt::string$, $trig::[s, e] Action$, $cond::[s] upred$, and $act::[s, e] Action$, that contain the source and target, the trigger, the condition, and the body. We then create a record type to represent the state machine.

Definition 5.2 (State Machine Record Type).

$$\textbf{record}\, [s, e] StMach \;=\; \begin{array}{ll} init::ID & finals::[ID] list \\ nodes::[[s, e] Node] list & transs::[[s, e] Transition] list \end{array}$$

It declares four fields for the initial state identifier (*init*), final states identifiers (*finals*), nodes definitions (*nodes*), and transition definitions (*transs*), and constitutes the static semantics. Since this corresponds to the meta-model, and to ensure a direct correspondence with the parser, we do not directly use sets and maps, but only lists in our structure. We will later derive views onto the data structure above, that build on well-formedness constraints.

Below, we show how syntactic machines are translated to Isabelle definitions.

Definition 5.3 (Static Semantics Translation).

$$
\begin{array}{l}
\textbf{statemachine}\, s \\
\textbf{vars}\, x_1 : \tau_1^v \;\cdots\; x_i : \tau_i^v \\
\textbf{events}\, e_1 : \tau_1^e \;\cdots\; e_j : \tau_j^e \\
\textbf{states}\, s_1 \cdots s_k\, \textbf{initial}\, ini \\
\textbf{finals}\, f_1 \cdots f_m \\
\textbf{transitions}\, t_1 \cdots t_n
\end{array}
\;\Longrightarrow\;
\begin{array}{l}
\textbf{alphabet}\, s\text{-}alpha = x_1 : \tau_1^v \;\cdots\; x_i : \tau_i^v \\
\textbf{datatype}\, s\text{-}ev = \epsilon \mid e_1\, t_1^e \mid \cdots \mid e_j\, t_j^e \\
\textbf{defn}\, machine::[s\text{-}alpha, s\text{-}ev] StMach \\
\quad (init = ini, \\
\textbf{where}\, machine = \begin{array}{l} finals = [f_1 \cdots f_m], \\ states = [s_1 \cdots s_k], \\ transs = [t_1 \cdots t_n]) \end{array} \\
\textbf{defn}\, semantics = [\![machine]\!]_{\mathsf{M}}
\end{array}
$$

For each machine, a new alphabet is created, which gives rise to a HOL record type $s\text{-}alpha$, and lenses for each field of the form $t_i^v \Longrightarrow s\text{-}alph$. For the events, an algebraic datatype $s\text{-}ev$ is created with constructors corresponding to each of them. We create a distinguished event ϵ that will be used in transitions with explicit trigger and ensures productivity. The overall machine static semantics is then contained in *machine*. We also define *semantics* that contains the dynamic semantics in terms of the semantic function $[\![\cdot]\!]_{\mathsf{M}}$ that we describe in Sect. 6.

Elements of the meta-model are potentially not well-formed, for example specifying an initial state without a corresponding state declaration, and therefore it is necessary to formalise well-formedness. RoboTool enforces a number of well-formedness constraints [2], and we here formalise the subset needed to ensure the dynamic semantics given in Sect. 6 can be generated. We need some derived functions for this, and so we define $nnames \triangleq set(map\, nname\, (nodes))$, which calculates the set of node names, and *fnames*, which calculates the set of final node names. We can now specify our well-formedness constraints.

Definition 5.4. *A state machine is well-formed if it satisfies these constraints:*

1. Each node identifier is distinct: $distinct(map\ nname\ (nodes))$
2. The initial identifier is defined: $init \in nnames$
3. The initial identifier is not final: $init \notin fnames$
4. Every transition's source node is defined and non-final:
   $\forall\, t \in transs \bullet src(t) \in nnames \setminus fnames$
5. Every transition's target node is defined: $\forall\, t \in transs \bullet tgt(t) \in nnames$

We have implemented them in Isabelle/HOL, along with a proof tactic called *check-machine* that discharges them automatically when a generated static semantics is well-formed, and ensure that crucial theorems are available to the dynamic semantics. In practice, any machine accepted by RoboTool is well-formed, and so this tactic simply provides a proof of that fact to Isabelle/HOL.

In a well-formed machine every node has a unique identifier. Therefore, using Definition 5.4, we construct two finite partial functions, $nmap :: ID \nrightarrow [s, e]Node$ and $tmap :: ID \nrightarrow [s, e]Transition\,list$, that obtain the node definition and list of transitions associated with a particular node identifier, respectively, whose domains are both equal to $nnames$. We also define $ninit \triangleq nmap\,init$, to be the definition of the initial node, and $inters$ to be the set of nodes that are not final. Using well-formedness we can then prove the following theorems.

Theorem 5.5 (Well-formedness Properties).

1. *All nodes are identified:* $\forall\, n \in set(nodes) \bullet nmap(nname(n)) = n$
2. *The initial node is defined:* $ninit \in set(nodes)$
3. *The name of the initial node is correct:* $nname(ninit) = init$

These theorems allow us to extract the unique node for each identifier, and in particular for the initial node. Thus, Isabelle/HOL can parse a state machine definition, construct a static semantics for it, and ensure that this semantics is both well-typed and well-formed. The resulting Isabelle command is illustrated in Fig. 2 that encodes the **GasAnalysis** state machine of Fig. 1.

6   Dynamic Semantics

In this section we describe the behaviour of a state machine using the reactive program domain we mechanised in Sect. 4. The RoboChart reference semantics [2] represents a state machine as a parallel composition of CSP processes that represent the individual variables and states. Variable access and state orchestration are modelled by communications between them. Here, we capture a simpler sequentialised semantics using guarded iteration, which eases verification. In particular, state variables have a direct semantics, and require no communication. The relation between these two semantics can be formalised by an automated refinement strategy that reduces parallel to sequential composition [4].

We first define alphabet type $[s]rcst$, parametrised by the state space type s, and consisting of lenses $actv :: ID \Longrightarrow [s]rcst$ and $r :: s \Longrightarrow [s]rcst$. The former

```
statemachine GasAnalysis [
  vars sts::Status  gs::"GasSensor list"  ins::Intensity  anl::real
  events resume  stop  turn::real  gas::"GasSensor list"
  states InitState NoGas Reading FinalState
        Analysis: "entry sts := «analysis»(&gs)ₐ"
        GasDetected: "entry ins := «intensity»(&gs)ₐ"
  initial InitState finals FinalState
  transitions
    t1: "from InitState to NoGas action gs := ⟨⟩; anl := 0"
    t2: "from NoGas to Analysis trigger gas?(gs)"
    t3: "from Analysis to NoGas condition &sts =ᵤ «noGas» action resume"
    t4: "from Analysis to GasDetected condition (&sts =ᵤ «gasD»)"
    t5: "from GasDetected to FinalState condition «goreq»(&ins,«thr»)ₐ action stop"
    t6: "from GasDetected to Reading condition ¬ «goreq»(&ins,«thr»)ₐ
         action anl := «location»(&gs)ₐ ; turn!(&anl)"
    t7: "from Reading to Analysis trigger gas?(gs)" ]
```

Fig. 2. State machine notation in Isabelle/UTP

lens records the currently active state, and the latter projects the state machine variable space. No action is permitted to refer to $actv$, a constraint that we impose through the frame extension $r:[P]^+$.

We describe the dynamic semantics of a state diagram using three functions.

Definition 6.1 (Dynamic Semantics).

$$[\![M]\!]_\mathsf{M} \triangleq \left(\begin{array}{l} actv := init_M \; ; \\ \mathbf{do} \, N \in set(inters_M) \bullet actv = nname(N) \rightarrow M \models [\![N]\!]_\mathsf{N} \; \mathbf{od} \end{array} \right)$$

$$M \models [\![N]\!]_\mathsf{N} \triangleq r:[nentry(N)]^+ \; ; \; (\square \, t \in tmap_M(nname(N)) \bullet M, N \models [\![t]\!]_\mathsf{T})$$

$$M, N \models [\![t]\!]_\mathsf{T} \triangleq r:[cond(t) \, \& \, trig(t) \; ; \; nexit(N) \; ; \; action(t)]^+ \; ; \; actv := tgt(t)$$

The function $[\![\cdot]\!]_\mathsf{M} :: [s, e] StMach \rightarrow [\![s]\!] rcst, e] Action$ calculates the overall behavioural semantics. It first sets $actv$ to the initial node identifier, and then enters a do iteration indexed by all non-final nodes. If a final node is selected, then the iteration terminates. In each iteration, the node N that is named by $actv$ is selected, and the semantics for it is calculated using $M \models [\![N]\!]_\mathsf{N}$.

When in a node, the entry action is first executed using $nentry$, and then an external choice is presented over all transitions associated with N, which are calculated using $tmap$. The entry and exit actions do not have $actv$ in their alphabet, and therefore we apply frame extensions to them. The semantics of a transition, $M, N \models [\![t]\!]_\mathsf{T}$, is guarded by the transition condition, and awaits the trigger event. Once this occurs, the exit action of N is executed, followed by the transition action, and finally $actv$ is updated with the target node identifier.

The output of the semantics is an iterative program with one branch for every non-final state. To illustrate, we below generate the denotational semantics for the GasAnalysis state machine given in Fig. 1.

*Example 6.2 (**GasAnalysis** Dynamic Semantics).*

$actv := InitState$ ⨟
do
$\quad actv = InitState \rightarrow \epsilon$ ⨟ $\boldsymbol{r}{:}gs := \langle\rangle$ ⨟ $\boldsymbol{r}{:}anl := 0$ ⨟ $actv := NoGas$
$\quad | \; actv = NoGas \rightarrow gas?\boldsymbol{r}{:}gs$ ⨟ $actv := Analysis$
$\quad | \; actv = Analysis \rightarrow$
$\qquad \boldsymbol{r}{:}sts := analysis(\boldsymbol{r}{:}gs)$ ⨟ $\left(\begin{array}{l} \boldsymbol{r}{:}sts = noGas \;\&\; \epsilon \text{ ⨟ } resume \text{ ⨟ } actv := NoGas \\ \square \; \boldsymbol{r}{:}sts = gasD \;\&\; \epsilon \text{ ⨟ } actv := GasDetected \end{array} \right)$
$\quad | \; actv = GasDetected \rightarrow \boldsymbol{r}{:}ins := intensity(\boldsymbol{r}{:}gs)$ ⨟
$\qquad \left(\begin{array}{l} goreq(ins, thr) \;\&\; \epsilon \text{ ⨟ } stop \text{ ⨟ } actv := FinalState \\ \square \; (\neg goreq(ins, thr)) \;\&\; \epsilon \text{ ⨟ } \begin{array}{l} \boldsymbol{r}{:}anl := location(\boldsymbol{r}{:}gs) \text{ ⨟} \\ turn!(\boldsymbol{r}{:}anl) \text{ ⨟ } actv := Reading \end{array} \end{array} \right)$
$\quad | \; actv = Reading \rightarrow gas?\boldsymbol{r}{:}gs$ ⨟ $actv := Analysis$
od

In order to yield a more concise definition, we have also applied the action simplification laws given in Sect. 4. In particular, the frame extensions have all been expanded so that the state variables are explicitly qualified by lens $\boldsymbol{r}$.

In order to verify such state machines, we need a specialised refinement introduction law. Using our well-formedness theorem, we can specialise Theorem 3.4.

Theorem 6.3. *The semantics of a state machine M refines a reactive invariant specification S, that is $S \sqsubseteq [\![M]\!]_{\mathsf{M}}$, provided that the following conditions hold:*

1. *M is well-formed according to Definition 5.4;*
2. *the initial node establishes the invariant — $S \sqsubseteq M \models [\![ninit_M]\!]_{\mathsf{N}}$;*
3. *every non-final node preserves S — $\forall N \in inters_M \bullet S \sqsubseteq S$ ⨟ $(M \models [\![N]\!]_{\mathsf{N}})$.*

Proof. By application of Theorem 3.4, and utilising trigger productivity.   □

We now have all the infrastructure needed for verification of state machines, and in the next section we describe our verification strategy and tool.

7   Verification Approach

In this section we use the collected results presented in the previous sections to define a verification strategy for state machines, and exemplify its use in verifying deadlock freedom. Our approach utilises Theorem 6.3 and our contractual refinement tactic, rdes-refine, to prove that every state of a state machine satisfies a given invariant, which is specified as a reactive contract. The overall workflow for description and verification of a state machine is given by the following steps:

1. parse, type check, and compile the state machine definition;
2. check well-formedness (Definition 5.4) using the *check-machine* tactic;
3. calculate denotational semantics, resulting in a reactive program;

4. perform algebraic simplification and symbolic evaluation (Theorems 2.2 and 4.1);
5. apply Theorem 6.3 to produce sequential refinement proof obligations;
6. apply **rdes-refine** to each goal, which may result in residual proof obligations;
7. attempt to discharge each remaining proof obligation using **sledgehammer** [10].

Diagrammatic editors, like RoboTool, can be integrated with this by implementing a serialiser for the underlying meta-model. The workflow can be completely automated since there is no need to enter manual proofs, and the final proof obligations are discharged by automated theorem provers. If proof fails, Isabelle/HOL has the **nitpick** [10] counterexample generator that can be used for debugging. This means that the workflow can be hidden behind a graphical tool.

We can use the verification procedure to check deadlock freedom of a state machine using the reactive contract $dlockf \triangleq [\,\mathbf{true} \vdash \exists\, e \bullet e \notin \mathsf{ref} \mid \mathbf{true}\,]$, an invariant specification which states that in all quiescent observations, there is always an event that is not being refused. In other words, at least one event is always enabled; this is the meaning of deadlock freedom. We can use this contract to check the **GasAnalysis** state machine. For a sequential machine, deadlock freedom means that it is not possible to enter a state and then make no further progress. Such a situation can occur if the outgoing transitions can all be disabled simultaneously if, for example, their guards do not cover all possibilities.

```
goal (6 subgoals):
 1. dlockf ⊑ ε ; ⟨[&r:gs ↦ₛ ⟨⟩, &r:anl ↦ₛ 0, &rc_ctrl ↦ₛ «''NoGas''»]⟩ₐ
 2. dlockf ⊑
     ((«analysis»(&r:gs)ₐ =ᵤ «gasD») &
      ε ; (r:sts), rc_ctrl := «analysis»(&r:gs)ₐ, «''GasDetected''») □
     ((«analysis»(&r:gs)ₐ =ᵤ «noGas») &
      ε ; resume ; (r:sts), rc_ctrl := «analysis»(&r:gs)ₐ, «''NoGas''»)
 3. dlockf ⊑
     ((¬ «goreq»((«intensity»(&r:gs)ₐ, «thr»)ᵤ)ₐ) &
      ε ; turn!(«location»(&r:gs)ₐ) ;
          ⟨[&r:ins ↦ₛ «intensity»(&r:gs)ₐ, &r:anl ↦ₛ «location»(&r:gs)ₐ, &rc_ctrl ↦ₛ
              «''Reading''»]⟩ₐ) □
     («goreq»((«intensity»(&r:gs)ₐ, «thr»)ᵤ)ₐ &
      ε ; stop ; (r:ins), rc_ctrl := «intensity»(&r:gs)ₐ, «''FinalState''»)
```

Fig. 3. Selection of deadlock freedom proof obligations in Isabelle/UTP

The result of applying the verification procedure up to step 5 is shown in Fig. 3. At this stage, the semantics for each node has been generated, and deadlock freedom refinement conjectures need to be proved. Isabelle generates 6 subgoals, 3 of which are shown, since it is necessary to demonstrate that the invariant is satisfied by the initial state and each non-final state. The first goal corresponds to the initial state, where no event occurs and the variables gs and anl, along with $actv$, are all assigned. The second goal corresponds to the **Analysis** state. The state body has been further simplified from the form shown in Fig. 6.2, since symbolic evaluation has pushed the entry action through the transition external choice, and into the two guards. This is also the case for the third goal, which corresponds to the more complex **GasDetected** state.

The penultimate step applies the **rdes-refine** tactic to each of the 6 goals. This produces 3 subgoals for each goal, a total of 18 first-order proof obligations, and invokes the relational calculus tactic **rel-auto** on each of them. The majority are discharged automatically, but in this case three HOL predicate subgoals remain. One of them relates to the **Analysis** state, and requires that the constructors *noGas* and *gasD* of *Status* are the only cases for *sts*. If there was a third case, there would be a deadlock as the outgoing transition guards don't cover this.

Finally, we execute **sledgehammer** on each of the three goals, which provides proofs and so completes the deadlock freedom check. Thus, we have engineered a fully automated deadlock freedom prover for state machines.

8   Conclusions and Related Work

In this paper we have presented a verification strategy for state machines in Isabelle/UTP by utilising the theory of stateful-failure reactive designs, and automated proof facilities. We have extended our UTP theory with the guarded iteration construct, which is the foundation of sequential state machines, proved a crucial induction law, and adapted it to an efficient implementation of reactive programs. We have created a static semantics of state machines in Isabelle/HOL, including well-formedness checks, and a dynamic semantics that generates a reactive program. Finally, we used this to describe a verification approach that utilises reactive contract refinement and iterative induction.

In future work, we will expand our semantics to handle additional features of RoboChart. Hierarchy, can be handled by having the *actv* variable hold a list of nodes, and during actions by implementing a reactive interruption operator [24]. Moreover, we are developing reasoning facilities for parallel composition and hiding to allow expression of concurrent state machines, which extends our existing work [6,7]. This will greatly increase verification capabilities for robotic and component-based systems, allow us to handle asynchronous communication and shared variables, and also to mechanise the CSP reference semantics [2].

A challenge that remains is handling assumptions and guarantees between parallel components, but we believe that abstraction of state machines to invariants, using our results, can make this tractable. We will also explore other reasoning approaches, such as use of the simplifier to algebraically transform state machines to equivalent forms. Going further, we emphasise that our UTP theory hierarchy supports more advanced semantic paradigms. We will therefore develop a mechanised theory of timed reactive designs, based on existing work [11,17], and use this to denote the timing constructs of RoboChart state machines. We are developing a UTP theory of probability [12], and will use it to handle probabilistic junctions. We also have a theory of hybrid reactive designs [13,17], which we believe can be used to support hybrid state machines.

In related work, while a number of state machine notations exist, such as UML and Stateflow, to the best of our knowledge, they provide limited support for formal verification by theorem proving. While formalisations have been proposed [25,26], they typically address a subset of the target notation or focus on model checking. Other approaches such as [27], similarly restrict themselves to model checking or other forms of automatic verification, which have limitations on both the types of systems that can be analysed (mostly finite) and the kinds of properties that can be checked (schedulability, temporal logic, etc). We differ in that our approach is extensible, fully automated, and can handle infinite state systems with non-trivial types. Also, our verification laws have been mechanically validated with respect only to the axioms of Isabelle/HOL.

Acknowledgments. This work is funded by the EPSRC projects RoboCalc (RoboCalc Project: https://www.cs.york.ac.uk/circus/RoboCalc/) (Grant EP/M025756/1) and CyPhyAssure (CyPhyAssure Project: https://www.cs.york.ac.uk/circus/CyPhyAssure/) (Grant EP/S001190/1), and the Royal Academy of Engineering.

References

1. Miyazawa, A., Ribieiro, P., Li, W., Cavalcanti, A., Timmis, J.: Automatic property checking of robotic applications. In: International Conference on Intelligent Robots and Systems (IROS), pp. 3869–3876. IEEE (2017)
2. Miyazawa, M., Cavalcanti, A., Ribeiro, P., Li, W., Woodcock, J., Timmis, J.: Robochart reference manual. Technical report, University of York (June 2018). https://cs.york.ac.uk/circus/RoboCalc/assets/robochart-reference.pdf
3. Hoare, T., He, J.: Unifying Theories of Programming. Prentice-Hall, London (1998)
4. Oliveira, M., Cavalcanti, A., Woodcock, J.: A UTP semantics for Circus. Form. Asp. Comput. **21**, 3–32 (2009)
5. Nipkow, T., Wenzel, M., Paulson, L.C. (eds.): Isabelle/HOL. LNCS, vol. 2283. Springer, Heidelberg (2002). https://doi.org/10.1007/3-540-45949-9
6. Foster, S., Cavalcanti, A., Canham, S., Woodcock, J., Zeyda, F.: Unifying theories of reactive design contracts. Submitted to Theoretical Computer Science (Dec 2017). Preprint: arXiv:1712.10233
7. Foster, S., Ye, K., Cavalcanti, A., Woodcock, J.: Calculational verification of reactive programs with reactive relations and Kleene algebra. In: Desharnais, J. et al. (eds.) RAMiCS 2018. LNCS, vol. 11194, pp. 205–224. Springer, Cham (2018). https://doi.org/10.1007/978-3-030-02149-8_13
8. Dijkstra, E.W.: Guarded commands, nondeterminacy and formal derivation of programs. Commun. ACM **18**(8), 453–457 (1975)
9. Foster, S., Zeyda, F., Woodcock, J.: Unifying heterogeneous state-spaces with lenses. In: Sampaio, A., Wang, F. (eds.) ICTAC 2016. LNCS, vol. 9965, pp. 295–314. Springer, Cham (2016). https://doi.org/10.1007/978-3-319-46750-4_17
10. Blanchette, J.C., Bulwahn, L., Nipkow, T.: Automatic proof and disproof in Isabelle/HOL. In: Tinelli, C., Sofronie-Stokkermans, V. (eds.) FroCoS 2011. LNCS (LNAI), vol. 6989, pp. 12–27. Springer, Heidelberg (2011). https://doi.org/10.1007/978-3-642-24364-6_2
11. Sherif, A., Cavalcanti, A., He, J., Sampaio, A.: A process algebraic framework for specification and validation of real-time systems. Form. Asp. Comput. **22**(2), 153–191 (2010)

12. Bresciani, R., Butterfield, A.: A UTP semantics of pGCL as a homogeneous relation. In: Derrick, J., Gnesi, S., Latella, D., Treharne, H. (eds.) IFM 2012. LNCS, vol. 7321, pp. 191–205. Springer, Heidelberg (2012). https://doi.org/10.1007/978-3-642-30729-4_14

13. Foster, S., Thiele, B., Cavalcanti, A., Woodcock, J.: Towards a UTP semantics for modelica. In: Bowen, J.P., Zhu, H. (eds.) UTP 2016. LNCS, vol. 10134, pp. 44–64. Springer, Cham (2017). https://doi.org/10.1007/978-3-319-52228-9_3

14. Hilder, J., Owens, N., Neal, M., Hickey, P., Cairns, S., Kilgour, D., Timmis, J., Tyrrell, A.: Chemical detection using the receptor density algorithm. IEEE Trans. Syst. Man Cybern. **42**(6), 1730–1741 (2012)

15. Cavalcanti, A., Woodcock, J.: A tutorial introduction to CSP in *Unifying Theories of Programming*. In: Cavalcanti, A., Sampaio, A., Woodcock, J. (eds.) PSSE 2004. LNCS, vol. 3167, pp. 220–268. Springer, Heidelberg (2006). https://doi.org/10.1007/11889229_6

16. Santos, T., Cavalcanti, A., Sampaio, A.: Object-orientation in the UTP. In: Dunne, S., Stoddart, B. (eds.) UTP 2006. LNCS, vol. 4010, pp. 18–37. Springer, Heidelberg (2006). https://doi.org/10.1007/11768173_2

17. Foster, S., Cavalcanti, A., Woodcock, J., Zeyda, F.: Unifying theories of time with generalised reactive processes. Inf. Process. Lett. **135**, 47–52 (2018)

18. Feliachi, A., Gaudel, M.-C., Wolff, B.: Unifying theories in Isabelle/HOL. In: Qin, S. (ed.) UTP 2010. LNCS, vol. 6445, pp. 188–206. Springer, Heidelberg (2010). https://doi.org/10.1007/978-3-642-16690-7_9

19. Foster, S., et al.: Stateful-failure reactive designs in Isabelle/UTP. Technical report, University of York (2018). http://eprints.whiterose.ac.uk/129768/

20. Zhan, N., Kang, E.Y., Liu, Z.: Component publications and compositions. In: Butterfield, A. (ed.) UTP 2008. LNCS, vol. 5713, pp. 238–257. Springer, Heidelberg (2010). https://doi.org/10.1007/978-3-642-14521-6_14

21. Back, R.J., Wright, J.: Refinement Calculus: A Systematic Introduction. Springer, Berlin (1998)

22. Morgan, C., Vickers, T.: On the Refinement Calculus. Springer, Berlin (1992)

23. Huffman, B., Kunčar, O.: Lifting and transfer: a modular design for quotients in Isabelle/HOL. In: Gonthier, G., Norrish, M. (eds.) CPP 2013. LNCS, vol. 8307, pp. 131–146. Springer, Cham (2013). https://doi.org/10.1007/978-3-319-03545-1_9

24. McEwan, A.: Concurrent Program Development in Circus. Ph.D. thesis, Oxford University (2006)

25. Schäfer, T., Knapp, A., Merz, S.: Model checking UML state machines and collaborations. ENCTS **55**(3), 357–369 (2001)

26. Miyazawa, A., Cavalcanti, A.: Refinement-oriented models of stateflow charts. Sci. Comput. Program. **77**(10–11) (2012)

27. Foughali, M., Berthomieu, B., Dal Zilio, S., Ingrand, F., Mallet, A.: Model checking real-time properties on the functional layer of autonomous robots. In: Ogata, K., Lawford, M., Liu, S. (eds.) ICFEM 2016. LNCS, vol. 10009, pp. 383–399. Springer, Cham (2016). https://doi.org/10.1007/978-3-319-47846-3_24

Using Coloured Petri Nets for Resource Analysis of Active Objects

Anastasia Gkolfi[1]($\boxtimes$), Einar Broch Johnsen[1]($\boxtimes$), Lars Michael Kristensen[2]($\boxtimes$), and Ingrid Chieh Yu[1]($\boxtimes$)

[1] Department of Informatics, University of Oslo, Oslo, Norway
{natasa,einarj,ingridcy}@ifi.uio.no
[2] Western Norway University of Applied Sciences, Bergen, Norway
lmkr@hvl.no

Abstract. Pay-on-demand resource provisioning is an important driver for cloud computing. Virtualized resources in cloud computing open for resource awareness, such that applications may contain resource management strategies to modify their deployment and reduce resource consumption. The ABS language supports the modelling of deployment decisions and resource management for active objects. In this paper, the semantics of ABS is captured directly as a Coloured Petri Net (CPN) model capable of representing any ABS program by an appropriate initial marking. We define an abstraction relation between the CPN model and the language semantics such that markings of the CPN model become abstract ABS configurations. We use a CPN model checker as an abstract interpreter to investigate resource distribution and starvation problems for deployed active objects in ABS.

1 Introduction

Pay-on-demand resource provisioning is an important driver for cloud computing. Using resources on the cloud, a service provider does not need to cater hardware resources upfront to deploy the service but can lease resources as required by the deployed service. Resources may be dynamically added or removed depending on the traffic to a service. The enabling virtualization technology introduces a software layer representing hardware resources, which means that deployment decisions can be programmed. Virtualized resources open for resource awareness, such that applications may contain resource management strategies to modify their deployment and reduce resource consumption. In this context, it is interesting to analyze deployment scenarios for services with respect to client traffic to, e.g., establish the amount of resources required for the timely delivery of a service.

Programming models which *decouple* control flow and communication, such as Actors [1,2] and active objects [9,16,26], inherently support both scalability (as argued with the Erlang programming language [5] and Scala's actors [22]) and compositional reasoning [12,17,18]. These features are also interesting for distributed services which should adapt to elastic cloud deployment.

© Springer Nature Switzerland AG 2018
K. Bae and P. C. Ölveczky (Eds.): FACS 2018, LNCS 11222, pp. 156–174, 2018.
https://doi.org/10.1007/978-3-030-02146-7_8

In this paper, we develop a method to investigate resource distribution for deployed active objects in ABS by a translation into Coloured Petri Nets (CPNs) [25]. ABS is a formally defined active object language [26,29] which directly supports the modelling of deployment decisions and resource management for active objects. CPNs extend the basic Petri net model [33] with data and data manipulation. We extend previous work [19] from behavioural models to deployment models such that the formal semantics of deployment models in ABS is captured directly as a hierarchical CPN. Consequently, the number of places in the CPN model is independent of the size of a program, and different programs are captured by changing the initial marking of the CPN model. This also allows the dynamic launch of virtual resources by the firing of CPN transitions. We define an abstraction relation between the CPN model and the language semantics. The model checker of CPN Tools is used as an abstract interpreter to investigate resource distribution and starvation problems for deployed active objects in ABS.

The main contributions of this paper are: (1) a *formal model* of deployed ABS programs as a hierarchical CPN that reflects the ABS semantics with markings as abstract configurations; (2) an *abstraction relation* translating resource-aware ABS programs into CPN markings and a *proof of correctness* of the abstraction relation; and (3) management support for deployment decisions in terms of *automated resource analysis* of starvation freedom and resource redistribution.

The paper is organized as follows: Sect. 2 introduces the ABS language, focusing on the modelling of deployment, and Sect. 3 briefly introduces CPNs. Section 4 presents the CPN model of the ABS semantics and Sect. 5 the abstraction relation between the CPN model and the ABS semantics, as well as the sketch of the soundness proof. The interested reader can find the full proof in a companion technical report [20]. Section 6 shows how the CPN Tools model checker can be used for the resource analysis of ABS programs. Finally, Sect. 7 draws some conclusions and discusses related work.

2 Deployment Modelling in ABS

ABS [26] is a formally defined actor-based language for the executable modelling of distributed, object-oriented systems. ABS supports *deployment modelling* by a separation of concerns between the resource costs of executions and the resource capacities of *deployment components* on which executions take place [29]; deployment components can be understood as (virtual) locations for computation. Deployment decisions can be made inside models, by allocating objects to deployment components with given resources at creation time (e.g., [4,27]).

ABS consists of a functional layer to express computation, an imperative layer to express communication and synchronization, and a deployment layer to express deployment decisions. In this paper we elide the functional layer to focus on control flow and deployment; the relevant syntax is shown in Fig. 1. A program consists of class definitions which contain field declarations and method definitions, and a main block. We follow the syntactic conventions of Java and only explain syntax that differs from Java.

Syntactic categories. Definitions.

s in STMT

e in EXPR

g in GUARD

$$P ::= \overline{CL} \, \{\overline{T} \; \overline{x}; \; ws \}$$

$$CL ::= \textbf{class} \, C \, (\overline{T} \; \overline{x}) \, \{\overline{T} \; \overline{x}; \; \overline{M} \}$$

$$M ::= T \; m \, (\overline{T} \; \overline{x}) \, \{\overline{T} \; \overline{x}; \; ws \}$$

$$s ::= \textbf{skip} \mid x = rhs \mid [\text{DC}{:}e] \; x = \textbf{new} \; C(\overline{e}) \mid \textbf{suspend} \mid \textbf{await} \; g$$

$$\mid \textbf{if} \; e \; \{ ws \} \; \textbf{else} \; \{ ws \} \mid \textbf{while} \; e \; \{ ws \} \mid \textbf{return} \; e$$

$$ws ::= s \mid [\text{Cost:} \; e] \; s \mid ws; ws$$

$$rhs ::= e \mid e!m(\overline{e}) \mid x.\textbf{get}$$

$$g ::= x? \mid \textbf{duration}(e, e) \mid g \wedge g$$

Fig. 1. ABS syntax. Overbar notation denotes lists.

The imperative layer of ABS is used for internal control flow, and for communication and synchronization between concurrent objects. Objects are instantiated from classes by the statement $[\text{DC}{:} \; server] \; o = \textbf{new} \; C(\overline{e})$, where the optional annotation DC: *server* expresses the deployment component on which the object should be created and $\overline{e}$ are constructor arguments. A reserved field **thisDC** points to the object's deployment component, just like **this** points to the object's identifier. Concurrent objects execute processes which stem from asynchronous method calls and terminate upon method completion. Asynchronous method calls $f = o!m(\overline{e})$ are non-blocking and return a future, i.e., a placeholder for the method reply (see, e.g., [9]). The blocking expression $f.\textbf{get}$ retrieves the return value from a future f.

Objects combine reactive and active behaviour (i.e., a **run** method is automatically activated upon object creation) by means of *cooperative scheduling*: Processes in an object may suspend at explicit scheduling points, allowing the scheduler to transfer control to another enabled process. Between the scheduling points, only one process is active in each object, so race conditions are avoided. Unconditional scheduling points are expressed by the statement **suspend**, conditional scheduling points by **await** g, where g may be a *synchronization condition* on a future, written $f?$ (where f points to a future) or a *duration guard*, written **duration**(b, w) where b and w are bounds on the time interval before the condition becomes true. ABS supports the modelling of dense time [8]; the local passage of time is expressed in terms of durations (as in, e.g., UPPAAL [31]).

Deployment models capture physical or virtual infrastructure in ABS using dynamically created *deployment components* [28,29] to represent computing environments. A deployment component is a modelling abstraction which captures locations offering (restricted) resources to computations. Deployment components are created as instances of a special class DC which takes as parameter a number expressing the resource capacity of the deployment component per time interval. These components implement a method **transfer**(dc, e) which enables *vertical scaling* by shifting up to e resources to a target deployment component dc. This is in contrast to the horizontal scaling which is realized by the dynamic allocation of deployment components. ABS also supports cost annotations to model resource consumption. Thus, *weighted statements ws* are statements [Cost: e] s which express that e resources are required to complete execution of the statement s. In this paper we model so-called elastic computing resources, where the computation *speed* of virtual machines is determined by the amount of elastic computing resources allocated to these machines per time interval. The computation time of processes depends on the available resources of their deployment component and on how many other processes are competing for these resources.

$$\frac{\text{(New-DC)} \quad fresh(dc) \quad [\![e]\!]_{aol} = n}{o(a, \{l \mid x = \textbf{new } \mathsf{DC}(e); s\}, q) \rightarrow o(a, \{l \mid x = dc; s\}, q) \, dc(n, 0, n)}$$

$$\frac{\text{(Run-To-New-Interval)} \quad blocked(cn, t)}{0 < d \le mte(cn, t) \quad \lceil t \rceil = t + d} \\ \frac{\{cn \; cl(t)\}}{\rightarrow_t \{timeAdv(rscRefill(cn), d) \; cl(t + d)\}}$$

$$\frac{\text{(Cost1)} \quad a(\mathsf{thisDC}) = dc \qquad an = \mathsf{Cost:} \, e \\ [\![e]\!]_{aol} = c \qquad\qquad c \le n - u}{o(a, \{l \mid [an] \, s\}, q) \, cn \rightarrow o(a', p', q') \, cn'}{o(a, \{l \mid [an] \, s\}, q) \, dc(n, u, k) \, cl(t) \, cn \\ \rightarrow o(a', p', q') \, dc(n, u + c, k) \, cl(t) \, cn'}$$

$$\frac{\text{(Cost2)} \quad a(\mathsf{thisDC}) = dc \qquad an = \mathsf{Cost:} \, e \\ [\![e]\!]_{aol} = c \qquad c > n - u \quad n \ne u \\ c' = c - (n - u) \qquad an' = \mathsf{Cost:} \, c'}{o(a, \{l \mid [an] \, s\}, q) \, dc(n, u, k) \, cn \\ \rightarrow o(a, \{l \mid [an'] \, s\}, q) \, dc(n, n, k) \, cn}$$

$$\frac{\text{(Transfer)} \quad fresh(f) \quad [\![e]\!]_{aol} = dc \quad [\![e']\!]_{aol} = dc' \quad [\![e'']\!]_{aol} = i \quad i' = min(i, k)}{o(a, \{l \mid x = e!\textbf{transfer}(e', e''); s\}, q) \, dc(n, u, k) \, dc'(n', u', k') \\ \rightarrow o(a, \{l \mid x = f; s\}, q) \, dc(n, u, k - i') \, dc'(n', u', k' + i') \, f(i')}$$

Fig. 2. Semantics of the deployment layer of ABS (based on [29]).

Semantics. The semantics of ABS is given by a (transitive) transition relation $\rightarrow$ over configurations realizing a maximal progress time model, in which time will only advance if the execution is otherwise blocked. We here focus on the transition rules formalizing the *cost and deployment aspects* of the execution of ABS programs. Configurations include *objects* $o(a, p, q)$, where o is the identifier, a the state, p the active process, and q the queue of suspended processes; *futures* $f(v)$ with identifier f and return value v; and *deployment components* $dc(n, u, k)$ with identifier dc, n resources available in the current time interval, u resources already used in the current time interval, and k resources available in the next time interval. Technically, the deployment components book-keep the resource consumption of their allocated objects per time interval. Thus, in New-DC (Fig. 2), a new deployment component with a fresh identifier dc is created, with n resources available in both the current and the next time interval. Rule Run-To-New-Interval captures the advance of time. Here, the brackets enclose all objects in the configuration as well as a global clock $cl(t)$ such that time advances uniformly. The predicate $blocked(cn, t)$ expresses that no (further) reduction is possible in cn at time t, so time may advance. Let $mte(cn', t)$ denote the maximal time advance until $enabled(cn')$. The condition $\lceil t \rceil = t + d$ expresses that time advance has arrived at the next resource provisioning (a corresponding rule without this condition advances time without resource provisioning). Two auxiliary functions recursively change the state cn': *timeAdv* decrements counters for **duration**-expressions and *rscRefill* provisions resources in the deployment components by changing each $dc(n, u, k)$ to $dc(k, 0, k)$.

Rule COST1 removes the cost annotation of a statement if the associated deployment component has sufficient resources to execute the statement in the current time interval. Rule COST2 reduces the remaining cost of executing a statement if the deployment component can provision some but not all of the required resources. Rule TRANSFER shifts e'' resources from a deployment component e to another deployment component e', up to the amount of resources that e has allocated for the next time interval. This change only affects e' for the next time interval. For further details on the semantics of deployment components in ABS, we refer to [29].

3   Coloured Petri Nets

Petri nets capture true concurrency in terms of causality and synchronization [33]. A basic (low-level) Petri net constitute a directed bipartite graph comprised of places and transitions connected by arcs. An arc (p, t) is outgoing for a place p and incoming for a transition t, whereas an arc (t, p) is incoming for p and outgoing for t. Places are used to model the states of the system and may hold tokens. A marking consists of a distribution of tokens on the places of the Petri net and represent a state of the modelled system. Transitions are used for modelling the actions of the system. A transition is enabled in a marking when there is a token on each of its input places. An enabled transition may occur (fire) and the effect of occurrence is to consume a token from each input place of the transition and add a token to each of its output places. This in turn changes the current marking of the Petri net model.

Coloured Petri Nets (CPNs) is a well-established form of high-level Petri nets [25]. High-level Petri nets extend the basic Petri net formalism to enable the modelling of data and data manipulation. Each place in a CPN has an associated type determining the data values that tokens residing on the place may have, i.e., the tokens in a place represent individual values of that type. The types, representing sets of values, are called *colour sets* and individual values are seen as colours. A type can be arbitrarily complex, defined by many sorted algebra in the same way as abstract data types. A place may in general hold a multi-set of token values over the type of the place. Arcs have associated arc expressions and transitions may have an associated boolean guard expression. These expressions may contain free variables which needs to be bound to values in order to determine whether a transition is enabled, i.e., whether the required tokens are present on input places and whether the guard evaluates to true. Similarly, the multi-set of tokens removed from input places and added to output places when an enabled transition occurs are determined by evaluating the arc expression of the transition according to the values bound to the free variables.

Below we formally define CPNs [25] in their basic form without hierarchical modules. In the rest of the paper we use hierarchical CPNs. Hierarchies enrich

CPNs with modularity in order to support the practical modelling of large systems. The basic definition of CPNs suffices for our purposes as any hierarchical CPN can be unfolded to a semantically equivalent non-hierarchical CPN.

Definition 1 (Coloured Petri net). *A coloured Petri net (CPN) is a tuple* $(P, T, A, \Sigma, V, C, G, E, I)$ *where*

1. P *is a finite set of places* P *and* T *is a finite set of transitions* T *such that* $P \cap T = \emptyset$;
2. A *is the set of arcs, such that* $A \subseteq (P \times T) \,\dot\cup\, (T \times P)$;
3. Σ *is a finite set of non-empty types (colour sets);*
4. V *is a set finite set of typed variables* V *such that* $type(v) \in \Sigma$ *for all* $v \in V$;
5. $C : P \to \Sigma$ *is a colouring function associating a type to each place;*
6. $G : T \to Expr_V$ *and* $E : A \to Expr_V$ *are labelling functions associating expressions with free variables from* V *to transitions and arcs, respectively such that* $type(G(t)) = bool$ *for all* $t \in T$ *and* $type(E(a)) = C(p)_{MS}$ *where* p *is the place connected to* a *and* $C(p)_{MS}$ *denotes the multi-set type over* $C(p)$.
7. $I : P \to Expr_{\emptyset}$ *is an initialization function associating a closed expression to each place specifying the initial marking of the place such that* $type(I(p)) = C(p)_{MS}$ *for all* $p \in P$

4   A CPN Model of ABS Semantics

In [19] the authors presented a CPN, modelling the concurrency of ABS. Active objects in [19] were represented as tokens whose colour contains their identifier and process pool. The process pool was implemented as a list, the head of which was the active process and the tail the list of the processes that were candidates to be activated by the scheduler. This list was being updated according to the calling methods of the other objects following the communication mechanism of ABS. In this paper, we focus on the deployment part of ABS. We present a new hierarchical CPN, modelling the deployment fragment of the language. Recall here, that hierarchies in CPNs introduce modularity. Each submodule can be seen as a "hidden part" of the net, named as the rectangular tag below the corresponding so-called *substitution transition* (in the figures they have double outer lines). Similarly, the double lined places keep the input/output marking of each submodule. In our CPN, we modelled the life time of program execution in a cyclic way, where the resources are refilled at the completion point of each cycle. This is illustrated in Fig. 3 where the top-layer of the model is shown. In the bottom part of this figure, we see the resource refill before the process execution in the next cycle.

We take as an input tokens that can be produced from the imperative part [19] of ABS as described above and we add information concerning the cost of each process and the deployment component they are located. This information, together with the deployment semantics of ABS can be used to verify starvation freedom of active objects and explore resource management strategies.

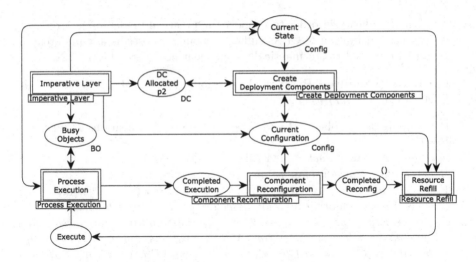

Fig. 3. Top-level module of the CPN deployment model

In the rest of the section, we present the CPN model which follows the corresponding semantic rules of ABS that add resource awareness through a running example. It is inspired from the change of the calling behaviours of cellphone clients during new year's eve midnight. Based on this example, we show in Sect. 6 how resource reallocation between deployment components can be used for load balancing purposes.

4.1   Telephone and SMS Services at Midnight on New Year's Eve

We use a running example inspired from cellphone clients behaviour in order to illustrate the relation between the CPN model and ABS programs and to show how we can use the model checker of CPN Tools for load balancing scenarios.

The average demand on phone calls and SMS messages from cellphone clients during the year is relatively low and the available resources suffice in a current distribution. There are some particular moments of the year like, for example, around the midnight of new year's eve, where this behaviour changes and a large number of SMS is requested by the clients while the call requests are negligible. Then, the initial distribution is not adequate, since there is a lack of resources for the SMS and an overplus for the calls.

In Fig. 4, we provide the ABS implementation of the above scenario [29] where telephone and SMS servers have been realised with the two corresponding classes and the operational cost annotated in square brackets at the beginning of the statements. We see that each SMS has cost 1 and each call has cost proportional to its duration. Cellphone clients can be implemented with corresponding classes allowing objects to make method calls to the SMS and telephone services.

As mentioned above, we use CPNs to model the deployment part of ABS. The markings shown in the current section are related to our running example.

```
 1  class TelephoneServer{
 2    Unit call (Int calltime) {
 3      while (calltime > 0) { [Cost:1] calltime = calltime − 1; await duration (1,1); }
 4    }
 5  }
 6  class SMSServer {
 7    Unit sendSMS () { [Cost:1] skip; }
 8  }
 9  {// Main block
10    DC telcomp = new DC(1);
11    DC smscomp = new DC(2);
12    [DC: smscomp] SMSServer sms = new SMSServer();
13    [DC: telcomp] TelephoneServer tel = new TelephoneServer();
14    // Start client handsets...
15  }
```

Fig. 4. Implementation of telephone and SMS service.

It is important to note that our CPN model is parametric and different ABS programs can be analysed by setting the initial marking accordingly. In our example, we modelled the SMS and the telephone servers in CPNs as two different tokens representing the corresponding objects of Fig. 4 (TelephoneServer and SMSServer). Those tokens have as colour triples of the form (ob, dc, lst), where ob is the object identifier and dc is the deployment component of the object execution. The last component (lst) models the client behaviour. In particular, it represents the process pool of the server object that keeps all the processes created from the clients calls to the corresponding service. Each process comes along with the cost of its execution, so lst is a list of triples $(proc, cost, bool)$, where $bool$ is a flag indicating whether the process has completed its execution.

Figure 5 shows the CPN module representing the imperative layer of ABS. Initially, the model has one token in place Ready and the transition Imperative Layer is enabled. Recall that the colour of the object tokens have the form (ob, dc, lst) as explained above. In Fig. 5, we have two tokens produced in place Busy Objects. The first one represents the object TelephoneServer with identifier 1 located in the first deployment component having in its process pool two processes: one with identifier 1 and cost 2 and one with identifier 2 and cost 4. The boolean flags set to *false* indicate that the processes have not been executed yet (it can be changed to true after firing Process Completed). Similarly, the second token represents the SMSServer object. Place DC Allocated is a counter of the deployment components created so far (for details, see [20]). Places Current State and Current Configuration have as a colour set a list of pairs (dc, cap) referring to the capacities of each deployment component. Place Current State keeps the current resource distribution while place Current Configuration records the distribution that will take place in the next cycle (resp. next time interval in ABS).

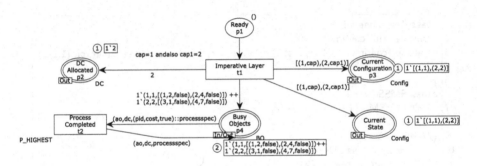

Fig. 5. CPN module of the imperative layer

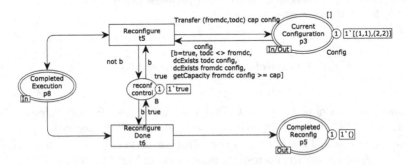

Fig. 6. CPN module for component reconfiguration

Figure 6 shows that when transition Reconfigure fires, the marking of the place Current Configuration is updated according to the function Transfer of its incoming arc inscription:

```
fun Transfer (fromdc,todc) cap config = List.map (fn (dc,ccap) =>
if (dc = fromdc) then (dc,ccap - cap) else (if (dc = todc) then
(dc,ccap+cap) else (dc,ccap))) config
```

This function transfers resources from one deployment component to another. When transition Reconfigure Done fires, the reconfiguration has been completed. Then the resources can be refilled (details of the related implementation can be found in [20]), and the marking of the place Current State can be updated according to the function Transfer and proceed to the execution.

Figure 7 shows the module related to the process execution and the resource consumption. Places Busy Objects and Current State are fusion places (i.e they appear in more than one module and share the same marking). Recall the meaning of their markings from Fig. 5. Object 2 needs for the execution of its first process in the list (having identifier 3) 1 resource and the availability of the second deployment component according to the marking of the place Current State is 2 resources (having colour $(2,2)$). As a result, transition Fully Executable (Fig. 7) can fire and set its cost to zero and the boolean flag to *true* (recall that the boolean flag is related to whether the process has been fully executed or

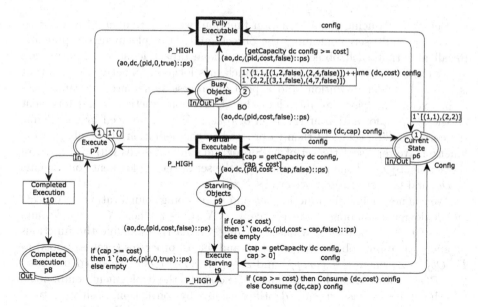

Fig. 7. CPN module for process execution

not). After this, transition Process Completed of Fig. 5 is enabled and the corresponding element of the list (head) is removed. Consider again Fig. 7: object 1 needs 2 resources to fully execute its first process while there is only 1 available, according to the marking of the place Current State. Hence it can only partially execute process 1 by consuming all available resources (here 1) when transition Partially Executable enabled. Then the token of the object 1 will be moved to the place Starving Objects with the remaining cost updated to 1, until the marking of place Current State will show resource availability at the deployment component greater or equal to 1. This can be done at a next cycle in the model, after possible resource transfer and refill. In such a case, transition Execute Starving will be enabled and send the token back to the Busy Objects place; otherwise, in case of insufficient resource for completion, it will be placed again to the place Starving Objects.

5 Abstraction Relation and Soundness

The model presented in Sect. 4 translates faithfully the fragment of ABS which is responsible for the resource awareness of the language. An abstraction function matching program configurations with CPN markings followed by a soundness proof guarantee the faithfulness of this translation. In this section, we define the abstraction relation α that associates each ABS program configuration with a marking of the CPN model and each small step semantics of ABS with a finite sequence of enabled CPN transitions. This relation is an *abstract simulation relation*, where the abstraction stands for the extraction of the elements related to the resources from each ABS configuration.

Before introducing the abstraction function, we note that in ABS, configurations are multi-sets containing the objects and the deployment components. Recall also that each object contains a unique object identifier, information about the deployment component to which it is located, an active process that is currently under execution, and a pool of processes that are the candidates to be executed. Below, we introduce the abstraction function α and represent all the above information at the level of tokens. Hence, we need first to define the corresponding sets and then to proceed to the definition of the abstraction function. We represent the set of ABS program configurations with $\mathcal{C}$, the set of the active objects of the program as Obj, the set of the deployment components as Dc, and the set of the processes as $Proc$.

We can now define the functions ob and dc mapping configurations to objects and deployment components, respectively, as $X : \mathcal{C} \to Y$ where $X \in \{ob, dc\}$ and $Y \in \{Obj, Dc\}$, with the obvious matching. Similarly, we define the functions pr and pp mapping objects to processes and sets of processes (process pools) as $F : Obj \to Z$, where $F \in \{pr, pp\}$ and $Z \in \{Proc, \mathcal{P}(Proc)\}$. We also define $pdc :$ $\mathcal{C} \to \mathcal{P}(Dc)$. Since each element among the objects, the deployment components and the processes has a unique identifier we use, by convention, positive natural numbers to translate it. This leads to the definition of the following injections: $L : W \to \mathbb{N}^*$ where $L \in \{obj\_id, dc\_id, proc\_id\}$ and $W \in \{Obj, Dc, Proc\}$ (with the obvious matching). We also define a cost function, assigning to each process the cost of its execution: $cost : Proc \to \mathbb{N}$ as well as two capacity functions cap and $ncap$ related to the resource capacity of each deployment component (cap for the current and $ncap$ for the next time interval), defined as $cap : Proc \to \mathbb{N}$ (resp. for $ncap$). Also, we define the function $cc : \mathcal{P}(Dc) \to \mathcal{P}(Dc \times \mathbb{N})$, where $cc(S) \overset{def}{=} \{(dc\_id(s), cap(s)) \in \mathbb{N}^* \times \mathbb{N} \mid s \in S\}$. Finally, we define the function $cpq : \mathcal{P}(Proc) \to \mathcal{P}(\mathbb{N}^* \times \mathbb{N} \times \mathbb{B})$, mapping the process pools (i.e. sets of processes) to sets of tuples, each representing the process identifier, the corresponding cost and a boolean flag (where $\mathbb{B}$ is the set of booleans). In particular, $cpq(S) \overset{def}{=}$ $\{(proc\_id(s), cost(s), b) \in \mathbb{N}^* \times \mathbb{N} \times \mathbb{B} \mid s \in S \wedge b \in \mathbb{B}\}$. Similarly to the function cc, we define the function ncc where, instead of the function $cap(s)$ of cc we use the function $ncap(s)$.

So far, we have defined elementary functions to represent the interesting information taken from ABS configurations in order to form the appropriate colour sets that are used in the model. Recall from Sect. 4 that the colour set of the tokens representing the objects of an ABS program is (ob, dc, lst) where ob is the object identifier, dc is the deployment component where the object is located, and lst is the process pool augmented with information about the cost. More concretely, lst is a list of triples $(proc, cost, bool)$ indicating the identifier of each process, its corresponding cost and a boolean flag showing whether the execution of a process has been completed or not. Recall also that the colour set of the deployment components is a pair (dc, cap) where dc is the deployment component identifier and cap its resource capacity. The colour set of the place Current State represents the current resource distribution and place Current Configuration the distribution that will take place at the next time interval.

Now, let us define the abstraction function, which induces an abstract simulation relation between ABS program configurations and CPN tokens. For all configurations $c \in \mathcal{C}$:

$$
\begin{aligned}
\alpha(c) = \bigcap \{ M \mid \exists\, p, p', p'' \in P \text{ s.t. } p \neq p' \neq p'' \text{ and for all } ob(c) \in Obj, \qquad (1) \\
((obj\_id \circ ob)(c), (dc\_id \circ dc)(c), (cpq \circ pr \circ ob)(c)) \in M(p) \\
\wedge\ (cc \circ pdc)(c) \in M(p') \\
\wedge\ (ncc \circ pdc)(c) \in M(p'') \}
\end{aligned}
$$

where $\bigcap$ is the intersection over sets of multi sets. Recall the colour sets of the places Busy Objects, Starving Objects, Current Configuration and Current State. The above function extracts information from ABS configurations and matches that information to the colour of the tokens of those places appropriately. At the second line of the equation, we have the information related to the tokens representing objects. They can be located either in Busy Objects or in Starving Objects place (hence the existential quantifier of the equation). The third and the fourth lines of the equation concern the deployment components and, in particular, the resource distributions for either the current or the next time interval. This information is also available at each ABS configuration, and hence the abstraction function retrieves it and matches it with the tokens located in places Current State and Current Configuration respectively.

Now, we can proceed to the correctness of the behaviour of our translation by establishing an abstract weak simulation relation between program configurations and CPN markings. For the full proof, see [20].

Theorem 1. *The markings of the CPN model are in abstract (weak) simulation relation with ABS program configurations.*

Proof. (sketch) We need to prove that, for any program configuration c, if $c \to_r c'$ for some ABS semantic rule r, then there exists a marking in the net M' and a *sequence* of enabled transitions w, such that $\alpha(c) \xrightarrow{w} M'$ and $\alpha(c') \subseteq M'$ (where, with $\subseteq$ we denote the subset relation between sets of multi sets) ☐

6   Resource Analysis and Management

We now show how state space exploration of the CPN model can be used to reason about starvation freedom of an ABS program. In presence of possible starvation, we show the state space of the CPN model can be used to synthesise a sequence of resource reconfigurations which can eliminate starvation. Finally, we show how the sequence of resource reconfiguration can be used to automatically obtain an implementation of a starvation free load balancer.

For the resource analysis, we rely on the model checker of CPN Tools applied on an Intel i7 3.4 GHz. We use the running example from the previous sections for illustration purposes, but our analysis approach generalises to instantiations of the CPN model. The state space for the running example has 776 nodes (states) and 1069 arcs (occurring events) and could be generated in less than 1 s.

For our analysis, we also rely on the strongly connected components (SCCs) of the state space. The SCCs could be generated in less than 1 s and contains 719 nodes (SCCs) and 988 arcs connecting the SCCs.

6.1   Resource Analysis

Section 4 covered the deployment layer as a CPN model. We obtained the execution cost of a program by adding cost tags to the tokens representing the active objects. More concretely, we matched each process of the process pool with the corresponding cost. Recall that the colour of an active object is represented as a triple (ob, dc, lst), where ob is the object identifier, dc is the deployment component where the object is being executed, and lst is the process pool of the objects. The latter is represented as a list of triples $(proc, cost, bool)$ where $proc$ is the process identifier, $cost$ is the related execution cost to the current process, and $bool$ is boolean flag indicating whether the process has fully executed (value $true$) or not (value $false$). The head of lst represents the active process.

As shown in Fig. 7, the model has been constructed with place Current State which record the resource availability of each deployment component by hosting the corresponding tokens of colour (dc, cap), where dc is the deployment component identifier and cap its resource capacity. In addition, the place Starving Objects holds tokens representing the objects whose execution has been blocked because of lack of resources at the current time interval. In the following, we explain in detail how to perform resource analysis using the markings of those places.

The first important information related to resource management is whether the current resource distribution provides sufficient resources for the full execution of the processes the objects have in their process pools. In other words, we need to check for *starvation freedom*. By model construction, place Starving Objects keeps track of the starving objects, if any. For the analysis, we implement the following Standard ML queries in CPN Tools for checking starvation freedom:

```
fun findStarvingObjects n =
 let
   val mSO  = Mark.Process_Execution'Starving_Objects_p9 1 n
   val soid = List.map (fn (ao,_,_) => ao) mSO
 in soid end

fun anyStarving n = (findStarvingObjects n) <> nil
fun anySO ()      = PredAllNodes anyStarving
```

Function findStarvingObjects takes a state (marking) n as argument and extract the list of object identifiers from any tokens on place Starving Objects. Such object identifiers represent objects that are starving in state n. This function is then used in the predicate anyStarving which can be used to determine whether or not there are any starving objects in state n. The anyStarving predicate is then used as a higher-order argument to the built-in query function `PredAllNodes` which returns the list of all those states where the `anyStarving` predicate holds, i.e., all states where there are some object starving.

For our running example, CPN Tools returns a non-empty list containing several states which imply that starvation is possible. Since the current resource distribution may lead to starvation, an interesting question is *whether there exists a resource reallocation strategy leading to starvation freedom*. For that, we need to check for the existence of any terminal SCC containing states where there are no starving objects and then ask for a path leading to that state. This involves writing queries of similar complexity as was shown above and consists of:

- a function that checks whether a SCC is non-starving, i.e. whether it consist of only states where the marking of place Starving Objects is empty.
- a function searching for a non-starving SCC among the terminal SCCs ones.
- a function that returns the path from the initial marking to a state in one on the non-starving terminal SCCs.

In the last case, we are interested only in the information related to resource transfer. Recall that the module Component Reconfiguration (see Fig. 6) is related to the resource refill, and the Reconfigure transition related to the resource transfer. We therefore filtered the path returned from CPN Tools to show only the occurrences and binding elements of this transition, where the binding specifies the values bound to the variables of the transition. This is the synthesised sequence of the resource transfers we need to perform in order to avoid starvation. For our running example, this resulted in the following sequence of resource transfers:

[Component Reconfiguration'Reconfigure
$(1, \{b = true, cap = 1, \text{config} = [(1,1),(2,2)], \text{fromdc} = 1, \text{todc} = 2\})$
$(1, \{b = true, cap = 3, \text{config} = [(1,0),(2,3)], \text{fromdc} = 2, \text{todc} = 1\})$
$(1, \{b = true, cap = 2, \text{config} = [(1,3),(2,0)], \text{fromdc} = 1, \text{todc} = 2\})]$

The first line shows the module and the transition of which we get the binding elements. In the tuples that follow, "*b*" is a guard of the transition, "*cap*" is the amount of the resources we need to move, "config" is the current resource distribution, "fromdc" is the source deployment component and "todc" is the target deployment component. The resource transfer represented by the sequence hence provides a non-starvation strategy.

6.2   Resource Management: Load Balancing

Above, we saw how the state space analysis of the CPN model can be used to prove starvation freedom or, in case of possible starvation to synthesise a path from the initial resource distribution to a starvation free state of a terminal SCC. In the rest of this section, we will see how this path can be used in load balancing.

Recall that in ABS, the discrete time follows maximal progress semantics: the time advances when no further execution can happen. In that case, the resources are refilled according to the transfer command, if any; otherwise they are updated as in the previous time interval. Recall also that the colour of the deployment components is (dc, cap) where the first element is the deployment component identifier and the second one its capacity. As an example, the pair $(1, 2)$ means that the deployment component 1 has a capacity of 2 resources.

Let us consider again our running example. Below follows a more detailed version of the path discussed in Sect. 6.1. For the sake of simplicity, we present only the name of the transition followed by the corresponding binding. The enumeration in the left corresponds to the respective ABS time point:

[Imperative Layer(1, {$cap = 1, cap1 = 2$})
t =0 Resource Refill(1, config = $[(1, 1), (2, 2), \text{oldconfig} = [(1, 1), (2, 2)]\}$)
...

Reconfigure(1, {$b = true, cap = 1, \text{config} = [(1, 1), (2, 2)], \text{fromdc} = 1, \text{todc} = 2$})
Reconfigure Done(1, {$b = false$})
t=1 Resource Refill(1, config = $[(1, 0), (2, 3), \text{oldconfig} = [(1, 0), (2, 0)]\}$)
...

Reconfigure Done(1, {$b = true$})
t=2 Resource Refill(1, config = $[(1, 0), (2, 3), \text{oldconfig} = [(1, 0), (2, 0)]\}$)
...

Reconfigure(1, {$b = true, cap = 3, \text{config} = [(1, 0), (2, 3)], \text{fromdc} = 2, \text{todc} = 1$})
Reconfigure Done(1, {$b = false$})
t=3 Resource Refill(1, config = $[(1, 3), (2, 0), \text{oldconfig} = [(1, 0), (2, 0)]\}$)
...

Reconfigure Done(1, {$b = true$})
t= 4 Resource Refill(1, config = $[(1, 3), (2, 0), \text{oldconfig} = [(1, 0), (2, 0)]\}$)
...

Reconfigure(1, {$b = true, cap = 2, \text{config} = [(1, 3), (2, 0)], \text{fromdc} = 1, \text{todc} = 2$})]
Reconfigure Done(1, {$b = false$})
t=5 Resource Refill(1, config = $[(1, 1), (2, 2), \text{oldconfig} = [(1, 1), (2, 0)]$)]

In the above path, the highlighted lines are resource transfers that will lead to a starvation free state, as we saw in Sect. 6.1. In our example, we consider two objects located in two deployment components. The first line shows the resource initialisation. The variables cap and $cap1$ refer, respectively, to the capacities of the first and the second deployment component. Hence we obtain the initial distribution: $(1, 1), (2, 2)$. During the first time interval, the highlighted line shows that we need to transfer 1 resource (variable cap) from the first deployment component (variable fromdc) to the second one (variable todc). Here, we notice that the variables are local to each transition, hence a possible name reuse (e.g. cap) should not create confusion. As a result of the first transfer, we obtain the distribution $(1, 0), (2, 3)$, as we can see at the corresponding resource refill (variable config) of the beginning of the second time interval (when $t = 1$). During the second time interval, we do not need to transfer resources, hence the refill of the beginning of the third time interval (when $t = 2$) updates the resources according to the last distribution, i.e. $(1, 0), (2, 3)$. Similarly, we obtain the distributions $(1, 3), (2, 0)$ when $t = 3$, $(1, 3), (2, 0)$ when $t = 4$ (no transfer) and $(1, 1), (2, 2)$ when $t = 5$.

```
 1  class Balancer(DC telcomp, DC smscomp) {
 2    Unit run() {
 3      telcomp!transfer(smscomp,1);
 4      await duration(2,2);
 5      smscomp!transfer(telcomp, 3);
 6      await duration(2,2);
 7      telcomp!transfer(smscomp,2);
 8  }}
 9  {// Main block
10    ... // deployment components, etc. as before
11    new Balancer(telcomp,smscomp);
12  }
```

Fig. 8. Implementation of load balancer.

The variable oldconfig of the transition Resource Refill shows the available resources that we have before time advances. Because of the maximal progress semantics of ABS, the second component of each pair should be zero in all the time intervals except the extremal ones: the first is the initialisation and the last one shows that we have remaining 1 resource at the first deployment component after the full execution of the processes of the first object. This is possible since the last state is starvation free.

From the above path information we can implement very easily a load balancer like the one of Fig. 8. We match object "1" with the telephone service and object "2" with the SMS service and we assume they are located at the deployment components "telcomp" and "smscomp", respectively, having the capacities as in the model, i.e. 1 and 2. In our load balancer we applied the strategy given by the path explained above, so we transfer 1 resource from the deployment component "telcomp" to the "smscomp" during the first time interval, 3 resources from the deployment component "smscomp" to the "telcomp" during the third time interval, and 2 resources from the deployment component "telcomp" to the "smscomp" during the fourth time interval. Notice here that each time we transfer resources, they take place at the next time interval according to the semantics of ABS.

7   Conclusions and Related Work

We have presented a CPN model of the deployment fragment of ABS [29], a resource aware programming language suitable for cloud applications. A key characteristics of our approach is that the compact modelling supported by CPNs allowed us to develop a CPN model capable of simulating any ABS program by only changing the initial marking. The main benefit of our approach is the ability to use model checking techniques to identify starvation of resource aware active objects, and to synthesise reconfiguration sequences that eliminates starvation and which in turn can be used to automatically obtain load-balancer implementations.

Some of the earliest applications of CPNs for analysis of distributed objects appeared in [30] focussing on spatial distribution of objects and not resource consumption. Early work [35] also considered simulation-based capacity planning of web-servers, but not in a context with dynamically configurable resources. CPNs have also recently been used to analyze deadlock situations for active objects with futures by de Boer et al. [10,11] and by the authors [19], as found in the ABS language. More recent work [14] has considered the COSTA language [3] for deployment and management of cloud applications. Their work, however, focused on the deployment language and management operations. COSTA is able to approximate the computational cost of a program, but do not provide resource management. Recent work [23] has also explored evaluation of cloud deployment strategies for distributed NoSQL databases using CPN simulation, but without dynamic reconfiguration. In contrast to previous modelling of programming languages into Petri nets like Ada, Java, Orc ([15,24,32]) where the model depends on the program, we suggest a fixed sized model where the markings are program configuration abstractions, hence different programs can be analysed by one single model upon different initialisation (according to the abstraction function).

More broadly, process algebras [7], priced [13] and probabilistic [6] automata have been proposed for performance analysis of embedded systems with resource constraints. Also, other resource analysis on resource aware programs like [34] and [21], target to guarantee that the program cost does not exceed a resource threshold. Our work is not restricted only to the guarantee of resource sufficiency, but also in case of possible starvation, proposes strategies for vertical scaling that can be retrieved by the counter examples of CPN Tools.

Our present work extends [19] by taking as input the communication status of resource aware active objects and performing resource analysis. We demonstrated how to statically construct a load balancer. A direction for future work will be to extend the model to support dynamic load balancing and investigate optimal vertical scaling using the CPN model checker. Another direction will be to perform a comprehensive experimental evaluation on a larger set of ABS programs.

References

1. Agha, G., Hewitt, C.: Concurrent programming using actors. Object-Oriented Concurrent Programming, pp. 37–53. The MIT Press, Cambridge (1987)
2. Agha, G.: ACTORS: A Model of Concurrent Computations in Distributed Systems. The MIT Press, Cambridge (1986)
3. Albert, E., Arenas, P., Genaim, S., Puebla, G., Zanardini, D.: Cost analysis of object-oriented bytecode programs. Theor. Comput. Sci. **413**(1), 142–159 (2012)
4. Albert, E., et al.: Formal modeling and analysis of resource management for cloud architectures: an industrial case study using real-time ABS. J. Serv.-Oriented Comput. Appl. **8**(4), 323–339 (2014)

5. Armstrong, J.: Programming Erlang: Software for a Concurrent World. Pragmatic Bookshelf, Dallas (2007)
6. Baier, C., Haverkort, B.R., Hermanns, H., Katoen, J.: Performance evaluation and model checking join forces. Commun. ACM **53**(9), 76–85 (2010)
7. Barbanera, F., Bugliesi, M., Dezani-Ciancaglini, M., Sassone, V.: Space-aware ambients and processes. Theor. Comput. Sci. **373**(1–2), 41–69 (2007)
8. Bjørk, J., de Boer, F.S., Johnsen, E.B., Schlatte, R., Tapia Tarifa, S.L.: User-defined schedulers for real-time concurrent objects. Innov. Syst. Softw. Eng. **9**(1), 29–43 (2013)
9. de Boer, F., et al.: A survey of active object languages. ACM Comput. Surv. **50**(5), 76:1–76:39 (2017)
10. de Boer, F.S., Bravetti, M., Grabe, I., Lee, M., Steffen, M., Zavattaro, G.: A petri net based analysis of deadlocks for active objects and futures. In: Păsăreanu, C.S., Salaün, G. (eds.) FACS 2012. LNCS, vol. 7684, pp. 110–127. Springer, Heidelberg (2013). https://doi.org/10.1007/978-3-642-35861-6_7
11. de Boer, F.S., Bravetti, M., Lee, M.D., Zavattaro, G.: A petri net based modeling of active objects and futures. Fundam. Inform. **159**(3), 197–256 (2018)
12. de Boer, F.S., Clarke, D., Johnsen, E.B.: A complete guide to the future. In: De Nicola, R. (ed.) ESOP 2007. LNCS, vol. 4421, pp. 316–330. Springer, Heidelberg (2007). https://doi.org/10.1007/978-3-540-71316-6_22
13. Bouyer, P., Fahrenberg, U., Larsen, K.G., Markey, N.: Quantitative analysis of real-time systems using priced timed automata. Commun. ACM **54**(9), 78–87 (2011)
14. Brogi, A., Canciani, A., Soldani, J., Wang, P.: Petri net-based approach to model and analyze the management of cloud applications. ToPNoC **XI**, 28–48 (2016)
15. Bruni, R., Melgratti, H., Tuosto, E.: Translating orc features into petri nets and the join calculus. In: Bravetti, M., Núñez, M., Zavattaro, G. (eds.) WS-FM 2006. LNCS, vol. 4184, pp. 123–137. Springer, Heidelberg (2006). https://doi.org/10.1007/11841197_8
16. Caromel, D., Henrio, L.: A Theory of Distributed Objects. Springer, Berlin (2005). https://doi.org/10.1007/b138812
17. Din, C.C., Bubel, R., Hähnle, R.: KeY-ABS: a deductive verification tool for the concurrent modelling language ABS. In: Felty, A.P., Middeldorp, A. (eds.) CADE 2015. LNCS (LNAI), vol. 9195, pp. 517–526. Springer, Cham (2015). https://doi.org/10.1007/978-3-319-21401-6_35
18. Din, C.C., Owe, O.: Compositional reasoning about active objects with shared futures. Formal Asp. Comput. **27**(3), 551–572 (2015)
19. Gkolfi, A., Din, C.C., Johnsen, E.B., Steffen, M., Yu, I.C.: Translating active objects into colored petri nets for communication analysis. In: Dastani, M., Sirjani, M. (eds.) FSEN 2017. LNCS, vol. 10522, pp. 84–99. Springer, Cham (2017). https://doi.org/10.1007/978-3-319-68972-2_6
20. Gkolfi, A., Johnsen, E.B., Kristensen, L.M., Yu, I.C.: Using coloured petri nets for resource analysis of active objects (full version). Technical report 484, Department of informatics, University of Oslo (2018)
21. Gordon, A.D. (ed.): ESOP 2010. LNCS, vol. 6012. Springer, Heidelberg (2010). https://doi.org/10.1007/978-3-642-11957-6
22. Haller, P., Odersky, M.: Scala actors: unifying thread-based and event-based programming. Theor. Comput. Sci. **410**(2–3), 202–220 (2009)
23. Huang, X., Wang, J., Qiao, J., Zheng, L., Zhang, J., Wong, R.K.: Performance and replica consistency simulation for quorum-based NoSQL system cassandra. In: van der Aalst, W., Best, E. (eds.) PETRI NETS 2017. LNCS, vol. 10258, pp. 78–98. Springer, Cham (2017). https://doi.org/10.1007/978-3-319-57861-3_6

24. Ichbiah, J., Barnes, J.G.P., Heliard, J.C., Krieg-Brückner, B., Roubine, O., Wichmann, B.A.: Modules and visibility in the Ada programming language. On the Construction of Programs, pp. 153–192. Cambridge University Press, Cambridge (1980)
25. Jensen, K., Kristensen, L.M.: Coloured Petri Nets - Modelling and Validation of Concurrent Systems. Springer, Berlin (2009). https://doi.org/10.1007/b95112
26. Johnsen, E.B., Hähnle, R., Schäfer, J., Schlatte, R., Steffen, M.: ABS: a core language for abstract behavioral specification. In: Aichernig, B.K., de Boer, F.S., Bonsangue, M.M. (eds.) FMCO 2010. LNCS, vol. 6957, pp. 142–164. Springer, Heidelberg (2011). https://doi.org/10.1007/978-3-642-25271-6_8
27. Johnsen, E.B., Owe, O., Schlatte, R., Tapia Tarifa, S.L.: Dynamic resource reallocation between deployment components. In: Dong, J.S., Zhu, H. (eds.) ICFEM 2010. LNCS, vol. 6447, pp. 646–661. Springer, Heidelberg (2010). https://doi.org/10.1007/978-3-642-16901-4_42
28. Johnsen, E.B., Schlatte, R., Tapia Tarifa, S.L.: Modeling resource-aware virtualized applications for the cloud in real-time ABS. In: Aoki, T., Taguchi, K. (eds.) ICFEM 2012. LNCS, vol. 7635, pp. 71–86. Springer, Heidelberg (2012). https://doi.org/10.1007/978-3-642-34281-3_8
29. Johnsen, E.B., Schlatte, R., Tapia Tarifa, S.L.: Integrating deployment architectures and resource consumption in timed object-oriented models. J. Log.Al Algebr. Methods Program. 84(1), 67–91 (2015)
30. Jørgensen, J.B., Mortensen, K.H.: Modelling and analysis of distributed program execution in BETA using coloured petri nets. In: Billington, J., Reisig, W. (eds.) ICATPN 1996. LNCS, vol. 1091, pp. 249–268. Springer, Heidelberg (1996). https://doi.org/10.1007/3-540-61363-3_14
31. Larsen, K.G., Pettersson, P., Yi, W.: UPPAAL in a nutshell. Int. J. Softw. Tools Technol. Transf. 1(1–2), 134–152 (1997)
32. Long, B., Strooper, P.A., Wildman, L.: A method for verifying concurrent Java components based on an analysis of concurrency failures. Concurr. Comput.: Pract. Exp. 19(3), 281–294 (2007)
33. Reisig, W., Rozenberg, G. (eds.): Lectures on Petri Nets I: Basic Models - Advances in Petri Nets. Springer, Berlin (1998). https://doi.org/10.1007/3-540-65306-6
34. Shao, Z., Pierce, B.C. (eds.): Proceedings of the 36th ACM SIGPLAN-SIGACT Symposium on Principles of Programming Languages, POPL 2009. ACM (2009)
35. Wells, L., Christensen, S., Kristensen, L.M., Mortensen, K.H.: Simulation based performance analysis of web servers. In: Proceedings of PNPM'01, pp. 59–68 (2001)

Adaptive Formal Framework for WMN Routing Protocols

Mojgan Kamali[1](✉) and Ansgar Fehnker[2](✉)

[1] Åbo Akademi University, Turku, Finland
[2] University of Twente, Enschede, The Netherlands
mojgan.kamali@abo.fi, ansgar.fehnker@utwente.nl

Abstract. Wireless Mesh Networks (WMNs) are self-organising and self-healing wireless networks that provide support for broadband communication without requiring fixed infrastructure. A determining factor for the performance and reliability of such networks is the routing protocols applied in these networks. Formal modelling and verification of routing protocols are challenging tasks, often skipped by protocol designers. Despite some commonality between different models of routing protocols that have been published, these models are often tailored to a specific protocol which precludes easily comparing models. This paper presents an adaptive, generic and reusable framework as well as crucial generic properties w.r.t. system requirements, to model and verify WMN routing protocols. In this way, protocol designers can adapt the generic models based on protocol specifications and verify routing protocols prior to implementation. This model uses Uppaal SMC to identify the main common components of routing protocols, capturing timing aspect of protocols, communication between nodes, probabilities of message loss and link breakage, etc.

1 Introduction

Wireless Mesh Networks (WMNs) are self-organising and self-healing wireless networks that provide support for broadband communication without requiring fixed infrastructure. They provide rapid and low-cost network deployment and have been applied in a wide range of application areas such as public safety, emergency response networks, battlefield areas, etc.

A determining factor for the performance and reliability of such networks is the routing protocols applied in these networks. Routing protocols specify the way of communication among nodes of the network and find appropriate paths on which data packets are sent. They are grouped into two main categories: proactive and reactive routing protocols. Proactive protocols rely on the periodic broadcasting of control messages through the network (time-dependent) and have the information available for routing data packets. Reactive protocols, in contrast, behave on-demand, meaning that when a packet targeting some destination is injected into the network they start the route discovery process.

© Springer Nature Switzerland AG 2018
K. Bae and P. C. Ölveczky (Eds.): FACS 2018, LNCS 11222, pp. 175–195, 2018.
https://doi.org/10.1007/978-3-030-02146-7_9

Previous studies of routing protocols mostly rely on simulation approaches and testbed experiments. These are appropriate techniques for performance analysis but are limited in the sense that it is not possible to simulate systems for all possible scenarios. Formal techniques, mathematically languages and approaches, are used to complement testbed experiments and simulation approaches. They provide tools to design and verify WMN routing protocols, allow to model protocols precisely and to provide counterexamples to diagnose their flaws.

Statistical Model checking (SMC) combines model checking with simulation techniques to overcome the barrier of analysing large systems as well as providing both qualitative and quantitative analysis. Uppaal SMC monitors simulation traces of the system and uses sequential hypothesis testing or Monte Carlo simulation (for qualitative and quantitative analysis respectively) to decide if the intended system property is satisfied with a given degree of confidence. Statistical model checking does not guarantee a 100% correct result, but it is able to provide limits on the probability that an error occurs. In this work, we apply Uppaal SMC [7], the statistical extension of Uppaal.

Contributions. Our work has been inspired by the fact that formal modelling and verification of routing protocols seem challenging tasks. Protocol designers often decide on skipping this level of development. We provide an adaptive, generic and reusable framework as well as crucial generic properties w.r.t. system requirements, to model and verify WMN routing protocols. In this way, protocol designers can adapt the generic models based on protocol specifications and verify routing protocols prior to implementation.

In particular, this study describes how to build reusable components within the constraints imposed by the Uppaal modelling language. It identifies the main components that routing protocols have in common, and how to map them to data structures, processes, channels, and timed automata in the Uppaal language. We show the validity and applicability of our models by modelling Better Approach To Mobile Ad-hoc Networking (BATMAN) [19], Optimised Link State Routing (OLSR) [5], and Ad-hoc On-demand Distance Vector version2 (AODVv2) [21] protocols using our framework.

Outline: The paper is structured as follows: in Sect. 2, we give an overview of the formal modelling language used in this paper. Then in Sect. 3, we shortly overview the general structure of WMN routing protocols. Section 4 is the core of this paper where we discuss our generic Uppaal framework as well as our generic Uppaal properties. Section 5 demonstrates the adaptability of our framework, sketching examples of BATMAN, OLSR, and AODVv2 protocols. We discuss related work in Sect. 6 and draw conclusions as well as propose future research directions in Sect. 7.

2   Modelling Language

Most routing protocols of WMNs have complex behaviour, e.g., real-time behaviour, and formal modelling and verification of such systems end up being

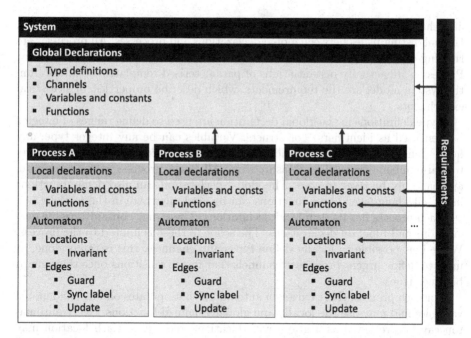

Fig. 1. Common structure of Uppaal models. Arrow denote access to variables and functions. Location names are treated like Booleans by the requirements.

a challenging task. Moreover, choosing a formal modelling language which considers the significant characteristic of these protocols is an important step in the development of a formal framework. In this work, we apply Uppaal SMC (which is based on stochastic time automata) to be able to realistically model timing behaviour, wireless communication, probabilistic behaviour, and complex data structure of routing protocols. In addition, the Uppaal GUI and Uppaal simulator provide a visualised interpretation of the system which makes the task of modelling easier. We describe the basic definitions that are used in Uppaal SMC.

2.1 Uppaal Timed Automata

The theory of timed automata [1] is applied for modelling, analysing and verifying the behaviour of real-time systems. A finite timed automaton is defined as a graph consisting of finite sets of locations and edges (transitions), together with a finite set of clocks having real values. The logical clocks of automata are initialised with zero and are increased with the same rate. Each location may have an invariant, and each edge may have guards (possibly clock guards) which allow a transition to be taken, and/or actions that can be updates of some variables and/or clocks.

The modelling language of Uppaal extends timed automata as defined by Alur and Dill [1] with various features, such as types, data structures, etc [2]. A system is a network of timed automata that can synchronise on channels and shared variables. Fig. 1 depicts the common structure of Uppaal models. Uppaal distinguishes between global declarations and processes. All processes are running concurrently at the same level, and the model has no further hierarchy. Processes are actually instantiations of parameterised templates. Separate from the system model are the requirements, which describe properties, or statistical experiments.

Type definitions in the global declaration are used to define ranges of integers – often used as identifiers – or structs. Variables can be any integer type, any newly defined type, channels, and arrays of these. Clock variables that evaluate to real numbers are used to measure time. All clocks progress at the same rate, and can only be reset to zero. The global declaration can also define functions in a C-like language. These functions can be used anywhere in the model.

Each process has its own local declarations. These may contain variable declarations and function declarations. The scope of these is limited to the process. While it is possible to locally define types and channels, this is rarely done; at most to define urgent broadcast channels that force transitions once their guard becomes true.

For each process, there exists an automaton that operates on local and global variables and may use the locally and globally defined functions. Every automaton can be presented as a graph with locations and edges. Each location may have an invariant, and each edge may have a guard, a synchronisation label, and/or an update of some variables.

Synchronisation between automata happens via channels. For every channel a there is one label $a!$ to identify the sender, and $a?$ to identify receivers. Transitions without a label are internal; all other transitions use either binary handshake or broadcast synchronisation. Uppaal SMC supports only broadcast channels [7]:

Broadcast synchronisation means that one automaton with a !-edge synchronises with several other automata that all have an edge with a relevant ?-label. The initiating automaton is able to change its location, and apply its update if and only if the guard on its edge is satisfied. It does not need a second automaton to synchronise with. Matching ?-edge automata must synchronise if their guards evaluate to true in the current state. They will change their location and update their states. First, the automaton with the !-edge updates its state, then the other automata follow. If more than one automaton can initiate a transition on a !-edge, the choice is made non-deterministically.

Due to the structure of the Uppaal model, automata cannot exchange data directly. A common workaround is the following: If an automaton wants to send data to another automaton, it synchronises on a channel. It writes the data to a global variable during an update, which is then copied by the second automaton to its local variable during its update.

Also, due to the scoping rules, one automaton cannot use a method of one of the other automata, for example, to query its state. The common workaround is to make either a duplicate of important information global, or to have the information global, and have a self-imposed rule on which a process can read and write and to what part of the global variables.

In addition to the system model, it is possible to define requirements. Requirements can access all global and local variables, and use global and local functions, as long as they are side-effect free, i.e. they do not change variables outside of the scope of the function. Requirements can iterate over finite ranges, using `forall`, `exists`, or sum iterators.

Uppaal has several other keywords to define the behaviour of delays and transitions, such as `urgent` or `priority`. The discussion of these is outside of the scope of this paper. The common structure of Uppaal, with its scoping rules, however, is relevant for this paper, as it sets the framework in which we have to develop our generic model.

2.2 Uppaal Stochastic Timed Automata

Uppaal SMC [7] is a trade off between classical model checking and simulation, monitoring only some simulation traces of the system and uses sequential hypothesis testing or Monte Carlo simulation (for qualitative and quantitative analysis respectively) to determine whether or not the intended system property is satisfied with a given degree of confidence.

The modelling formalism of Uppaal SMC is based on the extension of Uppaal timed automata described earlier in this section. For each timed automata component, non-deterministic choices between several enabled transitions assigned by probability choices, refine the stochastic interpretation. A model in Uppaal SMC can consist of a network of stochastic timed automata that communicate via broadcast channels and shared variables.

Classical Uppaal's verifier uses a fragment of Computation Tree Logic (CTL) to model system properties. Uppaal SMC adds to its query language elements of the Metric Interval Temporal Logic (MITL) to support probability estimation, hypothesis testing, and probability comparison, and in addition the evaluation of expected values [7].

The algorithm for probability estimation [12] computes the required number of runs to define an approximation interval $[p - \epsilon, p + \epsilon]$ where p is the probability with a confidence 1-α. The values of ϵ (probabilistic *uncertainty*) and α (*false negatives*) are selected by the user and the number of runs is calculated using the Chernoff–Hoeffding bound. In Uppaal SMC, the query has the form: $\Pr[bound](\phi)$, where *bound* shows the time bound of the simulations and ϕ is the expression (path formula).

Evaluation of expected values of a max of an expression which can be evaluated to a clock or an integer value is also supported by Uppaal SMC. In this case, the *bound* and the number of runs (N) are given explicitly and then max of the given expression (*expr*) is evaluated. The query has the form: $\mathrm{E}[bound; N](\mathtt{max} : expr))$; an explicit confidence interval is also required for these type of queries.

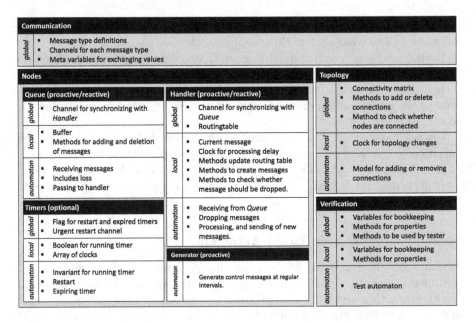

Fig. 2. Generic structure of a WMN routing protocol model for verification, with respect to typical structure of an Uppaal model.

3   Overview Uppaal Model of WMN Routing Protocols

WMN routing protocols disseminate information in the network to provide the basis for selecting routes. Routing protocols specify which control messages should be sent through the network. These messages are received/lost by other network nodes. Receiving nodes update their information about other nodes based on received messages. Network nodes can send data packets to destinations in the network using discovered paths. Figure 2 depicts the main components that define a routing protocol model.

Communication. The protocol has to specify the types of control messages and the information they contain. This information consists of originator address, originator sequence number, etc. The model has to specify whether a message is sent as a unicast or as a multicast message[1].

Topology. The network topology shows how nodes are connected to each other. Connectivity is commonly modelled as an adjacency matrix. The model should provide methods to add and delete connections, as well as a model that determines how the topology changes. This paper uses a simple model of link failure; a more elaborate study of dynamic topologies can be found in [10].

---

[1] To avoid confusion, we will refer to this type of communication as *multicast*, instead of *broadcast*. We reserve the term *broadcast* for Uppaal channels.

Node. The behaviour of a protocol is defined by the composition of a queue, a handler, and – if the protocol is proactive – by one or more generators, and possibly a number of timers.

Queue. Messages from other nodes should be stored in a buffer or queue. Based on the order of arrival they will be processed later by the handler (first in, first out method is applied for buffers). If different messages arrive to a node at the same time, the choice of the message reception happens non-deterministically. It will use the information in these messages to update the corresponding routing information about sender nodes.

Handler. The handler is the core of the protocol. The handler will receive messages from the queue and update the stored information, which is kept in the routing table. Depending on the content of the message, and the current state of the routing table, the handler further decides whether to drop the message, send a broadcast message to all other neighbouring nodes, or send a unicast message to another node (both broadcast and unicast message consider sending delays).

Different ways of nodes communication (multicast and unicast) are modelled illustrated schematically in Fig. 3. For multicast synchronisation, we use an array of broadcast channels Multicast[], one channel for each node. The invariant and the guard will encode the timing and duration of a transition (message delay). The guard of the corresponding edge of the receiving node – which will be part of its queue model– will encode the connectivity, i.e., it will not synchronise if the nodes are not connected. The sender will take the edge, regardless of whether other nodes are connected.

Unicast is modelled by a two-dimensional array of channels Unicast[][], one channel for each pair of nodes. Unicast messages assume that on a lower level reception is acknowledged. If this fails, for example, if the nodes are not connected, the sender has to take an alternative transition. A typical alternative would be to multicast an error message or initiate a route request.

Generator. Proactive protocols send control messages at regular intervals. They highly depend on on-time broadcasting of their control messages in order to keep track of network information. Hence, each node includes also a model to generate those messages.

Timers. A protocol may use simple timers that can be reset, and expire after a set time. They can be used by the handler, to time delays or the duration of different modes of operation.

Verification. Since the model will be used for verification, the models will include parts that are only included for this purpose. This will include variables for bookkeeping and methods that check conditions on existing data structures. For this reason, the routing table of the handler was made global, to give access to verifications methods. Otherwise, the routing tables could be a local variable of the corresponding handler. The verification part of the model also often includes a test automaton, which may insert messages, change the topology, and record progress in response to certain events.

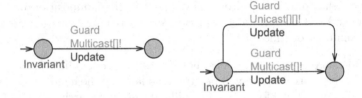

Fig. 3. Unicast and broadcast synchronisation.

The section omits the discussion of type definitions and constants that are used throughout the model. The next section will provide more detail on the various components of the Uppaal model.

4   Generic Uppaal Framework

Our framework consists of global declarations which are global in the system and accessible/updatable by all automata as well as local declarations that are exclusive to each automaton, i.e., these declarations can be accessed and updated only by the automaton itself. There are in total six templates for automata in our framework; four of them are used for modelling protocols and two are concerned with verification. The models are adaptable to protocol specifications, and they are available at http://users.abo.fi/mokamali/FACS2018.

4.1   Communication

To facilitate communication between network nodes in the model, there are a number of global declarations and type definitions. The number of nodes is `const int N`. Addresses of nodes are of type `typedef int[0, N - 1] IP`.

Communication can take place via unicast or multicast messages. The model includes the following channels:

```
broadcast chan   unicast[N][N];
broadcast chan multicast[N];
urgent broadcast chan tau[N];
broadcast chan   newpkt[N];
```

The `tau` channel is used to have internal transitions take place as soon as enabled. They are not used for synchronisation. The `newpkt` channel is used to insert a new packet at a given node.

A protocol must define for each type of message the message format. The reference implementation provides example for packets, route request messages, route reply messages, route error messages, and control messages, also known as TC messages. The format of a TC message, for example, is defined as:

```
typedef struct {
  IP oip;    //originator IP
```

```
    int hops; //hops
    TTLT ttl; //time-to-live
    IP sip;   //sender IP
    SQN osn;  //originator sequence number
} TCMSG;
```

The model will include a similar type definition for all types of messages. To make the treatment of message uniform we then define a generic message type as follows:

```
typedef struct {
    MSGTYPE msgtype; //Type of message
    TCMSG tc;        //TC message
    PACKET packet;   //Packet
    RREQMSG rreq;    //Route request msg
    RREPMSG rrep;    //Unicast route reply msg
    RERRMSG rerr;    //Route error msg
} MSG;
```

The field msgtype is an index into which type of message is being sent; only the corresponding field should be set. This construction is a work-around for not having *union types* in the Uppaal language.

Each type of message also comes with functions that generate a message of that type. They will be used for convenience and succinctness in the model. It also includes a global variable MSG msgglobal, which a sender copies into, and recipients copy from.

4.2   Topology

The network topology is defined by an adjacency matrix topology[N][N] with boolean type showing the directed connectivity between nodes, i.e., element 1 in the matrix shows that two nodes are directly connected and 0 indicates that two nodes are not connected directly, however they may be connected via some intermediate nodes. The connectivity between nodes is modelled by function bool isconnected(IP i, IP j), and links can be dropped by calling function void drop (IP i,IP j).

While protocols have to deal with mobility, the mobility models themselves are outside of the scope of this paper and these routing protocols. The processes that establish or delete links – and whether these processes are non-deterministic, stochastic, or probabilistic – are not part of the protocols themselves. The reference model includes a simple model TopologyChanger that drops between randomly selected nodes at a rate of 1 : 10. More elaborate models for changing topologies can be found in [10].

We should add here that even if we define a topology matrix to show the direct connectivity between nodes, the network is still wireless. It means that network nodes are not aware of each other before receiving the control messages, and they realise the connectivity only after they receive/process control messages from their neighbours.

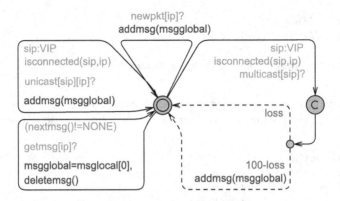

Fig. 4. *Queue* automaton.

4.3   Node

The model for a node using a reactive protocol comprises of two automata, the *Queue* and the *Handler*, proactive protocols also include a Generator. If the protocol uses timers, the model includes a fourth automaton to manage the timers. The generic model defines a number of global variables and channels to facilitate synchronisation between these parts. For instance, channel imsg[N] is an urgent channel which is used for synchronisation between *Handler* and *Queue* automata.

Queue. The template of the queue defines a number of local constants and variables to manage the stored messages. The most important variable is an array MSG msglocal[QLength]. The reference model includes methods void addmsg(MSG msg) and void deletemsg() to add or delete messages from the queue. For synchronisation with the *Handler* the model includes a global variable bool isMsgInQ[N] to encode whether a queue contains at least one message.

The automaton for the queue has essentially one control location, as depicted in Fig.4. It has one self-loop for unicast messages, and one loop for multicast messages that can be received, and one for new packets that are inserted by the tester. The latter loop includes a probabilistic choice to lose the message with probability of loss. The automaton also includes a loop, labelled getmsg?, for the handler to request the first element of the queue.

Handler (Reactive/Proactive). Nodes have routing tables that store information about other nodes of the network which are empty (initialised to 0 at the beginning) and may be updated when they receive control messages from their neighbour nodes (conditions on when to update routing tables can be specific to each protocol). The reference implementation defines an entry to the routing table as:

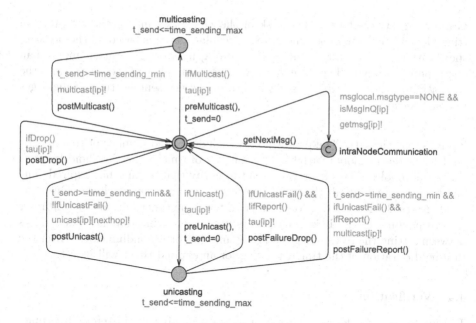

Fig. 5. *Handler* automaton.

```
typedef struct
{ IP dip;
  SQN dsn;
  int hops;
  IP nhop;
} rtentry;
```

The routing tables are then defined as rtentry art[N][N]. This is a global variable to allow the *Generator* and verification part read access. Protocols may define additional data structures, for example for error handling.

The handler has a main control location, as depicted in Fig. 5. It includes one loop for multicast messages. The transition to location multicasting prepares the message, and waiting in that location up to the permitted amount of time models the message delay, then the transition back to the main location, actually copies the message to the global variable msgglobal, for the queue of the receivers to read. The loop for unicast messages has a similar setup, except that includes the option of failure, as in Fig. 3. One option is to drop the message, the other is to multicast an error message. The model also includes for each message type a loop that drops the message, and a loop that requests a new message from the queue.

Most routing protocols use sequence numbers to keep track of newly received information. The reactive version of the handler includes the sequence number, in the proactive version this is a task for the *Generator*.

Generator (Proactive). The task of the *Generator* in a proactive protocol (time-dependent) is to create messages at regular intervals based on the protocol specification. There may be more than one generator, generating more than one type of message. The *Generator* will use a number of clocks to time the generation of those messages as well as to model the sending time of messages (message delays).

Timers (Optional). The protocol may include a fixed number of timers. The model includes as global variables the number of timers, the threshold for each timer, and boolean flags for restart, and to notify that a timer has expired. The automaton managing all timers of one node, has an array of clocks. Once the handler sets the restart flag for a timer to true, the timer automaton will reset a corresponding clock. This transition is urgent, ensuring that no time expires between setting the restart flag, and resetting the corresponding clock. After the threshold duration of the timer, the flag for an expired timer will be set.

4.4   Verification

The model includes for verification purposes a number of side-effect free functions, that can be used by the properties. This includes function to count the number of delivered packets, and how many routes have been established.

For verification the model also includes an automaton *Tester*. The reference model includes an automaton that injects one new packet after about 50 rounds of communication, after which it proceeds to location `final`.

The reference implementation focuses on three main properties, namely for route establishment, network knowledge and packet delivery. These properties verify the core functionality of protocols, e.g., routing data packets.

Route Establishment. The reference model includes the following property for route establishment:

```
Pr[<=1000](<>(route_establishment(OIP1,DIP1)))
```

The function `route_establishment()` returns true if the node `OIP1`, the source node, has the information about the destination node `DIP1` to later send data packet to the destination. The property computes the probability that the function `route_establishment()` returns true in less than or equal to 1000 time units (this value can be altered based on the system requirements).

Network Knowledge. The reference model includes the following property for the network knowledge:

```
E[<=1000;100](max:total_knowledge())
```

This property computes the expected number of connections that have been discovered by time 1000. The function `total_knowledge()` counts for how many originator/destination pairs a route is known.

Packet Delivery. The property for packet delivery is as follows:

```
E[<=1000;100](max:packet_delivered())
```

Packet delivery property shows the number of data packets being delivered at their destinations. The property returns the expected value during 1000 time units by 100 runs. Function `packet_delivered()` is used to count the number of delivered packets.

5   Experiments

We model three well-known routing protocols of WMNs, namely BATMAN, OLSR, AODVv2, to show the reusability and adaptability of our framework. We also verify these protocols for the three different properties discussed in the last section. Each of these is considered for the following scenarios: (1) 0% message loss and no link failures, (2) 80% message loss and no link failures, and (3) 0% message loss and possible link failures.

For all of our experiments, we inject one packet to an arbitrary source to be delivered to an arbitrary destination. We consider networks in a grid, a linear, a fully connected or a ring topology consisting of 9 nodes, as our framework is independent of the number of nodes in the network. It means that number of nodes in the network is adjustable (larger networks are allowed to have) as long as the tool can manage the number of states in the system (state space should be manageable by the tool). A detailed study of these protocols and verification of the models for all possible combinations and/or larger networks are out of the scope of this paper; we only illustrate the applicability and power of the proposed framework.

The automaton `TopologyChanger` is included in models that exhibits link failure. The rate of failure can be simply adjusted based on the protocol specification. We set this value as rate 1 : 10 for all of our models and experiments, e.g., BATMAN, OLSR, AODVv2 models. As none of the protocols that we considered for this study uses timers, we did not have to include the corresponding automaton.

We conduct our experiments using the following set-up: (i) 3.2 GHz Intel Core i5, with 8GB memory, running the Mac OS X 10.11.6 "El Capitan" operating system; (ii) Uppaal SMC model-checker 64-bit version 4.1.20. In Uppaal SMC, two main statistical parameters α and ϵ, in the interval $[0, 1]$, must be fixed by the user. These parameters indicate the probability of *false negatives* and probabilistic *uncertainty*, respectively. In our experiments, these values, i.e., false negatives (α) and probabilistic uncertainty (ϵ) are both set to 0.05, leading to a confidence level of 95%.

5.1   Better Approach to Mobile Ad-hoc Networking (BATMAN)

BATMAN [19] is a proactive protocol used in WMNs. It decentralises route information, i.e., no node has all the data. Each node only maintains information about the possible best next hop. The protocol has two main aims: first, it discovers all bidirectional links and then identifies the best next hop neighbour for all the other nodes in the network. To provide this information, each node broadcasts originator messages (OGMs) through the network at a regular interval. A node keeps track of the information about other known nodes, stored in the node's routing table. When a node receives a message from its neighbours, it updates this information.

Since BATMAN is a proactive protocol, we include a *Generator* for creating OGMs in addition to the *Handler* and the *Queue*. We adapted our framework based on the model of [4]. Table 1 shows the result of our verification for different topologies. We ran the same experiments for the original model of [4] and we got similar results as we got for our adjusted BATMAN model.

Results show that in case of reliable communication (0% loss), the source nodes can find a path to the destination of the injected packet with the probability in the interval [0.90–1.00] and the routing tables are all populated by periodic exchanging of control messages as they were expected by the specification. The injected packet is delivered at the destination in all types of topologies. When message loss increases to 80%, these values may decrease. The same happens also in case of possible link failures. The verification of the route establishment property (probability estimation) takes on average about 2 s whereas the verification for calculating the number of delivered packets and routing table entries (expected value evaluation) takes on average about 215 s (calculating the expected values is more time-consuming compared to estimating the probability).

5.2   Optimised Link State Routing (OLSR)

OLSR[5], a proactive protocol used in WMNs, bears the benefit of having routes to different destinations available to be used whenever needed. This is done by exchanging control messages, namely HELLO and Topology Control (TC), periodically through the network. Receiving nodes update their routing tables based on the information in the messages so that when a packet to be destined to some destination is injected, it can find the path in routing tables.

OLSR differs from other proactive protocols in the way that it minimises flooding of control messages by selecting so-called Multipoint Relays (MPRs). Informally, an MPR takes over the communication for a set of nodes that are one-hop neighbours of this node; these one-hop neighbours receive all the routing information from the MRPs and hence do not need to send and receive routing information from other parts of the network.

Our model for each node includes in addition to the routing table also data structures to manage the selection of MPRs. The model includes two *Generators*, one for HELLO and one for TC messages, the *Handler* and the *Queue*. We adapted our framework based on the model of [15] and verified our generic properties. Table 2 shows the result of our verification for different topologies. We ran the same experiments for the original model of [15] and we got similar results as we got for our adjusted OLSR model.

Table 1. BATMAN verification results

	Route establishment			Network knowledge			Packet delivery		
	0% loss	80% loss	link failure	0% loss	80% loss	link failure	0% loss	80% loss	link failure
Grid	0.90 − 1.00	0.00 − 0.10	0.88 − 0.98	72	7	70	1	0	0.4
Linear	0.90 − 1.00	0.00 − 0.10	0.00 − 0.10	72	4	36	1	0	0
Fully connected	0.90 − 1.00	0.25 − 0.35	0.90 − 1.00	72	22	72	1	0.1	0.8
Ring	0.90 − 1.00	0.24 − 0.34	0.85 − 0.95	72	4	58	1	0.1	0.6

Table 2. OLSR verification results

	Route establishment			Network knowledge			Packet delivery		
	0% loss	80% loss	link failure	0% loss	80% loss	link failure	0% loss	80% loss	link failure
Grid	0.90 − 1.00	0.33 − 0.43	0.90 − 1.00	72	65	70	1	0	0.3
Linear	0.90 − 1.00	0.00 − 0.10	0.18 − 0.28	72	34	50	1	0	0
Fully connected	0.90 − 1.00	0.90 − 1.00	0.89 − 0.99	72	72	72	1	1	0.5
Ring	0.90 − 1.00	0.90 − 1.00	0.89 − 0.99	72	43	63	1	1	0.6

Table 3. AODVv2 verification results

	Route establishment			Network knowledge			Packet delivery		
	0% loss	80% loss	link failure	0% loss	80% loss	link failure	0% loss	80% loss	link failure
Grid	0.90 − 1.00	0.00 − 0.10	0.14 − 0.24	28	3	21	1	0	0.3
Linear	0.90 − 1.00	0.00 − 0.10	0.00 − 0.10	72	1	8	1	0.1	0
Fully connected	0.90 − 1.00	0.16 − 0.26	0.90 − 1.00	9	21	11	1	0.1	0.8
Ring	0.90 − 1.00	0.11 − 0.21	0.79 − 0.89	30	2	10	1	0	0.7

Results indicate that in case of reliable communication (0% loss), the source nodes can find a path to the destination of the injected packet with the probability in the interval [0.90–1.00] and the routing tables are all populated by periodic exchanging of control messages as they were expected by the specification. The injected packet is delivered at the destination in all types of topologies. When message loss increases to 80%, these values may decrease. The same happens also in case of possible link failures. The verification regarding route establishment property (probability estimation) takes on average about 2 s whereas the verification for calculating the number of delivered packets and routing table entries (expected value evaluation) takes on average about 185 s (calculating the expected values is more time-consuming compared to estimating the probability).

5.3   Ad-Hoc On-Demand Distance Vector Version2 (AODVv2)

AODVv2 [21], a reactive protocol for WMNs, behaves on-demand. This means that it tries to find a route to the destination when a packet is injected into the network. The protocol initiates RREQ message and the receiving nodes update their routing tables and possibly rebroadcast the message until the RREQ is received by its destination. Then the destination sends a RREP message back to the source of the RREQ. In this way, a path from the source to the destination is created and the packet can be forwarded via that path. AODVv2 will report failure of links by multicasting RERR messages.

The model of AODVv2 protocol contains only models for the *Handler* and the *Queue*. As a reactive protocol, it does not need a generator. Compared to the other two models, AODVv2 has more message types, as it includes error reporting. This also means that in addition to routing information, each node maintains information of routing errors. We adapted our framework based on the model of [16] and verified our generic properties. Table 3 shows the result of our verification for different topologies. We ran the same experiments for the original model of [16] and we got similar results as we got for our adjusted AODVv2 model which shows the adaptability and reusability of our framework.

Results show that in case of reliable communication (0% loss), the source nodes can find a path to the destination of the injected packet with the probability in the interval [0.90–1.00]. Routing tables are partially populated by periodic exchanging of control messages as they were expected by the specification (reactive protocols find paths to destinations on-demand, so it is expectable that not all tables are updated). However in the linear topology, all routing tables are updated due to the path accumulation feature of AODVv2, meaning that whenever a control message travels via more than one node, information about all intermediate nodes is accumulated in the message and then is distributed to its recipients.

The injected packet is delivered at the destination in all types of topologies in case of reliable communication (0% message loss). When message loss increases to 80%, these values may decrease. The same happens also in case of possible link failures. The verification regarding route establishment property (probability estimation) takes on average about 2 s whereas the verification for calculating the number of delivered packets and routing table entries (expected value evaluation) takes on average about 15 s (calculating the expected values is more time-consuming compared to estimating the probability).

Evaluating the expected values for AODVv2 takes less time due to the reactive characteristic of AODVv2, meaning that since AODVv2 broadcasts control messages on demand it has less number of states compared to BATMAN and OLSR that broadcast control messages periodically which decreases the time spent for verification. As all the three protocols are modelled applying our framework, it is possible to easily compare the protocols w.r.t. the properties and verification time.

5.4   Discussion on BATMAN, OLSR and AODVv2 Models

Here, we discuss how much our framework needs the interaction from the modeller to be adjusted based on the protocol specification. In other words, how much the three case studies and our framework have in common and how much they are different. The general structure of our six automata (locations and transitions of the automata), i.e., *Handler*, *Queue*, *Generator*, *Timer*, *Topology-Changer* and *Tester*, and their synchronisation remain unchanged and only some declaration (code fragments) of the automata may need to be modified/added based on the specification of the protocol.

- Communication: format of each message has been separately modified using *typedef struct* (based on BATMAB, OLSR and AODVv2 specifications) and later is added in our generic message *MSG*. The *IP* address of nodes, *SQN* sequence numbers, channels, etc are borrowed from the framework.
- Topology: connectivity function, network topology and *TopologyChanger* automata remain unchanged. We have only borrowed them from our framework.
- Node: the *Queue* and the *Timer* automata remain unchanged and they have been only imported and used. Function *createMSG* in the *Generator* declaration which is applicable only for BATMAN and OLSR, has been modified based on the specification (as mentioned earlier, the format of messages for different protocols are unique to the protocol and must be changed based on the specification). The interval for sending periodic messages is a parameter of each protocol and should be set in the declarations.

  The *Handler* needs more interactions from the modeller when modifying the local declaration of the automaton. This is the case due to different behaviour of protocols, e.g., when to update a routing table, when to process/drop a message, when to multicast a message, etc. For instance, BATMAN protocol has a specific procedure for storing sequence numbers which is unique to this protocol, OLSR has a specific procedure for determining MPRs, and AODVv2 has a specific procedure for accumulating paths. These specific features need to be separately modelled for each protocol and our framework only supports the standardise behaviour of routing protocols which were discussed earlier. Our models move much of the logic to functions inside the model in order to have the core of the protocol as code fragments in the model which makes the modelling task easier.
- Verification: the three system requirements (properties) and their corresponding functions have also been imported without any modifications. The *Tester* automaton injects the packet in accordance to the category of the protocol; reactive or proactive protocol. If the protocol is proactive (BATMAN and OLSR), the *Tester* automaton injects the packet after routes are discovered; and if the protocol is reactive (AODVv2), the *Tester* injects the packet for route discovery process and the routes are discovered later after packet injection. It means that only the time interval that the *Tester* transition is enabled differs for reactive and proactive protocols.

6 Related Work

Formal modelling and analysis of the WMNs and Mobile Ad-hoc Networks (MANETs) and their routing protocols is among challenging tasks, and formal verification of such systems has attracted the attention from formal methods community [3,11,17]. Fehnker et al. [8] applied the Uppaal model checker [2] for analysing qualitative properties of the AODV protocol in all network topologies with five nodes. Kamali et al. [15] focused on formal modelling and verifying OLSR protocol in network topologies with five nodes. They have also applied

Event-B to model OLSR and have analysed this protocol in large networks (no size barrier w.r.t. the size of the network) [14]. Chaudhary et al. [4] formally modelled BATMAN routing protocol using Uppaal model checker revealing several ambiguities in the RFC. They verified their model for loop-freedom, bidirectional link discovery, and route-discovery. Fehnker et al. [9] modelled and verified LMAC protocol of wireless sensor networks applying Uppaal. Their study was carried out to detect and resolve collision in networks consisting of four and five nodes.

There are several studies using (statistical) model checking to analyse WMN and MANET routing protocols. Höfner and McIver [13] made a comparison of the AODV and DYMO protocols on arbitrary networks up to five nodes considering perfect communication among nodes, applying the Uppaal SMC model checker. Their analysis shows that DYMO has worsened performance compared to AODV. Dal Corso et al. [6] studied the extended and generalised work done by [13] to 4×3 grids with lossy communication. They showed contrary results, indicating that DYMO is performing better compared to AODV. Kamali et al. [16] investigated and compared the performance and looping property of the most recent version of AODV protocol [21] with DYMO on 3×3 grids. Their results indicate that the more recent version of AODV pays the price of degraded performance compared to DYMO to remain loop-free.

There are other studies providing formal frameworks for modelling and verifying MANETs. Liu et al. [18] presented a formal modelling framework for MANETs consisting of several mobility models together with wireless communication applying Real-Time Maude [20]. They analysed the AODV protocol using their framework and their mobility models. Their framework mainly focuses only on integrating a number of mobility models together with wireless communication. Yousefi et al. [22] have modelled MANETs using the extension of an actor-based modelling language bRebeca. They provided a framework to detect malfunctioning of MANET protocols, addressing local broadcast and topology changes. They have modelled the core functionality of AODV protocol and found some malfunctioning of this protocol (loop existence).

Our work differs from the other previous works in the sense that it models the core functionality of WMN routing protocols, considering wireless communication, topology, message loss, message queuing, link failure, etc. It is also possible to model timing aspects of protocols (both reactive and proactive) and to allow probabilities to have both qualitative and quantitative analysis.

In addition, networks of timed automata as the specification language used for introducing our generic framework (the main common components of routing protocols) are more manageable to alter based on the protocols specifications. It means that adapting our framework allows protocol designers to have an insight of the system before the deployment since timed automata is an easy-to-understand specification language and Uppaal SMC simulator provides the means to validate the system which later can be also used for verification. Protocol designers can simply modify the C-like code in the declarations based on the protocol specification where the general structure of networks of different automata remains unchanged.

7 Conclusion

This paper presented an adaptive, generic and reusable framework as well as crucial generic properties to model and verify WMN routing protocols. This framework uses Uppaal SMC to capture timing aspect of protocols, communication between nodes, and probabilities to model message loss, link breakage, etc.

This paper discussed the general structure of Uppaal models, and how this influences the design of models for network routing protocols. It described how to build reusable components within the constraints imposed by the Uppaal modelling language. It identified the main components that routing protocols have in common, and how to map them to data structures, processes, channels, and timed automata in the Uppaal language. We demonstrated the applicability of the approach by implementing three different protocols in this framework: AODVv2, OLSR and BATMAN.

One of the characteristics of these models is that they move much of the logic to functions inside of the Uppaal model. They rely less on the subtle interplay of channels, urgent locations, or committed locations. Instead, they standardise proven patterns that have been used in the community to model routing protocols. This also means that the core of the protocol resides as code fragments in the model, and becomes available to be standard code reviewing practices.

An observation that was made is that Uppaal as modelling language would benefit if it would adopt more mechanisms to structure code. It would be beneficial if the model could reflect that a number of templates share access to data structures to the exclusion of others. Often the workaround for sharing information is to make data global, without mechanisms to enforce its consistent use. Furthermore, code that is included for verification is currently scattered across the model. It might be worth to consider verification as a cross-cutting concern, similarly to how these are dealt with in aspect-oriented programming.

References

1. Alur, R., Dill, D.L.: A theory of timed automata. Theor. Comput. Sci. **126**(2), 183–235 (1994)
2. Behrmann, G., David, A., Larsen, K.G.: A tutorial on UPPAAL. In: Bernardo, M., Corradini, F. (eds.) SFM-RT 2004. LNCS, vol. 3185, pp. 200–236. Springer, Heidelberg (2004). https://doi.org/10.1007/978-3-540-30080-9_7
3. Bhargavan, K., Obradovic, D., Gunter, C.A.: Formal verification of standards for distance vector routing protocols. J. ACM **49**(4), 538–576 (2002)
4. Chaudhary, K., Fehnker, A., Mehta, V.: Modelling, verification, and comparative performance analysis of the B.A.T.M.A.N. protocol. In: Hermanns, H., Höfner, P. (eds.) MARS 2017, vol. 244, pp. 53–65 (2017)

5. Clausen, T., Jacquet, P.: Optimized link state routing protocol (OLSR). RFC3626 (2003). http://www.ietf.org/rfc/rfc3626
6. Dal Corso, A., Macedonio, D., Merro, M.: Statistical model checking of ad hoc routing protocols in lossy grid networks. In: Havelund, K., Holzmann, G., Joshi, R. (eds.) NFM 2015. LNCS, vol. 9058, pp. 112–126. Springer, Cham (2015). https://doi.org/10.1007/978-3-319-17524-9_9
7. David, A., Larsen, K.G., Legay, A., Mikučionis, M., Poulsen, D.B.: Uppaal SMC tutorial. STTT **17**(4), 397–415 (2015)
8. Fehnker, A., van Glabbeek, R., Höfner, P., McIver, A., Portmann, M., Tan, W.L.: Automated analysis of AODV using UPPAAL. In: Flanagan, C., König, B. (eds.) TACAS 2012. LNCS, vol. 7214, pp. 173–187. Springer, Heidelberg (2012). https://doi.org/10.1007/978-3-642-28756-5_13
9. Fehnker, A., van Hoesel, L., Mader, A.: Modelling and verification of the LMAC protocol for wireless sensor networks. In: Davies, J., Gibbons, J. (eds.) IFM 2007. LNCS, vol. 4591, pp. 253–272. Springer, Heidelberg (2007). https://doi.org/10.1007/978-3-540-73210-5_14
10. Fehnker, A., Höfner, P., Kamali, M., Mehta, V.: Topology-based mobility models for wireless networks. In: Joshi, K., Siegle, M., Stoelinga, M., D'Argenio, P.R. (eds.) QEST 2013. LNCS, vol. 8054, pp. 389–404. Springer, Heidelberg (2013). https://doi.org/10.1007/978-3-642-40196-1_32
11. van Glabbeek, R., Höfner, P., Portmann, M., Tan, W.L.: Modelling and verifying the AODV routing protocol. Distrib. Comput. **29**(4), 279–315 (2016)
12. Hérault, T., Lassaigne, R., Magniette, F., Peyronnet, S.: Approximate probabilistic model checking. In: Steffen, B., Levi, G. (eds.) Verification, Model Checking, and Abstract Interpretation, pp. 73–84. Springer, Berlin (2004)
13. Höfner, P., McIver, A.: Statistical model checking of wireless mesh routing protocols. In: Brat, G., Rungta, N., Venet, A. (eds.) NFM 2013. LNCS, vol. 7871, pp. 322–336. Springer, Heidelberg (2013). https://doi.org/10.1007/978-3-642-38088-4_22
14. Kamali, M., Petre, L.: Modelling link state routing in event-B. In: Wang, H., Mokhtari, M. (eds.) ICECCS 2016, pp. 207–210. IEEE (2016)
15. Kamali, M., Höfner, P., Kamali, M., Petre, L.: Formal analysis of proactive, distributed routing. In: Calinescu, R., Rumpe, B. (eds.) SEFM 2015. LNCS, vol. 9276, pp. 175–189. Springer, Cham (2015). https://doi.org/10.1007/978-3-319-22969-0_13
16. Kamali, M., Merro, M., Dal Corso, A.: AODVv2: performance vs. loop freedom. In: Tjoa, A.M., Bellatreche, L., Biffl, S., van Leeuwen, J., Wiedermann, J. (eds.) SOFSEM 2018. LNCS, vol. 10706, pp. 337–350. Springer, Cham (2018). https://doi.org/10.1007/978-3-319-73117-9_24
17. Kamali, M., Petre, L.: Improved recovery for proactive, distributed routing. In: ICECCS 2015, pp. 178–181. IEEE (2015)
18. Liu, S., Ölveczky, P.C., Meseguer, J.: A framework for mobile ad hoc networks in real-time maude. In: Escobar, S. (ed.) WRLA 2014. LNCS, vol. 8663, pp. 162–177. Springer, Cham (2014). https://doi.org/10.1007/978-3-319-12904-4_9
19. Neumann, A., Aichele, C., Lindner, M., Wunderlich, S.: Better approach to mobile ad-hoc networking (BATMAN). Internet draft00 (2008). https://tools.ietf.org/html/draft-wunderlich-openmesh-manet-routing-00
20. Ölveczky, P.C., Meseguer, J.: Semantics and pragmatics of Real-Time Maude. High.-Order Symb. Comput. **20**(1), 161–196 (2007)

21. Perkins, C., Stan, R., Dowdell, J., Steenbrink, L., Mercieca, V.: Ad hoc on-demand distance vector version 2 (AODVv2) routing. Internet Draft 16 (2016). https://datatracker.ietf.org/doc/draft-ietf-manet-aodvv2
22. Yousefi, B., Ghassemi, F., Khosravi, R.: Modeling and efficient verification of wireless ad hoc networks. Form. Asp. Comput. **29**(6), 1051–1086 (2017)

IsaK-Static: A Complete Static Semantics of $\mathbb{K}$

Liyi Li$^{(\boxtimes)}$ and Elsa L. Gunter$^{(\boxtimes)}$

Department of Computer Science, University of Illinois at Urbana-Champaign,
Champaign, USA
{liyili2,egunter}@illinois.edu

Abstract. $\mathbb{K}$ [1] is a rewrite-based executable semantic framework in which programming languages, type systems and formal analysis tools can be defined using configurations, computations and rules. $\mathbb{K}$ supports a module design for programming language specifications, with different language features separated in different modules. This is supported through a subsort system and $\mathbb{K}$ features called localization and concision. By these features and other features, language specifications can be defined in $\mathbb{K}$ effectively. In this paper we define a complete static semantics of $\mathbb{K}$ named **IsaK-Static**, in the interactive theorem prover Isabelle/HOL [2], to study these features. Specially, it defines the full static behavior of $\mathbb{K}$ a useful sort system for $\mathbb{K}$ and suggests several undesirable behaviors in the current $\mathbb{K}$ implementations ($\mathbb{K}$ 3.6 and $\mathbb{K}$ 4.0). To the best of our knowledge, **IsaK-Static** is the most complete of any existing $\mathbb{K}$ specification. We also provide an OCaml based executable full $\mathbb{K}$ interpreter generated automatically from the $\mathbb{K}$ specification in Isabelle.

1 Motivation and Overview

$\mathbb{K}$ is a domain specific language that takes a language specification as an input and generates an interpreter for the specification, including an execution engine to show trace behaviors of a program in the specification. There is a rich body of published work on $\mathbb{K}$ itself [3], and specifications given in $\mathbb{K}$, such as the Java semantics [4], the Javascript semantics [5], the PHP semantics [6] and the C semantics [7,8]. Despite the success of $\mathbb{K}$, there are issues. While there have been a number of papers published concerning theories related to $\mathbb{K}$, there is no source sufficiently complete to define the complete syntax and semantics of $\mathbb{K}$, or allow for rigorous proofs of properties of the languages defined in $\mathbb{K}$. In addition, while $\mathbb{K}$ supports specific tools for analyzing programs in a language defined in $\mathbb{K}$, it provides very little support for formal reasoning about the languages it defines. Finally, the fact that early versions of $\mathbb{K}$ had features that were dropped in intermediate versions, only to be reintroduced in the latest versions, and different versions have displayed different behaviors unveils the fact that researchers in the $\mathbb{K}$ community do not have a consensus on what $\mathbb{K}$ is. As an answer for these problems, we have created a complete formal semantics

© Springer Nature Switzerland AG 2018
K. Bae and P. C. Ölveczky (Eds.): FACS 2018, LNCS 11222, pp. 196–215, 2018.
https://doi.org/10.1007/978-3-030-02146-7_10

of $\mathbb{K}$ clarifying different aspects and features of $\mathbb{K}$. In this paper, we introduce the complete static semantics of $\mathbb{K}$, **IsaK-Static**. In particular, it gives semantics for the $\mathbb{K}$ modular system and concision features, especially, clarifying how $\mathbb{K}$ frontend AST (FAST) with modularity and concision features is translated into a standardized $\mathbb{K}$ backend AST (BAST) for defining dynamic semantics.

1.1 The $\mathbb{K}$ Framework

We will briefly introduce $\mathbb{K}$ in this subsection and state the challenges of formally defining these $\mathbb{K}$ features in the next subsection. The operational behavior of the $\mathbb{K}$ specification language contains four major steps: parsing, language compilation, sort checking, and semantic rewriting. In fact, parsing comes in two phases: one to learn the grammar of the object language (the programming language being defined), and a second to incorporate that grammar into the grammar of $\mathbb{K}$ to parse the definitions of the rules and semantic objects defining the executable behavior of programs of the object language. We assume the existence of two parsers, one for each of these phases, with the output of the first being passed to the second. Together these parsers translate the concrete syntax for both $\mathbb{K}$ and the object languages defined therein into concrete syntax, eliminating mixfix syntax and other syntactic sugar in the process.

$$\text{SYNTAX} \quad Exp ::= Exp \ / \ Exp \ [\text{strict}(1)]$$

(a)

$$\left\langle \begin{array}{l} \langle \$PGM : KItem \rangle_{\mathsf{k}} \ \langle .\texttt{Map} \rangle_{\mathsf{env}} \ \langle .\texttt{Map} \rangle_{\mathsf{heap}} \\ \langle\langle\langle .\mathtt{K} \rangle_{\mathsf{name}} \langle .\mathtt{K} \rangle_{\mathsf{body}} \rangle_{\mathsf{class}*} \rangle_{\mathsf{classes}} \end{array} \right\rangle_{\mathsf{T}}$$

(b)

$$\left\langle \frac{X}{E} \cdots \right\rangle_{\mathsf{k}} \langle \cdots X \mapsto N \cdots \rangle_{\mathsf{env}} \langle \cdots N \mapsto E \cdots \rangle_{\mathsf{heap}}$$

(c)

$$\frac{X : Int \ / \ Y : Int}{X : Int \ /\mathtt{Int} \ Y : Int}$$
$$requires \ Y \neq 0$$

(d)

$$\langle B : Bag \ \langle X \curvearrowright \kappa \rangle_{\mathsf{k}} \ \langle \rho_1, X \mapsto N, \rho_2 \rangle_{\mathsf{env}} \ \langle \rho_3, N \mapsto E, \rho_4 \rangle_{\mathsf{heap}} \rangle_{\mathsf{T}}$$
$$\Rightarrow \langle B : Bag \ \langle E \curvearrowright \kappa \rangle_{\mathsf{k}} \ \langle \rho_1, X \mapsto N, \rho_2 \rangle_{\mathsf{env}} \ \langle \rho_3, N \mapsto E, \rho_4 \rangle_{\mathsf{heap}} \rangle_{\mathsf{T}}$$

(e)

Fig. 1. A Briefing of $\mathbb{K}$

Figure 1a shows how a syntactic definition is defined in $\mathbb{K}$. It uses the assignment operator ($::=$) to connect a target sort with a list of terminals or non-terminals. After that, $\mathbb{K}$ automatically generates a `kLabel` name (having sort *KLabel*) representing the constructor and a sort *KList* term representing the argument list of the construct. Inside the bracket, $\mathbb{K}$ allows users to define attributes, some of which have semantic meanings. For example, the `strict(1)` attribute means to generate a pair of `heat`/`cool` rules for the first non-terminal position of the construct (described in Sect. 2). Two features that $\mathbb{K}$ uses to keep object language specifications succinct: localization and concision. Localization means to allow users to define language syntax by using conventional BNF anno-tated with semantic attributes, while the semantics based on the language syntax is given as a set of reduction equations and interpreted rules over a configuration mentioning only those components accessed or altered by the rule. Figure 1b is a over-simplified version of the Java configuration [4]. The configuration of a language is an algebraic structure of the program states, organized as nested labeled cells, in XML formats, holding semantic information, including the pro-gram itself. While the order of cells is irrelevant in a configuration (having *Bag* sort representing configuration cells in $\mathbb{K}$), the contextual relations between cells are relevant and must be preserved by rules defined by users and subsequently "completed" by the compilation step in $\mathbb{K}$ according to the configuration. Leaf cells represent pieces of the program state, like a computation stack or continu-ation (e.g., k), environments (e.g., env), heaps (e.g., heap), etc. For example, a typical rule for reading a variable would be in Fig. 1c. There are three cells in the rule: k, env and heap. The content of the k cell symbolizes a computation sequence waiting to be performed, while the head element in the cell represents the next item to be computed. The env cell contains a map of variables to loca-tion numbers, while the cell heap is a map of location numbers to expression values. The meaning of the rule above is that if the next computation to be exe-cuted is a variable lookup expression X, then we locate X in the environment to get its location number N in the location memory, and locate N in the heap to find its expression value E. With such, we transform the computation into that value, E; the horizontal line represents a transition. A cell with no horizontal line means that it is read but does not change during the transition.

The meaning of concision in rule Fig. 1c in $\mathbb{K}$ refers to the "…" operator, which represents portions of cells that are irrelevant and it could have different types depending on the context. This unconventional notation including the two features is useful in terms of allowing users to write less. The rule in Fig. 1c would be written out as a traditional rewrite rule (also allowed in $\mathbb{K}$) as Fig. 1e, which still relies on the $\mathbb{K}$ configuration but without localization and concision. We need to add the top cell T in the rule and a variable B with its sort *Bag* to indicate irrelevant program state pieces. Computations in the k cell are separated by "$\curvearrowright$" (a built-in sort *KItem* list concatenation operator in $\mathbb{K}$), which is now observable. The κ and ρ_1, ρ_2, ρ_3, ρ_4 fill in the place of the "…" above. The most important thing to notice is that many parts of the the rule are duplicated on the right-hand side. Duplication in a definition can lead to subtle semantic errors if users are not careful synchronizing their changes to their specifications in multiple places, once changes are made. In a big language like C, Java or LLVM, the configuration structure is very complicated, and would require actually including more cells than typical rule needs to mention. These intervening cells are automatically inferred in $\mathbb{K}$, which keeps the rules more succinct. Figure 1d shows another way of defining rules in $\mathbb{K}$. A rule without mentioning any cell structure means that the rule is matching with content in the k cell. $X : Int$ in the rule means that a variable X has sort Int. The *requires* keyword is a way of introducing a condition expression in a rule.

In addition, modularity is another important features of $\mathbb{K}$, and its module system can be classified as a set of separated files whose contents might not have relations between each other. In fact, the rules in Fig. 1 can be put in a single module by adding a module name. In defining specifications, users usually do not need to modify existing rules to add a new feature to the language. $\mathbb{K}$ maintains this feature by structuring the configuration as nested cells and by allowing users to design their specification rules by only mentioning the cells that are needed in those rules, and only the needed portions of those cells. For example, the above rule only refers to the k, env and heap cells, while the entire configuration contains other cells in Fig. 1b. The modularity of $\mathbb{K}$ not only allows users to create a compact and human readable specification, but also contributes to speeding up the semantics development process. For example, the above lookup rule does not change, even though a new cell is added to the configuration to support a new feature. The modular system of $\mathbb{K}$ also allows users to develop syntax and rules incrementally by allowing users to define a syntactic construct in a $\mathbb{K}$ module and define rules containing the construct in different $\mathbb{K}$ modules.

1.2 Challenges

Several formidable challenges are faced by the **IsaK-Static** project. First, other than the two simple descriptions of the theory behind $\mathbb{K}$ [1,9], there are no resources talking about its syntax and semantics. Indeed, all $\mathbb{K}$ implementations contain some undesirable behaviors, so it is hard to learn the exact meanings of $\mathbb{K}$ operators. In the process of defining $\mathbb{K}$, we needed to constantly interview the $\mathbb{K}$ team to understand the meanings of the $\mathbb{K}$ operators and look at the source code of the $\mathbb{K}$ implementation to understand how $\mathbb{K}$ is being defined. Second, the path compiling from the frontend language in $\mathbb{K}$ to the backend is not so clear. In the implementation of $\mathbb{K}$ 4.0 (in Java), there are 48 compilation steps to compile the front-end language to the back-end one. These 48 steps have different tasks. In particular, it takes several steps to compile out the localization features of $\mathbb{K}$. **IsaK-Static** must faithfully represent the meaning of the combination of these tasks. Third, the modular system in $\mathbb{K}$ is not independent of the context. Sometimes, it creates confusion. If one defines new syntax and subsort relations on top of an existing $\mathbb{K}$ definition, the $\mathbb{K}$ compilation step combines the existing $\mathbb{K}$ syntactic definitions with the new ones to create a new language. For any $\mathbb{K}$ specification, there is only one configuration, so whenever users define $\mathbb{K}$ rules in different $\mathbb{K}$ modules, these rules implicitly refer to the module in which the configuration resides. In addition, $\mathbb{K}$ allows users to define the evaluation result by giving subsorts to a special sort named *KResult*. Incrementally defining new subsorts of *KResult* actually means defining a series of new languages, each with its own evaluation result domain.

Fourth, the localization feature is also hard to compile in rules mentioning different cells, especially, when it is with the concision feature. The basic idea of the compilation step is to take the configuration in a language specification, compare it with a given rule, and fill the missing pieces in the rule to make the rule "complete". The problem is that adding the missing pieces is not so trivial. For example, assume that we have a configuration with thread structure like the one in the Java semantics [4]. We want to define a rule to remove all content in a cell named holds in a particular thread defined by its identifier (appearing in tid cell), one might think of two ways to define it as follows:

$$\left\langle \left\langle \frac{M}{\cdot} \right\rangle_{holds} \langle X \rangle_{tid} \cdots \right\rangle_{thread} \qquad \frac{\langle\langle M \rangle_{holds} \langle X \rangle_{tid} \cdots \rangle_{thread}}{\langle\langle \cdot \rangle_{holds} \langle X \rangle_{tid} \cdots \rangle_{thread}}$$

At first glance, people might think that the left-hand side rule (Rule 1) and the right-hand side rule (Rule 2) are the same, but they are not. To fully understand the difference between these two rules, we need to learn a little about the localization feature in $\mathbb{K}$. The localization feature means that users are able to define semantic rules for a language reflecting what happens within a small fragment of the whole program state. So, users can write less. Rule 1 reflects the feature. We are able to only mention the transition in the cell holds and keep other parts of the program state the same by using the "...". However, to allow users to write less, $\mathbb{K}$ has the second design goal for the localization feature. That is, it should have enough syntactic sugars to allow users to use. The "..." in the right hand side of a rule (the bottom line in Rule 2) means that we want to rewrite every program state pieces mentioned by the "..." to the state defined by the initial program state (In $\mathbb{K}$, users are able to define initial program state through the definition of configuration). Hence, based on these design features, we can see that rule 1 means that in a given thread with id X, we remove all the thread's holds (the · means the empty unit operator) and keep other parts of the program state the same as the previous state. Rule 2 means that for a given thread with id X, except the tid cell, we discard all the pieces in the program state in the thread and initialize them with the ones in the initial configuration (the initial values defined in the Java configuration). So, the hold cell is rewritten to empty, as well as other pieces are initialized to their initial values. The main problem here is that $\mathbb{K}$ puts too many design goals for the "..." operator so that it is not a simple syntactic sugar when it is associated with $\mathbb{K}$ cells. The compilation of the "..." in a sort *Bag* term desires a well-defined algorithm to accomplish this problem properly. In Sect. 2, we define how $\mathbb{K}$ translates the localization feature with concision, and in Sect. 3, we see some design issues of $\mathbb{K}$ related to these features.

2   The Static Semantics of $\mathbb{K}$

We briefly introduce the static semantics of $\mathbb{K}$ in this section and will discuss some design issues of $\mathbb{K}$, especially $\mathbb{K}$ modularity, localization and concision features in the next section. The static semantics of $\mathbb{K}$ describes how we compile away the localization, concision and modularity features of K to a uniformed backend AST. It contains several phases, as listed in Fig. 2. Each phase digs deeper into the syntactic structure of K and either performs a set of transformations over the user-defined K specifications or applies some checks on the input FAST of the specifications.

We assume that there is an external parser that parses user-input K object language specifications and object level programs to a FAST format. The parser is divided into two phases. In the first phase, it uses ocamllex and ocamlyacc (variants of lex and yacc for Ocaml) to read all syntactic definitions in a given specification, and then generates a symbol table based on the syntactic definitions. In the second phase, it uses the symbol table to generate lexers and parsers in the formats of ocamllex and Dypgen (a general LR parser) to parse rewrite rules and programs for the specification. The two-phase parser is a direct copy of the K parser (SDF-to-K adapter [10]) and is intended to be suitable for the OCaml-based K implementation extracted directly from **IsaK-Static** in Isabelle.

After the parsing, the static semantics takes as input the FAST representation of a user-defined language specification or programs that are allowed in the specification. Through the translation process in the static semantics, which performs computations that can be done statically (referred to as compile-time operations), the specification in FAST is processed and translated into a representation in BAST. Then the sort adjustment step in the static semantics outputs a sort-adjusted BAST, which is passed to the dynamic semantics for execution.

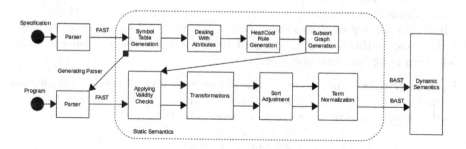

Fig. 2. The structure of **IsaK-Static**

Symbol Table Generation. In this phase, a symbol table is acquired from the syntactic definitions of a object specification, a database is formed for later phases to use, and a program parser is generated to parse object level programs. This symbol table is accumulated across all modules.

Dealing with Attributes and Heat/Cool Rules Generation. K provides syntactic and semantic attributes to allow for more succinct specifications, which are part of the concision feature and allow users to write less. For example, if we define an division operator as Fig. 1a, the `strict` attribute associated with the above syntactic definition means that a pair of `heat` and `cool` rules for the first non-terminal argument position is generated as follows:

$$\frac{X : Exp \ / \ Y : Exp}{\substack{X : Exp \curvearrowright (\square \ / \ Y : Exp) \\ requires \neg \ \mathtt{isKResult}(\ X \ )}} \qquad \frac{X : KResult \curvearrowright (\square \ / \ Y : Exp)}{X : KResult \ / \ Y : Exp}$$

The rule on the left takes a term $X : Exp \ / \ Y : Exp$, and splits it into a redex $X : Exp$ and a context $\square + Y : Exp$, provided that the term $X : Exp$ is not a subsort of $KResult$. The rule on the right merges a $KResult$ redex term $X : KResult$ and a context $\square + Y : Exp$ back to a term $X : KResult + Y : Exp$. As shown in the example in the previous paragraph, specifying a `strict` attribute in $\mathbb{K}$ is the same as generating a pair of `heat`/`cool` rules. The `heat`/`cool` rules in $\mathbb{K}$ work by separating context and redex in the evaluation context framework. A `heat` rule splits a term into a redex and a context with a hole ($\square$) in the specified position, and moves the redex to the front of the `kCell`, provided that the redex does not have a sort that is a subsort of $KResult$. A `cool` rule moves a $KResult$ redex back into the $\square$ in the context and merges them into a term without $\square$. In the later section, we will see that the meaning of a `heat`/`cool` rule pair might change due to the extention of $KResult$ sort in different modules of a $\mathbb{K}$ specification.

In this phase, we also take care of other syntactic attributes (associated with syntactic definitions) and semantic attributes (associated with rewrite rules) by grouping and collecting the parsed input language specification pieces. For example, if a syntactic definition is labeled with a `function` attribute, which is called a `function` operator (its `kLabel` name is called a `function kLabel`), we collect all rules across all modules whose left-hand side top-most `kLabel` name is the same as this definition, store all these rules in a set and label them as belonging to the function operator.

Subsort Graph Generation. In this phase, we collect all subsort information defined in a specification and form it into a graph. In $\mathbb{K}$, the only way to define a subsort relation is to use a syntactic definition like:

SYNTAX   Exp ::= Int

In this definition, sort Int is defined to be a subsort of sort Exp. $\mathbb{K}$ has a very special subsort structure. First, the subsort relation in a $\mathbb{K}$ specification is antisymmetric and transitive. Second, the sorts K, $KLabel$, $KList$, Set, $List$, Map and Bag are $\mathbb{K}$ built-in sorts representing the respective $\mathbb{K}$ built-in terms. Users cannot define subsort relations involving of these built-in sorts; otherwise, the specification is not well-formed. Third, the built-in sort $KItem$, representing the elements in a sort K (sort K means a list of $KItem$), is a subsort of the sort K implicitly, while all other user-defined sorts in a specification are subsorts of $KItem$ implicitly. Finally, users can define subsorts of the built-in sort $KResult$ representing the evaluation result terms of an execution. However, those user-defined sorts that have not been defined to be subsorts of $KResult$ through transitivity are implicit supersorts of *KResult*. Indeed, *KResult* is also a subsort of *KItem* implicitly.

We need to generate the subsort graph by combining the user-defined subsort relations and the implicit subsort relations above. In addition, we also need to apply checks, such as the well-formedness check above, to reject ill-formed specifications. Another important check is to see if there are cycles in the subsort graph, and reject those specifications as well.

Applying Validity Checks. In this phase, several checks are applied to a specification to rule out ill-formed specifications and programs. A lot of these checks are related to the improvement of $\mathbb{K}$ due to design issues in modularity, localization and concision features in Sect. 3. The first important check is to ensure that the kLabel names are used in a uniformly consistent manner. Second, users cannot define any new syntactic constructs or subsorts to the built-in sorts *K*, *KLabel*, *KList*, *Set*, *List*, *Map* and *Bag*, except with a function attribute. Third, at most one of the function, strict and seqstrict attributes is allowed to appear in a syntactic definition. Without this restriction, a syntactic definition could be both a function and generate heat/cool rules, which is not sound in $\mathbb{K}$. Also, the specified natural number for a strict attribute cannot exceed the total number of non-terminal positions in the syntactic definition it is associated with. Finally, any two user-defined lists cannot have the same target sort. For example, the following two syntactic definitions cannot appear in the same specification because they are adding two user defined lists with two different element sorts to the same target sort *Exp*.

SYNTAX $Exp ::= \text{List}\{\ Int\ ,","\ \}$ SYNTAX $Exp ::= \text{List}\{\ Bool\ ,","\ \}$

Transformation. We will select some important transformation steps to discuss here. Interesting readers can refer to our technical report [11] to get more information. There are some rewrite rules and programs that users are able to write down in FAST, but they have no meanings in $\mathbb{K}$ because the semantics of $\mathbb{K}$ terms are only defined if the terms can be written in BAST and the transformation from FAST to BAST is a partial function. The process of transforming FAST to BAST is both a transformation and a narrowing process. If a FAST term is transformable, we have a corresponding BAST term; if not, we reject the input specification or program.

$$X + (\ Y \Rightarrow (\ -\ Y\ )) \Rightarrow .K$$

$$\left\langle \begin{array}{c} \langle 1\ +\ 2\ +\ 3 \rangle_k \langle .\text{Bag} \rangle_{classes} \\ \langle .\text{Map} \rangle_{env} \langle .\text{Map} \rangle_{heap} \end{array} \right\rangle_T$$

(a)   (b)

Fig. 3. Transformation examples

The first step in the transformation process is to rule out some terms permissible in FAST but invalid in BAST. For example, Fig. 3a shows a rule that will be rejected in the transformation process because its LHS contains nested $\mathbb{K}$ rewrite operators ($\Rightarrow$). Usually, a rule will be translated into a five tuple format that BAST adopts. In BAST, the five tuple includes the rule label field indicating the type of the rule for execution, the pattern representing the LHS of the rule, the expression representing the RHS of the rule, the condition expression representing the condition of the rule, and a boolean flag indicating if the rule is a transition rule, which determines if the rule is part of multi-threaded behaviors in an object specification. For example, if we have a rule in Fig. 1d, what we get in the BAST form is a tuple like:

(KNormal, $X : Int$ / $Y : Int$, $X : Int$ /Int $Y : Int$, $Y : Int \neq 0$, true)

Recall in Sect. 1.1, we says that the configuration of an object language specification represents the program state that is necessary to describe the behaviors of the specification. Executing a program of a specification in $\mathbb{K}$ actually means that we apply semantic rules to a program state and generate a sequence of computations (or a set of sequences if we want to see multi-threaded behaviors). The generation of the initial program state is just to combine an object program with the configuration together. For example, if we define the configuration in Fig. 1b, and our program is 1 + 2 + 3, the initial state is generated as Fig. 3b. The cell class is replaced with a term .Bag as prescribed by the configuration because it is attributed with * keyword in the configuration which indicates that it should start with zero occurrences.

Before we transform a semantic rule in FAST to the tuple format in BAST as we described above, if the rule contains sort *Bag* terms (representing cells or the configuration), we need to perform a step called configuration concretization. It is the most difficult part of the transformation, because it mixes the localization and concision features together. The solution requires a combined process of splitting, "completing" and translating terms of sort *Bag*. The goal of the configuration concretization step is to regularize each rule involving sort *Bag* terms to a form where it only involves one rewrite operator, and the rule is spitted into a LHS and a RHS which have no rewrite operators inside them, and both the LHS and RHS are completed by filling those missing cells according to the configuration.

$$\left\langle \frac{\langle\langle \mathbf{f} \rangle_{\text{name}} \cdots \rangle_{\text{class}}}{\langle\langle \mathbf{g} \rangle_{\text{name}} \cdots \rangle_{\text{class}}} \cdots \right\rangle_{\text{classes}} \qquad \frac{\langle X : Bag \ \langle C : Bag \ \langle U : Bag \ \langle \mathbf{f} \rangle_{\text{name}} \rangle_{\text{class}} \rangle_{\text{classes}} \top}{\langle X : Bag \ \langle C : Bag \ \langle\langle . \mathbf{K} \rangle_{\text{body}} \langle \mathbf{g} \rangle_{\text{name}} \rangle_{\text{class}} \rangle_{\text{classes}} \top}$$

(a)   (b)

Fig. 4. Configuration concretization example

As we have seen in Sect. 1.2, the key difficulty is that the combination of a "…" operator in a sort *Bag* term and a rewrite operator cannot be understood as simple syntactic sugar for writing less cell information and term rewriting from left to right. The detail of the transformation algorithm is listed in the technical report [11]. There are two main tasks. First, the algorithm needs to compare a *Bag* rule with the configuration, find cells containing "…" operators in the *Bag* rule and replace those operators with correct values based on the configuration. Second, we need to split a *Bag* rule to have clear left-hand and right-hand sides. Figure 4 shows an example displaying the most important features of the transformation. We first locate all the rewrite operators ($\Rightarrow$) and their subterms in a rule, and take the left-hand sides of these ($\Rightarrow$) terms as patterns and right-hand sides as expressions. If there is a "…" in a pattern, we replace it with a variable with the correct sort indicated by the configuration, like the $U : Bag$ variable in Fig. 4b. For each "…" operator in an expression, we replace it with the correct terms according to the configuration, like the ⟨ .K ⟩ $_{body}$ in Fig. 4b. After finishing filling patterns and expressions, we put patterns in the pattern side and expressions in the expression side of the generated rule, and compare both sides and the remaining pieces with the configuration, and fill the gaps with variables or corresponding cells, like the cells classes, T, $C : Bag$ and $X : Bag$ in Fig. 4b.

Sort Adjustment. Previous materials about 𝕂 only briefly described the 𝕂 sort system. The implementations of 𝕂 have weak sort systems containing a lot of undesirable behaviors. One of the contributions of **IsaK-Static** is to fully propose a sort system for 𝕂 that is consistent with 𝕂's design goals. 𝕂 is a special purpose language that allows users to define an object language specification, and then allows execution of object programs by using the specification. The sort system design needs to check every rule in the specification to discover ill-formed rules, and adjust each metavariable in each rule to have the maximal lower bound sorts. This is called sort adjustment. Besides these design goals, we also need to consider the programs in the language being sort-checked. Once a rule has been sort adjusted and a program state has been sort-checked, applying the rule on the program state will not create a result that is ill-formed.

The complete story of the **IsaK-Static** sort system is described in the technical report [11]. Our sort system builds on the subsort graph defined in the **Subsort Graph Generation** paragraph of Page 7 and also the syntactic components of BAST, where a metavariable in BAST is not annotated by a sort but a set of sort (form: *Var* : *Sort* set). When we transform a FAST term to a BAST term, we transform the sort of a metavariable to a singleton set with an element of that sort for that metavariable. For a specification, we need to sort-adjust every rule after it is transformed into BAST format. The sort-adjustment is a partial function that takes in a BAST term t and outputs a new term t' if we can judge one set of maximal lower bound sorts (not equal to {T}) for each metavariable or subterm of sort *KItem* in t. Three things need to be clarified here. First, the top sort T is used to be assigned to metavariables for which users have not specified a particular sort in a FAST term. If the sort-adjustment function judges a BAST metavariable having a singleton set with an element of sort

⊤, it should fail to output a term because it means that users did not provide enough information for some metavariables in the term. Second, the output term t' of the sort-adjustment function has the same structure as the original term t, but all its metavariables or sort $KItem$ subterms have maximal lower bound sorts. Third, maximal lower bound sorts are a set of sorts, where for every occurrence of a particular metavariable or all sort $KItem$ subterm, every sort in the maximal lower bound sorts is a subsort of sorts of the occurrence. Additionally, there does not exist a strict supersort of any sort in a maximal lower bound sorts where the supersort is a subsort of all sorts from all occurrences.

The reason that we also need to sort-adjust sort $KItem$ subterms (having the form $KLabel(KList)$) is that users are allowed to define a term of sort $KItem$ with its $KLabel$ position being unspecified and being written as a $KLabel$ metavariable in $\mathbb{K}$. The metavariable has sort $KLabel$, but its instantiation also uniquely defines the target sort of the $KItem$ term. For example, assume that we have the following two syntactic definitions introducing + and `continuation`:

$$\text{SYNTAX} \quad Exp ::= Exp + Exp \ [\text{strict}(1)]$$
$$\text{SYNTAX} \quad Exp ::= \text{continuation}(\ KLabel \ , \ K \ , \ K \ )$$

Users might want to define the following rule to apply an input high-order function to the two following arguments and then add the results together.

$$\frac{\text{continuation}(\ F : KLabel \ , \ X : K \ , \ Y : K \ )}{F : KLabel \ (\ X : K \ ) + F : KLabel \ (\ Y : K \ )}$$

In this rule, while the metavariable F has sort $KLabel$, the application of the term $F : KLabel$ to $X : K$ ($F : KLabel \ (\ X : K \ )$) must be a subsort of sort Exp, because term + has the two argument sorts both restricted to sort Exp and term $F : KLabel \ (\ X : K \ )$ is located in the argument position of term +. Hence, after we apply the sort adjustment on the rule, the metavariable F has a value of sort $KLabel$ and it also determines the term $F : KLabel \ (\ X : K \ )$ with sort Exp.

$\mathbb{K}$ allows users to write semantic rules in a flexible way. We have shown an example above, where users are allowed to define some metarules without specifying the actual `kLabel` names (representing the names for constructs) for their constructs, but with using metavariables having target sort $KLabel$. In this case, these metarules can pattern match any program states regardless of the `kLabel` names in the constructs, as long as the the conditions of the pattern matching are satisfied. The sort system of $\mathbb{K}$ is explicitly first-order. It is impossible to define a strong sort system within first-order to catch the behavior of the flexibility, because it requires introducing function sorts. Designing a strong high-order sort system, such as the one in System F, can be done in the future, but it is beyond the scope of the paper because the **IsaK-Static** sort system is designed to capture behavior of $\mathbb{K}$.

Apart from the flexible situation, our $\mathbb{K}$ sort system can strongly guarantee that once a specification and its initial program states are sort adjusted and checked, executing the program states will not go wrong.

Term Normalization. Normalization is a process that happens after sort adjustment, to apply idempotent and functional equational rules to any sub-terms of rules and program states having the sort *Set* and *Map*. The process is to get rid of redundant child elements of *Set* or *Map* subterms and make sure every *Map* term is functional. Normalization also happens after sort checking when doing a pattern matching in the dynamic semantics.

3   The Design Issues and Improvement

In Sect. 2, we briefly describe how $\mathbb{K}$ compiles away its modularity, localization and concision features in the translation from FAST to a BAST format that is normalized for execution. We did not specify how to compile module systems in that section because the compilation of module systems in $\mathbb{K}$ is as easy as putting all files together. For a specification, different modules are not independent, so $\mathbb{K}$ has some unexpected behaviors. In this section, we mainly focus on the design issues of $\mathbb{K}$, especially the design issues of module systems in $\mathbb{K}$ and suggest ways to handle some of these problems.

Too Flexible FAST Semantic Rules. The LHS and the RHS of a $\mathbb{K}$ semantic rule have actually different tolerance on what can be correctly accepted. $\mathbb{K}$ views the LHS of a rule as the pattern and the RHS of a rule as the expression, and provides a different set of syntax for them in BAST. Their FAST formats are the same, and this can lead to confusion. For example, if we have the syntactic declaration and rule in Fig. 5a and 5b, the construct test takes an argument of sort *Set*. The rule tries to rewrite an element of value 1 to 2 in an element of a set. This rule is invalid in $\mathbb{K}$. As a pattern, $\mathbb{K}$ only allows one variable to represent elements of built-in term with sort *K*, *KList*, *Set*, *List*, *Map* or *Bag*. So, if we cut off the variable B in the rule, the rule becomes permissible. This design can allow $\mathbb{K}$ developers to design the $\mathbb{K}$ pattern matching algorithm simply, and avoid having exponential search steps in the algorithm that arise once we allow more than one variable for the elements of these built-in terms. The current $\mathbb{K}$ pattern matching algorithm is especially efficient when built-in terms having implicit equational rules.

SYNTAX   *Exp* ::= test(*Set*)

(a)

$$\frac{\text{test}(\ A : Set\ \text{SetItem(1)}\ B : Set\ )}{\text{test}(\ A : Set\ \text{SetItem(2)}\ B : Set\ )}$$

test(.Set)
― ―
test(.K)

(b)   (c)

Fig. 5. Pattern and expression being different example

Additionally, being overly flexible can be problematic in $\mathbb{K}$. For example, we found a bug in $\mathbb{K}$ which can allow the rule in Fig. 5c to compile. This rule basically allows $\mathbb{K}$ to rewrite a sort *Set* term to a sort K term. We disallow this rewrite in **IsaK-Static** by designing different types in Isabelle to represent different built-in terms of $\mathbb{K}$ and sort-checking each input rule.

Module Systems and Configurations. As we know in Sect. 1.1, each $\mathbb{K}$ object language specification has a unique configuration that provides users the localization property of $\mathbb{K}$. Users need to use a key word `configuration` in $\mathbb{K}$ to define it, and $\mathbb{K}$ does not restrict users where to place the configuration. Once a user declares `configuration` in a module A, it means that other modules depend on module A to direct how to interpret rules defined in them. This problem itself can be classified as a feature of $\mathbb{K}$ and only shows that $\mathbb{K}$ module system is not independent. However, if we define two configurations in two different modules in an object language specification, current $\mathbb{K}$ implementations can actually allow the specification to compile and execute programs. It will choose one of the configurations as the oracle. Which configuration will be pick is not clear. In **IsaK-Static**, we place a check to disallow two different configurations in a specification in the stage of **Applying Validity Checks** (in Sect. 2).

Module Systems and Extended Syntactic Definitions and Subsorts. The modularity of $\mathbb{K}$ allows users to define new syntactic constructs, new subsort relations or new semantic rules where they need. For an object language specification, users are able to define a new module with a new set of syntactic constructs and rules regarding the old modules. This brings problems. In the stage of **Heat/Cool Rules Generation** (Sect. 2), we see that a pair of `heat`/`cool` rules relying heavily on a built-in sort *KResult*. Defining new subsort relations in a new module with the sort *KResult* (which is a typical things to do in using $\mathbb{K}$) is in some sense changing the meaning of these `heat`/`cool` rules. It is completely possible that pattern matching a `heat` rule on a term might suddenly becomes invalid because we add a new module with a new subsort relation subsorting the target sort of a subterm in the term to *KResult*.

Moreover, extending a syntactic definition might invalidate an object language specification. In the **Applying Validity Checks** of the previous section, we have seen two such examples. If the two list syntactic definitions mentioned there are in two different modules, or if users define a new construct that has the same `kLabel` name as one in other modules, they will cause the object language specification to be invalid. In addition, if a rule is attributed with `function` in a new module, the rule might refer to be a part of semantics for a function application previous defined in other modules. The new rule might bring additional non-determinism for $\mathbb{K}$ functions in an object language specification. To solve the problem, our static semantics perform several checks in **Applying Validity Checks** to check if subsort relations are acyclic and anti-symmetric, if users define two syntactic definitions with the same `kLabel` name, and if two list syntactic definitions result in the conflict described in **Applying Validity Checks** (Sect. 2). If any of these is true, we recognize the input object language specification is not well-formed. For $\mathbb{K}$ functions, we only collect them and check if they follow certain formating such as having no more than one rule attributed with `owise` for a function construct, but we do not check if a function has non-determinism behaviors.

Failure in Generating Nested Cells. We have seen how K complies localization and concision features by "completing" a rule with configuration information in the **Transformation** stage in Sect. 2. Actually, current K implementations (K 3.6 and K 4.0) implicitly (without any error message or mention in any document) prevent people from defining in a configuration more than two levels of nested cells with the key word *, meaning that these cells can have zero or more copies through executions. What is more, there are some undesirable behaviors that happen when the nested * key word cell has only two levels. In K-Java [4], the method invocation rule connects an operator with a specific method body (some cells in the methodDec cell) in a specific class (the class cell). The method-Dec and class cells are both attributed with *. The method invocation rule in K-Java is valid but only by chance. If the author had changed the Java configuration by adding one more cell with the * key word inside the thread cell (labeled with * key word as well), an application of the method invocation rule would have crashed. This is not being picky because a lot of users might actually want to use the K-Java semantics to do further research. For example, when researchers want to enhance K-Java by making a better memory model, one thing they do is to change the stack structure. The current stack is implemented as a *List* data structure in K, but it is only used to store function information. Users might want to implement a real stack structure with stack range, types and map from byte location to value. We can model the stack structure as follows:

$$\langle\langle\langle StackType\rangle_{\text{stackType}}\ \langle Map\rangle_{\text{byteMap}}\ \langle(Int,Int)\rangle_{\text{stackRange}}\rangle_{\text{stackObject}*}\rangle_{\text{stack}}$$

The stackType stores the information about the types of the values stored in the stack piece; the byteMap cell stores the values for each byte location associated with the stack piece, and the stackRange cell determines the stack locations in the machine. By replacing the old stack cell with new stack structure in the K-Java configuration, we create two-level nested * cells in the configuration. The top level * cell is thread, and the inner level cell is stackObject. Suppose we define the semantics of an operator `getStackType` to lookup the type of a stack as:

$$\left\langle \frac{\textbf{getStackType}(X:Int)}{T:StackType} \cdots \right\rangle_{\text{k}}\ \langle\langle L:Int,R:Int\rangle\rangle_{\text{stackRange}}\ \langle T:StackType\rangle_{\text{stackType}}$$

requires $L:Int \le X:Int \le R:Int$

Once a program state requires this rule, the whole execution in the K 3.6 and K 4.0 crashes, because the special cell k representing the program computation sequence is inside a cell thread marked with the keyword *, and some variable inside the execution cell k is trying to match with some content inside another cell (stackObject) marked as *, which is inside the thread cell containing the execution cell k. Apparently, K 3.6 and K 4.0 do not allow this. If one is not a

$\mathbb{K}$ developer and is trying to define some language semantics with complicated stack or thread data structures, it is almost certain that they will need the special cell k inside a * keyword cell and define other cells in the * keyword cell with another * keyword. Nevertheless, determining there has been a crash, testing and finding the problem takes a $\mathbb{K}$ starter a great deal of effort and needless trouble because there are no error messages and the only way to locate it is to test each rule separately. Our **IsaK-Static** solve the problem by eliminating the restriction of level of nested cells with * keyword that users can write.

These are some design issues of $\mathbb{K}$ and our improvement, and we believe that this is one of the key advantages **IsaK-Static** is bringing to the $\mathbb{K}$ community.

4   Evaluation and Conclusion

Evaluating **IsaK-Static** took more than half of the development time. In testing it, we extracted OCaml code from **IsaK-Static** directly in Isabelle, and tested the $\mathbb{K}$ specifications and programs based on the extracted OCaml $\mathbb{K}$ interpreter. The extracted interpreter is using the dynamic semantics that we defined for $\mathbb{K}$ in the technical report [11]. The Ocaml interpreter is also a trivial utility of **IsaK-Static**, which is extracted directly from the Isabelle source code and users can use the krun function to execute a program of the specification and see a single trace of the program. In the following paragraphs, we describe our evaluation, especially the testing, which resulted in the first thorough set of bug reports for $\mathbb{K}$.

Testing process of IsaK-Static. The validation of language semantics is usually accomplished through the use of external test suites [6,7,12], which was also our strategy. A set of 13 specifications with 356 programs, which we call the $\mathbb{K}$ standard test suite, was the basis of our testing. It was used by the $\mathbb{K}$ team to test the $\mathbb{K}$ implementations.

Our methodology for developing **IsaK-Static** was through a strategy of combining Test Driven Development (TDD) with questioning the $\mathbb{K}$ team. We first talked to the $\mathbb{K}$ team in depth. In the first several months of our $\mathbb{K}$ semantics project, we only did multiple cycles of (1) discussing existing documents and materials with the $\mathbb{K}$ team, (2) implementing critical experiments of some small language specifications and running them in the $\mathbb{K}$ implementations, and (3) discussing more materials with them. After that, we developed our semantics largely by following the TDD process. The reason for employing this design methodology was because $\mathbb{K}$ had no semantics in print, so we needed to understand exactly what the $\mathbb{K}$ team was thinking. In addition, $\mathbb{K}$ is complicated enough that its design should be driven by tests. Our TDD design process required us to design our features carefully. When developing a new feature, we first tried to cover all corner cases of the feature under test in isolation, and then define it in the simplest way possible so as to pass all tests. The test suite also covered test cases when features overlapped, so we could make sure that the combinations of features in $\mathbb{K}$ were implemented correctly. This is extremely important in cases dealing with overlapped features.

We first used our design methodology to test our semantics with respect to the dynamic execution engine of K. We ran the K standard test suite, and our results showed that our K interpreter passed 338 of the programs. Among the test cases, we had no single specification that we could not handle. Our *kompile* function compiled all test specifications, but there were test programs that we could not handle with *krun* or *ksearch*. All of them related to the standard input channel. K allows users to define a cell as an input/output channel so that they can type in inputs to the cell from a keyboard, just as I/O operators in C and Java do. The behaviors of reading I/O input (the input channel) is hard to implement in Isabelle, and it is best to just define it with the K interpreter. We have not yet finished the job in the interpreter, but we believe that it will be an easy fix.

In the process of testing, we also questioned the behaviors of the current K implementations (K 3.6 and K 4.0). If we implemented a feature according to a K document and descriptions from the K team of the correct behaviors for it, and then found that test results for the feature were not what the K implementations did, we would extend the specifications or programs to include new aspects to see what the problems were. Thus, we found possible undesirable behaviors in the K implementations. Eventually, we located the bugs and made a new small K "program" (a small language specification and a single input program for the specification "k") to test against the bugs; we also added them to the test suite for later tests in the development process of **IsaK-Static**. In developing **IsaK-Static**, we identified 25 kinds of undesirable behavior in the K implementations. Each can have many different versions, and we specified a small K "program" for each of them in our test files.

These undesirable behaviors happen in very diverse circumstances. In fact, we have already seen one such failure in Sect. 3. Some implementations in K might have design problems. For example, rules labeled with a `macro` attribute (`macro` rules) are harmful and useless. There is no proper K documents suggesting the use of `macro` rules. When we test the rules, we find that applying such rules on a user defined program is error-prone. The only few cases when the `macro` rules can be applied successfully without any undesirable behaviors are those listed in the K test suites or in some previous defined language specifications in K [4–7]. In these cases, users always wanted to define a syntactic sugar and used a `macro` rule to rewrite the syntactic sugar to another term once in the beginning of a evaluation of input programs, which can be easily replaced by using `function` rules in K. Hence, `macro` rules are unnecessary in K.

Other undesirable behaviors are the implementation bugs in K. For example, some are related to sort checking/adjustment. The current K implementations allow users to write down rules rewriting a sort K term to a sort *List* or *Set* term, which are bugs because they do not allow users to write down rules rewriting a sort sort *List* or *Set* term to a sort K term. In addition, some undesirable behaviors are related to the pattern matching algorithm in K (the atomic step). The current K implementations allow some implicit associative and identity equational rules for user-defined list operators in a language specification.

However, there are some cases where the associative rewriting does not work, which is why we decided not to allow implicit associative and identity equational rules for user-defined list operators. Moreover, the implementation of the implicit commutative equational rule also fails in some cases. There are many of these undesirable behaviors, we will not list all of them here. Interested users can read the technical report [11] or go to https://github.com/liyili2/k-semantics to see these undesirable behaviors.

5   Related Work

We believe **IsaK-Static** is the first complete and formal static semantics of $\mathbb{K}$. In this section, we discuss related work on describing the $\mathbb{K}$ semantics, language semantics defined in $\mathbb{K}$ and other large scale language specifications.

$\mathbb{K}$ has a brief English description of its semantics and provides some examples in the $\mathbb{K}$ overview document [1]. In addition, there is a compiler implementation in Java to allow users to define their language specifications and show traces of execution programs. The compiler has almost fifty compilation steps, and eventually executes a program in a very small core language that has no English description to describe its grammar or semantics. In this sense, these $\mathbb{K}$ specifications are far from being formal. Matching Logic [13] is a logic system that is built on top of $\mathbb{K}$ for reasoning about structures. The current invention of Matching Logic is Reachability Logic [14,15]. It is a seven rule proof system and is language independent. It generalizes transitions of operational language specifications defined by users and the Hoare triples of axiomatic semantics [16] to prove properties about programs in the specifications, so that users do not need to define the axiomatic semantics of a specification. There is an ongoing project by Moore [17] that transfers the $\mathbb{K}$ specifications to Coq [18] and plans to prove properties of the programs of the specifications in Coq. The current state is that Moore has managed to define a useful co-induction tool in Coq and prove some properties by defining small language specifications in Coq. Big language specifications have been defined in $\mathbb{K}$ including C [7], PHP [6], JavaScript [5], and Java [4]. They are executable, have been validated by test banks, and, through the addition of some formal analysis tools produced by $\mathbb{K}$, have shown usefulness.

Standard ML by Milner, Tofte, Harper, and Macqueen [19] is one of the most prominent and mathematical programming language specifications, whose formal and executable specifications were given by Lee, Crary, and Harper [20], also by VanInwegen and Gunter [21], and by Maharaj and Gunter [22]. In contrast to ML, formalizing other real world language specifications is a challenge because they are designed without formalism in mind. There have been a number of formal language specifications given in the HOL and Coq. For example, A small step semantics of C in HOL was specified by Norrish [23], who proved substantial meta-properties, but the specification has not been tested for conformance with implementations. Blazy and Leroy [24] in the CompCert project have verified an optimizing compiler based on CLight, including compilation steps and

C-like modular systems. They used Coq to generate a compiled code behaving exactly as described by the specification of the language. Other projects based on CompCert include Appels, which combined program verification with a verified compilation software tool chain [25].

Other interesting work includes formal LLVM specification by Zhao et al. [26], a JavaScript specification by Bodin et al. [12], and formalized semantics of OCaml Light by Owens et al., which is built in Ott [27], which provides an easy way to write specifications, and automatically translates them into HOL, Isabelle, and Coq. HOL and Coq, being proof assistants, have a relatively steep learning curve, while Ott provides an easy way for researchers to explore specifications, which was one of the purposes for designing $\mathbb{K}$. Compared to Ott, $\mathbb{K}$ was designed as a programming language to allow users to define object language specifications by $\mathbb{K}$'s constructs that have modularity, localization and concision features.

We cannot list all interesting examples of formalized specifications in this paper for space reasons. Our **IsaK-Static** share many of the difficult challenges faced by the works described above, and involve many new ones due to the complex nature of $\mathbb{K}$. They are detailed in previous sections.

6 Conclusions and Future Directions

In this paper, we proposed **IsaK-Static**, which is a formal static semantics of $\mathbb{K}$ in Isabelle. It describes the behavior of how $\mathbb{K}$ is transformed from FAST to BAST; especially, how the concision, localization and modularity are transformed into a well structured BAST format. In addition, we discuss some potential design issues related to the concision, localization and modularity with respect to the transformation, and suggest some design changes. In the static semantics, we proposed a sort system for $\mathbb{K}$ which is the first complete sort system for $\mathbb{K}$. All of these processes involved discussion with the $\mathbb{K}$ team to make sure our $\mathbb{K}$ formal semantics behaved correctly. We also examined **IsaK-Static** by running tests against the extracted OCaml interpreter of **IsaK-Static** in Isabelle and found that our system passed all 13 test specifications and 338 out of 356 programs for these test specifications. We discovered 25 major undesirable behaviors of $\mathbb{K}$. We will continue to build the complete dynamic semantics of $\mathbb{K}$. After that, we will define and verify a compiler from $\mathbb{K}$ to Isabelle to build the bridge between the Isabelle community and the $\mathbb{K}$ group.

Acknowledgements. This material is based upon work supported in part by NSF Grant 0917218. Any opinions, findings, and conclusions or recommendations expressed in this material are those of the authors and do not necessarily reflect the views of the NSF.

References

1. Roşu, G., Şerbănuţă, T.F.: An overview of the K semantic framework. J. Logic Algebr. Program. **79**(6), 397–434 (2010)
2. Paulson, L.C.: Isabelle: The Next 700 Theorem Provers. In: Odifreddi, P. (ed.) Logic and Computer Science, pp. 361–386. Academic (1990)
3. Roşu, G.: K Publications (2017). http://www.kframework.org/index.php/K_Publications
4. Bogdănaş, D., Roşu, G.: K-Java: a complete semantics of java. In: Proceedings of the 42nd Symposium on Principles of Programming Languages (POPL 2015), pp. 445–456. ACM (January 2015)
5. Park, D., Ştefănescu, A., Roşu, G.: KJS: a complete formal semantics of javascript. In: Proceedings of the 36th ACM SIGPLAN Conference on Programming Language Design and Implementation (PLDI 2015), pp. 346–356 ACM (June 2015)
6. Filaretti, D., Maffeis, S.: An executable formal semantics of PHP. In: Jones, R. (ed.) ECOOP 2014. LNCS, vol. 8586, pp. 567–592. Springer, Heidelberg (2014). https://doi.org/10.1007/978-3-662-44202-9_23
7. Ellison, C., Rosu, G.: An executable formal semantics of C with applications. In: Proceedings of the 39th ACM SIGPLAN-SIGACT Symposium on Principles of Programming Languages (POPL2012), pp. 533–544. ACM (January 2012)
8. Hathhorn, C., Ellison, C., Roşu, G.: Defining the undefinedness of C. In: Proceedings of the 36th ACM SIGPLAN Conference on Programming Language Design and Implementation (PLDI 2015), pp. 336–345. ACM (June 2015)
9. Serbanuta, T.F., Arusoaie, A., Lazar, D., Ellison, C., Lucanu, D., Rosu, G.: The K primer (version 3.3). Electron. Notes Theore. Comput. Sci. **304**(Supplement C), 57–80 (2014). Proceedings of the Second International Workshop on the K Framework and its Applications (K 2011)
10. Bogdanas, D.: Label-based programming language semantics in K framework with SDF. In: Proceedings of the 2012 14th International Symposium on Symbolic and Numeric Algorithms for Scientific Computing. SYNASC 2012, Washington, DC, USA, pp. 160–167. IEEE Computer Society (2012)
11. Li, L., Gunter, E.L.: IsaK: A Complete Semantics of K. Technical Report , University of Illinois at Urbana-Champaign (June 2018). http://hdl.handle.net/2142/100116
12. Bodin, M., et al.: A trusted mechanised javascript specification. SIGPLAN Not. **49**(1), 87–100 (2014)
13. Roşu, G., Ştefănescu, A.: Matching logic: a new program verification approach. In: Proceedings of the 2010 Workshop on Usable Verification (UV 2010). Microsoft Research (2010)
14. Roşu, G., Ştefănescu, A., Ciobâcă, c., Moore, B.M.: One-path reachability logic. In: Proceedings of the 28th Symposium on Logic in Computer Science (LICS 2013), pp. 358–367. IEEE (June 2013)
15. Ştefănescu, A., e al.: All-path reachability logic. In: Dowek, G. (ed.) RTA 2014. LNCS, vol. 8560, pp. 425–440. Springer, Cham (2014). https://doi.org/10.1007/978-3-319-08918-8_29
16. Hoare, C.A.R.: An axiomatic basis for computer programming. Commun. ACM **12**(10), 576–580 (1969)
17. Moore, B., Roşu, G.: Program Verification by Coinduction. Technical Report University of Illinois (February 2015). http://hdl.handle.net/2142/73177

18. Corbineau, P.: A declarative language for the Coq proof assistant. In: Miculan, M., Scagnetto, I., Honsell, F. (eds.) TYPES 2007. LNCS, vol. 4941, pp. 69–84. Springer, Heidelberg (2008). https://doi.org/10.1007/978-3-540-68103-8_5

19. Milner, R., Tofte, M., Macqueen, D.: The Definition of Standard ML. MIT Press, Cambridge (1997)

20. Lee, D.K., Crary, K., Harper, R.: Towards a mechanized metatheory of standard ML. SIGPLAN Not. **42**(1), 173–184 (2007)

21. Vanlnwegen, M., Gunter, E.: HOL-ML. In: Joyce, J.J., Seger, C.-J.H. (eds.) HUG 1993. LNCS, vol. 780, pp. 61–74. Springer, Heidelberg (1994). https://doi.org/10.1007/3-540-57826-9_125

22. Maharaj, S., Gunter, E.: Studying the ML module system in HOL. In: Melham, T.F., Camilleri, J. (eds.) HUG 1994. LNCS, vol. 859, pp. 346–361. Springer, Heidelberg (1994). https://doi.org/10.1007/3-540-58450-1_53

23. Norrish, M.: C formalised in HOL. Technical Report UCAM-CL-TR-453, University of Cambridge, Computer Laboratory (December 1998)

24. Blazy, S., Leroy, X.: Mechanized semantics for the clight subset of the C language. J. Autom. Reason. **43**(3), 263–288 (2009)

25. Appel, A.W.: Verified software toolchain. In: Proceedings of the 20th European Conference on Programming Languages and Systems: Part of the Joint European Conferences on Theory and Practice of Software. ESOP 2011/ETAPS 2011, pp. 1–17 . Springer, Berlin (2011)

26. Zhao, J., Nagarakatte, S., Martin, M.M., Zdancewic, S.: Formalizing the LLVM intermediate representation for verified program transformations. SIGPLAN Not. **47**(1), 427–440 (2012)

27. Sewell, P. et al.: Ott: Effective Tool Support for the Working Semanticist. J. Funct. Program. **20**(1), 71–122 (2010)

Solving Parameterised Boolean Equation Systems with Infinite Data Through Quotienting

Thomas Neele[(✉)], Tim A.C. Willemse, and Jan Friso Groote

Eindhoven University of Technology, Eindhoven, The Netherlands
{T.S.Neele,T.A.C.Willemse,J.F.Groote}@tue.nl

Abstract. Parameterised Boolean Equation Systems (PBESs) can be used to represent many different kinds of decision problems. Most notably, model checking and equivalence problems can be encoded in a PBES. Traditional instantiation techniques cannot deal with PBESs with an infinite data domain. We propose an approach that can solve PBESs with infinite data by computing the bisimulation quotient of the underlying graph structure. Furthermore, we show how this technique can be improved by repeatedly searching for finite proofs. Unlike existing approaches, our technique is not restricted to subfragments of PBESs. Experimental results show that our ideas work well in practice and support a wider range of models and properties than state-of-the-art techniques.

1 Introduction

A *parameterised Boolean equation system* (PBES) [12] is a sequence of fixpoint equations over first-order logic formulae. Many different types of decision problems can be encoded in a PBES, for example model checking problems, as implemented by the toolsets CADP [11] and mCRL2 [6], and equivalence queries [4]. Model checking problems using the modal mu-calculus with data and time as well as CTL*/LTL formulas can be translated efficiently into PBESs. The answer to the encoded problem can be found by (partially) solving the PBES. In this way, PBESs and techniques to solve them are useful in the analysis of component systems.

Although finding the solution of a PBES is undecidable in general, in practice several efficient approaches to solve PBESs exist. Most notably, some PBESs can be solved efficiently by first simplifying it—if needed—using static analysis techniques, instantiating it to a finite *Boolean equation system* (BES) and subsequently solving this BES. However, for many types of problems, the corresponding PBES contains data taken from domains that are infinite. For example, a PBES encoding the mutual exclusion property for Lamport's bakery protocol requires data variables ranging over natural numbers. Similarly, PBESs encoding model checking problems for timed or hybrid systems, typically modelled by

K. Bae and P. C. Ölveczky (Eds.): FACS 2018, LNCS 11222, pp. 216–236, 2018.
https://doi.org/10.1007/978-3-030-02146-7_11

timed automata or hybrid automata, contain data variables that range over real numbers.

Several symbolic techniques have been proposed to deal with PBESs over infinite data domains [10,18,21], but their application is unfortunately limited to specific subclasses of PBESs. Typically, these fragments exclude PBESs in which both logical quantifiers occur; *i.e.* PBESs may only contain universal quantification or only existential quantification. Such constraints effectively limit the class of properties that can be encoded, excluding, *e.g.* most behavioural equivalence decision problems, but also many CTL* properties. In this paper, we present a more general approach that is applicable to the *full* class of PBESs, without such limitations. Our contributions are as follows:

- We introduce a new normal form for PBESs which we call *clustered recursive form* (CRF). This normal form facilitates reasoning about the dependencies between predicate variables in a PBES and enables capturing these in a *dependency graph*.
- We provide an algorithm that computes, using quotienting, a minimal reduced dependency graph from a symbolic representation of the dependency graph of a PBES. Upon termination of the algorithm, the computed artefact can then be used to solve the PBES. The correctness is given by Theorem 3.
- On top of this, we provide an algorithm that extracts finite partial solutions from PBESs that have an infinite minimal reduced dependency graph. The correctness of this approach is given by Theorem 4.

To validate the above, we perform a number of experiments with an implementation of our two algorithms and compare these to the approach of [18]. The results of this evaluation show that our technique is indeed capable of solving decision problems that existing approaches fail to solve so far. In particular, the experiments show that our technique is a promising generic approach for model checking of (timed) modal mu-calculus properties on systems with infinite data domains and also equivalence checking of systems with infinite data domains.

The rest of the paper is structured as follows: Sect. 2 introduces the basic theoretical concepts. Section 3 contains an example that shows how PBESs can be applied and what the shortcomings of current solving techniques are. Then, Sects. 4 and 5 show how a minimal representation of the semantics of a PBES can be computed. An improved algorithm is presented in Sect. 6, and the performance of an experimental implementation is evaluated in Sect. 7. Finally, Sect. 8 gives an overview of related work and Sect. 9 presents a conclusion and suggestions for future work. For detailed proofs of our lemmas and theorems we refer to a technical report [23].

2   Preliminaries

In this paper, we work with abstract data types and denote their non-empty data sorts with the letters $D, E, \ldots$ and their corresponding semantic domains by $\mathbb{D}, \mathbb{E}, \ldots$ In addition, we use B to denote the Booleans and N to denote the natural numbers $\{0, 1, 2, \ldots\}$, which have the semantic counterparts $\mathbb{B}$ and $\mathbb{N}$ respectively. We also have a singleton sort $D_\star = \{\star\}$ on which no operations are defined. Furthermore, we have a set of data variables $\mathcal{V}$. Expressions not containing variables are called *ground terms*. For expressions that do contain variables, we have a data environment δ that maps each variable in $\mathcal{V}$ to an element of the corresponding sort. The semantics of an expression f in the context of a data environment δ is denoted $[\![f]\!]\delta$. The set of all data environments is Δ. Updates to an environment δ are denoted by $\delta[v/d]$, which is defined as $\delta[v/d](d) = v$ and $\delta[v/d](d') = \delta(d')$ for all variables d, d' satisfying $d' \neq d$.

A parameterised Boolean equation system is a sequence of fixpoint equations over predicate formulae. We confine ourselves to giving a cursory overview of the syntax and semantics of the relevant theory and refer the interested reader to [12] for a more in-depth treatment and additional examples.

Definition 1. *A predicate formula is defined by the following grammar:*

$$\phi ::= b \mid \phi \vee \phi \mid \phi \wedge \phi \mid \phi \Rightarrow \phi \mid \exists e{:}E.\,\phi \mid \forall e{:}E.\,\phi \mid X(f)$$

where b is a data term of sort B, e is a variable of sort E, X is a predicate variable of sort $D \to B$, which is taken from some set $\mathcal{X}$ of sorted predicate variables and argument f is an expression of sort D. The interpretation of a predicate formula ϕ in the context of a predicate environment $\eta : \mathcal{X} \to 2^D$, providing an interpretation for predicate variables from $\mathcal{X}$, and a data environment δ is denoted by $[\![\phi]\!]\eta\delta$ and inductively defined as follows:

$$[\![b]\!]\eta\delta = [\![b]\!]\delta \qquad\qquad [\![X(f)]\!]\eta\delta = \begin{cases} true & if \; [\![f]\!]\delta \in \eta(X) \\ false & otherwise \end{cases}$$

$$[\![\varphi \wedge \psi]\!]\eta\delta \Leftrightarrow [\![\varphi]\!]\eta\delta \; and \; [\![\psi]\!]\eta\delta \; hold \qquad [\![\varphi \vee \psi]\!]\eta\delta \Leftrightarrow [\![\varphi]\!]\eta\delta \; or \; [\![\psi]\!]\eta\delta \; hold$$

$$[\![\varphi \Rightarrow \psi]\!]\eta\delta \Leftrightarrow [\![\varphi]\!]\eta\delta \; holds \; implies \; that \; [\![\psi]\!]\eta\delta \; holds$$

$$[\![\forall d : E.\; \varphi]\!]\eta\delta \Leftrightarrow for \; all \; v \in E, \; [\![\varphi]\!]\eta\delta[v/d] \; holds$$

$$[\![\exists d : E.\; \varphi]\!]\eta\delta \Leftrightarrow for \; some \; v \in E, \; [\![\varphi]\!]\eta\delta[v/d] \; holds$$

A predicate formula is *syntactically monotone* iff all its subformulae of the form $\varphi \Rightarrow \psi$ are such that φ contains no predicate variables. Without loss of generality, in the theory we develop in this paper we only consider parameterised Boolean equation systems where each equation carries the same single parameter of a given data sort D. In our examples, we use (multi-parameter) equations ranging over the Booleans (B) and the natural numbers (N).

Definition 2. *A parameterised Boolean equation system (PBES) is a sequence of equations as defined by the following grammar:*

$$\mathcal{E} ::= \emptyset \mid (\nu X(d{:}D) = \varphi)\mathcal{E} \mid (\mu X(d{:}D) = \varphi)\mathcal{E}$$

where $\emptyset$ is the empty PBES, μ and ν denote the least and greatest fixpoint operator, respectively, and $X \in \mathcal{X}$ is a predicate variable of sort $D \to B$. The right-hand side φ is a syntactically monotone predicate formula. Lastly, $d \in \mathcal{V}$ is a parameter of sort D.

We use bnd($\mathcal{E}$) to denote the predicate variables bound by $\mathcal{E}$, *i.e.*, those variables occurring at the left-hand side of an equation. For an equation for X, d_X denotes its parameter and φ_X denotes its right-hand side predicate formula. We omit the trailing $\emptyset$. We say a PBES is *closed* when it does not contain free variables, *i.e.*, all data variables that occur in a right-hand side φ_X are either bound by a quantifier or as a data parameter of X, whereas all predicate variables belong to bnd($\mathcal{E}$). A PBES $\mathcal{E}$ is called a *Boolean equation system* (BES) iff all predicate variables bound by $\mathcal{E}$ have type $D_\star \to B$ and every right-hand side only contains the operators $\wedge$ and $\vee$, constants *true* and *false* and $X(\star)$. We say that a PBES $\mathcal{E}$ is *well-formed* iff for every $X \in$ bnd($\mathcal{E}$) there is exactly one equation in $\mathcal{E}$. In the remainder of the paper we only reason about well-formed, closed PBESs.

Definition 3. *The solution $[\![\mathcal{E}]\!]\eta\delta$ of a PBES $\mathcal{E}$ in the context of a predicate environment η and a data environment δ, is a predicate environment that is defined inductively:*

$$[\![\emptyset]\!]\eta\delta = \eta$$
$$[\![(\mu X(d{:}D) = \varphi_X)\mathcal{E}]\!]\eta\delta = [\![\mathcal{E}]\!]\eta[\mu T_X/X]\delta$$
$$[\![(\nu X(d{:}D) = \varphi_X)\mathcal{E}]\!]\eta\delta = [\![\mathcal{E}]\!]\eta[\nu T_X/X]\delta$$

with $T_X(R) = \{v \in \mathbb{D} \mid [\![\varphi_X]\!]([\![\mathcal{E}]\!]\eta[R/X]\delta)\delta[v/d]\}$.

Intuitively, the solution of a PBES gives priority to fixpoints that occur early in the PBES, while satisfying the equalities that are specified by each equation. The monotonicity of the transformer $T_X : 2^{\mathbb{D}} \to 2^{\mathbb{D}}$, which follows from syntactic monotonicity of φ_X, guarantees the existence of the least fixpoint μT_X and greatest fixpoint νT_X in the complete lattice $(2^{\mathbb{D}}, \subseteq)$. Also, note that the solution of a bound variable in a closed PBES does not depend on the environments η and δ. For this reason, we often omit η and δ and simply write $[\![\mathcal{E}]\!]$ instead of $[\![\mathcal{E}]\!]\eta\delta$. Finally, for a PBES $\mathcal{E}$ and some $X \in$ bnd($\mathcal{E}$) we sometimes say that [the solution to] $X(v)$ is *true* iff $v \in [\![\mathcal{E}]\!](X)$.

Example 1. Consider the following PBES consisting of an equation for X and an equation for Y, both carrying a single parameter. Furthermore, the equation for X has a least fixpoint, and the equation for Y has a greatest fixpoint.

$$\mu X(n{:}N) = (\exists m{:}N. \, m \geq n \wedge X(m)) \wedge Y(false)$$
$$\nu Y(b{:}B) = Y(\neg b)$$

The solution η for this PBES satisfies $\eta(X) = \emptyset$ and $\eta(Y) = \mathbb{B}$. $\qquad\square$

The theory of this paper is built on the notion of *dependency graphs* and *proof graphs* explored in [8]. Intuitively, a proof graph is a witness providing an operational explanation for a (partial) solution of a PBES. Before we introduce these graphs formally, we need some additional concepts.

First, sig($\mathcal{E}$) is the signature of $\mathcal{E}$, defined as sig($\mathcal{E}$) $= \{(X, v) \mid X \in$ bnd($\mathcal{E}$), $v \in \mathbb{D}\}$. For a given set $S \subseteq$ sig($\mathcal{E}$), the predicate environment

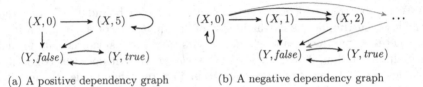

(a) A positive dependency graph   (b) A negative dependency graph

Fig. 1. Dependency graphs for the PBES from Example 1.

env$(S, true)$ that follows from it is defined as env$(S, true)(X) = \{v \in \mathbb{D} \mid (X, v) \in S\}$. Dually, we define env$(S, false)(X) = \mathbb{D} \setminus$ env$(S, true)(X)$. Furthermore, every predicate variable bound in $\mathcal{E} = (\sigma_1 X_1(d{:}D) = \varphi_1) \ldots (\sigma_n X_n(d{:}D) = \varphi_n)$ is assigned a *rank*, where rank$_{\mathcal{E}}(X_i)$ is the number of alternations in the sequence of fixpoint symbols $\nu\sigma_1\sigma_2 \ldots \sigma_i$. Observe that rank$_{\mathcal{E}}(X_i)$ is *even* iff $\sigma_i = \nu$.

Definition 4. *Let $\mathcal{E}$ be a PBES and $G = (V, E)$ be a directed graph, where $V \subseteq \text{sig}(\mathcal{E})$. We say G is a* dependency graph *for $r \in \mathbb{B}$ iff for every $(X, v) \in V$ and for all δ, $[\![\varphi_X]\!]\eta(\delta[v/d_X]) = r$ with $\eta = \text{env}((X, v)^\bullet, r)$, where $s^\bullet$ denotes the* successor set *of a node, defined as $s^\bullet = \{t \mid s \, E \, t\}$.*

Intuitively, in a *positive dependency graph* (where r is *true*), $\eta = \text{env}((X, v)^\bullet, r)$ is a predicate environment that maps all successors of (X, v) to *true* and all other nodes to *false*. Then, the requirement is that φ_X (and thus $X(v)$) is *true* under η and a data environment that maps d_X to v. In other words, the successors of a node (X, v) being *true* must imply that (X, v) is *true* as well. Dually, a *negative dependency graph* (where r is *false*) indicates a node (X, v) is *false*, because its successors are all *false*.

Example 2. Recall the PBES from Example 1. Figure 1 depicts a positive and a negative dependency graph for this PBES. We focus on node $(X, 0)$ in the positive dependency graph of Fig. 1(a). Its successors are $(X, 5)$ and $(Y, false)$. The environment η induced by these successors is given by env$((X, 0)^\bullet, true)$, which sets these successors to *true*; *i.e.* η is such that $\eta(X) = \{5\}$ and $\eta(Y) = \{false\}$. When we evaluate the right-hand side of the equation for X in the context of η and parameter n set to 0, we obtain $[\![(\exists m{:}N. \, m \geq n \wedge X(m)) \wedge Y(false)]\!]\eta(\delta[0/n]) = true$. Therefore, the positive dependency graph condition is satisfied for node $(X, 0)$.

Note that nodes $(Y, false)$ and $(Y, true)$ are dependent on each other in both dependency graphs. Furthermore, in the negative case, $(X, 0)$ needs no dependency on $(Y, false)$ as long as it depends on all (X, i) with $i \in \mathbb{N}$. $\square$

A dependency graph captures the logical structure of a PBES; it does not include the fixpoint semantics. If we want to reason about the actual solution of a PBES, we need an additional restriction on the infinite paths in a dependency graph. Dependency graphs that meet these restrictions are called *proof graphs*.

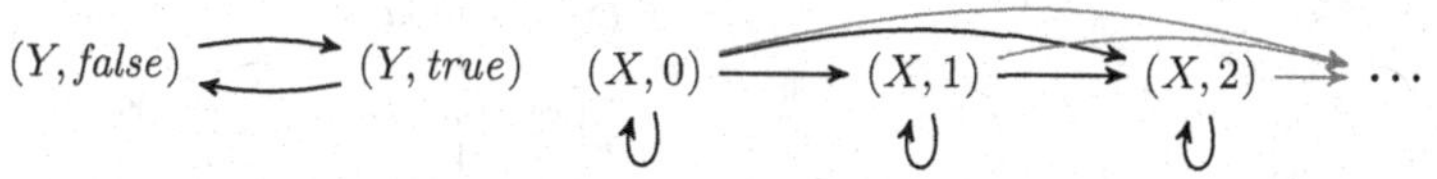

$(Y, false) \rightleftarrows (Y, true)$ $(X, 0) \rightrightarrows (X, 1) \rightrightarrows (X, 2) \rightrightarrows \cdots$

(a) A positive proof graph   (b) A negative proof graph

Fig. 2. Proof graphs for the PBES from Example 1.

Definition 5. *Let $G = (V, E)$ be a positive (respectively negative) dependency graph for a PBES $\mathcal{E}$. Then G is a positive proof graph (respectively negative proof graph) iff for all infinite paths π in G, the number $\min\{rank_{\mathcal{E}}(X) \mid X \in V^{\infty}(\pi)\}$ is even (respectively odd), where $V^{\infty}(\pi)$ is the set of predicate variables that occur infinitely often along π.*

Observe that predicate variables with a lower rank dominate those with a higher rank. This reflects the fact that fixpoint symbols that occur early in an equation system take priority over later ones (cf. Definition 3).

Example 3. Recall again the PBES from Example 1. In this PBES, the rank of X is 1, and the rank of Y is 2. Figure 2 depicts a positive and a negative proof graph for this PBES. Note that Fig. 2(a) depicts the smallest positive proof graph proving that $Y(false)$ is *true*. Larger proof graphs can be obtained by adding a self loop to $(Y, false)$ or $(Y, true)$. Similarly, the proof graph in Fig. 2(b) is the smallest negative proof graph explaining that $X(0)$ is *false*. However, there is a smaller negative proof graph showing that $X(1) = false$, *viz.* the graph that does not include $(X, 0)$.   □

The next theorem formally states the relationship between proof graphs and the solution of a PBES.

Theorem 1. ([8]) *Let $\mathcal{E}$ be a PBES with $X \in bnd(\mathcal{E})$. Then $v \in [\![\mathcal{E}]\!](X)$ iff there is a positive proof graph (V, E) such that $(X, v) \in V$. Dually, $v \notin [\![\mathcal{E}]\!](X)$ iff there is a negative proof graph containing (X, v).*

In [8], proof graphs were introduced mainly to formalise the concept of witnesses and counterexamples. Instead, we rely on the above theorem to (partially) *solve* PBESs by searching for concise representations of proof graphs. Before we explain this idea in detail, we illustrate how to apply PBESs in model checking with an example.

3   Motivating Example

To show how PBESs can be used for model checking and to motivate our approach, we introduce a slightly larger example in this section. The model we consider is a simplified version of Lamport's bakery protocol [19]. In our setting, there are only two processes (customer 0 and customer 1) and all writes and reads are atomic. When customer i enters the bakery, he/she does not have a

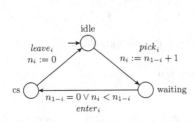

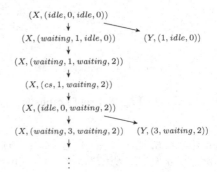

Fig. 3. Process i from the simplified bakery protocol.

Fig. 4. Part of the infinite proof graph of the bakery example.

number ($n = 0$). At any point, the customer can pick a number, which is one larger than the number of the other customer. If both customers are waiting, the customer with the smallest number can enter the critical section. When leaving the critical section, the number is discarded (n is reset to 0). See Fig. 3.

On this model, we would like to check the property "whenever customer 0 picks a number, it will unavoidably enter the critical section within a finite amount of time". This can be formalised with the modal mu-calculus formula $\nu X.([true]X \wedge [pick_0]\mu Y.([\overline{enter_0}]Y \wedge \langle true \rangle true))$. From the model and the formula, the following PBES can be constructed automatically:

$$\nu X(s_0{:}S, n_0{:}N, s_1{:}S, n_1{:}N) = \tag{1}$$
$$s_0 = idle \Rightarrow Y(n_1 + 1, s_1, n_1) \wedge \tag{2}$$
$$s_0 = idle \Rightarrow X(waiting, n_1 + 1, s_1, n_1) \wedge \tag{3}$$
$$s_0 = waiting \wedge (n_1 = 0 \vee n_0 < n_1) \Rightarrow X(cs, n_0, s_1, n_1) \wedge \tag{4}$$
$$s_0 = cs \Rightarrow X(idle, 0, s_1, n_1) \wedge \tag{5}$$
$$s_1 = idle \Rightarrow X(s_0, n_0, waiting, n_0 + 1) \wedge \tag{6}$$
$$s_1 = waiting \wedge (n_0 = 0 \vee n_1 < n_0) \Rightarrow X(s_0, n_0, cs, n_1) \wedge \tag{7}$$
$$s_1 = cs \Rightarrow X(s_0, n_0, idle, 0) \tag{8}$$
$$\mu Y(n_0{:}N, s_1{:}S, n_1{:}N) = \tag{9}$$
$$((n_1 = 0 \vee n_0 < n_1) \vee \tag{10}$$
$$s_1 = idle \vee (s_1 = waiting \wedge (n_0 = 0 \vee n_1 < n_0)) \vee s_1 = cs) \wedge \tag{11}$$
$$s_1 = idle \Rightarrow Y(n_0, waiting, n_0 + 1) \wedge \tag{12}$$
$$s_1 = waiting \wedge (n_1 = 0 \vee n_1 < n_0) \Rightarrow Y(n_0, cs, n_1) \wedge \tag{13}$$
$$s_1 = cs \Rightarrow Y(n_0, idle, 0) \tag{14}$$

In this encoding, s_i and n_i represent the state and number of customer i, respectively. Furthermore, the states of a single process are encoded in the sort S. Predicate variable X represents the fact that the property has to hold at any point in time. Therefore, it encodes the full behaviour of the system (lines 3–8) and is labelled with a greatest fixpoint. When customer 0 picks a number, we check the second half of the property using Y (line 2). For predicate variable Y, we assume that customer 0 is in the state *waiting*. Then, Y is *true* if customer 0 can enter the critical section (line 10) or customer 1 does something else after which Y holds (line 11 and lines 12–14). However, customer 1 is only allowed to do something finitely often, so the equation for Y is labelled with a least fixpoint. The property holds, since the solution for the initial state is *true*, i.e., $(X, (idle, 0, idle, 0)) \in [\![\mathcal{E}]\!](X)$.

There are a few interesting observations that we can make based on this PBES. Firstly, it is not possible to solve it with traditional instantiation-based techniques, since the dependency graph is infinite. Moreover, there is no finite proof graph that contains $(X, (idle, 0, idle, 0))$, so even the application of smart heuristics to guide the instantiation does not improve the situation. See Fig. 4 for a part of the infinite proof graph. Secondly, the actual value of n_0 and n_1 is not essential to the problem. What matters is which of the two is larger. This inspired us to investigate symbolic techniques for solving PBESs.

4   Standard and Clustered Recursive Form

To reason symbolically about the underlying dependency graph of a PBES $\mathcal{E}$, we need to rely on the information contained in $\mathcal{E}$. However, for PBESs with an arbitrary structure, that is not trivial [15]. Therefore, we introduce a normal form that simplifies the reasoning about transitions in the underlying proof graph.

A common normal form for Boolean equation systems is *standard recursive form* (SRF) [16]. This normal form is commonly used to translate a BES into a *parity game*, for which efficient solving techniques exist. We generalise the definition to PBESs.

Definition 6. *Let $\mathcal{E}$ be a PBES. Then $\mathcal{E}$ is in* standard recursive form *(SRF) iff for all $(\sigma_i X_i(d{:}D) = \phi) \in \mathcal{E}$, ϕ is either disjunctive or conjunctive, i.e., the equation for X_i has the shape*

$$\sigma_i X_i(d{:}D) = \bigvee_{j \in J_i} \exists e_j{:}E_j.\ f_j(d, e_j) \wedge X_j(g_j(d, e_j))$$

or

$$\sigma_i X_i(d{:}D) = \bigwedge_{j \in J_i} \forall e_j{:}E_j.\ f_j(d, e_j) \Rightarrow X_j(g_j(d, e_j))$$

Furthermore, we add the semantic restriction that for every $(X, v) \in \text{sig}(\mathcal{E})$, at least one condition f_j should evaluate to true, i.e., there is a $j \in J$, a data environment δ and a $v_j \in \mathbb{E}_j$ such that $[\![f_j(d, e_j)]\!]\delta[v_j/e_j, v/d]$ holds.

Standard recursive form is similar to the *parameterised parity game* form of [14]. We call each of the disjuncts or conjuncts of a right-hand side a *clause*.

For a PBES $\mathcal{E}$ in SRF, we define a function $op_{\mathcal{E}} : bnd(\mathcal{E}) \rightarrow \{\wedge, \vee\}$ that indicates for each predicate variable whether its equation is conjunctive or disjunctive. The next proposition states that SRF is a proper normal form, *i.e.*, every PBES can be transformed into SRF while preserving the solution of bound variables.

Proposition 1. *For every PBES $\mathcal{E}$, there is an $\mathcal{E}'$ in SRF such that $[\![\mathcal{E}]\!](X) = [\![\mathcal{E}']\!](X)$ for every $X \in bnd(\mathcal{E})$.*

Proof. For each equation in $\mathcal{E}$ that is not yet of the required form, we can stepwise transform it into one that is. This is done by eliminating nested conjunctions, disjunctions and quantifiers by introducing new predicate variables and extra equations for these variables, see [12]. For instance, an equation that is of the form $(\sigma X(d{:}D) = \forall e{:}E. \phi)$ can be replaced by two equations $(\sigma X(d{:}D) = \forall e{:}E. Y(d, e))$ $(\sigma Y(d{:}D, e{:}E) = \phi)$ for some fresh variable Y. Note that this results in at most a linear blow-up of the size of $\mathcal{E}$.

The semantic restriction that at least one clause should be satisfiable can be met by adding the equations $(\nu X_{true}(d{:}D_\star) = X_{true}(\star))$ and $(\mu X_{false}(d{:}D_\star) = X_{false}(\star))$ to $\mathcal{E}$, and adding a clause $X_{true}(\star)$ to every conjunctive right-hand side and a clause $X_{false}(\star)$ to every disjunctive right-hand side. $\qquad\square$

We say a formula is in *clustered recursive form* (CRF) iff the predicate variable in each of the clauses is unique, *i.e.*, $X_j \neq X_k$ for all distinct $j, k \in J$. A PBES is in CRF iff all its right-hand sides are CRF formulae. We observe that every PBES can be transformed to CRF by applying Proposition 1 and subsequently combining clauses that have the same predicate variable, relying on suitable pairing and projection operators for the data arguments.

Henceforward we only consider PBESs in CRF. The structure offered by CRF enables us to reason about the edges that exist in proof graphs. Intuitively, an outgoing edge from a node (X_i, v) must be based on some clause $j \in J_i$ whose guard $f_j(v, e_j)$ is *true* for some e_j of sort E_j. The target node of that edge is associated to predicate variable instance $X_j(g_j(v, e_j))$. The following definition formalises this.

Definition 7. *Let $\mathcal{E}$ be a PBES in CRF, where each equation has the same structure as in Definition 6. Then, the* dependency space *of $\mathcal{E}$ is a graph $G = (sig(\mathcal{E}), E)$, where E is the set satisfying $(X_i, v)E(X_j, w)$ for given X_i, X_j for $j \in J_i$, v and w iff for some δ and $v_j{\in}E_j$, both $w = [\![g_j(d, e_j)]\!]\delta[v_j/e_j, v/d]$ and $[\![f_j(d, e_j)]\!]\delta[v_j/e_j, v/d]$ hold.*

Definition 7 generalises the definition of a dependency space from [18]. Note that every node in a dependency space has an outgoing edge, since CRF imposes this semantic requirement. This is necessary for the validity of the next lemma.

Lemma 1. *The dependency space $G = (sig(\mathcal{E}), E)$ of $\mathcal{E}$ is both a positive and a negative dependency graph.*

Proof. Let (X_i, v) be a node of G. There are four cases that we must consider. Case 1: suppose the equation for X_i is conjunctive and we want to prove that

G is a positive dependency graph, *i.e.*, r (from Definition 4) is *true*. From the definition of env$(S, true)$ and Definition 7 we know the following:

$$\text{env}((X_i, v)^\bullet, true)(X_j) \\ = \{[\![g_j(d, e_j)]\!]\delta[v_j/e_j, v/d] \mid \delta \in \Delta, v_j \in \mathbb{E}_j. \ [\![f_j(d, e_j)]\!]\delta[v_j/e_j, v/d]\} \qquad (\dagger)$$

Using the definition of the semantics and $(\dagger)$, we can deduce that $[\![\varphi_{X_i}]\!]\eta\delta[v/d] = r$, where $\eta = \text{env}((X_i, v)^\bullet, true)$. With this, the condition on transitions in a positive dependency graph is satisfied. The proofs for the other three combinations are analogous. $\qquad\square$

Theorem 2. *The dependency space of a PBES $\mathcal{E}$ is the unique smallest dependency graph with $V = \text{sig}(\mathcal{E})$ that is both positive and negative.*

Proof. By contradiction. Let $G = (\text{sig}(\mathcal{E}), E)$ be the dependency space for some PBES $\mathcal{E}$ and let $G' = (\text{sig}(\mathcal{E}), E')$ be a dependency graph that is both positive and negative such that $E \not\subseteq E'$, *i.e.*, G is not strictly smaller than G'. That means that there is at least one edge in E that is missing from E'. Let $(X, v)E(Y, w)$ be such an edge. From the definition of a dependency space, we can deduce that there is some j such that $Y = X_j$. Furthermore, for some value of e_j, if d has value v, the condition $f_j(d, e_j)$ holds and $g_j(d, e_j)$ has value w. Therefore, (X, v) depends on (Y, w) in one of two ways:

- In case the equation for X is conjunctive, $Y(w)$ necessarily has to hold in order for $X(v)$ to hold. This is not reflected by G'. Therefore G' is not a positive dependency graph, contrary to our assumption.
- In case the equation for X is disjunctive, $Y(w)$ necessarily has to be false in order for $X(v)$ to be false. This is not reflected by G'. Therefore G' is not a negative dependency graph, again contrary to our assumption.

We conclude that G' is either not a positive or not a negative dependency graph, which contradicts our initial assumption. $\qquad\square$

5 Reduced Dependency Space

In the literature, different approaches to solving PBESs have been proposed. Many of those rely on instantiation of the PBES to a finite Boolean equation system. The BES can then be solved with Gaussian elimination or with a parity game solver. However, for PBESs with an underlying infinite BES, instantiation is not possible. Several symbolic approaches have been proposed to reason about the solution of such a PBES. Most notably, Koolen *et al.* [18] use SMT solvers to find proof graphs and Nagae *et al.* [21,22] compute reduced proof graphs that finitely represent an infinite proof graph. We extend that latter work to arbitrary PBESs and show how a reduced proof graph can be computed efficiently.

Definition 8. *Let $G = (V, E)$ be a dependency graph for a PBES $\mathcal{E}$. Then $G' = (V', E')$ is a reduced dependency graph, iff:*

- $V' \subseteq 2^V$ is a finite partition of V, i.e. $\bigcup V' = V$ and for all distinct $b, b' \in V'$ we have $b \cap b' \neq \emptyset$,
- $E' = \{(b, b') \in V' \times V' \mid \exists s \in b, t \in b'. s E t\}$.

We say G is the base graph of G'.

The intuition behind reduced dependency graphs is that nodes that are in some way equivalent, are grouped. In this way, some infinite dependency graphs can be represented finitely. As equivalence relation on nodes we use *bisimulation* [24].

Definition 9. *Let $G = (V, E)$ be a dependency graph for $\mathcal{E}$. A relation $\mathcal{R} \subseteq V \times V$ is a* bisimulation relation *iff for all $(X, v)\mathcal{R}(Y, w)$:*

- $rank_{\mathcal{E}}(X) = rank_{\mathcal{E}}(Y)$ *and* $op_{\mathcal{E}}(X) = op_{\mathcal{E}}(Y)$.
- *If $(X, v)E(X', v')$, then there is a (Y', w') such that $(Y, w)E(Y', w')$ and $(X', v')\mathcal{R}(Y', w')$.*
- *If $(Y, w)E(Y', w')$, then there is a (X', v') such that $(X, v)E(X', v')$ and $(X', v')\mathcal{R}(Y', w')$.*

We say that nodes (X, v) and (Y, w) are bisimilar, denoted $(X, v) \Leftrightarrow (Y, w)$, iff they are related by some bisimulation relation. We say two graphs G and H are bisimilar iff for every node in G there is a bisimilar node in H and vice versa.

Since bisimilarity is an equivalence relation it induces a partition of the node set V into equivalence classes. We call the reduced dependency graph $G_r = (V/\Leftrightarrow, E_r)$, that has G as its base graph (cf. Definition 8), the *bisimulation quotient* of G, notation $G/\Leftrightarrow$.

Partition refinement

To compute the bisimulation quotient, we rely on partition refinement. In this algorithm, a partition of the state space is iteratively refined until it becomes *stable* (a formal definition follows). The coarsest stable partition coincides with the equivalence classes under bisimulation.

In the context of partition refinement, a *block* is a set of nodes. A *partition* P of a set of nodes V is a set of blocks that are pairwise disjoint. Furthermore, the union over all blocks in P is equal to V. We say a partition P is *finer* than a partition P' iff all blocks of P are contained in some block of P'.

Algorithm 1 shows how to perform partition refinement on a dependency graph $G = (V, E)$ that underlies the PBES $\mathcal{E}$. The initial partition P_0 is set to $\{\{(X, v) \in V \mid v \in \mathbb{D} \wedge rank_{\mathcal{E}}(X) = rank_{\mathcal{E}}(Y) \wedge op_{\mathcal{E}}(X) = op_{\mathcal{E}}(Y)\} \mid Y \in bnd(\mathcal{E})\}$. In every iteration, we find two blocks $b, b' \in P$ and split b with respect to b' in the following way:

$$split(b, b') = \{s \in b \mid \exists t \in b'. s E t\}$$
$$co\text{-}split(b, b') = b \setminus split(b, b')$$

Then we update the partition to reflect this split (line 3). Note that each partition P_{i+1} is finer than partition P_i.

Algorithm 1: Partition refinement for PBESs

Input: PBES $\mathcal{E}$, **initial partition** P_0

1 $i \leftarrow 0$;
2 **while** P_i *is not stable* **do**
3      $P_{i+1} \leftarrow (P_i \setminus \{b\}) \cup \{split(b, b'), co\text{-}split(b, b')\}$ **for some** $b, b' \in P_i$ such that $split(b,' b)$ and $co\text{-}split(b, b')$ are non-empty;
4      $i \leftarrow i + 1$;
5 **return** P_i;

If a block b cannot be split with respect to a block b', we say b is *stable* with respect to b'. Block b is stable with respect to a set of blocks K if it is stable with respect to all the blocks in K. A partition P is stable (with respect to itself) iff all of the blocks in P are stable with respect to P. The partition refinement algorithm terminates when P is stable (line 2).

Since our goal is to enable reasoning about infinite dependency graphs, we cannot store blocks explicitly. Instead, we represent each block with a *characteristic function*.

Definition 10. *Let* $\mathcal{E}$ *be a PBES and b be a set of nodes in a dependency graph of* $\mathcal{E}$. *The corresponding* characteristic function $k_b : \text{sig}(\mathcal{E}) \to \mathbb{B}$ *is defined as:*

$$k_b(X, v) = \begin{cases} true & if\ (X, v) \in b \\ false & otherwise \end{cases}$$

With this representation, we can also provide a symbolic implementation of the split and co-split functions. In the following definitions, k and k' are Boolean expressions representing characteristic functions.

$$split(k, k') = \lambda X_i {\in} \mathcal{X}, d{:}D.\, k(X_i, d) \wedge \bigvee_{j \in J_i} \exists e_j{:}E_j.\, f_j(d, e_j) \wedge k'(X_j, g_j(d, e_j))$$

$$co\text{-}split(k, k') = \lambda X_i {\in} \mathcal{X}, d{:}D.\, k(X_i, d) \wedge \neg \bigvee_{j \in J_i} \exists e_j{:}E_j.\, f_j(d, e_j) \wedge k'(X_j, g_j(d, e_j))$$

Example 4. We revisit the bakery protocol example from Sect. 3. Running Algorithm 1 on that PBES yields a finite reduced dependency space (depicted in Fig. 5) which contains 14 reachable equivalence classes. Here, we abbreviated state names. For example, in state wi, process 0 is waiting and process 1 is idle. Furthermore, in state $ww0$, both processes are waiting, but process 0 has preference to enter the critical section first. States belonging to predicate variable Y are prefixed with Y-. We omitted the state containing X_{true} for simplicity (cf. proof of Proposition 1). Note the symmetry between process 0 and process 1 in those states belonging to variable X and also the parallels between X and Y. $\square$

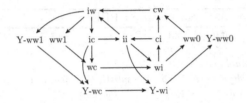

Fig. 5. Equivalence classes and transitions in the reduced dependency space of the bakery protocol example.

Algorithm 1 can be used to solve a PBES as follows. Upon its termination[1] a Boolean equation system or a parity game can be generated from the stable partition; either of them then finitely represents the dependency graph of the original PBES. For both possible types of outputs, there are existing solvers that can compute their solution. From these solutions we can then derive the solution to the original PBES. We next formalise these steps.

Since we are reasoning in the context of partition refinement, we know that all partitions that are finer than P_0 are (by definition of P_0 given above) such that all nodes in a block have the same rank and operand. We call a partition with this property *consistent*. We say that a reduced dependency graph is consistent iff its set of vertices is a consistent partition. The following definition shows how to construct a BES (in CRF) for a consistent reduced dependency graph.

Definition 11. *Let $G = (V, E)$ be a consistent reduced dependency graph of a PBES $\mathcal{E}$. The induced Boolean equation system, denoted $\mathcal{E}_G$, is the BES containing, per block $b \in V$, exactly one equation $(\sigma_b X_b(d{:}D_\star) = \phi_b)$ such that:*

- *$rank_{\mathcal{E}_G}(X_b) = rank_{\mathcal{E}}(X)$ for all $(X, v) \in b$,*
- *If $op_{\mathcal{E}}(X) = \wedge$ for all $(X, v) \in b$ then $\phi_b = \bigwedge_{(b,b') \in E}(true \Rightarrow X_{b'}(\star))$,*
- *If $op_{\mathcal{E}}(X) = \vee$ for all $(X, v) \in b$ then $\phi_b = \bigvee_{(b,b') \in E}(true \wedge X_{b'}(\star))$.*

Before we state several interesting properties of an induced BES, we introduce one additional notion. Given two (reduced) dependency graphs G and G' and their associated PBESs $\mathcal{E}$ and $\mathcal{E}'$, we say G and G' are *rank-operand-isomorph* when there is an isomorphism between them that preserves the rank and operand, which follow from $\mathcal{E}$ and $\mathcal{E}'$ respectively.

The following lemma formalises that the BES induced by a consistent reduced dependency graph is a correct representation of the reduced dependency graph.

Lemma 2. *Let G be a consistent reduced dependency graph of a PBES $\mathcal{E}$ and $\mathcal{E}_G$ be the induced BES. Then, the dependency space of $\mathcal{E}_G$ is rank-operand-isomorph to G.*

The following theorem states that the solution to the BES that is induced by the bisimulation quotient of the dependency space of a PBES $\mathcal{E}$, preserves and reflects the solution to that PBES.

---

[1] We remark that termination is not guaranteed as not every infinite dependency graph has a finite bisimulation quotient.

Theorem 3. *Let $\mathcal{E}$ be a PBES, $G = (V, E)$ be the dependency space of $\mathcal{E}$ and $\mathcal{E}'$ the BES induced by $G/{\leftrightarrow}$. Then, $v \in [\![\mathcal{E}]\!](X)$ iff $[\![\mathcal{E}']\!](X_b) = \{\star\}$, where $(X, v) \in b$.*

Proof. The proof is based on Theorem 1, Lemma 2, the reasoning that bisimulation reduction preserves bisimilarity and that bisimilarity is a *consistent correlation* [26], *i.e.*, bisimilarity preserves and reflects the solution of a PBES.
□

We remark that the algorithm presented in this section generalises the algorithms presented by Nagae *et al.* in [22] and [21], which only apply to PBESs consisting of predicate formulae that contain no predicate variables within the scope of universal quantifiers.

6   Computing Local Solutions

The approach presented in the previous section terminates when the bisimulation quotient is finite and all the operations on data are decidable. However, we are also interested in cases where the bisimulation quotient is not finite. Therefore, we propose an improvement that allows for reasoning about the solution of a single node (X, v), even when some part of the dependency space is not finitely representable. This is illustrated by the following example.

Example 5. Consider the following PBES:

$$\nu X(n{:}N) = X(n+1) \vee (n = 0 \wedge Y(0))$$
$$\mu Y(n{:}N) = Y(n+1) \wedge (n = 0 \Rightarrow X(0)) \wedge (n > 1 \Rightarrow Y(n-1))$$

The (stable) bisimulation quotient of the dependency space of this PBES is infinite and looks as follows:

$$\{(X, 0)\} \rightarrow \{(X, n) \mid n \geq 1\} \circlearrowright$$
$$\updownarrow$$
$$\{(Y, 0)\} \rightleftarrows \{(Y, 1)\} \rightleftarrows \{(Y, 2)\} \rightleftarrows \cdots$$

While this reduced dependency graph is infinite, there is a finite reduced proof graph for $X(0)$, namely the subgraph that only contains the blocks $\{(X, 0)\}$ and $\{(X, n) \mid n \geq 1\}$. Therefore, to draw conclusions about the solution for $X(0)$, it is not necessary to refine the part of the partition that concerns Y. □

The example suggests we may in general search for a proof graph in a—not yet stable—reduced dependency graph and use that to partially solve a PBES. However, not every proof graph obtained that way necessarily induces a proper proof graph for the original PBES: stability of the subgraph representing the proof graph is required. The following lemma and theorem formalise this.

Lemma 3. *Let $G = (V, E)$ be a dependency graph and $G_r = (V_r, E_r)$ a consistent reduced dependency graph of G. Furthermore, let $G'_r = (V'_r, E'_r)$ be a reduced dependency graph that is a subgraph of G_r and $G' = (V', E')$ its base graph. If $V'_r \subseteq V_r$ is stable with respect to itself then G'_r is bisimilar to G'.*

Proof. By proving that $\mathcal{R} = \{((X, v), b) \mid (X, v) \in b\}$ is a bisimulation relation, we show that G'_r is bisimilar to G'. □

Theorem 4. *Let* $G = (V, E)$ *be a dependency graph for a PBES* $\mathcal{E}$ *and* $G_r = (V_r, E_r)$ *a consistent reduced dependency graph of* G. *Furthermore, let* $G'_r = (V'_r, E'_r)$ *be a reduced dependency graph that is a subgraph of* G_r *and* $G' = (V', E')$ *its base graph. If* $V'_r \subseteq V_r$ *is stable with respect to itself and rank-operand-isomorph with a proof graph of the BES induced by* G_r, *then* G' *is a proof graph for* $\mathcal{E}$.

Proof. The proof proceeds by showing that G' satisfies the conditions of a dependency graph and of a proof graph, by applying Lemma 3. □

The following example illustrates that the assumptions from Theorem 4 are necessary conditions.

Example 6. Consider the PBES $(\nu X(n:N) = ((n \neq 0) \wedge X(n)) \vee Y)(\mu Y = Y)$. The figures below depict the initial partition of the dependency space of this PBES (on the left-hand side) and the stable partition (on the right-hand side).

$$\{(X, 0))\}$$

$$\{(X, n) \mid n \in N\} \longrightarrow \{Y\} \circlearrowright \qquad \qquad \longrightarrow \{Y\} \circlearrowright$$

$$\{(X, n) \mid n \neq 0\}$$

In the initial partition, there is a positive reduced proof graph that contains $(X, 0)$, *viz.* the graph containing only $\{(X, n) \mid n \in \mathbb{N}\}$. Note that this block is not stable with respect to itself. In contrast, in the stable partition, there is only a negative proof graph for $(X, 0)$. This shows that a reduced proof graph that is not stable with respect to itself can in general not be used to draw conclusions about the solution of the PBES under consideration. □

Based on this theorem, we propose the following changes to our approach: after every iteration, we search for a proof graph in the current partition. In the next iteration, only the blocks that are contained in the proof graph will

---

Algorithm 2: Computing local partitions

Input: PBES $\mathcal{E}$, initial partition P_0, initial node (X, v)

1   $U_0 \leftarrow \emptyset$;
2   $i \leftarrow 0$;
3   **while** P_i *is not stable* **do**
4      $Q \leftarrow (P_i \setminus \{k\}) \cup \{split(k, k'), co\text{-}split(k, k')\}$ **for some** $k, k' \in P_i$ such that $split(k, k')$ and $co\text{-}split(k, k')$ are non-empty;
5      $Q \leftarrow Q \cup U_i$;
6      $Q \leftarrow \texttt{computeReachableBlocks}(Q, (X, v))$;
7      $(P_{i+1}, U_{i+1}) \leftarrow \texttt{findProofGraph}(Q, (X, v))$;
8      $i \leftarrow i + 1$;
9   **return** P_i;

be refined. When the blocks in the proof graph are stable with respect to each other, we are finished (by Theorem 4). See Algorithm 2. We maintain two sets of blocks: P contains the blocks in the proof graph that we are currently considering and U contains the other blocks. At line 4, we split a block in P and temporarily store the resulting partition in Q. Then, the set of blocks of the whole partition, reachable from the block containing the initial node (X, v) is computed (lines 5 and 6). Thereby, blocks that are not reachable from the initial node are effectively "thrown away", *i.e.*, they are not considered during next iterations. Since unreachable blocks cannot be part of a minimal proof graph for the initial node, this does not affect the correctness of the algorithm. From the reachable blocks, we extract a proof graph for the initial node (X, v) (line 7). Searching for a proof graph can be done with existing techniques, such as a solver for Boolean equations systems or for parity games. The blocks contained in the proof graph are again stored in P, the remaining blocks are stored in U. After every iteration, we check whether P is stable (line 3). If so, the algorithm terminates.

7   Implementation and Experiments

We implemented Algorithms 1 and 2 in a tool called `pbessymbolicbisim` that is part of the mCRL2 toolset [6]. The implementation calls the Z3 SMT-solver to determine whether one of the sets $split(k, k')$ or $co\text{-}split(k, k')$ is empty, *i.e.*, whether its characteristic function is unsatisfiable. Further simplification of the characteristic functions is handled by the mCRL2 term rewrite system. Choosing which block to split each iteration (line 3 of Algorithm 1 and line 4 of Algorithm 2) is done in such a way that an unreachable block is never split, in similar vein to [20].

We compare the performance of three approaches: our implementation of Algorithms 1 and 2 and the `pbes-cvc4` tool from [18]. We originally also aimed to compare with the tool `PBESSolver` from [21]. However, their implementation has several practical limitations, making a fair comparison impossible. We therefore decided to exclude `PBESSolver` from our experiments. The experiments were performed on a machine with an Intel Core i5 3350P processor and 8GB of memory running Ubuntu 16.04 and mCRL2 commit 9068139379.

Our set of benchmarks consists of various PBESs that encode different types of decision problems, covering typical linear-time, branching-time and real-time model checking problems, a scheduling problem, recursive functions and behavioural equivalence checking problems. The PBESs encoding model checking problems mostly originate from the set of examples included in mCRL2, which in some cases have been modified to generate infinite state spaces. Classical approaches that generate the state-space explicitly fail for all of these models. We remark that most of the models contain multiple concurrent processes. Each model is combined with one or more formal properties in the form of a modal mu-calculus formula to obtain a PBES. More specifically, we verified the following properties:

- two *reachability* properties (the real-time ball game: winning impossible; and the real-time train gate system: action *go(1)* can be executed at time 20);
- two *invariants* (Fischer's real-time mutual exclusion protocol and Lamport's bakery protocol: no deadlock);
- six linear and branching-time properties (the ball game: infinitely often put ball; the train gate: fairness; Fischer's protocol and Lamport's bakery protocol: request must be served; the Concurrent Alternating Bit Protocol (CABP): a message can be received infinitely often; Hesselink's handshake register [13]: cache consistency, and all writes finish).

The scheduling problem we consider is due to [22]; it encodes a fair trading problem encoded as a PBES. Furthermore, two recursive functions we consider are based on classical benchmarks for verification tools [17]. A modified version of the McCarthy 91 function, as per [21], is represented with the following PBES:

$$\mu M(x, y{:}N) = (x > 10 \land x = y + 1) \lor \exists e{:}N.\, x \leq 10 \land M(x + 2, e) \land M(e, y)$$

Here, $M(x, y)$ is *true* if and only if (x, y) is a solution for the function we represent. In a similar fashion, we have a PBES for Takeuchi's function [17]:

$$\mu T(x, y, z, w{:}N) = (x \leq y \land y = w) \lor (\exists t_1, t_2, t_3{:}N.\, x > y \land$$
$$T(x - 1, y, z, t_1) \land T(y - 1, z, x, t_2) \land T(z - 1, x, y, t_3) \land T(t_1, t_2, t_3, w))$$

Finally, we consider the decision problem whether Alternating Bit Protocol (ABP) is branching bisimilar to a one-place buffer, both with infinite data. This PBES is encoded using the techniques in [4], as implemented in the mCRL2 tool `lpsbisim2pbes`.

The results are listed in Table 1. For each PBES, we report the solution for the initial node and the runtime in seconds for each approach. In addition, for Algorithm 1, we report the number of blocks in the reachable part of the bisimulation quotient as $|V|$. For Algorithm 2, we list the size of the reduced proof graph and the total number of blocks in memory at the moment the algorithm terminates. A timeout is represented with 't.o.', and an out-of-memory error with 'o.o.m.'. Furthermore, we write a cross for the PBESs that cannot be handled.

We observe that Algorithm 2 performs better than Algorithm 1 for nearly every PBES in our set of benchmarks. Algorithm 1 also runs into several out-of-memory errors, while Algorithm 2 manages to find a proof graph for every PBES. The runtime of `pbes-cvc4` is very small for the four cases it can solve. However, it fails to provide a solution in most cases.

The three cases where a timeout occurs for `pbes-cvc4` (trading, ball game and bakery) are similar: the models contain one or more variables that strictly increase. Since `pbes-cvc4` can only find lasso-shaped proof graphs, it does not terminate for PBESs with infinite proof graphs that are not lasso-shaped.

For Fischer and bakery with the no deadlock property and the equivalence problem on ABP and buffer, the reduced proof graph covers almost the entire reduced dependency space. Only the block containing X_{false} (cf. proof of Proposition 1) is not present in the proof graph. In those cases, Algorithm 2 does not perform better than Algorithm 1.

Table 1. Runtime comparison between `pbessymbolicbisim` and `pbes-cvc4`. All runtimes are in seconds. 't.o.' indicates a time-out, 'o.o.m' indicates an out-of-memory error and a cross indicates that a PBES cannot be handled.

PBES	Initial node/property	Solution	Algorithm 1		Algorithm 2		pbes-cvc4
			$|V|$	Time	$|V|$	Time	Time
Ball game	Winning impossible	*false*	12	0.55	12/12	0.65	0.27
	Infinitely often *put_ball*	*true*	3	0.006	1/3	0.006	t.o.
Train gate	*go(1)* at time 20	*true*	29	11.51	6/28	5.15	0.39
	Fairness	*false*	19	21.95	5/32	4.79	✗
Fischer (N = 3)	No deadlock	*true*	65	74.77	64/65	61.41	✗
Fischer (N = 4)	Request must serve	*false*		o.o.m.	5/38	20.87	✗
Bakery	No deadlock	*true*	23	3.08	23/23	2.26	t.o.
	Request must serve	*false*	123	85.02	14/111	14.52	0.44
Hesselink	Cache consistency	*false*		o.o.m.	21/1807	387.54	✗
	All writes finish	*false*		t.o.	13/724	117.47	✗
CABP	Receive infinitely often	*true*	260	267.95	25/702	61.02	✗
Trading	$X_a(1,1)$	*true*	7	0.02	5/7	0.02	t.o.
McCarthy	$M(0,10)$	*true*	1633	1299.17	14/405	59.46	✗
	$M(0,9)$	*false*	1633	1364.33	128/178	8.57	✗
Takeuchi	$T(3,2,1,3)$	*true*		t.o.	9/187	35.64	✗
	$T(3,2,1,2)$	*false*		t.o.	77/198	39.42	✗
ABP+buffer	Branching bisimilar	*true*	132	4.89	131/132	4.86	✗

8   Related Work

The first works on generating minimal representations from behavioural specifications were written by Bouajjani et al. [3]. Later, these ideas were applied to timed automata [1,25]. Similar to our approach, they rely on bisimulation to compute the minimal quotient directly from a specification. Fisler and Vardi [9] extended this work to include early termination when performing reachability analysis. Our work is similar in spirit to these methods, but it generalises these by allowing to verify properties expressed in the full modal mu-calculus and by supporting infinite-state systems, not limited to real-time systems.

The techniques and theory we present also generalise several other closely related works, such as [16,18,21,22]. Nagae et al. [22] transfer the ideas of Bouajjani et al. to disjunctive, quantifier-free PBESs and generate finite parity games that can be solved. They later expanded the work to existential PBESs [21]. These fragments of the PBES logic limit the type of properties one can verify. A small set of experimental results shows that their approach is feasible in practice for small academic examples.

Koolen et al. [18] use an SMT solver to search for linear proof graphs in disjunctive or conjunctive PBESs. Their technique manages to find solutions for model checking problems where traditional tools time out. Even if enumeration of the state-space is possible, an instantiation-based approach is not always faster. We remark that the number of unrollings performed by their tool gives a rough indication of the optimal size of the proof graph constructed with our techniques when applied to disjunctive or conjunctive PBESs.

In [16], Keiren *et al.* define two equivalence relations based on bisimulation for BESs. These relations are then used to minimise BESs that represent model checking problems. Experiments show that applying minimisation speeds up the solving procedure, *i.e.*, the time required for minimising and then solving the minimal BES is lower than the time required to solve the original BES. Whereas [16] applies explicit-state techniques by working directly on a BES, our work is based on a symbolic representation. The disadvantages of the explicit approach of [16] is that it requires one to instantiate a PBES to BES first. Therefore, it is not suitable for infinite-state systems.

Fontana *et al.* [10] construct symbolic proof trees to check alternation-free mu-calculus formulae on timed automata. To recursively prove (sub)formulas, they unfold the transition relation according to a set of proof rules they propose. This approach allows a larger class of properties than UPPAAL [2], which only supports a subset of TCTL. Contrary to our approach, the proof they produce is not necessarily minimal with respect to bisimulation.

Although our work was not inspired by counterexample-guided abstraction refinement (CEGAR) [5], we see many similarities. In this approach, an abstraction of the model under consideration is continuously refined based on spurious traces that are found by a model checker. Our second algorithm essentially refines with respect to 'spurious proof graphs'. Compared to our approach, CEGAR typically supports a less expressive class of properties, such as ACTL or LTL.

9   Conclusion

We presented an approach to solving arbitrarily-structured PBESs with infinite data, which enables solving of a larger set of PBESs than possible with existing tools. This improves the state-of-the-art for model checking and equivalence checking on (concurrent) systems with infinite data. A possible direction for future work is to weaken the equivalence relation on dependency graph nodes. Here, one can draw inspiration from equivalence relations defined on parity games, for instance as defined in [7]. We also want to investigate heuristics for the choice of blocks that are used for splitting in every iteration. The heuristics can for example be based on information obtained from static analysis of the PBES. We believe the choice of blocks during splitting can have a significant influence on the runtime.

Acknowledgements. We would like to thank the anonymous reviewers for their constructive feedback. Their suggestions helped us to improve the paper before publication.

References

1. Alur, R., Courcoubetis, C., Halbwachs, N., Dill, D., Wong-Toi, H.: Minimization of timed transition systems. In: Cleaveland, W.R. (ed.) CONCUR 1992. LNCS, vol. 630, pp. 340–354. Springer, Heidelberg (1992). https://doi.org/10.1007/BFb0084802

2. Behrmann, G., David, A., Larsen, K.G.: A tutorial on UPPAAL. In: Bernardo, M., Corradini, F. (eds.) SFM-RT 2004. LNCS, vol. 3185, pp. 200–236. Springer, Heidelberg (2004). https://doi.org/10.1007/978-3-540-30080-9_7

3. Bouajjani, A., Fernandez, J.-C., Halbwachs, N., Raymond, P., Ratel, C.: Minimal state graph generation. Sci. Comput. Programm. 18(3), 247–269 (1992)

4. Chen, T., Ploeger, B., van de Pol, J., Willemse, T.A.C.: Equivalence checking for infinite systems using parameterized boolean equation systems. In: Caires, L., Vasconcelos, V.T. (eds.) CONCUR 2007. LNCS, vol. 4703, pp. 120–135. Springer, Heidelberg (2007). https://doi.org/10.1007/978-3-540-74407-8_9

5. Clarke, E., Grumberg, O., Jha, S., Lu, Y., Veith, H.: Counterexample-guided abstraction refinement. In: Emerson, E.A., Sistla, A.P. (eds.) CAV 2000. LNCS, vol. 1855, pp. 154–169. Springer, Heidelberg (2000). https://doi.org/10.1007/10722167_15

6. Cranen, S., Groote, J.F., Keiren, J.J.A., Stappers, F.P.M., de Vink, E.P., Wesselink, W., Willemse, T.A.C.: An overview of the mCRL2 toolset and its recent advances. In: Piterman, N., Smolka, S.A. (eds.) TACAS 2013. LNCS, vol. 7795, pp. 199–213. Springer, Heidelberg (2013). https://doi.org/10.1007/978-3-642-36742-7_15

7. Cranen, S., Keiren, J.J.A., Willemse, T.A.C.: A cure for stuttering parity games. In: Roychoudhury, A., D'Souza, M. (eds.) ICTAC 2012. LNCS, vol. 7521, pp. 198–212. Springer, Heidelberg (2012). https://doi.org/10.1007/978-3-642-32943-2_16

8. Cranen, S., Luttik, B., Willemse, T.A.C.: Proof graphs for parameterised boolean equation systems. In: D'Argenio, P.R., Melgratti, H. (eds.) CONCUR 2013. LNCS, vol. 8052, pp. 470–484. Springer, Heidelberg (2013). https://doi.org/10.1007/978-3-642-40184-8_33

9. Fisler, K., Vardi, M.Y.: Bisimulation and Model Checking. In: Pierre, L., Kropf, T. (eds.) CHARME 1999. LNCS, vol. 1703, pp. 338–342. Springer, Heidelberg (1999). https://doi.org/10.1007/3-540-48153-2_29

10. Fontana, P., Cleaveland, R.: The power of proofs: new algorithms for timed automata model checking. In: Legay, A., Bozga, M. (eds.) FORMATS 2014. LNCS, vol. 8711, pp. 115–129. Springer, Cham (2014). https://doi.org/10.1007/978-3-319-10512-3_9

11. Garavel, H., Lang, F., Mateescu, R., Serwe, W.: CADP 2011: a toolbox for the construction and analysis of distributed processes. STTT 15(2), 89–107 (2013)

12. Groote, J.F., Willemse, T.A.C.: Parameterised boolean equation systems. Theor. Comput. Sci. 343(3), 332–369 (2005)

13. Hesselink, W.H.: Invariants for the construction of a handshake register. Inf. Process. Lett. 68(4), 173–177 (1998)

14. Kant, G., van de Pol, J.: Efficient instantiation of parameterised boolean equation systems to parity games. In: GRAPHITE 2012, volume 99 of EPTCS, pp. 50–65 (2012)

15. Keiren, J.J.A., Wesselink, W., Willemse, T.A.C.: Liveness analysis for parameterised boolean equation systems. In: Cassez, F., Raskin, J.-F. (eds.) ATVA 2014. LNCS, vol. 8837, pp. 219–234. Springer, Cham (2014). https://doi.org/10.1007/978-3-319-11936-6_16

16. Keiren, J.J.A., Willemse, T.A.C.: Bisimulation minimisations for boolean equation systems. In: Namjoshi, K., Zeller, A., Ziv, A. (eds.) HVC 2009. LNCS, vol. 6405, pp. 102–116. Springer, Heidelberg (2011). https://doi.org/10.1007/978-3-642-19237-1_12

17. Knuth, D.E.: Textbook examples of recursion. Artif. Math. Theory Comput. **91**, 207–229 (1991)

18. Koolen, R.P.J., Willemse, T.A.C., Zantema, H.: Using SMT for solving fragments of parameterised boolean equation systems. In: Finkbeiner, B., Pu, G., Zhang, L. (eds.) ATVA 2015. LNCS, vol. 9364, pp. 14–30. Springer, Cham (2015). https://doi.org/10.1007/978-3-319-24953-7_3

19. Lamport, L.: A new solution of Dijkstra's concurrent programming problem. Commun. ACM **17**(8), 453–455 (1974)

20. Lee, D., Yannakakis, M.: Online minimization of transition systems (extended abstract). In: STOC 1992, pp. 264–274 (1992)

21. Nagae, Y., Sakai, M.: Reduced dependency spaces for existential parameterised boolean equation systems. In: WPTE 2017, volume 265 of EPTCS, pp. 67–81 (2018)

22. Nagae, Y., Sakai, M., Seki, H.: An extension of proof graphs for disjunctive parameterised boolean equation systems. In: WPTE 2016, volume 235 of EPTCS, pp. 46–61 (2017)

23. Neele, T., Willemse, T.A.C., Groote, J.F.: Solving Parameterised Boolean Equation Systems with Infinite Data Through Quotienting (Technical Report). Technical report, Eindhoven University of Technology (2018)

24. Park, D.: Concurrency and automata on infinite sequences. In: Deussen, P. (ed.) GI-TCS 1981. LNCS, vol. 104, pp. 167–183. Springer, Heidelberg (1981). https://doi.org/10.1007/BFb0017309

25. Tripakis, S., Yovine, S.: Analysis of timed systems using time-abstracting bisimulations. FMSD **18**(1), 25–68 (2001)

26. Willemse, T.A.C.: Consistent correlations for parameterised boolean equation systems with applications in correctness proofs for manipulations. In: Gastin, P., Laroussinie, F. (eds.) CONCUR 2010. LNCS, vol. 6269, pp. 584–598. Springer, Heidelberg (2010). https://doi.org/10.1007/978-3-642-15375-4_40

Actors with Coroutine Support in Java

Vlad Serbanescu$^{(\boxtimes)}$, Frank de Boer, and Mohammad Mahdi Jaghoori

Centrum Wiskunde and Informatica, Amsterdam, The Netherlands
{vlad.serbanescu,frank.s.de.boer,jaghouri}@cwi.nl
http://www.cwi.nl

Abstract. In this paper, we introduce a Java library for actors integrated seamlessly with futures and supporting coroutines. Coroutines allow actors to suspend the execution of a message and possibly schedule other messages before resuming the suspended continuation. As such coroutines enhance actors as a major building block for constructing software components. The library is used together with a compiler to generate code from an application model into an executable program in Java. A formal description of the translation process is provided together with the most important library methods. We highlight the importance of having a scalable and efficient implementation by means of some typical benchmarks which model a large number of tasks, coroutines and actors.

Keywords: Asynchronous programming · Actors · Coroutines
Futures · Object-orientation · Java

1 Introduction

Asynchronous programming is becoming the standard programming paradigm. The Abstract Behavioral Specification (ABS) modeling language [12] provides a formal computational model which integrates actor-based programming with futures and coroutines.

An ABS model describes a dynamic system of actors which only interact by means of asynchronous method calls. This provides a "programming to interfaces" paradigm that enables static type checking of message passing at compile time. In contrast, in the typical approach of actors such as in Scala, messages are allowed to have any type and thus it is only checked at run-time whether the receiver can handle them. In ABS a future is generated only when a method is called asynchronously. This future can be passed around and actors holding a reference to it can check the completion of the corresponding method and then, if the method is not void, get its returned value.

Actor-based models of computation in general assume a run-to-completion mode of execution of the messages [2]. ABS extends the actor-based model with *coroutines* by introducing explicit suspend statements. Suspending the execution of a method allows the actor to execute another method invocation. This

© Springer Nature Switzerland AG 2018
K. Bae and P. C. Ölveczky (Eds.): FACS 2018, LNCS 11222, pp. 237–255, 2018.
https://doi.org/10.1007/978-3-030-02146-7_12

suspension and resumption mechanism thus gives rise to multiple control flows in a single actor. The suspension of a method invocation in ABS can have an enabling condition that controls when it can be resumed. Typical enabling conditions are awaiting completion of a future or awaiting until the internal state of the actor satisfies a given boolean condition.

Actors in ABS serve as a major building block for constructing software components. Actors in ABS can model a distributed environment as they interact via asynchronous communication. Internally with support for cooperative scheduling they allow for a fine-grained and powerful internal synchronization between the different method invocations of an actor. Therefore they are a natural and intuitive basis for component-based software engineering and service-oriented computing and related Internet- and web-based programming models [3]. ABS has been applied to several major case studies like in the domain of cloud computing [7], simulation of railway models [14] and modeling software product lines [13].

The main contribution of this paper is a Java library called JAAC[1] together with a compiler[2] which allows generation of programs in Java from ABS sources, as well as enabling writing Java programs directly following the ABS concurrency model. This library provides a bridge between modeling and programming: by *reverse engineering* the ABS model underlying such an application of the library API we can apply the formal development and analysis techniques supported by the ABS language, e.g. functional correctness [6] and deadlock analysis [8].

One of the major challenges addressed is the development of a Java library that *scales* in the number of executing actors and (suspended) method invocations on a single JVM. To reach this goal, we represent (suspended) method invocations in Java as a kind of `Callable` objects (referred to as tasks), which are stored into actor queues [1]. This representation allows the development of a library API which encapsulates a run-time system tailored to the efficient management of the dynamic generation, storage and execution of such tasks. The overall architecture of the system is based on the following. We submit one main task per actor to the thread pool which iteratively selects an enabled task from its queue and runs it. We make use of a system-wide thread pool where millions of actors can run on a limited number of threads efficiently. A key feature provided by our library is a new general mechanism for *spawning* tasks which allows an uniform modelling of both asynchronous method calls and suspension of a method invocation. Suspension of a method invocation, called synchronously or asynchronously, is modeled by spawning a new task in the actor queue which captures its continuation, i.e., the code to be executed upon its resumption.

Related Work. The library provides a scalable implementation of the ABS asynchronous programming model which integrates actors, futures and cooperative scheduling. In contrast, existing libraries in mainstream JVM languages, namely Java [20], Scala [9] and Kotlin [11], support actors, futures and coroutines mainly as independent mechanisms for asynchronous programming. Even though one

---

[1] https://github.com/JaacRepo/JAAC push-mechanism branch.
[2] https://github.com/JaacRepo/absCompiler.

can use them together, this in general only adds to the complexity of the program. For example in Scala, one can use a future to hold the result of an asynchronous message sent to an actor. But then one should either block the whole thread to await the completion of the future, or register a continuation that will possibly run in another thread in parallel to the actor's thread. It is the programmer's job to ensure that the thread running the continuation will not give rise to race conditions with the actor's thread. In JAAC, however, awaiting the result of an asynchronous message, which is automatically captured in a future, creates a continuation that will safely run in the actor's thread; thus no race conditions can happen.

The current existing support for coroutines in JVM can be categorized by two main approaches: one which operates on source code level and one which operates on the bytecode level.

Main examples of bytecode manipulation are Apache Commons Javaflow [4] and Kilim [17]. Even though bytecode manipulation allows for more flexibility, it has several disadvantages regarding maintainability and portability. Further, the application of debugging techniques becomes more involved and source-code based static analysis tools become unusable.

The ABCL language [19, 21] is a language similar to ABS in terms of asynchronous communication support and message suspension. However, messages are preempted without a user-defined condition, being based only on an assigned priority. To the best of our knowledge it does not have any formal semantics and an up to date status of its implementation available.

A straightforward way to support coroutines at source-code level in Java (see [15]) is by allocating a thread to every "routine" that can be suspended, since a thread naturally contains already all the information about the call stack and local variables. However that does not scale because threads are well known to be heavyweight in Java. In Scala, macros are also a viable approach to implementing coroutines. Macros are an experimental feature in Scala that allow a programmer to write code at the level of abstract syntax trees and thus to instruct the compiler to generate code differently. Scala-coroutines project [18] uses this feature to implement low-level coroutine support for Scala with explicit suspension and resume points which however in general are prone to errors.

Kotlin supports coroutines natively but actors are not first class citizens. Kotlin actors are implemented as coroutines, which by definition ensures a single thread of execution within the actor. However one cannot process the messages inside actors in a coroutine manner (as is the case in JAAC). In other words, it is not possible to process other messages if one message is suspended.

Our solution provides support for coroutines by only making changes at the source level and provides a higher-level mechanism for scheduling and resumption tailored towards actor-based systems. Unlike Scala coroutines, suspension and release points are done through the use of the API, allowing the programmer to specify resumption based on a particular actor state or task completion (done by either the same or different actor). Therefore the programmer does not need to explicitly resume control in the code. Our solution extends the Java implementation of ABS described in [16] with a new general mechanism for spawning tasks which allows for modeling suspension of entire call stacks and in general allows for a more efficient executable in terms of scalability and performance.

The rest of this paper is organized as follows: In Sect. 2 we give an overview of the main features that the target actor-based model has. Section 3 presents the formal aspects of pre-processing and compiling continuations together with the most important method from the library API. Section 4 describes the implementation of the run-time system of the JAAC library. In Sect. 5 we show the experimental evaluation of our solution followed by the conclusions drawn in Sect. 6.

2   Coroutine Support in ABS

In this section we informally describe the main features of the flow of control underlying the semantics of the coroutine abstraction as proposed by the ABS language. We describe the main concepts of (a)synchronous method invocation and their coroutine manner of execution through the example in Listing 1.1 which presents a general behaviour of a pool of workers. For a detailed description of the syntax of the ABS language we refer to [12].

The example sketches the behaviour of two kinds of actors: a WorkerPool and a Worker. A WorkerPool actor maintains a set of Worker actors (line 2). An asynchronous invocation of the method sendWork (line 4) suspends until the set of workers is non-empty (line 5). It then selects a worker from the set and asynchronously calls its doWork method (line 8). The future uniquely associated with this call is used to store the return value of this call. Note that in this manner asynchronous method calls in ABS by default return futures (see [5] for details about the type system for ABS which covers futures). An asynchronous invocation of the method finished simply adds the Worker parameter back to the set of workers (lines 12 and 13). Each worker actor stores a reference to its worker pool p which is passed as a parameter upon instantiation (line 16). Before returning the result (line 21) the method doWork asynchronously calls the method finished of its associated WorkerPool reference (line 20). The suspension mechanism underlying the await statement in line 5 allows to schedule any update of the set of worker actors by a call of the method finished. Such an update then will allow the resumption of the execution of the method sendWork.

In ABS a statement of the form await f? suspends the executing method invocation which can only be rescheduled if the method invocation corresponding to the future f has computed the return value. In contrast, the evaluation of the expression f.get blocks all the method invocations of an actor until the return value has been computed.

A key feature of the coroutine execution of messages in ABS is that it does *not* provide an explicit command for resuming a message. Messages are resumed for execution only by the underlying scheduler. This implicit resumption by the underlying scheduler allows for an important improvement of the program quality and avoids the error-prone usage of explicit resumption, i.e., resuming a routine twice in Scala [18] raises an exception.

Listing 1.1. Example of a pool of workers

```
1   class WorkerPool(){
2     Set<Worker> workers; // initialization omitted for brevity
3
4     Result sendWork() {
5       await !(emptySet(workers));
6       Worker w = take(workers);
7       workers = remove(workers, w);
8       Fut<Result> f = w ! doWork();
9       return f.get;
10     }
11
12     Unit finished(Worker w) {
13       workers = insertElement(workers, w);
14   } }
15
16   class Worker(WorkerPool p) implements Worker{
17     Result doWork(){
18       Result r;
19       // computation
20       p ! finished(this);
21       return r;
22   }  }
```

Line 1 of Listing 1.1 depicts a sugared syntax in ABS of the `await` construct. This construct is used to suspend execution of an asynchronous invocation and retrieve its result once the implicitly generated future holds the computed return value. It is a shortened version of lines 3–5. It is important to observe that evaluation of `fut.get` will never block because of the successful execution of `await fut?`.

Listing 1.2. ABS Await sugared syntax

```
1   Result result = await w ! doWork();
2   //can be expanded to
3   Fut<Result> fut = w ! doWork();
4   await fut?;
5   Result result = fut.get;
```

In ABS, actors which form so-called concurrent object groups also may invoke their own methods synchronously. For example, we may want to move the functionality of obtaining a worker in the `doWork` method to a separate method `getWorker` such as in Listing 1.3. We can then call this method synchronously like in line 8. It is important to observe that suspension of a synchronous method call gives rise to suspension of an entire call stack. In our example, suspension of the await statement in line 3 gives rise to a stack which consists of a top frame that holds the suspended synchronous call and as bottom frame the continuation of the asynchronous method invocation of `sendWork` upon return of the synchronous call in line 8. In contrast to multi-threading in Java, these call stacks cannot be interleaved arbitrarily, only one call stack in an actor is executing until it is either terminated or suspended.

Listing 1.3. Synchronous Call in ABS

```
1
2    Worker getWorker(){
3        await !(emptySet(workers));
4        Worker w = take(workers);
5    }
6
7    Result sendWork() {
8        Worker w = this.getWorker();
9        workers = remove(workers, w);
10       Fut<Result> f = w ! doWork();
11       return f.get;
12   }
```

3   Emulating Coroutines Through Spawning Tasks

To emulate the coroutines of ABS we introduce a new general mechanism of spawning tasks. This mechanism is a lightweight alternative to JVM threads and by generating code in a certain design pattern, the state from which to resume can be saved as part of the spawned task, such that it is equivalent to the resumption point of the coroutine. As described in Sect. 2 an actor can resume a method once the guard suspending it has been satisfied. The local environment of the method together with any possible call stack that built up before the **await** statement must be reloaded. This mechanism avoids the need to reload the local environment and call stack as will be explained later in this section.

3.1   Spawning Tasks

Library Methods. The API provides several methods that can be used both by the compiler from ABS to Java or as a standalone Java library. We highlight three important methods that support the simulation of ABS features in the Java language.

The first method is called **spawn** and its usage is highlighted is Listing 1.4. It is used to implement the suspension point in the `sendWork` method of the actor class `WorkerPool` in Listing 1.1. The method generates a new task (in the form of a Callable). In Java 8 lambda expressions have been introduced to allow a block of code to be passed as an argument and be treated as data (implicitly converted into a Callable or Runnable). This is the syntax used on line 3 of Listing 1.4.

Note that the return type of `sendWork` is an `ABSFuture`. This is special future type defined in the library that cannot block a thread when trying to retrieve its result. Instead it is used in conjunction with **getSpawn** (to be described later in this section) to spawn a new task that uses its result once the `ABSFuture` is ready. More implementation details about the `ABSFuture` will be presented in Sect. 4.1.

The `guard` parameter (`nonEmpty`) represents the associated enabling condition that can be either the completion of a future or a condition based on the actor's internal state. Here the abstract class `Guard` allows for multiple types of enabling conditions to be evaluated. The aforementioned enabling conditions are subclasses of `Guard` known as `FutureGuard` and `PureExpressionGuard`. The static overloaded method `convert` creates instances of these subclasses depending on the instance type of `Guard` parameter passed. As the enabling condition has to verify an actor's state, it needs to be checked every time the actor attempts to schedule the task (i.e. the block of code that starts on line 4). Therefore we transform this enabling condition into a guard from a lambda expression that verifies if the set of available workers is non-empty (line 2).

It is important to note that the intended target object for calling **spawn** is **this** (also known as a self call) as guards always refer to the local environment of an object (either future references or local variables and fields) and thus should not be passed to different objects as part of the guard as it would break actor semantics. The other two methods (whose usage is already shown on lines 5 and 6) represent particular cases of this method. These two methods along with their usage and parameters will be explained next in this section.

Listing 1.4. Spawn Method Intended Usage

```
1   public ABSFuture<Result> sendWork() {
2       Guard nonEmpty = Guard.convert(() -> ! workers.isEmpty());
3       return spawn(nonEmpty, () -> {
4         Worker w = workers.pop();
5         ABSFuture<Result> f = w.send( () -> w.doWork());
6         return getSpawn(f, (r)->{ return ABSFuture.done(r);}, HIGH, STRICT);
7       });
8   }
```

The **send** method is used to model ABS asynchronous method invocations. It is a particular case of spawning a task without a guard. Unlike **spawn**, its intended use can be both a self call or a different target object (as it does not have a guard). Without a guard the newly spawned task will be ready for execution on the target object. It is also important to note that actor semantics of ABS impose that the spawned task be a method exposed by the target object's interface. As of now the library does not enforce this semantics, but we recommend as a general programming practice to avoid sending a task represented by an arbitrary block of code to the target object.

Using a lambda expression as shown in Listing 1.5 we model an asynchronous invocation of the `sendWork` method of the newly created `WorkerPool`. The **send** method returns a future that will eventually contain the result of running the `Callable` parameter. The task itself will be stored in the internal task queue of the actor (see Sect. 4).

Listing 1.5. Sending an Asynchronous Call

```
1   WorkerPool pool = new WorkerPool();
2   ABSFuture<Result> fut = pool.send(() -> pool.sendWork());
```

The **getSpawn** method is a particular case of spawning a task that is used only together with a future guard. This guard's result is passed as a parameter to the spawned task making it available to use once the future is complete (the task is ready to be scheduled). Listing 1.6 shows how to model an ABS

await syntactic sugar illustrated in Listing 1.2. The task represents a `Callable` instance that in the method application in line 2 (Listing 1.6) *implicitly* binds its parameter `result` to the (completed) value stored in the future `fut`. This provides a cleaner, more intuitive way of retrieving and using a future's result as part of the block of code to be run by the actor when the future completes.

Listing 1.6. getSpawn Method Intended Usage

```
1   ABSFuture<Result> fut = w.send( () -> w.doWork());
2   getSpawn(fut, (result) -> {...});
```

Call Stack and Priorities. In ABS an asynchronous method invocation may in general generate a stack of synchronous calls. In the JAAC API we can model such a call stack by generating for each call a corresponding task as a `Callable` instance that represents the code to be resumed after the return of the call and that is parameterized by an enabling condition on a future uniquely associated with the call (see Listing 1.7 for a simple example of a synchronous call). To ensure that these tasks are executed in the right order, that is, tasks belonging to different call stacks are not interleaved, we assign them a HIGH priority. But if one of these instances should suspend (an **await** construct is encountered), it will use **spawn** for suspension (line!3). By default tasks that are created by **spawn** or **send** are set with a LOW priority. The default priority, when **getSpawn** is used without priority arguments is LOW. The default scheduling policy of an actor is to schedule one of the enabled tasks with highest priority. If all such tasks are disabled the scheduler moves to the next priority. As a result, when a synchronous call returns, the task representing its return will have priority over all other tasks (note that the enabling conditions of these tasks ensure the LIFO execution of the tasks representing a call stack).

The additional `strictness` parameter allows the following refinement of the scheduling policy: an enabled task of a lower priority can only be scheduled if all higher priority tasks are disabled and *non strict*. As an example of the use of this additional parameter, the modeling of the `f.get` is illustrated on line 6 of Listing 1.4. Note that this combination of HIGH priority and STRICT does not allow scheduling of any other tasks (of the given actor).

Listing 1.7. Usage of getSpawn to emulate a synchronous call of an Actor

```
1    public ABSFuture<Worker> getWorker() {
2        Guard nonEmpty = Guard.convert(() -> ! workers.isEmpty());
3        return spawn(nonEmpty, () -> {
4            Worker w = workers.pop();
5            return ABSFuture.done(w);
6        });
7    }
8
9    ABSFuture<Result> sendWork() {
10       ABSFuture<Worker> fw = this.getWorker();
11       return getSpawn(fw, (w)->{
12           ABSFuture<Result> f = w ! doWork();
13           return f;
14       }, HIGH, NON_STRICT);
15   }
```

3.2   Compiler Correctness

The basic idea underlying the compiler is to model both method calls and the suspension mechanism in ABS by a general mechanism of spawning tasks. In this section we focus on the correctness of the translation of the await statement. We do so by considering a language ABS-SPAWN which is obtained from ABS by using instead of the await construct the **spawn**(g, S) statement for spawning subtasks (the unconditional release statement in ABS we view as an abbreviation of **await true**). Note that in ABS-SPAWN method invocations are thus executed in a run-to-completion mode.

The basic idea underlying the compilation of await statements then can be formalized by a formal translation of ABS statements into corresponding statements of ABS-SPAWN (we refer to the syntax of ABS in [12]). This translation is applied to every class in the ABS program. For each class, every method body is viewed as a sequential composition of the first instruction followed by its (sequential) continuation and translated accordingly. We only highlight the main rules of this translation in Fig. 1 which affect the first instruction (in all other cases, e.g., that of method calls, the first instruction is not affected and the translation is only applied to its sequential continuation). For technical convenience only, we assume that repetitive (while) statements are rewritten using tail-recursion[3]. This allows us to syntactically identify the continuation of an **await** statement as its sequential continuation in the body of the method and does not require any loop-unfolding.

$$
\begin{aligned}
T(\epsilon) &:= & \epsilon \\
T(\textbf{await } g;\ S) &:= & \textbf{spawn}(g,\ T(S)\ ) \\
T(\textbf{if } b\ \{S_1\}\ \textbf{else}\ \{S_2\}; S) &:= & \textbf{if } b\ \{T(S_1;\ S;)\}\ \textbf{else}\ \{T(S_2;\ S)\} \\
T(\textbf{case } e\ \{ &:= & \textbf{case } e\ \{ \\
P_1 \Rightarrow S_1 & & P_1 \Rightarrow T(S_1;\ S) \\
P_2 \Rightarrow S_2 & & P_2 \Rightarrow T(S_2;\ S) \\
\ldots & & \ldots \\
P_n \Rightarrow S_n & & P_n \Rightarrow T(S_n;\ S) \\
\};S & & \}
\end{aligned}
$$

Fig. 1. Translation of ABS syntax

In Fig. 1 the empty statement is denoted by ϵ (we assume here the syntactical equivalence $S; \epsilon \equiv S$). The translation of an **await** construct with guard g followed by a (sequential) continuation S results simply in a **spawn** statement with

---

[3] In practice, running applications using tail-recursion are affected by the program's memory limits due to the buildup of the program's stack memory. The compiler of ABS into Java using the library, avoids this by converting tail-recursion into a set of spawned tasks representing each iteration of the loop.

two parameters: the guard g and the task representing the translation applied to the continuation $(T(S))$. A conditional statement is translated by "absorbing" the sequential continuation that follows into the two branches of the statement. This also applies to the translation of the case statement (or pattern matching statement) where the continuation has to capture for each possible pattern (P_i) both the block to be executed on that pattern branch (S_i) as well as the rest of the control flow that follows the statement (S).

The translation thus captures the whole syntactic continuation that follows an **await** statement as the new task to be spawned. Therefore the translation of the method containing the **await** statement will terminate directly after having spawned the corresponding subtask, thus emulating an implicit suspension point.

In order to establish formally the correctness of this translation we first introduce a formal operational semantics of the ABS-SPAWN language.

Operational semantics. We introduce object configurations of the form (σ, S, Q), where:

- σ assigns values to the instance variables (fields) of the class (we treat the keyword **this** as a distinguished instance variable identifying the object) and all the fresh variables generated for the local variables of the different method invocations.
- S represents the current statement of the active process that is run by the actor.
- Q is a (multi-)set of statements which represent suspended processes. As a special case, we introduce a run-time syntax of the form $(g \rightarrow S)$ that represents a (top-level) statement (S) that is guarded by an enabling condition (g).

As described below, to model sharing of the local variables of a method among its generated subtasks, for each method invocation fresh variables are introduced in σ for the local variables (including the formal parameters).

A global configuration G then is a set of object configurations. We highlight the following rules of the transition system for deriving transitions $G \rightarrow G'$.

Asynchronous Invocation Rule. For notational convenience only we describe the semantics of an invocation of a void method (thus abstracting from the generation of a future).

$$\{(\sigma, x!m(\bar{e}); S, Q), (\sigma', S', Q')\} \cup G \rightarrow \{(\sigma, S, Q), (\sigma'', S', Q'')\} \cup G$$

where $\sigma'(\textbf{this}) = \sigma(x)$ (i.e., $\sigma'(\textbf{this})$ is the callee of the method call $x!m(\bar{e})$), σ'' extends σ' by assigning to the fresh variables introduced for the local variables of m the values of the actual parameters $\bar{e}$ in σ, and, finally, Q'' is obtained from Q' by adding the body of m with its local variables renamed. In case of an assignment $y = x!m(\bar{e})$, we assign to the future variable a pair $(f, \bot)$, where f is the (unique) identity used as a reference to the return value which is initialised by $\bot$ (which stands for "undefined").

Spawning Subtasks. Spawning a sub-task simply consists of adding a corresponding statement with enabling condition to the set Q of suspended processes:

$$\{(\sigma, \mathbf{spawn}(g, S); S', Q)\} \cup G \rightarrow \{(\sigma, S', \{g \rightarrow S\} \uplus Q)\} \cup G$$

Scheduling Rule. The following rule describes the scheduling of an enabled suspended task.

$$\{(\sigma, \epsilon, \{g \rightarrow S\} \uplus Q)\} \cup G \rightarrow \{(\sigma, S, Q)\} \cup G$$

where σ validates the guard g (i.e., σ satisfies any Boolean condition of g and $\sigma(x) = (f, v)$, for some value $v \neq \bot$, for any query x? of a future variable x). Note that only when the current statement has terminated a new statement is selected for execution.

It is straightforward to define a transition system for deriving transitions $G \rightarrow_{abs} G'$ modeling execution steps of an ABS program, where G (and G') now only contain ABS statements. (The main difference with the standard semantics of ABS ([12]) is the use of fresh variables for the local variables of a method instead of a local environment.)

Let $T(G)$, for any global ABS configuration G, denote the result of applying the translation to all the *executing* ABS statements in G and translating any *suspended* statement **await** $g; S$ in G by $g \rightarrow T(S)$. We now can state the following theorem which states the correctness of the translation of await statements in ABS, the proof of which proceeds by a straightforward case analysis of the first instruction of an executing statement.

Theorem 1. *For every global ABS configuration G we have*

$$G \rightarrow_{abs} G' \text{ iff } T(G) \rightarrow T(G')$$

4   Library Implementation in Java

A naive approach to implementing actors in ABS is to generate a thread for every asynchronous method call and introduce a lock for each actor to ensure that at most one thread per actor is executing [15]. In such an approach suspending execution of a method would be as easy as parking the thread and resuming it later on. This however does not scale because an application will require a large number of JVM threads which are very expensive in terms of memory.

Instead of generating a thread for every asynchronous method call, in our approach such calls are stored as `Callable` objects which we call *tasks*. The overall architecture for the execution, suspension and resumption of such tasks consists of the following main basic ideas:

- A system-wide thread-pool that assigns at most one thread to each actor.
- A task queue for each actor.
- Each actor thread runs a main task which iteratively selects from its queue an enabled task and runs it.
- Newly generated tasks are stored in the corresponding actor's queue.

In the following we first describe in more detail the generation and completion of tasks and then the mechanism for task scheduling and execution.

4.1   Task Generation and Completion

Every call to **send**, **spawn** or **getSpawn** creates a new task as an instance of the class ABSTask(Listing 1.8) and stores it into the task queue of the actor callee. In all these cases the field resultFuture will contain a newly created instance of ABSFuture(Listing 1.9) which uniquely identifies this task and which is returned to the caller (of the **send**, **spawn** or **getSpawn** method). Upon termination of a task, the return value will be wrapped in an ABSFuture instance created by the done() method with a set completed flag and an assigned value. This new instance is subsequently assigned to the target field of the ABSFuture identifying the completed task. Note that thus upon termination of the task the target field of the future returned by the **send**, **spawn** or **getSpawn** method will hold a reference to the future returned by the generated task. Consequently for checking the availability and retrieval of value of a future, in general one needs to follow a chain of future references until a future with a null target field is found. This scheme fully integrates futures with the mechanism of spawning new tasks and supports the delegation of the computation of return values.

Listing 1.8. ABSTaskClass

```
1   public class ABSTask<V> implements Serializable, Runnable {
2       protected Guard enablingCondition = null;
3       protected final ABSFuture<V> resultFuture;
4       protected Callable<ABSFuture<V>> task;
5       //implementation and functionality
6   }
```

Listing 1.9. ABSFutureClass

```
1   public class ABSFuture<V> {
2       private V value = null;
3       private boolean completed = false;
4       private ABSFuture<V> target = null;
5       private Set<Actor> awaitingActors = ConcurrentHashMap.newKeySet();
6       //implementation and functionality
7   }
```

In order to avoid busy-waiting on futures, the class ABSFuture implements a push mechanism to notify the actors that are awaiting its completion (which are stored in the field awaitingActors). Whenever an actor passes a future to the **getSpawn** method, this actor is added to the list of awaiting actors of that future and will also be propagated through the target chain. We explain in the next subsection how the notification mechanism works together with the scheduling mechanism of actors.

Using JVM Garbage Collection. The only extra references we need for the actors (i.e., in addition to what is used in the program) are the ones required for the notification mechanism for futures. Once the future is completed and notifications are sent, these extra references are deleted. Therefore we can leave the entire garbage collection process to the Java Runtime Environment as no other bookkeeping mechanisms are required. This way we do not need to keep a registry of the actors like the context in Scala and Akka.

In this setup we completely encapsulate the generation and completion of futures and they are an integral part of the asynchronous method invocation and

return, and as such are not exposed to the user of the API. Furthermore, the
ABSFuture class is implemented completely lock-free and therefore the chaining
of futures performs very efficiently.

4.2   Task Scheduling and Execution

The LocalActor class implements the functionality of scheduling and executing
tasks in an actor in a scalable manner that ensures fairness between the actors
when competing for the system threads. The internal part of this class, which is
hidden from the user of the API, is presented in Listing 1.10. Inside the class there
is a taskQueue which holds all tasks of an actor. Tasks are defined as instances
of class ABSTask (for example on line 30). To allow for concurrent access and an
efficient scheduling of these tasks we use a hashmap (ConcurrentSkipListMap
on line 4) that orders tasks into buckets (queues of tasks defined by assigned
priorities).

Listing 1.10. Local Actor Class

```
1    abstract class LocalActor implements Actor {
2        private ABSTask<?> runningTask;
3        private final AtomicBoolean mainTaskIsRunning = new AtomicBoolean(false);
4        private ConcurrentSkipListMap<...> taskQueue
5            = new ConcurrentSkipListMap<>();
6
7        class MainTask implements Runnable{
8            public void run() {
9                if (!takeOrDie()) return;
10               runningTask.run();
11               ActorSystem.submit(this);
12       }  }
13
14       private boolean takeOrDie() {
15           synchronized (mainTaskIsRunning) {
16               // iterate through queue and take one ready task
17               // if it exists set it the next runningTask and then
18               return true;
19               // if the queue if empty or no task is able to run
20               mainTaskIsRunning.set(false);
21               return false;
22       }  }
23
24       private boolean notRunningThenStart() {
25           synchronized (mainTaskIsRunning) {
26               return mainTaskIsRunning.compareAndSet(false, true);
27       }  }
28
29       public final <V> ABSFuture<V> send(Callable<ABSFuture<V>> message) {
30           ABSTask<V> m = new ABSTask<>(message);
31           // add m to the task queue with low priority and no strictness
32           if (notRunningThenStart()) {
33               ActorSystem.submit(new MainTask());
34           }
35           return m.resultFuture;
36   }  }
```

The implementation defines an inner class MainTask which is responsible
for selecting an enabled task from the queue (via the takeOrDie method) and
running it. Being a Runnable, the main task of an actor can be submitted to
the system-wide thread pool and thus actors are put to compete for available

threads in a scalable way. This fairness policy may also be fine-tuned to allow the `MainTask` to execute a fixed chunk of tasks at a time before releasing the thread in order to reduce context switches.

The `MainTask` avoids busy-waiting in cases that all tasks in the queue are disabled. In such cases, `takeOrDie` returns false and then the `MainTask` simply terminates. It is reactivated upon generation of any new task in the queue (line 33). To make sure there is no more than one instance of the `MainTask` running for an actor, we use the `mainTaskIsRunning` flag. As the task queue is accessed concurrently by the `MainTask` performing the queue traversal and other actors sending method invocations, it is important to avoid race conditions. A race condition may happen if after `MainTask` finds no enabled messages in the queue and just before it resets the `mainTaskIsRunning` flag, a new message is sent to the actor; if this happens, the current `MainTask` will terminate and the new message also creates no new `MainTask`. We avoid this situation by the synchronized blocks in `takeOrDie` and `notRunningThenStart`.

In case `MainTask` terminates because all tasks in the queue are disabled and one task that was awaiting completion of a future becomes enabled, the corresponding future is made responsible for reactivating the `MainTask`. As mentioned in the previous subsection, every future has a list of awaiting actors. Upon completion, each future will send a special *empty* message to the awaiting actors. To avoid performance penalties, the actor scheduler skips such empty messages and will continue to the next message immediately. Nevertheless, this empty message will reactivate the `MainTask` if it was terminated. As already stated above a big advantage of this approach is that there is no need for any centralized registry of awaiting actors and also eliminates any busy waiting by actor schedulers.

5   Benchmarking and Evaluation

This section shows the comparison of having coroutine support available in Java through either thread-abstraction or spawning tasks. The comparison is first made through an example that relies heavily on coroutines, such that we can measure the overhead that programming with coroutines has on a program. The second example is selected from the Savina benchmark for programming with actors [10]. All the benchmarks are ran a core i5 machine which supports hyper-threading and 8GB of RAM on a single JVM. In the library repository[4] we provide implementations of several examples in the benchmark suite directly using the library, while in the compiler repository[5] we have several ABS models of these benchmarks.

5.1   Coroutine "Heavy" Benchmark

First the library is evaluated in terms of the impact that programming with coroutines has on performance. The first benchmark involves a large number of

---

[4] https://github.com/JaacRepo/JAAC.
[5] https://github.com/JaacRepo/absCompiler.

suspension and release points in an actor's life cycle in order to compare the spawning approach to the thread-abstraction approach when translating from ABS to Java. In Java using threads and context switches heavily limits the application to the number of native threads that can be created. To measure the improvement provided by our Java library features we use a simple example that creates a recursive stack of synchronous calls. A sketch of the ABS model is presented in Listing 1.11.

Listing 1.11. Benchmark Example

```
1    interface Ainterface {
2        Int recursive_m(Int i, Int id);
3    }
4
5    class A() implements Ainterface{
6        Int result=0;
7        Int recursive_m(Int i, Int id){
8            if (i>0){
9                this.recursive_m(i − 1,id);
10           }else{
11               Fut<Int> f = this ! compute( );
12               await f ?;
13           }
14           return 1;
15       }
16       Int compute( ){
17           return result + 1;  //no significant computation }  }
18   { // Main block:
19       Int i = 0;
20       Ainterface master = new A ( );
21       List<Fut<Int>> futures = Nil;
22       while( i < 500){
23           Fut<Int> f = master ! recursive_m (5, i);
24           futures = Cons( f, futures );
25           i = i + 1 ;
26       }
27       while ( futures != Nil ){
28           Fut<Int> f1 = head(futures);
29           futures = tail(futures);
30           Int r = f1.get;
31   }  }
```

The model creates an Actor of type "A" and sends a large number of messages to it to execute a method `recursive_m(5,id)`. This method creates a call chain of size 5 before sending an asynchronous message to itself to execute method compute() and awaits on its result. Although simple, this example allows us to benchmark the pure overhead that arises from having a runtime system with coroutine support, both in a thread-based approach and through spawning of tasks. The results are shown in Fig. 2. The performance figures presented are for one actor that is running 500–2500 method invocations. It is important to observe that each invocation generates 2 tasks in the actors queue, so as the number of calls increases, the number of tasks doubles. The figures show that the trade-off for storing continuations and context as tasks into heap memory instead of saving them in native threads removes limitations on the application and significantly reduces overhead.

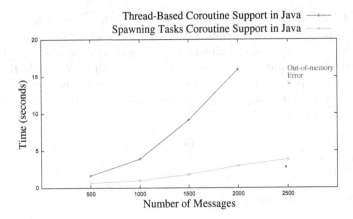

Fig. 2. Performance figures for coroutine overhead

5.2 NQueens Benchmark

From the Savina test suite, we selected the NQueens problem as it is a typical problem with both memory operations and CPU-intensive tasks. Listings 1.2 and 1.3 describe in ABS the problem of arranging N queens on a $N \times N$ chessboard. It provides a master-slave model that illustrates very well the advantage of using actors together with coroutines.

Listing 1.12. NQueens Master Class Snippet

```
1   class Master (Int numWorkers, Int threshold, Int boardSize, ...) implements IMaster {
2       List<IWorker> workers = Nil;
3       //... constructor and initializations
4       {
5           Int i = 0;
6           while (i <= numWorkers) {
7               IWorker w = new Worker(this,threshold,size);
8               workers = Cons(w,workers);
9               i = i+1;
10          }
11          this!sendWork(Nil, 0, ...); // triggers computation
12      }
13      //method for receiving solutions
14
15      Unit sendWork(List<Int> board, Int depth, ...){
16          Fut<Unit> f = nth(workers,messageCounter)!nqueensKernelPar(board,depth,priorities);
17          messageCounter = (messageCounter + 1) \% numWorkers;
18          if(depth==0){
19              await f? ;
20              //handling program completion
21  } } }
```

The benchmark divides the task of finding all the valid solutions to the N queens problem into subtasks sent to a fixed number of workers. The **board** is defined as a list of integers where the index of each element represents the line (equivalent to the **depth** of the board) and the number represents the column. Each subtask sent to a worker (line 16 in Listing 1.12) requires finding all possible valid solutions of placing the next queen on a **board** filled up to the current

depth. Once an intermediary solution is found the worker sends an asynchronous call to the **master** (line 12 in Listing 1.13) to create a new subtask for the new board and the incremented **depth.** The master aggregates the results using a coroutine model (line 19) to await all the solutions starting at depth 0.

Listing 1.13. NQueens Worker Class Snippet

```
1   class Worker(IMaster master, Int threshold, Int size) implements IWorker {
2
3       Unit nqueensKernelPar(List<Int> board, Int depth, ...) {
4           Int i = 0;
5           if (size != depth) {
6               if (depth >= threshold) {
7                   //handle the rest of the solution sequentially and send it to the master
8               } else {
9                   while (i < size) {
10                      List<Int> newboard = appendright(board,i);
11                      if (boardValid(0, newboard,depth+1)) {
12                          master!sendWork(newboard,depth+1, ...);
13                      }
14                      i = i+1;
15          } } }
16          else { //send a solution to the master
17   } } }
```

We ran the benchmark with a board size varying from 7 to 14 with a fixed number of 4 workers. The results compare the implementations of the NQueens problem and are shown in Fig. 3. The first two implementations are direct translations in Java from ABS source code with the two co-routine approaches (thread-abstraction and JAAC(spawning)). It is important to observe that as the board size increases, the number of solutions grows from 40 to 14200. The results show that using thread abstraction (where each method invocation generates a corresponding thread) the time taken grows exponentially and cannot complete once the board size reaches 11 while the approach that uses tasks remains unaffected.

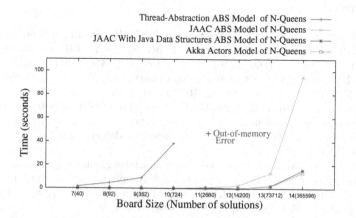

Fig. 3. Results for the N-Queens problem using two different coroutine approaches

The next result (the blue plot) shows the improvement brought by using Java data structures. These results are at a comparable level with the Savina implementation using Akka actors(orange plot). ABS has limited support for data structures (offering only lists, sets and associative lists that can be used as maps) and by changing the **board** from an ABS list to a Java Array we obtain a significant improvement. This enforces the need of a foreign language interface for ABS to be used a full-fledged programming language.

6   Conclusions

In this paper we have formally described a translation scheme together with a Java library for efficiently simulating the behaviour of ABS coroutines. The coroutine abstraction is a powerful programming technique in a software development context. Having a scalable JVM library with support for coroutine emulation gives us a basis for industrial adoption of the ABS language for component-based software engineering. It makes ABS a powerful extension of Java with support for formal verification, resource analysis and deadlock detection.

We plan to extend the library to statically type-check the message submitted via the **send** method in order to prevent the user from running unwanted code on the actors. To this end we already provide a syntactic sugar in Scala for an asynchronous invocation that can be used directly to send a message to an actor and restricts the messages to methods supported by the actor in question.

We also plan to implement a foreign language interface for ABS such that existing libraries may be used directly in the ABS model. This requires extending the type-checker to verify correct foreign types in ABS source code. This in turn would allow for creating both a model on which formal analysis tools can be applied and that would be scalable and efficient once deployed.

References

1. Azadbakht, K., de Boer, F.S., Serbanescu, V.: Multi-threaded actors. In: Proceedings 9th Interaction and Concurrency Experience, ICE 2016, Heraklion, Greece, 8–9 June 2016, pp. 51–66 (2016). https://doi.org/10.4204/EPTCS.223.4
2. Boer, F.D., et al.: A survey of active object languages. ACM Comput. Surv. **50**(5), 76:1–76:39 (2017). https://doi.org/10.1145/3122848
3. Clarke, D., Johnsen, E.B., Owe, O.: Concurrent objects à la carte. In: Dams, D., Hannemann, U., Steffen, M. (eds.) Concurrency, Compositionality, and Correctness. LNCS, vol. 5930, pp. 185–206. Springer, Heidelberg (2010). https://doi.org/10.1007/978-3-642-11512-7_12
4. Commons, A.: Javaflow. http://commons.apache.org/sandbox/javaflow
5. de Boer, F.S., Clarke, D., Johnsen, E.B.: A complete guide to the future. In: De Nicola, R. (ed.) ESOP 2007. LNCS, vol. 4421, pp. 316–330. Springer, Heidelberg (2007). https://doi.org/10.1007/978-3-540-71316-6_22
6. Din, C.C., Bubel, R., Hähnle, R.: KeY-ABS: a deductive verification tool for the concurrent modelling language ABS. In: Felty, A.P., Middeldorp, A. (eds.) CADE 2015. LNCS (LNAI), vol. 9195, pp. 517–526. Springer, Cham (2015). https://doi.org/10.1007/978-3-319-21401-6_35

7. Flores-Montoya, A.E., Albert, E., Genaim, S.: May-happen-in-parallel based dead-lock analysis for concurrent objects. In: Beyer, D., Boreale, M. (eds.) FMOODS/-FORTE -2013. LNCS, vol. 7892, pp. 273–288. Springer, Heidelberg (2013). https://doi.org/10.1007/978-3-642-38592-6_19

8. Giachino, E., Laneve, C., Lienhardt, M.: A framework for deadlock detection in core ABS. Softw. Syst. Model. **15**(4), 1013–1048 (2016)

9. Haller, P., Odersky, M.: Scala actors: unifying thread-based and event-based programming. Theor. Comput. Sci. **410**(2), 202–220 (2009)

10. Imam, S.M., Sarkar, V.: Savina-an actor benchmark suite: enabling empirical evaluation of actor libraries. In: 4th International Workshop on Programming based on Actors Agents and Decentralized Control, pp. 67–80. ACM (2014)

11. Jangid, M.: Kotlin the unrivalled android programming language lineage. Imp. J. Interdiscip. Res. **3**(8) (2017), http://imperialjournals.com/index.php/IJIR/article/view/5491

12. Johnsen, E.B., Hähnle, R., Schäfer, J., Schlatte, R., Steffen, M.: ABS: a core language for abstract behavioral specification. In: Aichernig, B.K., de Boer, F.S., Bonsangue, M.M. (eds.) FMCO 2010. LNCS, vol. 6957, pp. 142–164. Springer, Heidelberg (2011). https://doi.org/10.1007/978-3-642-25271-6_8

13. Kamburjan, E., Hähnle, R.: Uniform modeling of railway operations. In: Artho, C., Ölveczky, P.C. (eds.) FTSCS 2016. CCIS, vol. 694, pp. 55–71. Springer, Cham (2017). https://doi.org/10.1007/978-3-319-53946-1_4

14. Kamburjan, E., Hähnle, R.: Deductive verification of railway operations. In: International Conference on Reliability, Safety and Security of Railway Systems, pp. 131–147. Springer (2017)

15. Schäfer, J.: A programming model and language for concurrent and distributed object-oriented systems. Ph.D. thesis, University of Kaiserslautern (2011)

16. Serbanescu, V., Nagarajagowda, C., Azadbakht, K., de Boer, F., Nobakht, B.: Towards type-based optimizations in distributed applications using ABS and JAVA 8. In: Pop, F., Potop-Butucaru, M. (eds.) ARMS-CC 2014. LNCS, vol. 8907, pp. 103–112. Springer, Cham (2014). https://doi.org/10.1007/978-3-319-13464-2_8

17. Srinivasan, S., Mycroft, A.: Kilim: isolation-typed actors for java. In: Vitek, J. (ed.) ECOOP 2008. LNCS, vol. 5142, pp. 104–128. Springer, Heidelberg (2008). https://doi.org/10.1007/978-3-540-70592-5_6

18. Storm, E.: Scala coroutines. http://storm-enroute.com/coroutines/

19. Taura, K., Matsuoka, S., Yonezawa, A.: ABCL/f: a future-based polymorphic typed concurrent object-oriented language - its design and implementation. In: Proceedings of the DIMACS Workshop on Specification of Parallel Algorithms, pp. 275–292. American Mathematical Society (1994)

20. Wong, P.Y.H., Albert, E., Muschevici, R., Proença, J., Schäfer, J., Schlatte, R.: The ABS tool suite: modelling, executing and analysing distributed adaptable object-oriented systems. Int. J. Softw. Tools Technol. Transf. **14**(5), 567–588 (2012). https://doi.org/10.1007/s10009-012-0250-1

21. Yonezawa, A., Briot, J.-P., Shibayama, E.: Object-oriented concurrent programming in ABCL/1. In: Agha, G., Igarashi, A., Kobayashi, N., Masuhara, H., Matsuoka, S., Shibayama, E., Taura, K. (eds.) Concurrent Objects and Beyond. LNCS, vol. 8665, pp. 18–43. Springer, Heidelberg (2014). https://doi.org/10.1007/978-3-662-44471-9_2

Dynamic Cut-Off Algorithm for Parameterised Refinement Checking

Antti Siirtola[1]($\boxtimes$)(iD) and Keijo Heljanko[2,3,4](iD)

[1] Faculty of Information Technology and Electrical Engineering,
M3S Research Group, University of Oulu, Oulu, Finland
`antti.siirtola@oulu.fi`
[2] Department of Computer Science, Aalto University, Helsinki, Finland
`keijo.heljanko@iki.fi`
[3] Department of Computer Science, University of Helsinki, Helsinki, Finland
[4] Helsinki Institute for Information Technology (HIIT), Helsinki, Finland

Abstract. The verification of contemporary software systems is challenging, because they are heavily parameterised containing components, the number and connections of which cannot be a priori fixed. We consider the multi-parameterised verification of safety properties by refinement checking in the context of labelled transition systems (LTSs). The LTSs are parameterised by using first-order constructs, sorts, variables, and predicates, while preserving compositionality. This allows us to parameterise not only the number of replicated components but also the system topology, the connections between the components. We aim to solve a verification task in the parameterised LTS formalism by determining cut-offs for the parameters. As the main contribution, we convert this problem into the unsatisfiability of a first-order formula and provide a SAT modulo theories (SMT)-based semi-algorithm for dynamically, i.e., iteratively, computing the cut-offs. The algorithm will always terminate for topologies expressible in the $\exists^*\forall^*$ fragment of first-order logic. It also enables us to consider systems with topologies beyond this fragment, but for these systems, the algorithm is not guaranteed to terminate. We have implemented the approach on top of the Z3 SMT solver and successfully applied it to several system models. As a running example, we consider the leader election phase of the Raft consensus algorithm and prove a cut-off of three servers which we conjecture to be the optimal one.

Keywords: Labelled transition systems · Refinement checking
Safety properties · Compositional verification · Parameterized systems
Cut-off · First-order logic · Satisfiability modulo theories

1 Introduction

Contemporary software systems are not only highly concurrent and distributed but also heavily parameterised containing components, the number and connections of which cannot be a priori fixed. Since these systems are everywhere

© Springer Nature Switzerland AG 2018
K. Bae and P. C. Ölveczky (Eds.): FACS 2018, LNCS 11222, pp. 256–276, 2018.
https://doi.org/10.1007/978-3-030-02146-7_13

around us, it is essential to verify that at least the most critical of them operate properly in all circumstances, i.e., for all possible parameter values. Moreover, since some subsystems (e.g., external software packages and subsystems concurrently under construction) can only be available in an interface specification form, we often need to be able to do their verification in a compositional way.

Contribution. We consider the multi-parameterised verification of safety properties in the context of labelled transition systems (LTSs) with trace refinement preorder and parallel composition and hiding operators. The LTSs are parameterised by using the constructs of first-order logic (FOL), *sorts* (a.k.a. *types*), typed *variables*, and *predicates*, such that compositional verification is possible in the parameterised setting, too. Sorts are used to parameterise the number of replicated components whereas predicates enable us to parameterise the system topology, i.e., the connections between the components.

Our goal is to solve a verification task in the parameterised LTS (PLTS) formalism by determining cut-offs for the parameters such that in order to prove a parameterised system implementation correct with respect to its specification, it is sufficient to consider only finitely many instances up to the cut-offs. As the main result, we show how this problem can be converted into the unsatisfiability of a first-order formula (Theorem 23). The result is accompanied by a SAT modulo theories (SMT)-based semi-algorithm for computing the cut-offs. The algorithm is called dynamic because it computes the cut-offs iteratively until the unsatisfiability condition is met. The algorithm is implemented and successfully applied to several parameterised system models, including the repeatable read property of taDOM2+ XML database protocol [10] with the tree topology and the leader election phase of the Raft consensus protocol with the quorum topology [17,21].

Our approach is based on the precongruence reduction (PR) technique previously used to prove *static* cut-offs for PLTSs with predicates defined in the universal fragment ($\forall^*$) of FOL [24] and for PLTSs with special quorum functions [21]. The technique is also adapted to parameterised modal interface automata without predicates [23]. In general, the PR technique applies to implementation-specification pairs the topology of which is downward-closed in the sense that any (big) instance can be represented as a composition of smaller instances. For example star, bipartite, totally connected, linear, tree, and quorum topologies are such, but not all their combinations.

Static cut-off results [21,24] are syntax-based and restricted to topologies specifiable in fragments of FOL. Consequently, a separate result is needed for each such fragment. The dynamic algorithm introduced here is not restricted to any syntactic fragment and we can basically use the full expressive power of FOL. The dynamic algorithm will always terminate for topologies expressible in the $\exists^*\forall^*$ fragment of first-order logic, because the fragment is decidable [8] and such topologies are downward-closed [24]. The algorithm also enables us to consider systems with downward-closed topologies beyond this fragment, but for these systems, termination depends on the capabilities of the used SMT solver. Nevertheless, the dynamic algorithm not only enables us to treat the parameters of [21,24] in a uniform way but it also allows for the use of parameters that are beyond those handled by the static methods. Moreover, based on our experiments, the dynamic algorithm produces at least as tight or even smaller cut-offs than the static cut-off methods. For example, the static cut-off for the number of servers in Raft is seven whereas the computed dynamic cut-off is only three, which we conjecture to be the optimal one. Earlier, the cut-offs of 5-7 are proved for other consensus algorithms [15].

Related Work. The distinctive features of our solution to the parameterised verification problem are compositionality, the support for multiple and topology related parameters, and the dynamic computation of cut-offs.

As regards compositionality, the process algebraic approaches of Valmari & Tienari [25], Lazić [13], and Creese [2] are the closest works. Valmari & Tienari [25] present a generic induction method for parameterised verification. However, a crucial part of the technique is to come up with an invariant process which is a task that cannot be automated in general. Lazić considers data-independent systems which can handle infinite or arbitrarily large data types. His approach allows multiple parameters and provides static cut-offs for the size of data types. There is also a more general version of the results based on infinite automata [14] but in this context, compositionality is not considered. Moreover, neither approach allows the number of concurrent components nor the system topology to be parameterised. The limitation is overcome by Creese who combines the data-independence results with the induction method [2]. Simultaneously, however, full automation is lost.

Multi-parameterised verification is also considered by Emerson & Kahlon [4], Hanna et al. [9], and Yang & Li [26]. The approaches [4,26] are based on static cut-offs, whereas [9] uses the iterative computation of cut-offs. The methods apply to systems with guarded broadcasts [4], shared actions [9], or rendezvous communication [26] and specifications are given in temporal logic [4,9] or as property automata [26]. However, the formalisms do not lend support to compositionality. In addition to [2,9,25], dynamic cut-off computation is previously considered by Kaiser, Kroening & Wahl [12], too. Their approach can be used for the verification of reachability in boolean programs, but it does not lend support to multiple parameters nor compositional reasoning.

Completely different approaches to parameterised verification are based on abstract interpretation [27] and infinite-state verification algorithms [5]. While some of these techniques lend support to multiple parameters, they are typically not compositional. The additional benefit of our approach over these techniques is that we can exploit efficient finite-state model checkers for verification and since abstraction is not involved, false error traces are avoided.

Outline. The next three sections are preliminaries; they cover the basics of LTSs, FOL, and PLTSs. In Sect. 5, we present our main contribution, the dynamic cut-off algorithm. The paper concludes with discussion on future research.

2 Labelled Transition Systems

In this section, we briefly recall a Communicating Sequential Processes (CSP)-like LTS-based process calculus with parallel composition and hiding operators and trace refinement preorder [18]. We use LTSs to express system components.

We assume a countably infinite set of *events*. One of the events is *invisible*, denoted τ, and the other ones are *visible*. The visible events have an explicit channel and data part; we assume countably infinite sets $\mathbb{C}$ and $\mathbb{A}$ of, respectively, *channels* and *atoms* and that each visible event is of the form $c(a_1, \ldots, a_n)$, where c is a channel and $a_1, \ldots, a_n \in \mathbb{A}$ are atoms.

A *labelled transition system (LTS)* is a four-tuple $L := (S, E, R, \dot{s})$, where (1) S is a finite non-empty set of *states*, (2) E is a finite set of *visible events*, also called an *alphabet*, (3) $R \subseteq S \times (E \cup \{\tau\}) \times S$ is a set of *transitions*, and (4) $\dot{s}$ is the *initial* state.

Let L_i be an LTS $(S_i, E_i, R_i, \dot{s}_i)$ for both $i \in \{1, 2\}$. The *parallel composition* (of L_1 and L_2) is an LTS $(L_1 \parallel L_2) := (S_1 \times S_2, E_1 \cup E_2, R_\parallel, (\dot{s}_1, \dot{s}_2))$, where $R_\parallel$ is the set of all triples $((s_1, s_2), \alpha, (s_1', s_2'))$ such that either (1) $\alpha \neq \tau$ and $(s_i, \alpha, s_i') \in R_i$ for both $i \in \{1, 2\}$; (2) $(s_1, \alpha, s_1') \in R_1$, $\alpha \notin E_2$, $s_2 \in S_2$, and $s_2' = s_2$; or (3) $(s_2, \alpha, s_2') \in R_2$, $\alpha \notin E_1$, $s_1 \in S_1$, and $s_1' = s_1$.

Let L be an LTS $(S, E, R, \dot{s})$ and E' a set of visible events. The LTS L *after hiding* E' is an LTS $(L \setminus E') := (S, E \setminus E', R_\setminus, \dot{s})$, where $R_\setminus$ is the set of (1) all triples $(s, \alpha, s') \in R$ such that $\alpha \notin E'$; and (2) all triples (s, τ, s') such that $(s, \alpha, s') \in R$ for some $\alpha \in E'$.

A finite alternating sequence $(s_0, \alpha_1, s_1, \ldots, \alpha_n, s_n)$ of states and events of L is an *execution of L* if s_0 is the initial state and (s_{i-1}, α_i, s_i) is a transition of L for every $i \in \{1, \ldots, n\}$. A finite sequence of visible events is a *trace (of L)*, if there is an execution of L such that the sequence can be obtained from the execution by erasing all the states and the invisible events. The set of all the traces of L is denoted by $\mathrm{tr}(L)$. An LTS L_1 is a *trace refinement* of an LTS L_2, denoted $L_1 \preceq_{\mathrm{tr}} L_2$, if L_1 and L_2 have the same alphabet and $\mathrm{tr}(L_1) \subseteq \mathrm{tr}(L_2)$ [11]. The LTSs L_1 and L_2 are *trace equivalent*, denoted $L_1 \equiv_{\mathrm{tr}} L_2$, if and only if $L_1 \preceq_{\mathrm{tr}} L_2$ and $L_2 \preceq_{\mathrm{tr}} L_1$. Clearly, $\preceq_{\mathrm{tr}}$ is a preorder (i.e., a reflexive and transitive relation) and $\equiv_{\mathrm{tr}}$ an equivalence relation on the set of LTSs.

The operators and the trace relations have many useful properties [11,18,24], which are also exploited in the proofs. The parallel composition is commutative, associative, and idempotent with respect to $\equiv_{\mathrm{tr}}$ (i.e., $L \parallel L \equiv_{\mathrm{tr}} L$ for all LTSs L) and a single-state LTS $L_{id} := (\{\dot{s}\}, \emptyset, \emptyset, \dot{s})$ with the empty alphabet and no transition is the identity element of $\parallel$. This allows us to extend $\parallel$ to every finite set $I = \{i_1, \ldots, i_n\}$ and all LTSs $L_{i_1}, \ldots, L_{i_n}$ by defining $(\parallel_{i \in I} L_i) = (\parallel_{k=1}^{n} L_{i_k}) := (L_{i_1} \parallel (\parallel_{i \in I \setminus \{i_1\}} L_i))$, when $n > 0$, and $(\parallel_{i \in I} L_i) = (\parallel_{k=1}^{n} L_{i_k}) := L_{id}$, when $n = 0$. Moreover, distributing hiding over parallel composition results in an LTS greater in the preorder; $(L_1 \parallel L_2) \setminus E \preceq_{\mathrm{tr}} (L_1 \setminus E) \parallel (L_2 \setminus E)$ for all LTSs L_1, L_2 and every set E of visible events [24]. Finally, $\equiv_{\mathrm{tr}}$ is compositional with respect to the parallel composition and hiding operators; if $L_1 \preceq_{\mathrm{tr}} L_2$, then $L_1 \parallel L_3 \preceq_{\mathrm{tr}} L_2 \parallel L_3$ and $L_1 \setminus E \preceq_{\mathrm{tr}} L_2 \setminus E$ for all LTSs L_1, L_2, L_3 and all sets E of visible events. Hence, $\preceq_{\mathrm{tr}}$ is a precongruence and $\equiv_{\mathrm{tr}}$ a congruence on LTSs.

3 Many-Sorted First-Order Logic

In this section, we introduce first-order logic (FOL) [6] with *sorts* (a.k.a. *types*), *variables*, and *predicates*. We use FOL to express system topologies.

We assume sets of sorts, variables, and predicates, denoted by $\mathbb{T}$, $\mathbb{X}$, and $\mathbb{F}$, respectively, that are disjoint and countably infinite. We assume that for each atom $a \in \mathbb{A}$, there is a sort $T_a \in \mathbb{T}$ and for each sort $T \in \mathbb{T}$, the set $\mathbb{A}_T := \{a \in \mathbb{A} \mid T_a = T\}$ is countably infinite. Hence, $\mathbb{A}_T$ and $\mathbb{A}_S$ are disjoint whenever T and S are different sorts. Moreover, we assume that for each variable $x \in \mathbb{X}$ there is a sort $T_x \in \mathbb{T}$, and for each predicate F there is an arity $n_F \in \mathbb{Z}_+$ and a tuple of sorts $\mathbf{T}_F = (T_F^1, \ldots, T_F^{n_F})$ specifying the domain of the predicate.

The *atomic propositions* are of the form $\top$ (always true), $x = y$ (equivalence), and $F(x_1, \ldots, x_n)$ (predicate application), where x and y are variables, F is a predicate with arity n, and $x_1, \ldots, x_n$ are variables of the sort $T_F^1, \ldots, T_F^n$, respectively. The *formulae* of FOL are defined by the grammar

$$\mathcal{V} ::= p \mid \neg\mathcal{V} \mid \mathcal{V} \wedge \mathcal{V} \mid \mathcal{V} \vee \mathcal{V} \mid \forall x.\mathcal{V} \mid \exists x.\mathcal{V} \,,$$

where x denotes a variable and p an atomic proposition. We also write $x \neq y$ (inequivalence) and $\mathcal{V}_1 \rightarrow \mathcal{V}_2$ (implication) short for $\neg(x = y)$ and $(\neg\mathcal{V}_1) \vee \mathcal{V}_2$, respectively. A *propositional formula* or a *guard* is a formula without quantified structures of the form $\forall x.\mathcal{V}$ and $\exists x.\mathcal{V}$. A formula is in the *prenex normal form* with *quantifier alternation* $Q_1, \ldots, Q_n$ if it is of the form $Q_1 x_1. \cdots .Q_n x_n.\mathcal{V}$, where $Q_1, \ldots, Q_n \in \{\forall, \exists\}$ are quantifiers and $\mathcal{V}$ is propositional.

A *signature function* maps a formula $\mathcal{V}$ to a finite set of sorts, variables, and predicates, which are the parameters of $\mathcal{V}$. The signature function, denoted par, is defined inductively:

1. $\mathrm{par}(\top) = \emptyset$,
2. $\mathrm{par}(x = y) = \{x, y, T_x, T_y\}$,
3. $\mathrm{par}(F(x_1, \ldots, x_n)) = \{F, x_1, \ldots, x_n, T_{x_1}, \ldots, T_{x_n}\}$,
4. $\mathrm{par}(\neg\mathcal{V}) = \mathrm{par}(\mathcal{V})$,
5. $\mathrm{par}(\mathcal{V}_1 \wedge \mathcal{V}_2) = \mathrm{par}(\mathcal{V}_1 \vee \mathcal{V}_2) = \mathrm{par}(\mathcal{V}_1) \cup \mathrm{par}(\mathcal{V}_2)$,
6. $\mathrm{par}(\forall x.\mathcal{V}) = \mathrm{par}(\exists x.\mathcal{V}) = (\mathrm{par}(\mathcal{V}) \setminus \{x\}) \cup \{T_x\}$ (x is considered bound).

We write $\mathrm{par}_X(\mathcal{V})$ for the restriction $\mathrm{par}(\mathcal{V}) \cap X$ of the signature to a set X.

A formula is evaluated by using a *valuation* function which assigns values to sorts, variables, and predicates.

Definition 1 (Valuation). *A valuation is a function ϕ such that*

1. *the domain of ϕ is a finite set of sorts, variables, and predicates,*
2. *for each sort $T \in \mathrm{dom}(\phi)$, $\phi(T)$ is a finite non-empty subset of $\mathbb{A}_T$,*
3. *for each variable $x \in \mathrm{dom}(\phi)$, $T_x \in \mathrm{dom}(\phi)$ and $\phi(x) \in \phi(T_x)$, and*
4. *for each predicate $F \in \mathrm{dom}(\phi)$, $T_F^1, \ldots, T_F^{n_F} \in \mathrm{dom}(\phi)$ and $\phi(F)$ is a subset of $\phi(T_F^1) \times \ldots \times \phi(T_F^{n_F})$.*

We write $\mathrm{dom}_X(\phi)$ for the restriction $\mathrm{dom}(\phi) \cap X$ of the domain to a set X and $\mathrm{Im}(\phi)$ for the set $\bigcup_{T \in \mathrm{dom}_\mathbb{T}(\phi)} \phi(T)$ of all atoms in the image of ϕ. The complement $\overline{\phi(F)}$ of the value of a predicate F is the set $\phi(T_F^1) \times \ldots \times \phi(T_F^{n_F}) \setminus \phi(F)$. A valuation ϕ is *compatible* with a formula $\mathcal{V}$ if $\mathrm{par}(\mathcal{V}) \subseteq \mathrm{dom}(\phi)$. The *instance* of $\mathcal{V}$ *generated by* a compatible valuation ϕ, denoted $[\![\mathcal{V}]\!]_\phi$, is a truth value obtained in the usual way by substituting $\phi(T)$ for each sort T, $\phi(x)$ for each variable x not bound in $\mathcal{V}$, and $\phi(F)$ for each predicate F occurring in $\mathcal{V}$ and by evaluating the operators. We say that ϕ *satisfies* $\mathcal{V}$, if $[\![\mathcal{V}]\!]_\phi$ is true. The satisfiability problem in FOL asks whether for a given formula $\mathcal{V}$, there is a valuation satisfying $\mathcal{V}$. The problem is undecidable in general, but the fragment consisting of the formulae with the quantifier alternation $\exists^* \forall^*$ is decidable [8]. Many-sorted FOL considered here has several other known decidable fragments [1], too, but since many of them do not contain full $\exists^* \forall^*$, they are of limited use from the viewpoint of our algorithm introduced in Sect. 5.

4   Parameterised Labelled Transition Systems

In this section, we parameterise LTSs with first-order constructs, sorts, variables, and predicates, while preserving compositionality. With minor syntactic differences, this is done as in [24]. Parameterised LTSs can express systems with an unbounded number of replicated components and we use them to model both system implementations and specifications.

Example 2. As a running example, we consider the leader election phase of the Raft consensus algorithm [17]. In Raft, time is divided into *terms* of arbitrary length and a server can crash at any moment. When a server is running, it is in one of the three states, a follower, candidate, or leader. A server always (re)starts as a follower. A follower can vote for at most one server in a term. If a follower does not regularly receive messages from the leader, it increases its term and promotes itself to a candidate. A candidate sends vote requests to the other servers and if it receives a quorum of votes, it becomes a leader. Our goal is to formally prove that in each term, there is at most one leader independent of the number of terms and the size of the cluster.

For our Raft model, we pick a sort T_S to represent the set $\{s_1, \ldots, s_n\} \subseteq \mathbb{A}_{T_S}$ of the identifiers of servers and a sort T_T to represent the set $\{t_1, \ldots, t_m\} \subseteq \mathbb{A}_{T_T}$ of the identifiers of terms. We also use a predicate Q_S with $\mathbf{T}_{Q_S} = (T_S, T_T, T_S)$ to assign each server and each term a set of servers from which the server needs a vote in order to become a leader in the term. Variables x_i of the sort T_S are used to refer to individual servers and a variable y of the sort T_T is used to refer to a specific term.

Next, we specify the values of Q_S. We require that for each server x_0 and each term y, the set $Q_{x_0, y} := \{x_1 \mid Q_S(x_0, y, x_1)\}$ of servers, from which x_1 needs a vote in order to became a leader in the term y, is a quorum set (the set covers more than half the servers including x_0 itself) or the empty set (the server cannot become a leader in the term y). Allowing the empty set is needed to make the topology downward-closed so that our approach, introduced in the next section, can be successfully applied. Since we do not have an explicit construct for restricting the size of a set, we require that whenever $Q_{x_0,y}$ is non-empty then for every $x_1 \notin Q_{x_0,y}$, there is a unique $x_2 \in Q_{x_0,y}$. For this purpose, we introduce a partial function $f : (x_0, y, x_1) \mapsto x_2$ which is encoded as a predicate F_S with $\mathbf{T}_{F_S} = (T_S, T_T, T_S, T_S)$ such that $f(x_0, y, x_1) = x_2$ if and only if $F_S(x_0, y, x_1, x_2)$. The values of Q_S and F_S are expressed as a formula

$$Qrm := \forall x_0. \forall y. ((\forall x_1. \neg Q_S(x_0, y, x_1)) \vee$$
$$(Q_S(x_0, y, x_0) \wedge \forall x_1. (\neg Q_S(x_0, y, x_1) \to \exists x_2. F_S(x_0, y, x_1, x_2)))) \wedge$$
$$\forall x_0. \forall x_1. \forall x_2. \forall y. (F_S(x_0, y, x_1, x_2) \to (Q_S(x_0, y, x_2) \wedge \neg Q_S(x_0, y, x_1))) \wedge$$
$$\forall x_0. \forall x_1. \forall x_2. \forall x_3. \forall y. ((F_S(x_0, y, x_1, x_3) \wedge F_S(x_0, y, x_2, x_3)) \to x_1 = x_2) \wedge$$
$$\forall x_0. \forall y. \exists x_1. \forall x_2. (\neg F_S(x_0, y, x_2, x_1) \wedge \neg F_S(x_0, y, x_1, x_2)) \ .$$

The first three lines of the formula state the relationship between Q_S and F_S, the next line says that the function represented by F_S is injective, and the last line indirectly guarantees that if $Q_{x_0,y}$ is non-empty then it is larger than its complement, i.e., a quorum set covers more than half the servers. The formula is outside the decidable fragment $\exists^* \forall^*$, because it involves a quantifier alternation $\forall \exists \forall$, but our algorithm still terminates on this running example. □

Parameterised LTSs are constructed from LTSs with variables substituted for the atoms, propositional formulae used as guards, and (replicated) parallel composition and hiding constructs which can be thought as operators on parameterised LTSs. Replicated parallel composition allows for parameterising the number of components while guards are used to restrict the system topology.

Definition 3 (PLTS). *Parameterised LTSs (PLTSs) are defined inductively:*

1. *If L is an LTS, $a_1, \ldots, a_n$ are the atoms occurring in its alphabet, and $x_1, \ldots, x_n$ are variables such that $T_{a_i} = T_{x_i}$ for all $i \in \{1, \ldots, n\}$, then a function $L(x_1, \ldots, x_n) := \lambda a_1, \ldots, a_n.L$ is an (elementary) PLTS.*
2. *If $\mathcal{P}$ is a PLTS and G a guard, then $([G]\mathcal{P})$ is a (guarded) PLTS.*
3. *If $\mathcal{P}_1$ and $\mathcal{P}_2$ are PLTSs, then $(\mathcal{P}_1 \parallel \mathcal{P}_2)$ is a (parallel) PLTS.*
4. *If $\mathcal{P}$ is a PLTS and x a variable, then $(\parallel_x \mathcal{P})$ is a (replicated parallel) PLTS.*
5. *If $\mathcal{P}$ is a PLTS and C a finite set of channels, $(\mathcal{P} \setminus C)$ is a (hiding) PLTS.*

The signature function is extended to the set of PLTSs by setting:

1. $\mathrm{par}(L(x_1, \ldots, x_n)) = \{x_1, \ldots, x_n, T_{x_1}, \ldots, T_{x_n}\}$,
2. $\mathrm{par}([G]\mathcal{P}) = \mathrm{par}(G) \cup \mathrm{par}(\mathcal{P})$,
3. $\mathrm{par}(\mathcal{P}_1 \parallel \mathcal{P}_2) = \mathrm{par}(\mathcal{P}_1) \cup \mathrm{par}(\mathcal{P}_2)$,
4. $\mathrm{par}(\parallel_x \mathcal{P}) = (\mathrm{par}(\mathcal{P}) \setminus \{x\}) \cup \{T_x\}$ (x is considered bound), and
5. $\mathrm{par}(\mathcal{P} \setminus C) = \mathrm{par}(\mathcal{P})$.

The signature determines the *parameters* of the PLTS and a valuation ϕ is said to be *compatible* with a PLTS $\mathcal{P}$ if $\mathrm{par}(\mathcal{P}) \subseteq \mathrm{dom}(\phi)$. We sometimes write $\mathcal{P}(x_1, \ldots, x_n)$ to emphasise that $\mathcal{P}$ has the variables $x_1, \ldots, x_n$ as parameters.

A PLTS is evaluated to an LTS by fixing the values of the parameters and by evaluating the operators. Handling binary operators is straightforward, but in order to evaluate a replicated construct $\|_x \mathcal{P}$ by using a compatible valuation ϕ, we need to iterate over all the extensions of ϕ to $\{x\}$. Let ϕ be a valuation and X a set of variables such that $T_x \in \mathrm{dom}_\mathrm{T}(\phi)$ for all $x \in X$. We write $\mathrm{ext}(\phi, X)$ for the set of all valuations ϕ' with the domain $\mathrm{dom}(\phi) \cup X$ such that $\phi'(x) \in \phi(T_x)$ for all $x \in X$ and $\phi'|_{\mathrm{dom}(\phi) \setminus X} = \phi|_{\mathrm{dom}(\phi) \setminus X}$, i.e., ϕ and ϕ' agree on the values of the parameters outside X. We can now extend the instantiation function $[\![\cdot]\!]_\phi$ to PLTSs $\mathcal{P}$ for which $\mathrm{par}(\mathcal{P}) \subseteq \mathrm{dom}(\phi)$.

Definition 4 (Instance of a PLTS). *Let $\mathcal{P}$ be a PLTS and ϕ a compatible valuation. The ϕ-instance of $\mathcal{P}$ or the instance of $\mathcal{P}$ (generated by ϕ) is denoted by $[\![\mathcal{P}]\!]_\phi$ and determined inductively as follows:*

1. $[\![L(x_1, \ldots, x_n)]\!]_\phi = L(\phi(x_1), \ldots, \phi(x_n))$,
2. $[\![[G]\mathcal{P}']\!]_\phi = \begin{cases} [\![\mathcal{P}']\!]_\phi, & \text{if } [\![G]\!]_\phi \text{ is true,} \\ L_{id}, & \text{if } [\![G]\!]_\phi \text{ is false (the instance has no behaviour),} \end{cases}$
3. $[\![\mathcal{P}_1 \| \mathcal{P}_2]\!]_\phi = [\![\mathcal{P}_1]\!]_\phi \| [\![\mathcal{P}_2]\!]_\phi$,
4. $[\![\|_x \mathcal{P}']\!]_\phi = \|_{\phi' \in \mathrm{ext}(\phi, \{x\})} [\![\mathcal{P}']\!]_{\phi'}$,
5. $[\![\mathcal{P}' \setminus C]\!]_\phi = [\![\mathcal{P}']\!]_\phi \setminus \{c(a_1, \ldots, a_n) \mid c \in C, a_1, \ldots, a_n \in \mathbb{A}\}$.

Example 5. For the Raft specification, we use an event $leader(x_0, y)$ to denote that the server x_0 is chosen as a leader in the term y. First, we consider the specification from the viewpoint of two servers, x_0 and x_1, and a term y. PLTS $Spec2(x_0, x_1, y)$ on the left of Fig. 1 formally says that no two servers can become a leader during the same term but repeating a leader notification is fine.

Recall the definition of the predicate Q_S from Ex. 2. As we let the variable y to range over all term identifiers and x_0, x_1, and x_2 over all server identifiers, we obtain the model of the full specification as a PLTS

$$Spec := \|_{x_0} \|_{x_1} \|_{x_2} \|_y [Q_S(x_0, y, x_2) \wedge Q_S(x_1, y, x_2)] Spec2(x_0, x_1, y),$$

which says that for each term, there is at most one leader. The guard guarantees that for each term, we only consider servers with (non-empty) overlapping quorum sets. This is not a restriction since any two quorum sets are overlapping. Since $Spec2(x_0, x_1, y)$ has no bound variable, $\mathrm{par}(Spec2(x_0, x_1, y)) = \{x_0, x_1, y, T_S, T_T\}$, but $\mathrm{par}(Spec) = \{Q_S, T_S, T_T\}$ as $Spec$ has only bound variables.

In order to visualize $Spec$, let us consider a valuation ϕ such that $\phi(T_T) = \{t_1\}$, $\phi(T_S) = \{s_1, \ldots, s_n\}$, and $\{x \mid (s_i, t_1, x) \in \phi(Q_S)\}$ is a quorum set for all $i \in \{1, \ldots, n\}$. Obviously, the valuation is compatible with $Spec$ and the ϕ-instance of $Spec$ is a star-shaped LTS on the right of Fig. 1, which indeed says that there is at most one leader for the term t_1. □

We complete the PLTS formalism by extending the trace refinement relation to the set of PLTSs while preserving compositionality. However, instead of a single relation, there will be infinitely many, since we use formulae to define the allowed values of parameters.

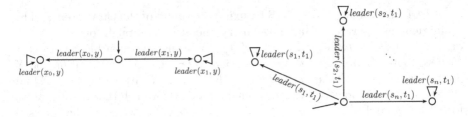

Fig. 1. On the left: PLTS $Spec2(x_0, x_1, y)$ representing the Raft specification from the viewpoint of two servers, x_0 and x_1, and a term y. On the right: the instance of $Spec$ representing the Raft specification from the viewpoint of n servers $s_1, \ldots, s_n$ and a term t_1.

Definition 6 (Trace refinement on PLTSs). *Let $\mathcal{P}$ and $\mathcal{Q}$ be PLTSs and $\mathcal{V}$ a formula. We write $\mathcal{P} \preceq_{tr}^{\mathcal{V}} \mathcal{Q}$, if $[\![\mathcal{P}]\!]_\phi \preceq_{tr} [\![\mathcal{Q}]\!]_\phi$ for all valuations ϕ that are compatible with $\mathcal{P}$ and $\mathcal{Q}$ and satisfy $\mathcal{V}$.*

Obviously, the definition can also be restricted to valuations with the minimal domain $par(\mathcal{P} \parallel \mathcal{Q}) \cup par(\mathcal{V})$. Therefore, we write $va(\mathcal{V} \mid \mathcal{P}, \mathcal{Q})$ for the set of all valuations ϕ which have the domain $par(\mathcal{P} \parallel \mathcal{Q}) \cup par(\mathcal{V})$ and satisfy $\mathcal{V}$.

Parameterised verification tasks can now be expressed as follows: Given an implementation PLTS $\mathcal{P}$, a specification PLTS $\mathcal{Q}$, and a topology formula $\mathcal{V}$, we consider $\mathcal{P}$ to be *correct (with respect to $\mathcal{Q}$) (when $\mathcal{V}$)*, if $\mathcal{P} \preceq_{tr}^{\mathcal{V}} \mathcal{Q}$. This allows for the verification of safety properties. Parameterised trace refinement relations also enable compositional verification since they are precongruences. This follows from Definition 4 and the precongruence of $\preceq_{tr}$.

Proposition 7. *For all formulae $\mathcal{V}$, the relation $\preceq_{tr}^{\mathcal{V}}$ is a precongruence on the set of PLTSs [24].*

Example 8. For the Raft implementation, we use an event $vote(x_0, y, x_1)$ to denote that the server x_0 votes for the server x_1 in the term y and an event $candidate(x_0, y)$ to denote that the server x_0 promotes itself to a candidate in the term y. The behaviour of the Raft implementation is modelled in the same fashion as the specification. First, we capture it in the follower/candidate mode from the viewpoint of three servers x_0, x_1, x_2 and a term y in a PLTS $Flw3(x_0, x_1, x_2, y)$ on the left of Fig. 2. The PLTS says that in the term y, the server x_0 can vote for either x_1, x_2, or itself or become a candidate and vote for itself. When we let the variables x_1, x_2, and y to range over all values in their domain (with the restriction that the values of x_1 and x_2 are different), we obtain the model of a single server x_0 running in the follower/candidate mode as a PLTS

$$Flw(x_0) := \mathop{\parallel}_{x_1} \mathop{\parallel}_{x_2} [x_1 \neq x_2] \mathop{\parallel}_{y} Flw3(x_0, x_1, x_2, y) \,,$$

which states that a server can vote for at most one server in the term or become a candidate.

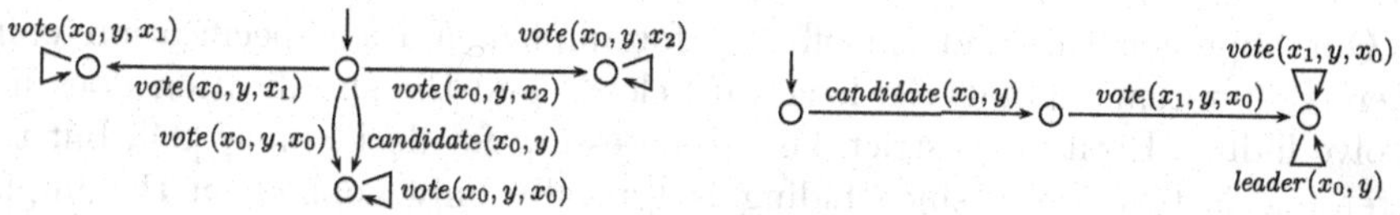

Fig. 2. On the left: PLTS $Flw3(x_0, x_1, x_2, y)$ representing the Raft implementation in the follower/candidate mode from the viewpoint of three servers x_0, x_1, x_2 and a term y. On the right: PLTS $Ldr2(x_0, x_1, y)$ representing the Raft implementation in the candidate/leader mode from the viewpoint of two servers x_0, x_1 and a term y.

Second, we model the Raft implementation in the candidate/leader mode from the viewpoint of two servers x_0, x_1 and a term y as a PLTS $Ldr2(x_0, x_1, y)$ on the right of Fig. 2. This model says that once the server x_0 becomes a candidate and receives a vote from the server x_1, it can promote itself to a leader in the term y. As we let y to range over all term ids and x_1 to range over all server ids in the quorum set of the server x_0 for the term y, the model of a single server x_0 running in the candidate/leader mode is obtained as a PLTS

$$Ldr(x_0) := \underset{y\ x_1}{\|\ \|} [Q_S(x_0, y, x_0) \wedge Q_S(x_0, y, x_1)] Ldr2(x_0, x_1, y) ,$$

which says that in order for a server to become a leader, it needs to become a candidate and then receive a vote from a quorum of servers, including itself.

When we compose the partial models in parallel and let x_0 to range over all server ids, we obtain the model of the Raft implementation with an arbitrary many servers and terms as a PLTS $Raft := \|_{x_0}(Ldr(x_0) \| Flw(x_0))$. Finally, we hide the events irrelevant to the specification yielding to a PLTS $Raft' := Raft \setminus \{vote, candidate\}$. Now, the problem on the correctness of Raft can be formalised as the question whether $Raft' \preceq_{tr}^{Qrm} Spec$ holds. Code for the Raft example is found in the online appendix [22]. □

5   Dynamic Cut-Off Algorithm

In this section, we show how a parameterised trace refinement checking task can be reduced to finitely many refinement checks among LTSs by determining a cut-off set. As the main result, we convert the problem of determining a cut-off set into the unsatisfiability in FOL and introduce an SMT-based semi-algorithm for computing such a set.

Definition 9 (Cut-off set). *Let $\mathcal{P}$ be an implementation PLTS, $\mathcal{Q}$ a specification PLTS, $\mathcal{V}$ a topology formula, and $\Phi \subseteq va(\mathcal{V} \mid \mathcal{P}, \mathcal{Q})$ a finite set of valuations. The set Φ is a cut-off set (for $\mathcal{P}$, $\mathcal{Q}$, and $\mathcal{V}$), if $\mathcal{P} \preceq_{tr}^{\mathcal{V}} \mathcal{Q}$ if and only if $[\![\mathcal{P}]\!]_\phi \preceq [\![\mathcal{Q}]\!]_\phi$ for all $\phi \in \Phi$.*

Our approach can find cut-off sets for implementation-specification pairs where the system topology is downward-closed and the specification does not involve hiding. Both the restrictions are necessary for decidability [24], but the latter one is less severe since hiding is typically only applied on the implementation side. Hence, from now on, *an implementation PLTS* refers to any PLTS, whereas *a specification PLTS* means a PLTS which does not involve hiding. Results similar to Proposition 15 are proved in [21,23,24] but the main result, Theorem 23, the supporting lemmata, Lemmata 20 and 22, and the related dynamic cut-off algorithm are completely new.

Intuitively, our verification technique consists of the following steps. First, we show that if a big instance of the implementation PLTS $\mathcal{P}$ (resp., a specification PLTS $\mathcal{Q}$) is composed of the same components as a set of small instances and each small instance of $\mathcal{P}$ is a trace refinement of the corresponding instance of $\mathcal{Q}$, then the big instance of $\mathcal{P}$ is a trace refinement of the big instance of $\mathcal{Q}$, too (Proposition 15). Second, if the system topology is downward-closed, i.e, all the instances are covered by a finite set of small instances, then we can reduce a refinement checking on PLTSs to finitely many refinement checks on LTSs (Proposition 18). Third, we convert the sufficient condition for a cut-off set into the unsatisfiability of a first-order formula (Theorem 23). Finally, we give an SMT-based semi-algorithm for computing a cut-off set and successfully apply it to several system models (Algorithm 1).

In order to present the technique in detail, we first formalise the notion of a small instance. After that, in Lemma 14, we show that small instances are generated by small valuations, called subvaluations.

Definition 10. *Let $\mathcal{P}$ be a PLTS and ϕ a compatible valuation. The set of the components (of the ϕ-instance of $\mathcal{P}$), denoted by $\mathrm{comp}(\mathcal{P}, \phi)$, is defined inductively:*

1. $\mathrm{comp}(L(x_1, \ldots, x_n), \phi) = \{L(\phi(x_1), \ldots, \phi(x_n))\}$,
2. $\mathrm{comp}([G]\mathcal{P}', \phi) = \begin{cases} \mathrm{comp}(\mathcal{P}', \phi), & \text{if } [\![G]\!]_\phi \text{ is true}, \\ \emptyset, & \text{otherwise}, \end{cases}$
3. $\mathrm{comp}(\mathcal{P}_1 \parallel \mathcal{P}_2, \phi) = \bigcup_{i \in \{1,2\}} (\{i\} \times \mathrm{comp}(\mathcal{P}_i, \phi))$,
4. $\mathrm{comp}(\parallel_x \mathcal{P}', \phi) = \bigcup_{\phi' \in \mathrm{ext}(\phi, \{x\})} (\{\phi'(x)\} \times \mathrm{comp}(\mathcal{P}', \phi'))$, *and*
5. $\mathrm{comp}(\mathcal{P}' \setminus C, \phi) = \mathrm{comp}(\mathcal{P}', \phi)$.

We say that the ϕ-instance of $\mathcal{P}$ is smaller than (or equal to) the ψ-instance of $\mathcal{P}$ if $\mathrm{comp}(\mathcal{P}, \phi)$ is a subset of $\mathrm{comp}(\mathcal{P}, \psi)$.

Example 11. Recall our Raft model and the definition of $Q_{x_0,y}$ from Ex. 2. Let $\theta \in \mathrm{va}(Qrm \mid Raft', Spec)$ such that $\theta(T_S) = \{s_1, \ldots, s_n\}$, $\theta(T_T) = \{t_1, \ldots, t_m\}$, and $\{x \mid (s_i, t_l, x) \in \theta(Q_S)\}$ is a quorum set with $(s_i, t_l, s_i) \in \theta(Q_S)$ for all $i \in \{1, \ldots, n\}$ and $l \in \{1, \ldots, m\}$. Then

$$\mathrm{comp}(Spec, \theta) = \bigcup_{i=1}^{n} \bigcup_{j=1}^{n} \bigcup_{l=1}^{m} \bigcup_{\substack{k=1 \\ s_k \in Q_{s_i,t_l} \cap Q_{s_j,t_l}}}^{n} \{(s_i, (s_j, (s_k, (t_l, Spec2(s_i, s_j, t_l)))))\} . \qquad \square$$

Definition 12 (Subvaluation). *Let Π and Ξ be sets of predicates. A valuation ϕ is a (Π, Ξ)-subvaluation of a valuation ψ if and only if*

1. *the valuations have the same domain,*
2. *$\phi(T) \subseteq \psi(T)$ for all sorts $T \in \mathrm{dom}_T(\phi)$,*
3. *$\phi(x) = \psi(x)$ for all variables $x \in \mathrm{dom}_X(\phi)$,*
4. *$\phi(F) \subseteq \psi(F)$ for all predicates $F \in \mathrm{dom}_F(\phi) \cap \Pi$, and*
5. *$\phi(F) \subseteq \psi(F)$ for all predicates $F \in \mathrm{dom}_F(\phi) \cap \Xi$.*

The fact that ϕ is (not) a (Π, Ξ)-*subvaluation* of ψ is denoted $\phi \sqsubseteq^{\Pi}_{\Xi} \psi$ (respectively, $\phi \not\sqsubseteq^{\Pi}_{\Xi} \psi$). Given a propositional formula G, we write $\mathrm{pr}^+(G)$ and $\mathrm{pr}^-(G)$ for the set of predicates occurring within, respectively, even and odd number of negations in G. The notation is extended to PLTSs $\mathcal{P}$ by defining $\mathrm{pr}^{\oplus}(\mathcal{P})$, where $\oplus \in \{+, -\}$, as the union of all $\mathrm{pr}^{\oplus}(G)$ as G ranges over all guards in $\mathcal{P}$.

Example 13. Let θ be a valuation as in Ex. 11 and Θ the set of all valuations $\theta' \in \mathrm{va}(Qrm \mid Raft', Spec)$ such that $\theta'(T_T) = \{t_l\}$, $\theta'(T_S) = \{s_i, s_j, s_k\}$, and $\theta'(Q_S) \subseteq \theta(Q_S)$ for some $l \in \{1, \ldots, m\}$ and $i, j, k \in \{1, \ldots, n\}$. Since $Spec$ involves a single predicate, Q_S, without negation, $\mathrm{pr}^+(Spec) = \{Q_S\}$ and $\mathrm{pr}^-(Spec) = \emptyset$. This implies that Θ is a finite set of $(\mathrm{pr}^+(Spec), \mathrm{pr}^-(Spec))$-subvaluations of θ. It is also easy to see that for all $\theta' \in \Theta$, $\mathrm{comp}(Spec, \theta')$ is a subset of $\mathrm{comp}(Spec, \theta)$, i.e., $[\![Spec]\!]_{\theta'}$ is smaller than $[\![Spec]\!]_{\theta}$. □

Lemma 14. *Let $\mathcal{P}$ be a PLTS, G a propositional formula, and ψ, ϕ valuations compatible with $\mathcal{P}$ and G such that ϕ is a $(\emptyset, \emptyset)$-subvaluation of ψ.*

1. *If $\mathcal{P}$ is an elementary PLTS, then $[\![\mathcal{P}]\!]_{\psi} = [\![\mathcal{P}]\!]_{\phi}$.*
2. *If ϕ is a $(\mathrm{pr}^+(G), \mathrm{pr}^-(G))$-subvaluation of ψ and $[\![G]\!]_{\phi}$, then $[\![G]\!]_{\psi}$.*
3. *If ϕ is a $(\mathrm{pr}^+(\mathcal{P}), \mathrm{pr}^-(\mathcal{P}))$-subvaluation of ψ, then $[\![\mathcal{P}]\!]_{\phi}$ is smaller than $[\![\mathcal{P}]\!]_{\psi}$.*

Proof. (1) Since $\phi|_X = \psi|_X$ and an instance of $\mathcal{P}$ is completely defined by the values of variables, the claim is evident. (2) Put G into negation normal form $\overline{G}$ and argue by induction on the structure of $\overline{G}$ by using the claim as an induction hypothesis. (3) By induction on the structure of $\mathcal{P}$ by using (1) and (2) and the lemma as an induction hypothesis. □

With the aid of the lemma above, we can show that the correctness of a (big) implementation instance can be derived from the correctness of smaller instances if the big implementation and specification instances are composed of the same components as the smaller, respectively, implementation and specification instances. This is formalised as Proposition 15.

Proposition 15. *Let $\mathcal{P}$ be an implementation PLTS, $\mathcal{Q}$ a specification PLTS, ψ a valuation compatible with $\mathcal{P}$ and $\mathcal{Q}$, and Φ a finite set of $(\mathrm{pr}^+(\mathcal{P} \| \mathcal{Q}), \mathrm{pr}^-(\mathcal{P} \| \mathcal{Q}))$-subvaluations of ψ. If $\mathrm{comp}(\mathcal{P} \| \mathcal{Q}, \psi) = \bigcup_{\phi \in \Phi} \mathrm{comp}(\mathcal{P} \| \mathcal{Q}, \phi)$ and $[\![\mathcal{P}]\!]_{\phi} \preceq_{\mathrm{tr}} [\![\mathcal{Q}]\!]_{\phi}$ for all $\phi \in \Phi$, then $[\![\mathcal{P}]\!]_{\psi} \preceq_{\mathrm{tr}} \|_{\phi \in \Phi} [\![\mathcal{P}]\!]_{\phi} \preceq_{\mathrm{tr}} \|_{\phi \in \Phi} [\![\mathcal{Q}]\!]_{\phi} \preceq_{\mathrm{tr}} [\![\mathcal{Q}]\!]_{\psi}$.*

Proof. First, we argue that if $\text{comp}(\mathcal{P}, \psi) = \bigcup_{\phi \in \Phi} \text{comp}(\mathcal{P}, \phi)$, then $[\![\mathcal{P}]\!]_\psi \preceq_{\text{tr}}$ $\|_{\phi \in \Phi}[\![\mathcal{P}]\!]_\phi$. The proof proceeds by induction on the structure of $\mathcal{P}$ by using the claim as an induction hypothesis.

The cases when $\mathcal{P}$ is an elementary PLTS, a (replicated) parallel PLTS, or a hiding PLTS are similar to the proofs of Lemmata 23 and 25 in [24]: the base case (an elementary PLTS) follows from the idempotence of $\|$, the case when $\mathcal{P}$ is a (replicated) parallel PLTS utilises the associativity and commutativity of $\|$ (and, respectively, the identity property), and the case when $\mathcal{P}$ is a hiding PLTS follows from the distributivity of hiding over parallel composition. Hence, we only need to consider the case when $\mathcal{P}$ is $[G]\mathcal{P}'$. If $[\![G]\!]_\psi$ is false, then by the second item of Lemma 14, $[\![G]\!]_\phi$ is false for all $\phi \in \Phi$. This implies that $[\![\mathcal{P}]\!]_\psi \equiv_{\text{tr}}$ $L_{id} \equiv_{\text{tr}} \|_{\phi \in \Phi}[\![\mathcal{P}]\!]_\phi$. Let us then assume that $[\![G]\!]_\psi$ is true and let Φ_t be the set of all $\phi \in \Phi$ such that $[\![G]\!]_\phi$ is true. Since $\text{comp}(\mathcal{P}, \phi)$ is empty for all $\phi \in \Phi \setminus \Phi_t$, it means that $\text{comp}(\mathcal{P}, \psi) = \bigcup_{\phi \in \Phi_t} \text{comp}(\mathcal{P}, \phi)$. By the induction hypothesis and the identity of L_{id}, it implies that $[\![\mathcal{P}]\!]_\psi \equiv_{\text{tr}} [\![\mathcal{P}']\!]_\psi \preceq_{\text{tr}} \|_{\phi \in \Phi_t}[\![\mathcal{P}']\!]_\phi \equiv_{\text{tr}} \|_{\phi \in \Phi}[\![\mathcal{P}]\!]_\phi$.

The proof that $\text{comp}(\mathcal{Q}, \psi) = \bigcup_{\phi \in \Phi} \text{comp}(\mathcal{Q}, \phi)$ implies $\|_{\phi \in \Phi}[\![\mathcal{Q}]\!]_\phi \preceq_{\text{tr}} [\![\mathcal{Q}]\!]_\psi$ is similar but simpler because there is no need to consider the case with hiding.

Finally, we argue like in the proof of Proposition 27 in [24]. If $\text{comp}(\mathcal{P} \| \mathcal{Q}, \psi) = \bigcup_{\phi \in \Phi} \text{comp}(\mathcal{P} \| \mathcal{Q}, \phi)$ and $[\![\mathcal{P}]\!]_\phi \preceq_{\text{tr}} [\![\mathcal{Q}]\!]_\phi$ for all $\phi \in \Phi$, then by above and the precongruence of $\preceq_{\text{tr}}$, $[\![\mathcal{P}]\!]_\psi \preceq_{\text{tr}} \|_{\phi \in \Phi}[\![\mathcal{P}]\!]_\phi \preceq_{\text{tr}} \|_{\phi \in \Phi}[\![\mathcal{Q}]\!]_\phi \preceq_{\text{tr}} [\![\mathcal{Q}]\!]_\psi$. □

Example 16. Let θ and Θ be as in Ex. 11 and 13. Since every element of $\text{comp}(Spec, \theta)$ depends on the identifiers of at most three servers and one term, it is easy to see that $\text{comp}(Spec, \theta) = \bigcup_{\theta' \in \Theta} \text{comp}(Spec, \theta')$, i.e., the θ-instance of *Spec* is composed of the same components as the set of θ'-instances, where $\theta' \in \Theta$. Similarly, we can see that every element of $\text{comp}(Raft', \theta)$ depends on the identifiers of at most three servers and one term, which implies that $\text{comp}(Raft', \theta) = \bigcup_{\theta' \in \Theta} \text{comp}(Raft', \theta')$. Since Θ is finite, by Proposition 15, it means that if $[\![Raft']\!]_{\theta'} \preceq_{\text{tr}} [\![Spec]\!]_{\theta'}$ for all $\theta' \in \Theta$, then $[\![Raft']\!]_\theta \preceq_{\text{tr}} [\![Spec]\!]_\theta$, too. □

Valuations that can be obtained from each other by injective renaming result in equivalent verification tasks. A function (injection) $g : A \to B$, where $A, B \subseteq \mathbb{A}$, is a *sortwise function* (respectively, *injection*) if $g(a) \in \mathbb{A}_{T_a}$ for each $a \in A$. Let ϕ be a valuation and g a sortwise function. We write $g(\phi)$ for a valuation ϕ' which is obtained from ϕ by mapping the atoms in the image using g. Valuations ϕ_1 and ϕ_2 are *(non-)isomorphic*, if there is (respectively, not) a sortwise injection $g : \text{Im}(\phi_1) \to \text{Im}(\phi_2)$ such that $\phi_2 = g(\phi_1)$. It is easy to see that for isomorphic valuations ϕ_1 and ϕ_2, $[\![\mathcal{P}]\!]_{\phi_1} \preceq [\![\mathcal{Q}]\!]_{\phi_1}$ if and only if $[\![\mathcal{P}]\!]_{\phi_2} \preceq [\![\mathcal{Q}]\!]_{\phi_2}$ [24].

Proposition 15 and the notion above imply that if the system topology is downward-closed in the sense that all the instances are covered by a finite set of (injectively renamed) small instances, then we can reduce a refinement checking on PLTSs to finitely many refinement checks on LTSs. This is stated formally as Proposition 18.

Definition 17 (Downward-closed topology). *A topology $\mathcal{V}$ of an implementation-specification pair $(\mathcal{P}, \mathcal{Q})$ is downward-closed, if there is a finite set $\Phi \subseteq$*

$\mathrm{va}(\mathcal{V} \mid \mathcal{P}, \mathcal{Q})$ of valuations for which the following holds: For all $\psi \in \mathrm{va}(\mathcal{V} \mid \mathcal{P}, \mathcal{Q})$ and all $P \in \mathrm{comp}(\mathcal{P} \parallel \mathcal{Q}, \psi)$, there is a valuation $\phi \in \Phi$ and a sortwise injection g from $\mathrm{Im}(\phi)$ such that $P \in \mathrm{comp}(\mathcal{P} \parallel \mathcal{Q}, g(\phi))$ and $g(\phi)$ is a $(\mathrm{pr}^+(\mathcal{P} \parallel \mathcal{Q}), \mathrm{pr}^-(\mathcal{P} \parallel \mathcal{Q}))$-subvaluation of ψ. The set Φ is called a witness for downward-closedness.

Proposition 18. Let $\mathcal{V}$ be a downward-closed topology for $(\mathcal{P}, \mathcal{Q})$ and Φ a witness for downward-closedness. Then Φ is a cut-off set for $\mathcal{P}$, $\mathcal{Q}$, and $\mathcal{V}$.

Proof. In order to prove that Φ is a cut-off set for $\mathcal{P}$, $\mathcal{Q}$, and $\mathcal{V}$, it is sufficient to show that if $[\![\mathcal{P}]\!]_\phi \preceq_{\mathrm{tr}} [\![\mathcal{Q}]\!]_\phi$ for all $\phi \in \Phi$, then $[\![\mathcal{P}]\!]_\psi \preceq_{\mathrm{tr}} [\![\mathcal{Q}]\!]_\psi$ for all $\psi \in \mathrm{va}(\mathcal{V} \mid \mathcal{P}, \mathcal{Q})$, because the opposite implication is trivial. Hence, let us assume that $[\![\mathcal{P}]\!]_\phi \preceq_{\mathrm{tr}} [\![\mathcal{Q}]\!]_\phi$ for all $\phi \in \Phi$ and let $\psi \in \mathrm{va}(\mathcal{V} \mid \mathcal{P}, \mathcal{Q})$. Since Φ is a witness for downward-closedness, for every $P \in \mathrm{comp}(\mathcal{P} \parallel \mathcal{Q}, \psi)$, there is a valuation $\phi_P \in \Phi$ and a sortwise injection g_P from $\mathrm{Im}(\phi_P)$ such that $P \in \mathrm{comp}(\mathcal{P} \parallel \mathcal{Q}, g_P(\phi_P))$ and $g_P(\phi_P)$ is a $(\mathrm{pr}^+(\mathcal{P} \parallel \mathcal{Q}), \mathrm{pr}^-(\mathcal{P} \parallel \mathcal{Q}))$-subvaluation of ψ. By the third item of Lemma 14, $[\![\mathcal{P} \parallel \mathcal{Q}]\!]_{g_P(\phi_P)}$ is smaller than $[\![\mathcal{P} \parallel \mathcal{Q}]\!]_\psi$ for all $P \in \mathrm{comp}(\mathcal{P} \parallel \mathcal{Q}, \psi)$, which implies that $\mathrm{comp}(\mathcal{P} \parallel \mathcal{Q}, \psi) = \bigcup_{P \in \mathrm{comp}(\mathcal{P} \parallel \mathcal{Q}, \psi)} \mathrm{comp}(\mathcal{P} \parallel \mathcal{Q}, g_P(\phi_P))$. Since $[\![\mathcal{P}]\!]_\phi \preceq_{\mathrm{tr}} [\![\mathcal{Q}]\!]_\phi$ for any $\phi \in \Phi$, we know that $[\![\mathcal{P}]\!]_{g(\phi)} \preceq_{\mathrm{tr}} [\![\mathcal{Q}]\!]_{g(\phi)}$ for all sortwise injections g such that $\mathrm{dom}(g) = \mathrm{Im}(\phi)$, too. Hence, $[\![\mathcal{P}]\!]_{g_P(\phi_P)} \preceq_{\mathrm{tr}} [\![\mathcal{Q}]\!]_{g_P(\phi_P)}$ for all $P \in \mathrm{comp}(\mathcal{P} \parallel \mathcal{Q}, \psi)$. By Proposition 15, it implies that $[\![\mathcal{P}]\!]_\psi \preceq_{\mathrm{tr}} [\![\mathcal{Q}]\!]_\psi$. Therefore, Φ is a cut-off set. □

Proposition 18 gives a sufficient condition for a cut-off set, but it does not clearly say which valuations should be included in the set. That is why we will transform the condition of downward-closedness into a first-order formula, the satisfaction of which can be, in decidable cases, analysed by using existing tools. For that purpose, we introduce Lemmata 20 and 22, which tell how the tests for $P \in \mathrm{comp}(\mathcal{P}, \phi)$ and $g(\phi) \sqsubseteq_{\Xi}^\Pi \psi$ occurring in the condition are converted in FOL. In order to present the results, we assume that $\mathbb{X}$ is partitioned into sets $\mathbb{X}^0$, $\mathbb{X}'$, and $\mathbb{X}''$, each containing infinitely many variables for each sort. Moreover, we assume that only the variables in $\mathbb{X}^0$ are used in PLTSs and topology formulae and for each atom $a \in \mathbb{A}$ there is a unique variable $x_a'' \in \mathbb{X}''$ such that $T_a = T_{x_a''}$.

Definition 19 (Branch). The set of the branches of a PLTS $\mathcal{P}$, denoted $\mathrm{br}(\mathcal{P})$, is defined inductively as follows:

1. $\mathrm{br}(L(x_1, \ldots, x_n)) = \{\top\}$,
2. $\mathrm{br}([G]\mathcal{P}') = \{G \wedge \mathcal{B} \mid \mathcal{B} \in \mathrm{br}(\mathcal{P}')\}$,
3. $\mathrm{br}(\mathcal{P}_1 \parallel \mathcal{P}_2) = \mathrm{br}(\mathcal{P}_1) \cup \mathrm{br}(\mathcal{P}_2)$,
4. $\mathrm{br}(\parallel_x \mathcal{P}') = \{\exists x.(x' = x \wedge \mathcal{B}) \mid \mathcal{B} \in \mathrm{br}(\mathcal{P}')\}$, where $x' \in \mathbb{X}'$ is a variable of the sort T_x not occurring in $\mathrm{br}(\mathcal{P}')$, and
5. $\mathrm{br}(\mathcal{P}' \setminus C) = \mathrm{br}(\mathcal{P}')$.

Lemma 20. Let $\mathcal{P}$ be a PLTS and ϕ and ψ compatible valuations. There is $P \in \mathrm{comp}(\mathcal{P}, \phi) \cap \mathrm{comp}(\mathcal{P}, \psi)$ if and only if there are $\mathcal{B} \in \mathrm{br}(\mathcal{P})$, $\phi' \in \mathrm{ext}(\phi, \mathrm{par}_{\mathbb{X}'}(\mathcal{B}))$ and $\psi' \in \mathrm{ext}(\psi, \mathrm{par}_{\mathbb{X}'}(\mathcal{B}))$ such that $[\![\mathcal{B}]\!]_{\phi'}$ and $[\![\mathcal{B}]\!]_{\psi'}$ are true and $\psi'|_{\mathbb{X}} = \phi'|_{\mathbb{X}}$.

Proof. By induction on the structure of $\mathcal{P}$ by using the lemma as an induction hypothesis. □

Example 21. Recall the Raft specification *Spec* and the valuation θ from Ex. 11. Since only the parameterised version of the parallel composition is used it *Spec*, there is a single branch

$$\exists x_0.(x_0' = x_0 \wedge \exists x_1.(x_1' = x_1 \wedge \exists x_2.(x_2' = x_2 \wedge \exists y.(y' = y \wedge$$
$$Q_S(x_0, y, x_2) \wedge Q_S(x_1, y, x_2) \wedge \top)))) \,.$$

For every $(s_i, (s_j, (s_k, (t_l, Spec2(s_i, s_j, t_l))))) \in \text{comp}(Spec, \theta)$, there is an extension θ' of θ to $\{x_0', x_1', x_2', y'\}$ such that $\theta'(x_0') = s_i$, $\theta'(x_1') = s_j$, $\theta'(x_2') = s_k$, and $\theta'(y') = t_l$. It is also easy to see that θ' satisfies the branch above. $\square$

Lemma 22. *Let ϕ and ψ be valuations with the same domain, $\Pi, \Xi \subseteq \text{dom}_\mathbb{F}(\phi)$ sets of predicates, $g : \text{Im}(\phi) \to \text{Im}(\psi)$ a sortwise function, and ψ_g a valuation in $\text{ext}(\psi, \{x_a'' \mid a \in \text{Im}(\phi)\})$ such that $\psi_g(x_a'') = g(a)$ for all $a \in \text{Im}(\phi)$. Then g is an injection and $g(\phi) \subseteq_\Xi^\Pi \psi$, if $[\![NoSval(\phi, \Pi, \Xi)]\!]_{\psi_g}$ is false, where*

$$NoSval(\phi, \Pi, \Xi) := (\bigvee_{\substack{\{a,b\} \subseteq \text{Im}(\phi) \\ a \neq b}} x_a'' = x_b'') \vee (\bigvee_{x \in \text{dom}_\mathbb{X}(\phi)} x_{\phi(x)}'' \neq x) \vee$$

$$(\bigvee_{F \in \Pi} \bigvee_{(a_1,\dots,a_n) \in \phi(F)} \neg F(x_{a_1}'', \dots, x_{a_n}'')) \vee (\bigvee_{F \in \Xi} \bigvee_{(a_1,\dots,a_n) \in \overline{\phi(F)}} F(x_{a_1}'', \dots, x_{a_n}'')) \,.$$

Proof. Let us assume that $[\![NoSval(\phi, \Pi, \Xi)]\!]_{\psi_g}$ is false. Because the first big disjunction is false, it implies that the variables x_a'', where $a \in \text{Im}(\phi)$, representing the image of g are mapped to different values. Hence, g is an injection.

In order to prove that $g(\phi) \subseteq_\Xi^\Pi \psi$, we will show that the conditions (1)–(5) of Definition 12 are met. (1) By the assumption, $\text{dom}(g(\phi)) = \text{dom}(\phi) = \text{dom}(\psi)$. (2) Because g is a sortwise function: $\text{Im}(\phi) \to \text{Im}(\psi)$, $(g(\phi))(T) \subseteq \psi(T)$ for all sorts $T \in \text{dom}_\mathbb{T}(\phi)$. (3) Since the second big disjunction is false, $(g(\phi))(x) = \psi_g(x_{\phi(x)}'') = \psi_g(x) = \psi(x)$ for all $x \in \text{dom}(\phi)$, (4) If $F \in \Pi$ and $(a_1, \dots, a_n) \in (g(\phi))(F)$, then $(g^{-1}(a_1), \dots, g^{-1}(a_n)) \in \phi(F)$. Because the third big disjunction is false, it implies that $(\psi_g(x_{g^{-1}(a_1)}''), \dots, \psi_g(x_{g^{-1}(a_n)}'')) \in \psi_g(F)$. Since $(\psi_g(x_{g^{-1}(a_1)}''), \dots, \psi_g(x_{g^{-1}(a_n)}'')) = (g(g^{-1}(a_1)), \dots, g(g^{-1}(a_n))) = (a_1, \dots, a_n)$ and $\psi_g(F) = \psi(F)$, it means that $(a_1, \dots, a_n) \in \psi(F)$. (5) Similar to (4). $\square$

By combining Proposition 18 and Lemmata 20 and 22, a sufficient condition for a cut-off set can be converted into the unsatisfiability of a first-order formula.

Theorem 23 (Cut-off theorem). *Let $\mathcal{P}$ be an implementation PLTS, $\mathcal{Q}$ a specification PLTS, $\mathcal{V}$ a topology formula, and $\Phi \subseteq \text{va}(\mathcal{V} \mid \mathcal{P}, \mathcal{Q})$ a finite set of valuations. The set Φ is a cut-off set for $\mathcal{P}$, $\mathcal{Q}$, and $\mathcal{V}$, if the first-order formula*

$$\mathcal{V} \wedge \mathcal{B} \wedge \bigwedge_{\phi \in \Phi_\mathcal{B}} (\forall x_{a_1}'' . \cdots . \forall x_{a_n}'' . NoSval(\phi, \text{pr}^+(\mathcal{P} \parallel \mathcal{Q}), \text{pr}^-(\mathcal{P} \parallel \mathcal{Q}))) \tag{1}$$

is unsatisfiable for all $\mathcal{B} \in \text{br}(\mathcal{P} \parallel \mathcal{Q})$, where $\Phi_\mathcal{B} = \{\phi' \in \text{ext}(\phi, \text{par}_{\mathbb{X}'}(\mathcal{B})) \mid \phi \in \Phi, [\![\mathcal{B}]\!]_{\phi'}\}$ is the set of the extensions of the valuations in Φ to $\text{par}_{\mathbb{X}'}(\mathcal{B})$ satisfying $\mathcal{B}$ and for every $\phi \in \Phi_\mathcal{B}$, $a_1, \dots, a_n$ are the atoms in $\text{Im}(\phi)$.

Proof. We will show that if Φ is not a witness for downward-closedness, then Formula 1 is satisfiable for some branch $\mathcal{B} \in \mathrm{br}(\mathcal{P} \parallel \mathcal{Q})$, which by Proposition 18 implies the theorem.

By Definition 17, Φ is not a witness for downward-closedness if the following condition holds: There is a valuation $\psi \in \mathrm{va}(\mathcal{V} \mid \mathcal{P}, \mathcal{Q})$ and $P \in \mathrm{comp}(\mathcal{P} \parallel \mathcal{Q}, \psi)$ such that for every valuation $\phi \in \Phi$ and a sortwise injection g from $\mathrm{Im}(\phi)$, if $P \in \mathrm{comp}(\mathcal{P} \parallel \mathcal{Q}, g(\phi))$ then $g(\phi)$ is not a $(\mathrm{pr}^+(\mathcal{P} \parallel \mathcal{Q}), \mathrm{pr}^-(\mathcal{P} \parallel \mathcal{Q}))$-subvaluation of ψ.

By Lemma 20, the condition can be converted into the form: There is a valuation $\psi \in \mathrm{va}(\mathcal{V} \mid \mathcal{P}, \mathcal{Q})$, a branch $\mathcal{B} \in \mathrm{br}(\mathcal{P} \parallel \mathcal{Q})$, and $\psi' \in \mathrm{ext}(\psi, \mathrm{par}_{\mathrm{X}'}(\mathcal{B}))$ such that $[\![\mathcal{B}]\!]_{\psi'}$ and for every valuation $\phi \in \Phi$ and a sortwise injection g from $\mathrm{Im}(\phi)$, if $[\![\mathcal{B}]\!]_{\phi'}$ for some $\phi' \in \mathrm{ext}(g(\phi), \mathrm{par}_{\mathrm{X}'}(\mathcal{B}))$ with $\psi'|_{\mathrm{x}} = \phi'|_{\mathrm{x}}$ then $g(\phi)$ is not a $(\mathrm{pr}^+(\mathcal{P} \parallel \mathcal{Q}), \mathrm{pr}^-(\mathcal{P} \parallel \mathcal{Q}))$-subvaluation of ψ.

After simplification, the condition can be put as follows: There is a branch $\mathcal{B} \in \mathrm{br}(\mathcal{P} \parallel \mathcal{Q})$ and a valuation $\psi' \in \mathrm{va}(\mathcal{V} \wedge \mathcal{B} \mid \mathcal{P}, \mathcal{Q})$ such that for every valuation $\phi' \in \Phi_{\mathcal{B}}$ and for every sortwise function $g : \mathrm{Im}(\phi') \to \mathrm{Im}(\psi')$, g is not an injection or $g(\phi')$ is not a $(\mathrm{pr}^+(\mathcal{P} \parallel \mathcal{Q}), \mathrm{pr}^-(\mathcal{P} \parallel \mathcal{Q}))$-subvaluation of ψ'.

Next, we apply Lemma 22 and convert the condition into the form: There is a branch $\mathcal{B} \in \mathrm{br}(\mathcal{P} \parallel \mathcal{Q})$ and a valuation $\psi' \in \mathrm{va}(\mathcal{V} \wedge \mathcal{B} \mid \mathcal{P}, \mathcal{Q})$ such that for all valuations $\phi' \in \Phi_{\mathcal{B}}$ and for all sortwise functions $g : \mathrm{Im}(\phi') \to \mathrm{Im}(\psi')$, $[\![NoSval(\phi', \mathrm{pr}^+(\mathcal{P} \parallel \mathcal{Q}), \mathrm{pr}^-(\mathcal{P} \parallel \mathcal{Q}))]\!]_{\psi'_g}$ is true.

Since Φ is finite and each valuation only has finitely many extensions to $\mathrm{par}_{\mathrm{X}'}(\mathcal{B})$, universal quantification over the valuations in $\Phi_{\mathcal{B}}$ can be substituted by a finite conjunction. Universal quantification over sortwise functions is, in general, a second-order construct. However, since the image of each function $g : \mathrm{Im}(\phi') \to \mathrm{Im}(\psi')$ is finite and represented by the variables in $\{x''_a \mid a \in \mathrm{Im}(\phi')\}$, the universal quantification over sortwise functions can be replaced by the universal quantification over these variables. Hence, the condition gets the form: There is a branch $\mathcal{B} \in \mathrm{br}(\mathcal{P} \parallel \mathcal{Q})$ and a valuation $\psi' \in \mathrm{va}(\mathcal{V} \wedge \mathcal{B} \mid \mathcal{P}, \mathcal{Q})$ such that $[\![\bigwedge_{\phi' \in \Phi_{\mathcal{B}}} (\forall x''_{a_1}. \cdots . \forall x''_{a_n}. NoSval(\phi', \mathrm{pr}^+(\mathcal{P} \parallel \mathcal{Q}), \mathrm{pr}^-(\mathcal{P} \parallel \mathcal{Q})))]\!]_{\psi'}$ is true.

Finally, the existence of $\psi' \in \mathrm{va}(\mathcal{V} \wedge \mathcal{B} \mid \mathcal{P}, \mathcal{Q})$ can be simply encoded as the satisfaction of the formula $\mathcal{V} \wedge \mathcal{B}$. This means that Φ is not a witness for downward-closedness, if there is a branch $\mathcal{B} \in \mathrm{br}(\mathcal{P} \parallel \mathcal{Q})$ such that Formula 1 is satisfiable, which by Proposition 18 implies the theorem. Obviously, the formula is also in FOL since it only involves first-order constructs. □

The iterative application of Theorem 23 results in Algorithm 1 that allows us to determine a cut-off set for systems with a downward-closed topology by starting from the empty set and appending the set with non-isomorphic valuations of increasing size until the Formula 1 becomes unsatisfiable for all branches. The removal of isomorphs is implemented by converting the valuations into coloured graphs as described in [19] and by using the nauty library [16] to compute a canonical form for each graph. Finally, the valuations with redundant canonical graph representations are removed.

There are two points in the algorithm that are critical for termination. The one is the condition of the while loop, Formula 1. The formula consists of several conjuncts: the topology $\mathcal{V}$, a branch $\mathcal{B}$ involving only conjunctions and existential quantification, and universally quantified conjuncts. Since quantification (over non-empty sets) can be pushed outside the conjunctions, the condition is of the form $\mathcal{V} \wedge \mathcal{U}$, where $\mathcal{U}$ is in the $\exists^*\forall^*$ fragment. Therefore, the whole condition is within the decidable $\exists^*\forall^*$ fragment if the topology $\mathcal{V}$ is.

The other critical point is querying a sort from an oracle and incrementing the cut-off, because the cut-offs heavily affect the length of Formula 1. In the worst case, when predicates are involved, the formula grows exponentially in the size of the cut-offs, and even when predicates are not used, the length of the formula is quadratic in the size of the cut-offs. Of course, a non-deterministic oracle can guess the optimal order, but also in practice, the algorithm will always compute some (not necessarily an optimal) cut-off set as long as incrementing is done fairly, i.e., the incrementation of a sort cannot be omitted infinitely many times consecutively. Hence, the algorithm will always terminate for topologies expressible in the $\exists^*\forall^*$ fragment of FOL, because as stated in Lemma 24, the fragment is decidable and such topologies are downward-closed. The algorithm also enables us to consider systems with downward-closed topologies beyond this fragment, but termination depends on the capabilities of the used SMT solver. If the solver is unable to decide the satisfiability of the equation and consequently, returns the unknown value, it is always safe to consider the equation satisfiable. This may lead to an infinite execution loop but guarantees the correctness of the algorithm.

---

input : implementation PLTS $\mathcal{P}$, specification PLTS $\mathcal{Q}$, topology formula $\mathcal{V}$
output: cut-off set Φ for $\mathcal{P}$, $\mathcal{Q}$, and $\mathcal{V}$

foreach $T \in \text{par}_{\mathbb{T}}(\mathcal{P} \parallel \mathcal{Q}) \cup \text{par}_{\mathbb{T}}(\mathcal{V})$ **do** $cutoff_T \leftarrow 1$;
$\Phi \leftarrow$ the set of all non-isomorphic valuations $\phi \in \text{va}(\mathcal{V} \mid \mathcal{P}, \mathcal{Q})$ such that $|\phi(T)| = 1$ for all $T \in \text{dom}_{\mathbb{T}}(\phi)$;
foreach $\mathcal{B} \in \text{br}(\mathcal{P} \parallel \mathcal{Q})$ **do**
> **while** *Formula 1 of Theorem 23 is satisfiable* **do**
> > get a sort $T_o \in \text{par}_{\mathbb{T}}(\mathcal{P} \parallel \mathcal{Q}) \cup \text{par}_{\mathbb{T}}(\mathcal{V})$ from an oracle and increment $cutoff_{T_o}$;
> > append the set Φ with all non-isomorphic valuations $\phi \in \text{va}(\mathcal{V} \mid \mathcal{P}, \mathcal{Q})$ such that $|\phi(T_o)| = cutoff_{T_o}$ and $|\phi(T)| \leq cutoff_T$ for all $T \in \text{dom}_{\mathbb{T}}(\phi) \setminus \{T_o\}$;
> **end**
end

Algorithm 1: Dynamic cut-off algorithm

Lemma 24. *Let $\mathcal{V}$ be a formula in the $\exists^*\forall^*$ fragment of FOL. Then the satisfiability of $\mathcal{V}$ is decidable and the topology $\mathcal{V}$ of any implementation-specification pair is downward-closed.*

Proof. The decidability of the $\exists^*\forall^*$ fragment is well-known [1,8].

Let us then consider a topology $\mathcal{V} := \exists x_1. \cdots .\exists x_n. \mathcal{U}$, where $\mathcal{U}$ is in the $\forall^*$ fragment. Without the loss of generality, we may assume that the variables $x_1, \ldots, x_n$ do not occur in $\mathcal{P}$ and $\mathcal{Q}$. By Theorem 50 in [24], we know that there is a witness Φ' for downward-closedness for the topology $\mathcal{U}$ of $(\mathcal{P}, \mathcal{Q})$.

Next, we will show that $\Phi := \{\phi'|_{\operatorname{dom}(\phi')\backslash\{x_1,\ldots,x_n\}} \mid \phi' \in \Phi'\}$ is a witness for downward-closedness for the topology $\mathcal{V}$ of $(\mathcal{P}, \mathcal{Q})$. Let $\psi \in \operatorname{va}(\mathcal{V} \mid \mathcal{P}, \mathcal{Q})$ and $P \in \operatorname{comp}(\mathcal{P} \parallel \mathcal{Q}, \psi)$. Then there is $\psi' \in \operatorname{ext}(\psi, \{x_1, \ldots, x_n\})$ such that $\psi' \in \operatorname{va}(\mathcal{U} \mid \mathcal{P}, \mathcal{Q})$ and $P \in \operatorname{comp}(\mathcal{P} \parallel \mathcal{Q}, \psi')$. Since Φ' is a witness for downward-closedness for $\mathcal{U}$, there is a valuation $\phi' \in \Phi'$ and a sortwise injection g such that $P \in \operatorname{comp}(\mathcal{P}\|\mathcal{Q}, g(\phi'))$ and $g(\phi')$ is a $(\operatorname{pr}^+(\mathcal{P}\|\mathcal{Q}), \operatorname{pr}^-(\mathcal{P}\|\mathcal{Q}))$-subvaluation of ψ'. Because $x_1, \ldots, x_n$ do not occur in $\mathcal{P}\|\mathcal{Q}$, it implies that $\phi := \phi'|_{\operatorname{dom}(\phi')\backslash\{x_1,\ldots,x_n\}}$ is a valuation in Φ such that $P \in \operatorname{comp}(\mathcal{P} \parallel \mathcal{Q}, g(\phi))$ and $g(\phi)$ is a $(\operatorname{pr}^+(\mathcal{P} \parallel \mathcal{Q}), \operatorname{pr}^-(\mathcal{P}\|\mathcal{Q}))$-subvaluation of ψ. Hence, Φ is a witness for downward-closedness for the topology $\mathcal{V}$. $\qquad\square$

Corollary 25 (Soundness and completeness). *Let $\mathcal{P}$ be an implementation PLTS, $\mathcal{Q}$ a specification PLTS, and $\mathcal{V}$ a topology formula.*

1. *If Algorithm 1 terminates with Φ, then Φ is a cut-off set for $\mathcal{P}$, $\mathcal{Q}$, and $\mathcal{V}$.*
2. *If $\mathcal{V}$ is downward-closed and there is a decision procedure for formulas of the form $\mathcal{V} \wedge \mathcal{U}$ (where $\mathcal{U}$ is in the $\exists^*\forall^*$ fragment), then Algorithm 1 terminates.*
3. *If $\mathcal{V}$ is in the $\exists^*\forall^*$ fragment, then Algorithm 1 terminates.*

Proof. (1) Follows from Theorem 23. (2) Follows from the facts that downward-closed topologies have a witness and the algorithm will eventually compute some witness. (3) Follows from Lemma 24 and (2). $\qquad\square$

We have implemented a prototype version of Algorithm 1 in Bounds tool [20]. The tool uses the Z3 SMT solver [3] for testing satisfiability and the oracle is implemented as a fair heuristic. The heuristic uses the satisfying valuation provided by Z3 and favours the incrementation of sorts which the valuation maps to a set larger than the current cut-off. The tool takes a parameterised verification task as an input, computes a cut-off set by using the dynamic cut-off algorithm, and provided the algorithm terminates, produces an LTS refinement checking task for each valuation in the cut-off set. After that, the verification is completed by refinement checking the instances by using FDR [7]. Once we have proved that a system implementation refines its specification, we can use the specification, which is usually much smaller, in place of the system implementation in further verification efforts. This is possible since our PLTS formalism is compositional.

Example 26. We have applied Bounds to several system models by using both the dynamic and static cut-off algorithms (Table 1). The Raft model for the static algorithm uses specific *quorum function variables* [21] which in our formalism are modelled in FOL. The tree topology of taDOM2+ and the lower bound for the number of transactions are naturally modelled by using existential quantification but for the static algorithm, which does not support it, they

Table 1. The performance of the dynamic cut-off algorithm with respect to the static ones, $|T|$ is the cut-off size for a sort T, $|\Phi|$ is the size of the cut-off set, and t is the time taken (in seconds) by the computation of the cut-off set Φ plus refinement checking the ϕ-instances for all $\phi \in \Phi$.

System	Parameters	Dynamic		Static	
		cut-offs	t(s)	cut-offs	t(s)
Raft [21]	servers (S), terms (T), quorum topology	$\mathbf{|S| = 3, |T| = 1, |\Phi| = 20}$	**7+2**	$|S| = 7, |T| = 1, |\Phi| > 10^5$	dnf
Shared resources [24]	users (U), resources (R), forest topology	$|U| = 2, |R| = 3, |\Phi| = 6$	1+6	$|U| = 2, |R| = 3, |\Phi| = 6$	1+6
Shared resources [24]	users (U), resources (R), ring topology	$|U| = 4, |R| = 1, |\Phi| = 4$	1+1	$|U| = 4, |R| = 1, |\Phi| = 4$	1+1
taDOM2+ [24]	transactions (T), nodes (N), forest topology	$|T| = 2, |N| = 3, |\Phi| = 14$	1+1122	$|T| = 2, |N| = 3, |\Phi| = 14$	1+1130
taDOM2+ [24]	2+ transactions (T), nodes (N), tree topology	$\mathbf{|T| = 2, |N| = 3, |\Phi| = 7}$	**1+1121**	$|T| = 4, |N| = 4, |\Phi| = 45$	11+dnf
Token ring [20]	users (U), ring topology	$|U| = 4, |\Phi| = 3$	1+1	$|U| = 4, |\Phi| = 3$	1+1
Ring with 2 tokens [24]	users (U), ring topology	$|U| = 5, |\Phi| = 30$	10+7	$|U| = 5, |\Phi| = 30$	25+7

are modelled by using free variables. Otherwise the models are identical. In each case, the dynamic algorithm performs at least as well as the static one in terms of running time and the size of a cut-off set. In the case of Raft and tree-based taDOM2+, the implementation based on static cut-offs ran out of memory, whereas the dynamic one terminated with very small cut-offs, which we claim to be optimal. Hence, the dynamic algorithm not only enables extending the application domain of static ones but also provides more compact cut-offs. All experiments were made on an 8-thread Intel i7-4790 with 16GB of memory running Ubuntu 16.04 LTS. An example run of Bounds on the Raft model is in the online appendix [22]. □

6   Conclusions and Future Work

We have provided a semi-algorithm for reducing a refinement checking task in the parameterised LTS formalism to a finite set of refinement checks between LTSs. The algorithm is implemented in a tool and applied to several system models. The novelty of the algorithm is in its generality; it not only combines existing static cut-off techniques but also extends their application domain beyond known decidable fragments. In future, we aim to extend the algorithm to other process algebraic formalisms such as modal interface automata [23].

References

1. Abadi, A., Rabinovich, A., Sagiv, M.: Decidable fragments of many-sorted logic. J. Symb. Comput. **45**(2), 153–172 (2010)
2. Creese, S.J.: Data Independent Induction: CSP Model Checking of Arbitrary Sized Networks. Ph.D. thesis, Oxford University (2001)
3. de Moura, L., Bjørner, N.: Z3: an efficient SMT solver. In: Ramakrishnan, C.R., Rehof, J. (eds.) TACAS 2008. LNCS, vol. 4963, pp. 337–340. Springer, Heidelberg (2008). https://doi.org/10.1007/978-3-540-78800-3_24
4. Emerson, E.A., Kahlon, V.: Reducing model checking of the many to the few. In: McAllester, D. (ed.) CADE 2000. LNCS (LNAI), vol. 1831, pp. 236–254. Springer, Heidelberg (2000). https://doi.org/10.1007/10721959_19
5. Finkel, A., Schnoebelen, P.: Well-structured transition systems everywhere!. Theor. Comput. Sci. **256**(1), 63–92 (2001)
6. Gallier, J.H.: Logic for Computer Science: Foundations of Automatic Theorem Proving. Courier Dover Publications, New York (2015)
7. Gibson-Robinson, T., Armstrong, P., Boulgakov, A., Roscoe, A.W.: FDR3: a parallel refinement checker for CSP. STTT **18**(2), 149–167 (2016)
8. Gurevich, Y.: On the classical decision problem. In: Rozenberg, G., Salomaa, A. (eds.) Current Trends in Theoretical Computer Science: Essays and Tutorials. World Scientific Series in Computer Science, vol. 40, pp. 254–265. World Scientific, Singapore (1993)
9. Hanna, Y., Samuelson, D., Basu, S., Rajan, H.: Automating cut-off for multi-parameterized systems. In: Dong, J.S., Zhu, H. (eds.) ICFEM 2010. LNCS, vol. 6447, pp. 338–354. Springer, Heidelberg (2010). https://doi.org/10.1007/978-3-642-16901-4_23

10. Haustein, M., Härder, T.: Optimizing lock protocols for native XML processing. Data Knowl. Eng. **65**(1), 147–173 (2008)
11. Hoare, C.A.R.: Communicating Sequential Processes. Prentice-Hall, New York (1985)
12. Kaiser, A., Kroening, D., Wahl, T.: Dynamic cutoff detection in parameterized concurrent programs. In: Touili, T., Cook, B., Jackson, P. (eds.) CAV 2010. LNCS, vol. 6174, pp. 645–659. Springer, Heidelberg (2010). https://doi.org/10.1007/978-3-642-14295-6_55
13. Lazić, R.: A Semantic Study of Data Independence with Applications to Model Checking. Ph.D. thesis, Oxford University (1999)
14. Lazić, R., Nowak, D.: A unifying approach to data-independence. In: Palamidessi, C. (ed.) CONCUR 2000. LNCS, vol. 1877, pp. 581–596. Springer, Heidelberg (2000). https://doi.org/10.1007/3-540-44618-4_41
15. Marić, O., Sprenger, C., Basin, D.: Cutoff bounds for consensus algorithms. In: Majumdar, R., Kunčak, V. (eds.) CAV 2017. LNCS, vol. 10427, pp. 217–237. Springer, Cham (2017). https://doi.org/10.1007/978-3-319-63390-9_12
16. McKay, B.D., Piperno, A.: Practical graph isomorphism II. J. Symb. Comput. **60**, 94–112 (2014)
17. Ongaro, D., Ousterhout, J.: In search of an understandable consensus algorithm. In: Gibson, G., Zeldovich, N. (eds.) USENIX ATC 2014, pp. 305–320. USENIX Association (2014)
18. Roscoe, A.W.: Understanding Concurrent Systems. Springer, Berlin (2010)
19. Siirtola, A.: Algorithmic Multiparameterised Verification of Safety Properties. Process Algebraic Approach. Ph.D. thesis, University of Oulu (2010)
20. Siirtola, A.: Bounds2: a tool for compositional multi-parametrised verification. In: Ábrahám, E., Havelund, K. (eds.) TACAS 2014. LNCS, vol. 8413, pp. 599–604. Springer, Heidelberg (2014). https://doi.org/10.1007/978-3-642-54862-8_52
21. Siirtola, A.: Refinement checking parameterised quorum systems. In: Legay, A., Schneider, K. (eds.) ACSD 2017, pp. 39–48. IEEE (2017)
22. Siirtola, A., Heljanko, K.: Online appendix, http://cc.oulu.fi/~asiirtol/papers/dyncutoffapp.pdf
23. Siirtola, A., Heljanko, K.: Parametrised modal interface automata. ACM Trans. Embed. Comput. Syst. **14**(4), 65:1–65:25 (2015)
24. Siirtola, A., Kortelainen, J.: Multi-parameterised compositional verification of safety properties. Inform. Comput. **244**, 23–48 (2015)
25. Valmari, A., Tienari, M.: An improved failures equivalence for finite-state systems with a reduction algorithm. In: Jonsson, B., Parrow, J., Pehrson, B. (eds.) PSTV 1991, pp. 3–18. North-Holland (1991)
26. Yang, Q., Li, M.: A cut-off approach for bounded verification of parameterized systems. In: Kramer, J., Bishop, J., Devanbu, P.T., Uchitel, S. (eds.) ICSE 2010, pp. 345–354. ACM (2010)
27. Zuck, L., Pnueli, A.: Model checking and abstraction to the aid of parameterized systems (a survey). Comput. Lang. Syst. Struct. **30**(3), 139–169 (2004)

Tool Papers

FACTum Studio: A Tool for the Axiomatic Specification and Verification of Architectural Design Patterns

Diego Marmsoler$^{(\boxtimes)}$ (iD) and Habtom Kahsay Gidey

Technische Universität München, München, Germany
`diego.marmsoler@tum.de, habtom@habtom.org`

Abstract. Architectural Design Patterns (ADPs) restrict the design of an architecture with the aim to guarantee certain properties. Verifying ADPs requires to show that the imposed constraints indeed lead to the claimed guarantees and it is best done using interactive theorem proving (ITP). ITP, however, requires knowledge which is usually not available in the architecture community, which is why the technology is rarely used for the verification of patterns. To address this problem, we are working on a tool which supports the interactive verification of ADPs at a level of abstraction familiar to an architect. In the following paper, we introduce the tool and demonstrate it by means of a running example: we model a version of the Publisher-Subscriber pattern with a corresponding guarantee and verify it in a generated Isabelle/HOL theory.

Keywords: Architectural design patterns
Interactive theorem proving · FACTum · Eclipse/EMF

1 Introduction

Architectural design patterns (ADPs) are an important concept in software engineering and regarded as one of the major tools to support an architect in the conceptualization and analysis of software systems [16]. They capture architectural design experience and provide abstract solutions to recurring architectural design problems. Thereby, they constrain an architectural design and guarantee some desired safety/liveness properties for architectures implementing the pattern. Thus, verifying ADPs requires to show that the constraints imposed by an ADP indeed lead to architectures satisfying the claimed guarantees. Due to the abstract nature of patterns, verification requires axiomatic reasoning and is usually done using interactive theorem proving (ITP) [12]. ITP, however, has a steep learning curve and requires expertise which is not always available in the

Electronic supplementary material The online version of this chapter (https://doi.org/10.1007/978-3-030-02146-7_14) contains supplementary material, which is available to authorized users.

K. Bae and P. C. Ölveczky (Eds.): FACS 2018, LNCS 11222, pp. 279–287, 2018.
https://doi.org/10.1007/978-3-030-02146-7_14

architecture community. Thus, the potential of the technology is not yet fully explored for the verification of ADPs.

In an effort to lower the entry barriers and make the technology available to the broader software community, we are developing FACTUM Studio, a tool which supports the interactive verification of ADPs at a level of abstraction familiar to an architect. Currently, its main features include support for the modeling of ADPs and the generation of corresponding Isabelle/HOL [15] theories. Thereby, it implements several languages, graphical as well as textual, to model different aspects of an ADP: abstract datatypes, component types, architectural constraints, and architectural guarantees. In this paper, we introduce FACTUM Studio: We describe its main features and demonstrate it in terms of a small, running example. The tool itself, as well as a step-by-step tutorial to reconstruct the running example, is provided online [7].

2   Overview of Core Features

Currently, FACTUM Studio provides the following core features to support the axiomatic specification of ADPs:

- Specification of abstract datatypes.
- Graphical modeling of component types.
- Specification of architectural constraints.
- Specification of architectural guarantees.

Thereby, FACTUM Studio provides rigorous type-checking mechanisms to support a user in the specification. Moreover, the tool allows to automatically generate a corresponding Isabelle/HOL theory from a given specification according to the algorithm presented in [12]. In the following, we describe each of the features in more detail and demonstrate them by means of a running example [1].

Example 1 (Running example: Publisher-Subscriber architectures). The purpose of the Publisher-Subscriber pattern is to achieve a "flexible" way of communication between components of an architecture. Thereby, the pattern requires the existence of two types of components: *publisher* and *subscriber* components. Subscribers can register for certain events by sending special subscription messages to publisher components. Publishers, on the other hand, can send out messages which are associated to certain events. Moreover, the pattern requires that a subscriber component is connected to a publisher, whenever the latter sends out a message for which the former previously subscribed. In return, the pattern guarantees for an architecture which satisfies these requirements, that a subscriber indeed receives all the messages associated to events for which he is subscribed.   □

---

[1] Note that the example is intentionally kept simple since its purpose is to demonstrate the tool's main features, rather than evaluating it in a real-world setting.

3 Specifying Data Types

Data types in FACTUM Studio are specified using traditional, *algebraic specification* techniques [3,17]. Therefore, for each datatype specification, we first provide a list of sorts. Then, we may use the sorts to specify characteristic functions for a data type. Finally, we may add axioms to characterize the behavior of the different functions. FACTUM Studio supports the specification of data types by means of two features: (i) First, it ensures that sorts used in a function specification do indeed exist. (ii) Moreover, it ensures that the parameters provided to a function in the specification of the axioms are consistent with the function's signature.

Example 2 (Datatypes for Publisher-Subscriber architectures). The left-hand side of Fig. 1 depicts the specification of data types for the Publisher-Subscriber example in FACTUM Studio. It contains two datatype specifications: Event and Subscription. Specification Event contains the events (and sets of events) for which subscribers may subscribe as well as corresponding messages. Moreover, it declares a function evt to associate messages with events, and a predicate in to check whether an event is indeed contained within a set of events. Specification *Subscription*, on the other hand, contains identifiers SID for subscriber components and the actual subscriptions SBS. Moreover, it declares corresponding functions, sub and unsub, to subscribe to, and unsubscribe from events.

The right-hand side of Fig. 1 demonstrates a situation in which we used a *non-existent* sort ABC to specify operation sub. As shown in the figure, FACTUM Studio notifies the user about such erroneous situations. Moreover, it even suggests a list of existing sorts which may be used to fix the problem.   □

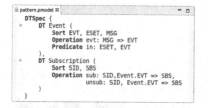 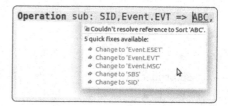

Fig. 1. Datatype specification for Publisher-Subscriber architectures

Note that for our simple example, we did not even require to characterize the meaning of our declared functions and thus we did not specify any axioms for them. In more complicated examples, however, we may also specify axioms for datatype functions, which can then be used for the verification of the pattern. FACTUM Studio would support such specifications and ensure that the parameters provided to a function reference do indeed match the function's signature.

4   Modeling Interfaces

Interfaces for components are modeled in FACTUM Studio using so-called *architecture diagrams* [12]. Thereby, an interface is represented as a labeled rectangle with empty and filled circles, denoting input and output ports, respectively. Ports are typed by the datatypes introduced for the pattern by assigning a corresponding sort from the pattern's datatype specification to each port. In addition to specify interfaces, architecture diagrams may also be used to graphically express common architectural constraints. To this end, interfaces may be annotated with constraints about the activation of components. Moreover, connections between interface ports denote constraints about the connections between the corresponding ports of components.

Example 3 (Architecture   diagram   for   Publisher-Subscriber   architectures). Figure 2 depicts the specification of interfaces in FACTUM Studio for the Publisher-Subscriber example. The left-hand side shows the corresponding architecture diagram: It consists of two interfaces, `Publisher` and `Subscriber`, with one corresponding input and output port for both of them. Input port `psb` of the `Publisher` interface and output port `ssb` of the `Subscriber` interface are both typed by sort `EVT` introduced in Example 2. Moreover, the `Publisher`'s output port `pnt` and the `Subscriber`'s input port `snt` are both typed by sort `MSG`. The connection between ports `ssb` and `psb` specifies a constraint regarding the connection of corresponding ports for publisher and subscriber components, and it is discussed in more detail in the next section.

The right-hand side of Fig. 2 depicts the property panel for the publisher's input port `psb`: it contains its name and the names of connected ports, and allows to set the type of the port by assigning a corresponding sort from the pattern's datatype specification.   □

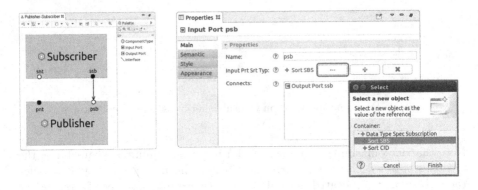

Fig. 2. Architecture diagram for Publisher-Subscriber architectures.

5   Adding Architectural Constraints

As discussed in [9,13], there exist 4 types of constraints for ADPs: (i) constraints for datatypes, (ii) constraints about the behavior of components, (iii) constraints about component activation, and (iv) connection between component ports. FACTUM Studio implements languages for the specification of all of these types of constraints and provides rigorous type checking to support a user in their specification. Constraints for data types are specified in terms of axioms for the datatypes functions as already discussed in Sect. 3.

Constraints about component behavior are specified for interfaces in terms of so-called *behavior trace assertions* [10]: linear temporal logic formulæ with terms formulated by port names and datatype functions. By adding a behavior trace assertion to an interface, we obtain a corresponding *component type*, i.e., an interface with assertions about the behavior of corresponding components.

Constraints about component activation and connections between ports are expressed by means of so-called *architecture trace assertions*: linear temporal logic formulæ with special predicates to denote component activation and port connection. Compared to behavior trace assertions (which are specified over a single interface), architecture trace assertions are specified over an architecture (a set of components). Thus, their specification relies on the concept of *component variables*: variables which are interpreted by components of a certain type.

Example 4 (Architectural constraints for Publisher-Subscriber architectures). The left-hand side of Fig. 3 depicts the specification of two architectural constraints for Publisher-Subscriber architectures in FACTUM Studio: **act_pb** requires that a publisher component is always activated and *unique* and **conn_sb** requires that a subscriber component is connected to the unique publisher component, whenever the latter sends out a message for which the subscriber is subscribed. To specify the constraints, we first declared three component variables: a *rigid*[2] one p and a *flexible*[3] one q for publisher components as well as a rigid one s for subscriber components. In addition, we declared one rigid datatype variable e for events, i.e., messages of type **EVT**. Then, we specified the two constraints in terms of two linear temporal logic formulæ over these variables. Therefore, we use four, so-called, *architecture predicates* to denote i. valuation of component ports with certain messages (**val**), ii. component activation (**cAct**), iii. connection between component ports (**conn**), and iv. equality of components (**eq**).

The right-hand side of Fig. 3 demonstrates some of FACTUM Studio's features to support the specification of architectural constraints. One convenient feature, which is demonstrated at the top of the figure, is its support to specify component ports: whenever such a port is used in the specification, the tool ensures that the port is indeed consistent with the type of the corresponding component variable. Thus, since variable s is of type **Subscriber**, only ports **snt** and **ssb**, declared

---

[2] A rigid variable keeps its value over time.

[3] A flexible variable is newly interpreted at each point in time.

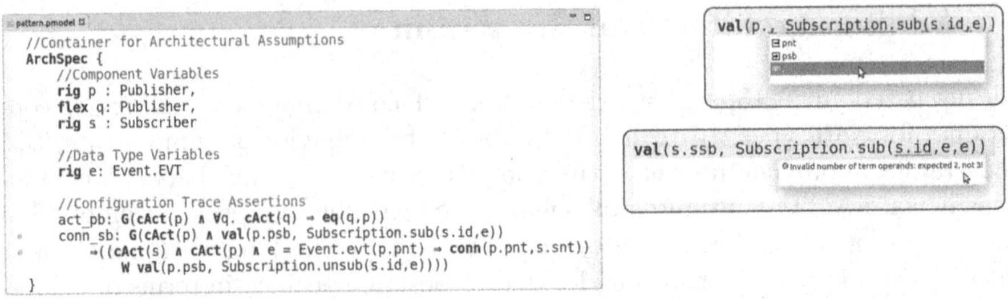

Fig. 3. Architectural constraints for Publisher-Subscriber architectures.

for a subscriber interface, can be referenced. Another convenient feature is the signature check, as demonstrated at the bottom of the figure: whenever we use a datatype function, FACTUM Studio ensures that the parameters passed to the function (either port values or other functions) are indeed consistent with the function's signature (as specified in the corresponding datatype specification). Thus, since function **sub** was declared to take two parameters only (see Sect. 2), we are indeed not allowed to pass more than two parameter to **sub**.

6   Specifying Architectural Guarantees

Architectural guarantees are specified similar to activation or connection constraints using *architecture trace assertions* (as introduced in Sect. 5). Consequently, FACTUM Studio supports its specification with the same features as described in Sect. 5 for the specification of architectural constraints.

Example 5 (A guarantee for Publisher-Subscriber architectures) Figure 4 depicts the specification of an architectural guarantee **delivery** for Publisher-Subscriber architectures in FACTUM Studio. It ensures that a subscriber indeed receives all the messages for which he is subscribed and it is specified in a similar manner as the architectural assumptions discussed in Example 4 using component variables and architecture predicates. As mentioned before, FACTUM Studio provides similar support for the specification of architectural guarantees as it does for architectural assumptions: correct use of component variables and architecture predicates as well as type checking for datatype functions and ports.

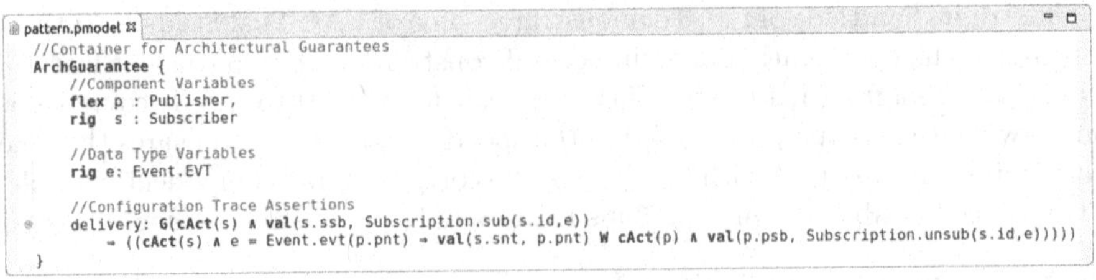

Fig. 4. A guarantee for Publisher-Subscriber architectures.

7   Verifying the Pattern

After specifying a pattern in FACTum Studio, we can generate corresponding Isabelle/HOL theories. The theory consists of an Isabelle/HOL locale [2]
specification, which contains corresponding assumptions for each architectural
constraint. Moreover, the pattern's guarantee is used to generate a corresponding Isabelle/HOL theorem for the locale which can then be proved using our
calculus for dynamic architectures [11].

Example 6 (Mapping Publisher-Subscriber architectures). Using FACTum Studio, we can create an Isabelle/HOL theory for the Publisher-Subscriber pattern containing assumptions for all the architectural constraints specified so far.
Moreover, the theory contains also a theorem derived from the corresponding
architectural guarantee. The generated theorem can be easily proved from the
assumptions using Isabelle/Isar [4].

8   Related Work

In the following, we present reviews of related tools that provide support for
software architecture specification and verification. For instance, The Alloy Analyzer [8] is an automated modeling and analysis tool, based on a declarative language named Alloy. It supports the specification of constraints which can then
be transformed to a corresponding specification for the Boolean SAT Solver
Kodkod for analysis. Acme Studio [6] is a tool which focuses on the structural
representations of architectural designs and which provides an editor and visu-
alization environment. It supports analysis of specifications by means of static
checks using the Armani constraint checker. ArchStudio [5] provides an Eclipse-
based environment for architecture specifications. It uses the Schematron XML
constraint engine for static analyses. RoboCalc [14] supports the modeling and
analysis of autonomous mobile robots, based on an UML-like notation called
RoboChart. It supports analyses of such models using model checking. AutoFocus [1] supports the development process of software-intensive, embedded
systems, starting from requirements to code generation. It allows translating
models to the NuSMV/nuXmv model checker for analysis. VerCors (VCE) [4] is
a platform to support the graphical specification of architectures based on the
Grid Component Model (GCM). It supports the analysis of such models through
model checking and equivalence checking.

While all these tools can be used to specify and analyze architectures or
even architectural constraints, they focus mainly on automatic analyses and
thus lack the support for component types. With the work presented in this
paper, we complement these approaches by providing an alternative approach to
architecture analysis, based on axiomatic specification techniques and interactive
theorem proving.

---

[4] A corresponding proof is provided online in this paper's supplementary electronic
material.

9   Conclusion

In this paper, we introduced FACTUM Studio, a tool to support the axiomatic specification and verification of architectural design patterns (ADPs). The tool allows to specify an ADP using a combination of graphical and textual elements and supports the specification by various type checking mechanisms. Then, a corresponding Isabelle/HOL theory can be generated out of the specification.

Our overall goal is the development of tools to support the interactive verification of ADPs. With the work presented in this paper, we provide an important, first step towards this goal. There is, however, still some missing elements to fully achieve this goal, which leads to future work: (i) The specification language should be extended to deal with more advanced features, such as parametric component types and hierarchical specifications. (ii) The output of Isabelle/HOL should be interpreted back into the modeling environment. (iii) In the long term, FACTUM Studio should also support modeling of proofs at the architecture level.

Acknowledgments. We would like to thank Dominik Ascher and Sebastian Wilzbach for their valuable support on Eclipse/EMF. Parts of the work on which we report in this paper was funded by the German Federal Ministry of Economics and Technology (BMWi) under grant no. 0325811A.

References

1. Aravantinos, V., Voss, S., Teufl, S., Hölzl, F., Schätz, B.: Autofocus 3: Tooling concepts for seamless, model-based development of embedded systems. In: CEUR Workshop Proceedings, vol. 1508, pp. 19–26. CEUR-WS.org (2015)
2. Ballarin, C.: Locales and locale expressions in Isabelle/Isar. In: Berardi, S., Coppo, M., Damiani, F. (eds.) TYPES 2003. LNCS, vol. 3085, pp. 34–50. Springer, Heidelberg (2004). https://doi.org/10.1007/978-3-540-24849-1_3
3. Broy, M.: Algebraic specification of reactive systems. Theor. Comput. Sci. **239**(1), 3–40 (2000)
4. Cansado, A., Madelaine, E., Valenzuela, P.: VCE: A graphical tool for architectural definitions of GCM components. In: 5th workshop on Formal Aspects of Component Systems (FACS'08) (2008)
5. Dashofy, E.M.: Supporting stakeholder-driven, multi-view software architecture modeling. Ph.D. thesis, University of California, Irvine (2007)
6. Garlan, D., Monroe, R.T., Wile, D.: Acme: architectural description of component-based systems. Foundations of Component-Based Systems, vol. 68, pp. 47–68 (2000)
7. Gidey, H.K., Marmsoler, D.: FACTUM Studio (2018). https://habtom.github.io/factum/
8. Jackson, D.: Alloy: a lightweight object modelling notation. ACM Trans. Softw. Eng. Methodol. (TOSEM) **11**(2), 256–290 (2002)
9. Marmsoler, D., Gleirscher, M.: On activation, connection, and behavior in dynamic architectures. Sci. Ann. Comput. Sci. **26**(2), 187–248 (2016)
10. Marmsoler, D.: On the semantics of temporal specifications of component-behavior for dynamic architectures. In: 11th International Symposium on Theoretical Aspects of Software Engineering, pp. 1–6. Springer, Berlin (2017)

11. Marmsoler, D.: Towards a calculus for dynamic architectures. In: Hung, D.V., Kapur, D. (eds.): Theoretical Aspects of Computing - ICTAC 2017–14th International Colloquium, Proceedings. Lecture Notes in Computer Science, vol. 10580. Springer, Berlin (2017)
12. Marmsoler, D.: Hierarchical specification and verification of architectural design patterns. In: Russo, A., Schürr, A. (eds.) FASE 2018. LNCS, vol. 10802, pp. 149–168. Springer, Cham (2018). https://doi.org/10.1007/978-3-319-89363-1_9
13. Marmsoler, D., Gleirscher, M.: Specifying properties of dynamic architectures using configuration traces. In: Sampaio, A., Wang, F. (eds.) ICTAC 2016. LNCS, vol. 9965, pp. 235–254. Springer, Cham (2016). https://doi.org/10.1007/978-3-319-46750-4_14
14. Miyazawa, A., Cavalcanti, A., Ribeiro, P., Li, W., Woodcock, J., Timmis, J.: Robochart reference manual. Technical report, University of York (2017)
15. Nipkow, T., Wenzel, M., Paulson, L.C. (eds.): Isabelle/HOL. LNCS, vol. 2283. Springer, Heidelberg (2002). https://doi.org/10.1007/3-540-45949-9
16. Taylor, R.N., Medvidovic, N., Dashofy, E.M.: Software Architecture: Foundations, Theory, and Practice. Wiley Publishing (2009)
17. Wirsing, M.: Algebraic specification. In van Leeuwen, J. (ed.): Handbook of Theoretical Computer Science, vol. B, pp. 675–788. MIT Press, Cambridge (1990)

The SLCO Framework for Verified, Model-Driven Construction of Component Software

Sander de Putter[1]([✉]), Anton Wijs[1], and Dan Zhang[1,2]

[1] Eindhoven University of Technology, Eindhoven, Netherlands
{s.m.j.d.putter,a.j.wijs,d.zhang}@tue.nl
[2] University of Twente, Enschede, Netherlands
d.zhang-3@utwente.nl

Abstract. We present the Simple Language of Communicating Objects (SLCO) framework, which has resulted from our research on applying formal methods for correct and efficient model-driven development of multi-component software. At the core is a domain specific language called SLCO that specifies software behaviour. In this paper, we discuss the language, give an overview of the features of the framework, and discuss our roadmap for the future.

1 Introduction

The development of complex, multi-component software is time-consuming and error-prone. One important cause is that there are multiple concerns to address. In particular, the software should be functionally correct, but also efficient. Careless optimisation of code may introduce bugs and make it less obvious to reason about the core functionality. To improve this, it is crucial that techniques are developed that make every step in the development work flow systematic and transparent.

With the Simple Language of Communicating Objects (SLCO) framework, we conduct research on the development of techniques for this purpose. Key characteristics are (1) the use of a Domain-Specific Language (DSL) based on well-known software engineering concepts, i.e., objects, variables, state machines, and sequences of instructions, (2) formal verification in every development step, from model to code, that does not require expert verification knowledge from the developer, and (3) (optimised) code generation, by which (parallel) programming challenges are hidden from the developer.

The framework uses the *model-driven software development* methodology, in which models are constructed and transformed to other models and code by means of *model transformations*. The framework makes use of a verified code

Sander de Putter—This work is supported by ARTEMIS Joint Undertaking project EMC2 (grant nr. 621429).
Dan Zhang—This work is supported by the 4TU-NIRICT project ViGARO.

K. Bae and P. C. Ölveczky (Eds.): FACS 2018, LNCS 11222, pp. 288–296, 2018.
https://doi.org/10.1007/978-3-030-02146-7_15

generator [27,28]. Furthermore, the framework supports some verification of model-transformations; support will be extended in the near future.

2   Related Work

In most related work, no verification is done (e.g. [9,20]) or only on either model-to-model or model-to-code transformations [19]. Some techniques cover both, e.g. [14], but they do not address the *direct* verification of transformations. This means that correctness of a transformation cannot be determined once-and-for-all; instead, every time it is applied, its result has to be checked. Furthermore, a few transformation steps may quickly render verification infeasible [2]. In contrast, the SLCO framework supports direct verification of transformations. We have yet to achieve direct verification of *all* transformations, but transformations of transition sequences consisting of user-defined actions can already be verified.

SCADE 6 [10], SIMULINK [21], and EVENT-B [1] are frameworks offering features similar to SLCO. All frameworks offer verification methods for their models and automatic code generation. SCADE can make use of Lustre's verified compiler [5] to generated code. Both SIMULINK and EVENT-B support verification of generated code [11,15], however, to our knowledge the generators are not mechanically verified and, thus, require some form of consistency verification between model and code.

Unlike SCADE, SLCO is not limited to the sampling-actuating model of control engineering, and can be used to specify such systems via user-defined actions serving as sampling and actuating calls. Of the frameworks mentioned above, only EVENT-B offers verification of refinement transformations. SLCO, in addition, also supports verification of other kinds of transformations. Finally, similar to SCADE, the SLCO code generator is mechanically verified and preserves certain correctness criteria, such as atomicity preservation and lock-deadlock freedom, without the need for a consistency check.

3   The SLCO 2.0 Language

The second version of SLCO is the core of the framework. The SLCO DSL should be used in the first development step to specify the intended functionality of the system. SLCO has been designed to model systems consisting of concurrent, communicating components at a convenient level of abstraction. It has a formal semantics.[1] New to version 2 is the support for arrays, user-defined actions, composite statements, the specification of a channel's buffer capacity, and transition priorities. We will introduce these additions together with the rest of SLCO.

SLCO models consist of a finite number of *classes*, which can be instantiated as *objects*, *channels* for communication between objects, and user-defined *actions*; each are declared in their own section of the model.

---

[1] See http://www.win.tue.nl/~awijs/SLCO/SLCO2doc.pdf.

A *class* consists of a finite number of concurrent *state machines*, and *ports* and *variables* shared by them that can be used for communication. Thus, SLCO supports components at two levels: each object forms a component that can communicate with other objects via message-passing, while inside an object multiple components may exist that can interact via shared variables.

Variables are of type `Integer`, `Byte`, `Boolean`, or Array of one of these. Furthermore, state machines can have private variables that are only accessible by the owning state machine. Variables are declared in the `variables` section of classes or state machines: `Integer x := y + 1` declares an integer variable named `x` that initially has the value of the expression `y + 1`.

A *channel* connects two ports of two objects; they are used to send messages between state machines of two different objects. A channel accepts messages (optionally with parameters of types `Integer`, `Byte`, or `Boolean`), it is either synchronous or asynchronous and in the latter case either lossless or lossy (lossy means that it may lose messages at any time). In case a channel is asynchronous, a buffer size can be defined, which is by default 1. Let `p` and `q` be objects with ports `InOut`, `In`, and `Out`; `c(Byte) sync between p.InOut and q.InOut` and `c(Byte) async[2] lossy from p.Out to q.In` respectively denote a synchronous and a lossy asynchronous channel named `c` that accepts messages with one `Byte` parameter. The asynchronous channel may buffer up to two messages. A *port* is attached to at most one channel. Furthermore, messages sent over ports have a *name* and optionally a number of parameters with the same types as defined on the connected channel.

A state machine consists of local variables, a finite number of states, an initial state, and transitions between states. Transitions have an optional priority and a (possibly empty) sequence of *statements* associated with it; for instance, given user-defined action a and variable x, `1: s1 -> s2 {x := x + 1; a}` denotes a transition, with the priority 1, starting at state `s1` that first performs the statement `x := x + 1` and then performs the action `a`. Upon completion of the statements the state `s2` is reached. A lower number indicates higher priority. Higher priority transitions are considered for firing before lower priority ones. Transitions with the same priority are fired non-deterministically. By default, a transition has priority 0.

Parallel execution of transitions is formalised using an interleaving semantics, in which SLCO statements are atomic, i.e., the transition with sequence of statements is equivalent to a sequence of transitions each executing one of the statements in the same order. No finer-grained interleaving is allowed. SLCO offers five types of statements, some of which may sometimes be blocked from execution. When this is the case, then the associated transition is blocked as well. The five types of statements are:

1. *(Boolean) Expression*: a condition that is blocked if it evaluates to `false`. In an expression, state machine-local and object-local variables may be referenced.
2. *Assignment*: `x := e` indicates that the evaluation of an expression e is assigned to variable x. The expression may be a logical (boolean) or arith-

```
1  model Test {
2    actions init
3    classes
4    P { ... }
5    Q {
6      variables Integer x y
7      ports Out1 Out2 InOut
8      state machines
9      SM1 {
10       variables Boolean started:=false
11       initial Com0 states Com1 Com2
12       transitions
13         Com0 -> Com1 { send M(false,0) to Out1;
14                        started:=true }
15         Com1 -> Com1 { [x > 0; x:=x-1; y:=y+1];
16                        send N(y) to Out2}
17       1: Com1 -> Com2 { receive S() from InOut }
18         Com2 -> Com0 { init }
19     }
20     SM2 { ... }
21   }
22   objects p: P(), q: Q(x:=10, y:=0)
23   channels
24     c1(Boolean, Integer) async[2] lossless
25       from q.Out1 to p.In1
26     c2(Integer) async lossy from q.Out2 to p.In2
27     c3() sync between p.InOut and q.InOut
28 }
```

```
1  ...
2  case Com1:
3    // [x > 0; x := x - 1; y := y + 1]
4    java_lockIDs[0] = 0; java_lockIDs[1] = 1;
5    java_kp.lock(java_lockIDs,2);
6    if (!(x > 0)) {
7      // receive S() from InOut
8      SignalMessage m = c3.receive("S");
9      java_kp.unlock(java_lockIDs,2);
10     if (!(m == null)) {
11       // Change state
12       java_currentState =
13         Test.java_State.Com2;
14     }
15     break;
16   }
17   x = x - 1; y = y + 1;
18   java_kp.unlock(java_lockIDs,2);
19   // send N(y) to Out2
20   java_lockIDs[0] = 1;
21   java_kp.lock(java_lockIDs,1);
22   c2.blocked_send("N", y);
23   java_kp.unlock(java_lockIDs,1);
24   // Change state
25   java_currentState = Test.java_State.Com1;
26   break;
27 case Com2:
28   ...
```

Fig. 1. An example SLCO model (left) and part of its Java implementation (right)

metic expression. Again, both state machine-local and object-local variables may be referenced. An assignment is always able to fire.

3. *Composite*: a statement grouping an optional boolean expression and one or more assignments (in that order). It is enabled iff the expression at the head is enabled. If no expression is included, it is always able to fire. For instance, [x>0; x:=x-1; y:=y+1] (the square brackets denote a composite statement) indicates that in case x is greater than 0, x is decremented and y is incremented, all in one atomic step.

4. *Send* and *Receive*: these statements attempt to send or receive a message to or from a particular channel, respectively. If the buffer associated to the channel is full, a send operation is blocked. A receive operation is blocked if the buffer is empty, or if the next message is not as expected; the receive statement can store the received parameter values in variables, and check whether an expression related to these values evaluates to true. If not, the receive statement is not enabled, and communication fails.

5. *User-defined action*: an action that indicates yet-unspecified behaviour. User-defined actions can be implemented in code or transformed to concrete behaviour.

Figure 1 presents part of an SLCO model Test on the left. It defines classes P, Q (lines 4, 5). At line 6–7 variables x and y and ports Out1, Out2 and InOut are defined. Class Q contains state machines SM1, SM2 (lines 9–20). At line 22, objects p and q are declared as instances of P and Q, respectively. The object ports are attached to channels at lines 24–27. Channel c1 accepts messages with a Boolean and an Integer parameter.

State machine SM1 has a boolean local variable started (line 10), an initial state Com0, and other states Com1 and Com2 (line 11).

Between the states, transitions with sequences of atomic statements are defined (lines 12–18). The priority of the transition at line 17 enforces SM1 in

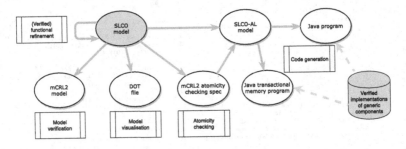

Fig. 2. An overview of the SLCO framework

state Com1 to consider the Com1 self-loop (line 15) before the transition to Com2 at line 17, i.e., it is first checked whether x > 0, only if this is not the case the transition to Com2 is considered. A message named M with parameters false and 0 is sent at line 13, while the transition at line 17 attempts to receive a message named S without parameters. At line 18, a user-defined action init is used, to indicate that some unspecified initialisation procedure is to be performed when moving from Com2 to Com0.

4   Features of the Framework

Figure 2 provides an overview of the SLCO framework. The framework[2] is implemented in Python, using TEXTX [8] for meta-modelling and JINJA2[3] for model transformation. Given an SLCO model (top-left corner), a number of features can be used.

Formal verification of SLCO *models.* To formally verify that an SLCO model satisfies desirable functional properties, it can be transformed to an MCRL2 model. With the MCRL2 toolset [7], it is then possible to apply model checking [3]. Properties specified as μ-calculus formulas can be checked by first combining model and property into a Parameterised Boolean Equation System, and then checking the latter's state space.

Model visualisation. SLCO models can be transformed to DOT files to visualise the state machines, thereby providing more insight into the structure of a model.

SLCO *model-to-model transformations.* Transformations can be used to iteratively refactor or refine SLCO models, for instance rewrite state machines or replace user-defined actions with concrete behaviour. Some user-defined transformations, specifically the ones between patterns of user-defined actions, can be verified directly for the preservation of functional properties, using our transformation verification technique [16,22] implemented in the REFINER tool [23]. It checks whether a transformation introduces patterns that are branching bisimilar to the replaced patterns after abstraction w.r.t. a given property. In other

---

[2] Git repository of the framework: https://gitlab.tue.nl/SLCO/SLCO.git.
[3] http://jinja.pocoo.org.

cases, preservation of properties can be determined for specific transformation applications by verifying the resulting SLCO model via MCRL2.

Transformation to multi-threaded Java. Before code is generated an SLCO model is translated to an SLCO-AL (SLCO Annotated Level) model. An SLCO-AL model is an SLCO model that is more specific on how and where to ensure atomicity.

The SLCO framework offers two partly verified code generators that take an SLCO-AL model and generate multi-threaded Java code. The generators use different methods to ensure atomicity of statements: the first generator uses a locking mechanism, while the second generator uses transactional memory.

In both generators, each state machine in the given SLCO-AL model is mapped to an individual thread. Hence, any variables shared by state machines correspond with shared variables in the Java code. The code is constructed modularly: implementations of generic concepts that are reusable in the generated code, such as channel and a locking mechanism for shared variables, have been added to a *generic component library* [27]. We have proven functional correctness of these parts of the generator [6] using VERIFAST [13]: (1) the atomicity of statements is preserved in generated code, (2) messages sent over lossless channels are eventually received, and (3) generated code does not introduce deadlocks. In addition, we have verified a robustness mechanism called *Failbox* [27] that is applied in the code to ensure that in case of a malfunctioning thread, dependent threads are notified if a thread fails.

The *first generator* enforces the use of a nested locking mechanism [28] to ensure that variables are safely shared. Each variable (and each array cell) is associated with an individual lock, and whenever for the execution of a statement a number of shared variables needs to be accessed, it is attempted to acquire the corresponding locks in a predefined order. The use of the fixed order prevents deadlocks and we have proven that it ensures the preservation of the atomicity of SLCO statements [28].

On the right in Fig. 1, part of the Java implementation of model `Test` produced by the first generator is presented. This part covers the transitions at lines 15–17 in the SLCO model and is part of a `switch` construct inside a `while` loop. This loop is responsible for the continuous movement between state machine states.

In the SLCO composite construct at line 15 in the SLCO model, class variables x and y are accessed. For this reason, locks need to be acquired in the generated code for both variables before the statement can be executed. At line 4 in the code, the IDs for both variables are added to array `java_lockIDs` in a sorted way to ensure ordered locking. Next, the locks are requested (line 5). If the locks are granted and the guard expression evaluates to `true`, the assignments of the composite statement are executed (line 17). Note the releasing of the locks once a statement has been executed. Alternatively, if the locks were not acquired or the guard expression evaluated to `false`, it is attempted to perform the `receive` statement specified at line 17 of the SLCO model. If the `receive` statement succeeded (line 10), the code 'changes state' according to the SLCO transition description (lines 12–13). Finally, at lines 19–23, the `send` statement at line 16 of the SLCO model is executed. It is executed as a possibly blocking send operation, since in the model, the state machine is in the middle of executing the statements of the transition at lines 15–16, and cannot consider alternatives.

The *second generator* enforces the use of transactional memory, relying on the ATOMJAVA code translation [12]. Instead of our nested locking mechanism, `atomic` blocks are used, to indicate that whenever the execution of a statement accesses a variable simultaneously accessed by another thread, the execution should be rolled back.

Reducing the use of synchronisation constructs with SLCO-AL. Naively using nested locking or `atomic` blocks for *all* statements often leads to congestion and, thus, results in under-performing parallel programs. As previously mentioned, SLCO-AL can be used to instruct code generators. It extends SLCO with constructs to indicate synchronisation.

Some statements do not actually need protection by a synchronisation mechanism; in such a case, the lack of such synchronisations is not *observable*. Furthermore, it is possible that statements within a composite statements can be factored out in a way that the model remains *observably* equivalent. To detect such situations, the framework provides a transformation to MCRL2 that encodes an atomicity detection and avoidance algorithm based on work on atomicity checking of parallel programs [18]. This algorithm checks which specified data accesses in a model need to be protected in the code by a synchronisation mechanism in order to avoid potential *atomicity violations*. Furthermore, the algorithm determines when a fence suffices as an alternative to the more heavy-weight locks or atomic blocks. With the output of the algorithm, composite statements can be decomposed and the need for synchronisations can be indicated in an SLCO-AL model. In the adapted model the use of these synchronisations is restricted to the absolutely necessary and least costly ones. The adapted model is semantically indistinguishable from the original one during execution of their respective generated code.

5   Roadmap

In the near future, we will continue our research in a number of directions. For instance, it is our goal that most, if not all, SLCO model transformations will be directly verifiable. Our current technique in REFINER [16, 23] is restricted to transformations between action patterns, as opposed to the transformation of (patterns of) other types of SLCO statements. Establishing that a transformation preserves properties for arbitrary input is stronger than having to verify resulting models each time the transformation is applied.

Regarding model verification, we plan to work on a new version of our GPU accelerated model checker GPUEXPLORE [26] that accepts SLCO models as input. Great speedups over 500× have been reported with this tool, and connecting SLCO will make it feasible to rapidly produce verification results for larger models. We will also continue our research on compositional model checking [17], to modularly verify SLCO models.

Regarding the SLCO-AL language, we will consider extending it to cover various other optimisation possibilities. In that respect, one can also think of optimising code w.r.t. other criteria than performance, such as power efficiency and security. To make smart decisions regarding quantitative characteristics of models, it may be required to extend our analysis towards probabilistic or stochastic model checking [3], and to add support for modelling quantitative aspects [24,25].

Research on verified code generation will focus on verifying complete programs, as opposed to only verifying generic components. We plan to use VERCORS [4] for this.

We plan to address the development of GPU software. For this, we need to extend SLCO to model such systems, and construct additional code generators.

Finally, we are considering to integrate our tool chain into the ECLIPSE IDE, to create one environment in which all tools in the framework can be accessed.

References

1. Abrial, J.R., Abrial, J.R.: The B-Book: Assigning Programs to Meanings. Cambridge University Press, Cambridge (2005)
2. Andova, S., van den Brand, M.G.J., Engelen, L.: Reusable and correct endogenous model transformations. In: Hu, Z., de Lara, J. (eds.) ICMT 2012. LNCS, vol. 7307, pp. 72–88. Springer, Heidelberg (2012). https://doi.org/10.1007/978-3-642-30476-7_5
3. Baier, C., Katoen, J.P.: Principles of Model Checking. MIT Press, Cambridge (2008)
4. Blom, S., Darabi, S., Huisman, M., Oortwijn, W.: The vercors tool set: verification of parallel and concurrent software. In: Polikarpova, N., Schneider, S. (eds.) IFM 2017. LNCS, vol. 10510, pp. 102–110. Springer, Cham (2017). https://doi.org/10.1007/978-3-319-66845-1_7
5. Bourke, T., Brun, L., Dagand, P.E., Leroy, X., Pouzet, M., Rieg, L.: A formally verified compiler for lustre. In: PLDI, pp. 586–601. ACM SIGPLAN Notices. ACM, New York (2017)
6. Bošnački, D., et al.: Towards modular verification of threaded concurrent executable code generated from DSL models. In: Braga, C., Ölveczky, P.C. (eds.) FACS 2015. LNCS, vol. 9539, pp. 141–160. Springer, Cham (2016). https://doi.org/10.1007/978-3-319-28934-2_8
7. Cranen, S., et al.: An overview of the mCRL2 toolset and its recent advances. In: Piterman, N., Smolka, S.A. (eds.) TACAS 2013. LNCS, vol. 7795, pp. 199–213. Springer, Heidelberg (2013). https://doi.org/10.1007/978-3-642-36742-7_15
8. Dejanović, I., Vaderna, R., Milosavljević, G., Vuković, Ž.: TextX: a python tool for Domain-Specific Languages implementation. Knowl.-Based Syst. 115, 1–4 (2017)
9. Deligiannis, P., Donaldson, A., Ketema, J., Lal, A., Thomson, P.: Asynchronous programming, analysis and testing with state machines. In: PLD, vol. 50, pp. 154–164. ACM SIGPLAN Notices. ACM Press (2015)
10. Dormoy, F.X.: Scade 6: a model based solution for safety critical software development. In: ERTS, pp. 1–9 (2008)
11. Fürst, A., Hoang, T.S., Basin, D., Desai, K., Sato, N., Miyazaki, K.: Code generation for event-B. In: Albert, E., Sekerinski, E. (eds.) IFM 2014. LNCS, vol. 8739, pp. 323–338. Springer, Cham (2014). https://doi.org/10.1007/978-3-319-10181-1_20

12. Hindman, B., Grossman, D.: Atomicity via source-to-source translation. In: MSPC, pp. 82–91. ACM Press (2006)

13. Jacobs, B., Smans, J., Philippaerts, P., Vogels, F., Penninckx, W., Piessens, F.: VeriFast: a powerful, sound, predictable, fast verifier for C and java. In: Bobaru, M., Havelund, K., Holzmann, G.J., Joshi, R. (eds.) NFM 2011. LNCS, vol. 6617, pp. 41–55. Springer, Heidelberg (2011). https://doi.org/10.1007/978-3-642-20398-5_4

14. Narayanan, A., Karsai, G.: Towards verifying model transformations. In: GT-VMT. ENTCS, vol. 211, pp. 191–200. Elsevier (2008)

15. O'Halloran, C.: Automated verification of code automatically generated from simulink®. Autom. Softw. Eng. **20**(2), 237–264 (2013)

16. de Putter, S., Wijs, A.: A formal verification technique for behavioural model-to-model transformations. Form. Asp. Comput. **30**(1), 3–43 (2017)

17. de Putter, S., Wijs, A.: Compositional model checking is lively. In: Proença, J., Lumpe, M. (eds.) FACS 2017. LNCS, vol. 10487, pp. 117–136. Springer, Cham (2017). https://doi.org/10.1007/978-3-319-68034-7_7

18. de Putter, S., Wijs, A., Zhang, D.: Model Driven Avoidance of Atomicity Violations under Relaxed-Memory Models (2018, Submitted)

19. Rahim, L., Whittle, J.: A survey of approaches for verifying model transformations. Software and Systems Modeling pp. 1–26 (2013)

20. Rompf, T., Odersky, M.: Lightweight Modular Staging: A Pragmatic Approach to Runtime Code Generation and Compiled DSLs. Commun. ACM **55**(6), 121–130 (2012)

21. The MathWorks Inc., Simulink®. www.mathworks.com/products/simulink

22. Wijs, A., Engelen, L.: Efficient property preservation checking of model refinements. In: Piterman, N., Smolka, S.A. (eds.) TACAS 2013. LNCS, vol. 7795, pp. 565–579. Springer, Heidelberg (2013). https://doi.org/10.1007/978-3-642-36742-7_41

23. Wijs, A., Engelen, L.: REFINER: Towards formal verification of model transformations. In: Badger, J.M., Rozier, K.Y. (eds.) NFM 2014. LNCS, vol. 8430, pp. 258–263. Springer, Cham (2014). https://doi.org/10.1007/978-3-319-06200-6_21

24. Wijs, A.: Achieving discrete relative timing with untimed process algebra. In: ICECCS, pp. 35–44. IEEE (2007)

25. Wijs, A., Fokkink, W.: From χ_t to μCRL: combining performance and functional analysis. In: ICECCS, pp. 184–193. IEEE (2005)

26. Wijs, A., Neele, T., Bošnački, D.: GPUexplore 2.0: unleashing GPU explicit-state model checking. In: Fitzgerald, J., Heitmeyer, C., Gnesi, S., Philippou, A. (eds.) FM 2016. LNCS, vol. 9995, pp. 694–701. Springer, Cham (2016). https://doi.org/10.1007/978-3-319-48989-6_42

27. Zhang, D.: From Concurrent State Machines to Reliable Multi-threaded Java Code. Ph.D. thesis, Eindhoven University of Technology (2018)

28. Zhang, D., et al.: Verifying atomicity preservation and deadlock freedom of a generic shared variable mechanism used in model-to-code transformations. In: Hammoudi, S., Pires, L.F., Selic, B., Desfray, P. (eds.) MODELSWARD 2016. CCIS, vol. 692, pp. 249–273. Springer, Cham (2017). https://doi.org/10.1007/978-3-319-66302-9_13

Author Index

Printed in the United States
by Bookmasters

Printed in the United States
By Bookmasters